CONTEMPORARY
ISRAEL

CONTEMPORARY
ISRAEL

Domestic Politics, Foreign Policy, and Security Challenges

edited by

Robert O. Freedman

Johns Hopkins University

Westview
PRESS
A Member of the Perseus Books Group

Library of Congress Cataloging-in-Publication Data
    Contemporary Israel : domestic politics, foreign policy, and security challenges / edited by
Robert O. Freedman.
        p. cm.
    Includes bibliographical references and index.
    ISBN 978-0-8133-4385-3
    1. Israel—History—21st century. 2. Israel—Politics and government—21st century. 3. Israel—
Foreign relations . 4. Arab-Israeli conflict—Influence. I. Freedman, Robert Owen.

DS126.5.C5936 2009
956.9405'4—dc22
                                                                            2008015527

10 9 8 7 6 5 4 3 2 1

This book is dedicated to my grandsons,
Zachary and Dylan,
in the hope that in their lifetimes
the Israeli people will live in peace
with all their Arab neighbors.

Contents

PART TWO — ISRAEL'S FOREIGN POLICY

PART THREE — ISRAEL'S SECURITY CHALLENGES

Preface

Anyone preparing a textbook on Israeli politics faces a series of challenges. First, should he or she write the textbook alone, or should a group of scholars be invited to make their contributions? In the case of Israeli politics, the subject has become increasingly complex in the sixty years Israel has been in existence as a state, and especially since the assassination of Prime Minister Yitzhak Rabin in 1995. Indeed, since 1995, the field of Israel studies has grown tremendously. There are now centers for the study of Israel not only in Israel itself, but also in the United States, Europe, and Russia. In addition, in the English language alone there are now three major journals dealing exclusively with Israel: *Israel Affairs, Israel Studies,* and *The Israel Studies Forum.* Consequently, given the increasing complexity of Israeli politics, I made the decision to invite scholars to write chapters in their fields of expertise for the text, rather than undertake to write the entire text by myself.

A second challenge is to choose the topics to be included in the book. Since security issues have been a dominant aspect of Israeli politics (and Israeli life) since 1948, a number of chapters have been devoted to Israeli security and foreign policy issues. In the realm of security policy, one chapter is devoted to an analysis of the existential threats facing Israel and another to the Israel-Hizbollah war of 2006, after which Israel's deterrence capability, hitherto the bedrock of its security strategy, was called into question. In the area of foreign policy, chapters are devoted to Israel's most important foreign relationships: with the Palestinians, the Arab world, and the United States. In addition, in recent years Israel has developed close relations with both India, a rising world power, and Turkey, a key country in the Muslim world, and it was felt that a chapter should be devoted to Israel's relationships with those countries as well.

Another key aspect of Israeli life since 1948 has been the growth and development of its very vibrant political party system. In addition to being divided into right and left on the political spectrum—in the Israeli context this means hawkish and dovish on their readiness to make peace with the Arabs—Israeli parties also represent special-interest groups. Thus, while chapters in this book are devoted to Israel's right-wing and left-wing parties, other chapters are devoted to the main interest-group parties in Israel: the religious parties, the Arab parties, and the Russian parties.

Finally, since 1995, two other major developments have occurred in Israel that have had a very significant impact on its politics. The first is the rise in importance of the Israeli Supreme Court, whose role in Israeli politics now approaches that of the US Supreme Court in American politics. The second is the radical change in the Israeli economy, which has moved from a socialist orientation to a capitalist one. Consequently, chapters have been devoted to both the Israeli Supreme Court and the Israeli economy.

A third challenge in preparing a text of this type is to find the proper mix of scholars to contribute. Since the field of Israel studies (represented, since 1985, by the Association for Israel Studies), like many other scholarly fields, has scholars from all over the world, embracing a wide spectrum of viewpoints, I have felt it important to have those differing viewpoints reflected in the text. Thus the reader will find contributors from both Israel and North America, as well as perspectives ranging from hawkish to dovish on the Arab-Israeli conflict. It is hoped that a book of this type will not only provide stimulating reading but will also provide the reader with a balanced understanding of both the dynamism and the complexity of Israeli politics.

ROBERT O. FREEDMAN
Baltimore, Maryland
November 2007

Acknowledgments

A book such as this is the result of the collective effort of a number of people, whom I would like to thank. First and foremost, my thanks go to Dr. Norman Levy and Mrs. Marian Levy, who provided the support for the conference "Israel since Rabin," held at Johns Hopkins University in March 2007, which was the basis of this book. Second, I would like to thank Dr. David Nirenberg, now of the University of Chicago, and Dr. Steven David, professor of political science and vice dean for programs and centers at the Johns Hopkins University Krieger School of Arts and Sciences, for their assistance in making the conference possible. Third, I would like to thank Ms. Ayana Teal, administrative assistant at the Department of History of Johns Hopkins University, for her help with conference logistics. Fourth, I would like to thank one of my PhD students, Mr. Neil Rubin (who is also managing editor of the *Baltimore Jewish Times*), who came to me with the original idea for the conference, and for the support the *Baltimore Jewish Times* gave in publicizing the conference. Fifth, I would like to thank Mr. Karl Yambert, my editor at Westview Press, for his enthusiasm in promoting the project, and Ms. Meredith Smith, my project editor at Westview, who saw the manuscript through to publication. Sixth, I would like to thank the Baltimore Jewish Council for their support of the conference. Seventh, I would like to thank Ms. Elise Baron, my typist, who has now typed my twentieth book. Finally, I would like to thank my wife, Sharon, without whose devoted support the book might never have been finished.

About the Authors

Steven R. David is professor of international relations, vice dean for Centers and Programs, and director of Jewish Studies at Johns Hopkins University. Among his publications are *Choosing Sides: Alignment and Realignment in the Third World, Third World Coups d'Etats and International Security,* and the forthcoming *Catastrophic Consequences: Civil Wars and American Interests.*

Robert O. Freedman is Peggy Meyerhoff Pearlstone Professor of Political Science Emeritus at Baltimore Hebrew University and is visiting professor of political science at Johns Hopkins University, where he teaches courses on the Arab-Israeli conflict and Russian foreign policy. Among his publications are *Moscow and the Middle East, Israel under Rabin,* and *Israel's First Fifty Years.*

Hillel Frisch is associate professor in the Departments of Political Studies and Middle East History at Bar-Ilan University, Israel, and is senior researcher at the Begin-Sadat (BESA) Center for Strategic Studies. Among his publications are *The Palestinian Military: Between Militias and Armies* and *Islamic Radicalism and International Security: Challenges and Response* (coedited with Efraim Inbar).

Efraim Inbar is professor of political studies at Bar-Ilan University and director of the Begin-Sadat Center for Strategic Studies. Among his publications are *War and Peace in Israeli Politics, Rabin and Israel's National Security, The Israeli-Turkish Entente,* and *Israel's National Security: Issues and Challenges since the Yom Kippur War.*

Vladimir (Ze'ev) Khanin is lecturer in the Department of Political Studies at Bar-Ilan University; director of academic programs of the Institute for Eurasian Studies at the Interdisciplinary Studies Center (IDC), Herzliya, Israel; and visiting professor of Israeli government and politics at Moscow State University. Among his publications is *The "Russians" and Power in the State of Israel: The Establishment of the USSR/CIS Immigrant Community and Its Impact on the Political Structure of the Country.*

Pnina Lahav is professor of law and Law Alumni Scholar at Boston University and is currently a fellow of the Center for Advanced Studies at the Hebrew University of Jerusalem. Among her publications is *Judgment in Jerusalem: Chief Justice Agranat and the Zionist Century.*

David W. Lesch is professor of Middle East history at Trinity University in San Antonio, Texas. Among his publications are *The Arab-Israeli Conflict: A History, The Middle East and the United States: A Historical and Political Reassessment,* and *The New Lion of Damascus: Bashar Al-Assad and Modern Syria.*

Elli Lieberman is a consultant on security and deterrence issues and is adjunct assistant professor of Middle East studies at Baltimore Hebrew University, where he teaches courses on Israeli politics. Among his publications are *Deterrence Theory: Success or Failure in Arab-Israeli Wars* and *What Makes Deterrence Work: Lessons from the Egyptian-Israeli Enduring Rivalry.*

Ilan Peleg is Charles Dana Professor of Government and Law, Lafayette College. Among his publications are *Begin's Foreign Policy 1977–1983: Israel's Turn to the Right, Human Rights in the West Bank and Gaza: Legacy and Politics,* and *Democratizing the Hegemonic State: Political Transformation in the Age of Identity.*

Mark Rosenblum is associate professor of history at Queens College of the City of New York, where he is director of the Michael Harrington Center. Among his publications are *Israel and the PLO: From Negotiating a "Piece of Paper" to Implementing "Peace on the Ground"* and *Euphoria with the King, Angst with Arafat, Anticipation with Assad: Hope without Delusion.*

Barry Rubin is director of the Global Research in International Affairs Center (GLORIA) and is editor of both *The Middle East Review of International Affairs (MERIA)* and *Turkish Studies.* Among his publications are *The Truth about Syria* and *The Long War for Freedom: The Arab Struggle for Democracy in the Middle East.*

Shmuel Sandler is the Sara and Simha Lainer Professor of Civility and Democracy and dean of the faculty of social sciences at Bar-Ilan University, Israel. He also serves as editor of the *Jewish Political Studies Review.* Among his publications are *The State of Israel, The Land of Israel: The Statist and Ethnonational Dimensions of Foreign Policy,* and *Bringing Religion into International Relations* (coauthored with Jonathan Fox). Aaron Kampinsky recently received his PhD from Bar-Ilan University, where his dissertation was written on the Rabbinate Department of the Israel Defense Forces.

Ofira Seliktar is professor of political science at Gratz College in Philadelphia. Among her publications are *The Transition to a Market Economy: The Road Half Taken, The New Zionism and the Foreign Policy System of Israel,* and *The Politics of Intelligence and American Wars with Iraq.*

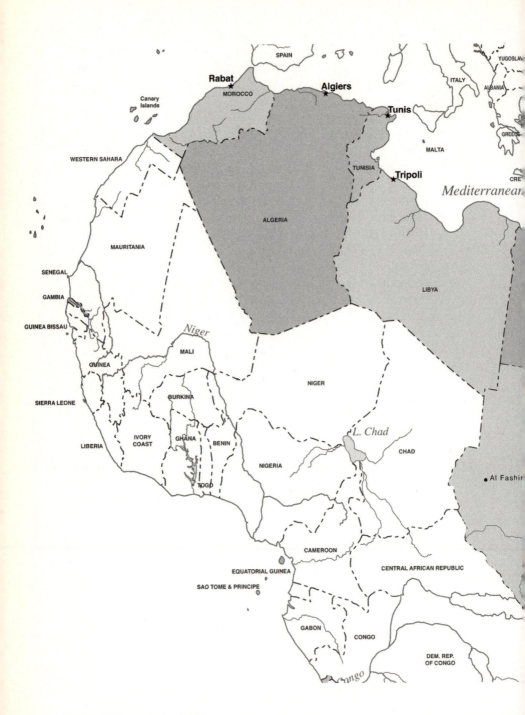

The Middle East and North Africa

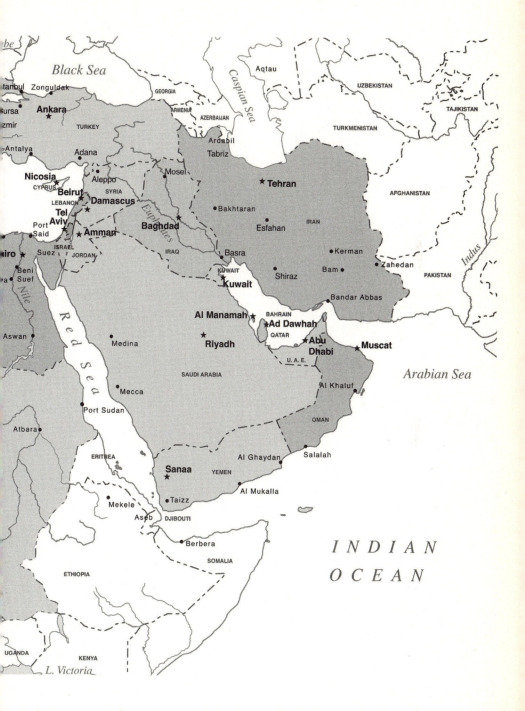

Israel

- ━━━ International boundary
- ─·─·─ District (mehoz) boundary
- ★ National capital
- ⊕ District (mehoz) center
- Railroad
- Divided highway
- Other road

0 _____ 40 Kilometers
0 _____ 40 Miles
Lambert Conformal Conic Projection, SP 30N / 36N

Israel proclaimed Jerusalem as
its capital in 1950, but the US,
like nearly all other countries,
maintains its embassy in Tel Aviv.

The West Bank and Gaza Strip
are Israeli-occupied with current
status subject to the Israeli-
Palestinian Interim Agreement –
permanent status to be determined through further negotiation.

LEBANON
UNDOF Zone
Tyre
Qiryat Shemona
Az Qunaytirah
Nahariyya
GOLAN HEIGHTS (Israeli occupied)
SYRIA
'Akko
Haifa
NORTHERN
As Suwaydā'
HAIFA
Tiberias
Lake Tiberias
Nazareth
Dar'ā
Irbid
Busrā ash Shām
Hadera
Janin
Al Mafraq
Netanya
Tulkarm
CENTRAL
Herzliyya
Nablus
Jarash
TEL AVIV
Tel Aviv-Yafo
WEST BANK
Bat Yam
Ram Allah
1994 Treaty Line
Az Zarqā
Rehovot
Ramla
Amman
Ashdod
Jericho
Jerusalem
Mādabā
Ashqelon
JERUSALEM
Bethlehem
Gaza
Qiryat Gat
Dead Sea
GAZA STRIP
Hebron
Khān Yūnis
1949 Armistice Line
Al 'Arish
Beersheba
Al Karak
Al Qaţrānah
Dimona
Zefa'
Aş Şafi
JORDAN
Bi'r Lahfān
NEGEV
Abū 'Ujaylah
Zin
'Ayn al Qusaymah
Mizpe Ramon
Bi'r Hasanah
Ma'ān
Al Jafr
EGYPT
SINAI
Al Kuntillah
Ra's an Naqb
An Nakhl
Yotvata
SOUTHERN
Mediterranean Sea
'Elat
Tābā
Al 'Aqabah
Gulf of Aqaba
Al Mudawwarah
SAUDI ARABIA

Boundary representation is
not necessarily authoritative.

Base 802833 (A00853) 9-01

Acronyms

AAMs	air-to-air missiles
ABM	antiballistic missile
ACRI	Association for Civil Rights and Civil Liberties
ADP	Arab Democratic Party
AIPAC	American-Israel Public Affairs Committee
AJC	American Jewish Committee
AKP	Turkish Justice and Development Party
ALH	advanced light helicopter
AMAN	Israeli Military Intelligence
AMC	Arab Movement for Change
ASAT	antisatellite
AWACS	airborne warning and control system
BJP	Bharatiya Janata Party
BMD	ballistic missile defense
CEC	Central Elections Committee
CIA	Central Intelligence Agency
CIS	Commonwealth of Independent States
DA	Democracy and Aliya (political party)
DFLP	Democratic Front for the Liberation of Palestine
DFPE	Democratic Front for Peace and Equality
DRDL	Defense and Research Development Laboratory
EU	European Union
FBI	Federal Bureau of Investigation
FSU	Former Soviet Union
GAHAL	Herut-Liberal Bloc
GDP	gross domestic product
GSS	General Security Services
HAL	Hindustani Aeronautics Limited
IAI	Israel Aircraft Industries
IB	Israel Beiteinu Party
IBA	Yisrael B'aliya Party
IDF	Israel Defense Forces
IDI	Israel Democracy Institute
IMF	International Monetary Fund
IMI	Israel Military Industries

IRAC	Religion Action Center
IT	information technology
IZL	Irgun Zvai Leumi
LIC	low-intensity conflict
LOMI	Lev Olim Lemaan Yisrael
LORROS	long-range reconnaissance and observation system
MASHAV	Israeli foreign ministry Center for International Cooperation
MENL	Middle East News Line
MERIA	*Middle East Review of International Affairs*
NAM	Nonaligned Movement
NATO	North Atlantic Treaty Organization
NGOs	nongovernmental organizations
NII	National Insurance Institute
NPT	Nonproliferation Treaty
NRP	National Religious Party
OECD	Organization for Economic Cooperation and Development
OIC	Organization of Islamic Countries
PA	Palestinian Authority
PFLP	Popular Front for the Liberation of Palestine
PKK	Kurdish Workers Party
PLC	Palestinian Legislative Council
PLO	Palestine Liberation Organization
PLP	Progressive List for Peace
PNC	Palestine National Council
PPP	purchasing power parity
SAMs	surface-to-air missiles
SEATO	Southeast Asia Treaty Organization
TALI	Movement for Israeli Renewal
TAMI	Movement for Israel's Tradition
TI	Transparency International Global Corruption Barometer
TISAS	thermal-imaging stand-alone system
UAL	United Arab List
UAVs	unmanned aerial vehicles
UN	United Nations
UNEF	United Nations Expeditionary Force
UNIFIL	United Nations Interim Force in Lebanon
UNSCOP	UN Special Committee on Palestine
UPA	United Progressive Alliance
UTJ	United Torah Judaism
WMD	weapons of mass destruction

Introduction

Robert O. Freedman

ISRAEL WAS BORN ON MAY 15, 1948. It was a child of the European nationalism of the nineteenth century, much as was Arab nationalism. On that date a group of Palestinian Jewish leaders, operating on the basis of the Zionist ideology, proclaimed the state of Israel. Their basic precept was that—just as the French had France; the Germans, Germany; the English, England; and the Italians, Italy—so, too, should the Jews have a state of their own. Israel, however, was also born in conflict with its Arab neighbors, who invaded Israel seeking to destroy it. That conflict, which became known as the Arab-Israeli conflict, has heavily influenced Israel's development, as security issues have dominated Israeli politics and society since 1948. A second major factor influencing Israel was immigration. Israel, whose ethos was the ingathering of Jews from around the world, particularly where they lived under conditions of persecution, has absorbed millions of immigrants since 1948, beginning with the survivors of the Holocaust, who were followed by Jews from Arab countries in the 1940s, 1950s, and 1960s, and Jews from the former Soviet Union in the 1970s, 1980s, and early 1990s. Even in 2007, fifty-nine years after the state of Israel was proclaimed, immigrants form a large percentage of its population, which now numbers more than seven million. Israel has also become a center for a revived Hebrew language and literature, as well as a source of pride for Jewish communities around the world, although differences with Diaspora Jewish communities, especially that of the United States, over religious issues and Israeli foreign policy have occasionally caused conflicts.

History Before 1948

Modern Israel had its political origins in the doctrine of nationalism, which was precipitated by the French Revolution and permeated Europe in the nineteenth century. Nationalism led to the unification of Germany and Italy, revolts by the Poles against the Russians, and the Hungarians against the Austrians, and to the gradual weakening of Ottoman control in the Balkans, which began with the independence movement in Greece in the 1820s. These events led a number of Jewish thinkers, such as Yehudah Alkelai, Zvi Kallischer, and Moses Hess, looking at the examples of Greece, Germany, and Italy, to suggest that the time had come for the Jews, as an ethnoreligious national group, to have their own homeland. Indeed, the title of Hess's seminal book, *Rome and Jerusalem: The Last Nationality Question,* specifically stated that just as the Italians were creating a new state on the ruins of ancient Rome, so, too, should the Jews recreate their state in Palestine, which, until the Romans conquered it and destroyed the Jewish Temple in 70 CE, had been the Jewish state.[1]

The ideas of Alkelai, Kallischer, and Hess were reinforced by the pogroms in Czarist Russia in 1881, which transformed a group of Russian Jewish intellectuals, such as Peretz Smolenskin, Moshe Lilienblum, and Leo Pinsker, from Russian assimilationists into ardent Zionists. The most important Zionist thinker in the nineteenth century was Theodore Herzl, an Austro-Hungarian Jewish journalist who was not only a Zionist theoretician but also an effective organizer. In 1896, after witnessing the anti-Jewish rioting in France connected to the Dreyfus affair, in which a French Jewish army officer was falsely accused of giving military secrets to the Germans, Herzl concluded that there was no safe place for the Jews of Europe and that assimilation was not possible. In 1896 he wrote the book *Der Judenstaat (The Jewish State),* which called for a Jewish state in Palestine, and in 1897 he organized the first international Zionist congress in Basle, Switzerland. The conference called for international support for the establishment of a Jewish state in Palestine, and for Jewish efforts to settle it. In sum, by the end of the nineteenth century, Zionist thinkers had concluded that a Jewish state was needed, both to provide a safe haven for persecuted Jews and to raise the national dignity of the Jewish people. A few Zionist leaders went further, arguing that a Jewish state would be "a light unto the nations."

While Herzl ran into opposition from both Orthodox and Reform Jews for religious reasons (the Orthodox Jews felt that only the Messiah could reestablish a Jewish state, while the Reform Jews asserted that it was God's will to scatter the Jews around the world so that they could teach God's laws), and from assimilated Jews in Europe and the United States, who did not share Herzl's concern about rising anti-Semitism, he continued his Zionist efforts.

Between 1897 and 1903, he visited the main chancelleries of Europe, trying to gain support for his plan. Herzl's greatest success came in England, where he found a receptive audience, especially among "Christian Zionists" such as Arthur Balfour. Indeed, his discussions with English leaders were to set the stage for British promises to the Zionist movement during World War I.[2]

World War I

During World War I, England had a number of objectives besides the defeat of the Central Powers (Germany, Austria-Hungary, and the Ottoman Empire). One of these was to secure a land route to the Persian Gulf, from Egypt to Iran, in lands then occupied by the Ottoman Empire, in order to secure the route to India. British possession of Palestine, as well as Iraq, was critical to achieving this goal. In order to both gain support against the Central Powers and gain the land bridge to the Persian Gulf, English officials made three conflicting promises during the war. The first was to Sherif Hussein of Mecca (the Hussein-McMahon correspondence of 1915–1916), in which the Arab leader, who then controlled only the land around Mecca, was vaguely promised an independent Arab state from southern Anatolia to the Arabian Sea, but with so many territorial exclusions as to make the promise almost meaningless. The second promise was in the 1916 Sykes-Picot agreement with France, under which England got most of modern-day Iraq and Jordan; France got modern-day Syria and Lebanon, as well as part of southern Anatolia and northern Iraq; and Palestine, west of the Jordan River, was to be an internationally controlled zone—the latter stipulation to satisfy czarist Russia, which was an ally of Britain and France during the war, and which had interests in Palestine. The third promise, the Balfour Declaration of November 1917, was to the Zionist movement, which during World War I had its primary headquarters in England. The Balfour Declaration was another vague promise, this time of a Jewish "national home in Palestine"; it did not stipulate the meaning of the term *national home* (state? autonomous area?) or where "in Palestine" the national home was to be (all of it? part of it?). At the peace conferences following the war, the czarist regime in Russia having been overthrown by the Bolsheviks and not participating in the conferences, England and France could more freely deal with Palestine, which England received as a League of Nations Mandate, along with Iraq, while France received Lebanon and Syria.[3]

The British Mandate over Palestine

Just as England had made conflicting promises during World War I, so, too, did it pursue conflicting policies during the Mandate period (1922–1948), favoring the Zionists as in the Mandate document itself, which stated that England would facilitate Jewish immigration to Palestine, and favoring the Arabs, as in the Passfield White Paper (1930; later rescinded), which stated that England would terminate immigration. As the conflict between Palestine's Jewish and Arab communities intensified during the 1930s, the British were hard put to work out a settlement between the two communities and never did succeed. The Peel Commission, sent to Palestine to investigate the causes of the Arab riots of 1936, urged the partition of the Mandate, which then included all the land from the Mediterranean to the Jordan River (Transjordan having been separated from British-controlled Palestine in 1921), into separate areas for Palestine's four hundred thousand Jews and almost one million Arabs. This partition was rejected by the Palestinian Arabs, but its suggestion did provide an important precedent for the UN Partition decision ten years later. In 1939, with World War II on the horizon and the continuing Arab revolt tying down large numbers of English troops, England again moved to pacify the Palestinian Arabs with the March 1939 White Paper, which limited Jewish immigration to Palestine to only seventy-five thousand over the next five years, no additional immigration to be allowed without the agreement of Palestine's Arabs—a highly unlikely possibility. The White Paper also limited Jewish land purchase possibilities to only 5 percent of the Mandate. The White Paper's limitation on immigration and land purchase infuriated the Palestinian Jewish community. More important, it cost the lives of perhaps one million European Jews, who died in the Holocaust and otherwise might have made it to Palestine, something that still angers Israeli Jews today.

During the Mandate period, the Jewish community of Palestine, in addition to absorbing hundreds of thousands of immigrants (mostly from Eastern and Central Europe) who augmented the almost eighty-four thousand Jews living in Palestine when the Mandate was proclaimed, developed the skills of self-government that were to serve it well during the postindependence period. The main contenders for power over the Jewish Agency for Israel (a branch of the World Zionist Organization) was Mapai (the forerunner of Israel's Labor Party), which was led by Chaim Arlosoroff and David Ben-Gurion, and the Revisionist Party (the forerunner of the Herut and Likud parties), which was led by Vladimir Jabotinsky. The political conflicts between Mapai and the Revisionists were to mirror, in many ways, the conflicts between the Labor Party and first Herut and then Likud after the establishment of the state of Israel in 1948. The conflicts included differences over the optimal economic system for the Jewish community, Mapai favoring socialism and the Revisionists, capitalism. In addition, the Revisionists, who had not reconciled themselves to the loss of the land east of the Jordan River given to Transjordan by Britain, also wanted a tougher Jewish response to continuing

Arab attacks than did Mapai. Finally, the Revisionists wanted to pressure England to call for the immediate establishment of a Jewish state, while Mapai wanted to wait until more Jews had immigrated to the country and the diplomatic situation was more favorable. The two main parties also had their own militias, Mapai controlling the Haganah and the Revisionists somewhat more loosely tied to the Irgun.

In addition, during the British Mandate, the Palestinian Jewish community developed a number of key institutions, including the Histadrut, a huge labor union, which, besides protecting its workers, carried out a great deal of construction, had an extensive health care program, and provided numerous cultural services. Other institutions, some of which had their origins in the pre-Mandate period, also developed, including agricultural cooperatives like the Kibbutz, Moshav, and Moshav-Shitufi. The Mandate also saw the development of major Jewish urban centers in Palestine, including Tel Aviv, Haifa, and West Jerusalem.[4]

With the outbreak of World War II, most of the Palestinian Jewish community supported the English, despite the 1939 White Paper, although there was a fringe group, Lehi, which opposed them. By 1943, however, with the Allies (the United States, England, the United Kingdom, and the USSR) having taken the offensive against the Axis powers (Nazi Germany, Italy, and Japan), the Irgun, now under the leadership of Menahem Begin, began to launch attacks against the English to break their blockade of the coast of Palestine, which was preventing some of the surviving Jews of Europe from escaping to Palestine. These attacks were opposed by Mapai and the Haganah because they damaged the Jewish community's diplomatic position as the war was coming to a close, even though the main Palestinian Arab leader, Hajj Amin al-Husseini, had actively cooperated with the Nazis during the war.

Following the war, a weakened England became economically dependent on the United States and therefore could not simply reject US president Harry Truman's call for one hundred thousand European Jewish survivors of the Holocaust to be permitted to emigrate to Palestine (Britain had kept the White Paper limits on immigration). Consequently, England's foreign minister, Ernest Bevin, suggested the establishment of an Anglo-American Committee of Inquiry to study the refugee problem and the situation in Palestine. He also promised that if the six Americans and six English who made up the committee issued a unanimous report, he would implement it. However, he subsequently rejected the committee's 1946 unanimous recommendation that one hundred thousand Jews be allowed to emigrate to Palestine. This refusal led the Haganah to join the Irgun in attacks on the British, which in turn led to a British crackdown on the Jewish Agency. Nonetheless, the British, war weary and economically exhausted, brought the issue of Palestine to the

United Nations in February 1947. The UN set up its own investigatory commission, the UN Special Committee on Palestine (UNSCOP), which, after visiting Palestine, made two recommendations. The majority recommendation
was for the partition of the British Mandate into Palestinian Arab and Palestinian Jewish states, with Jerusalem and its environs becoming an international zone. The minority recommendation was for a Jewish-Arab Federation.
With the support of both the United States and the Soviet Union, the majority
recommendation was passed by the UN General Assembly in November 1947,
calling for an end to the Mandate and for the establishment of the two states.
Following the UN decision, which the Palestinian Jews accepted and the
Palestinian Arabs rejected, guerrilla war broke out between the two communities, with volunteers from neighboring Arab countries entering Palestine to
help the Palestinian Arabs. The volunteers, however, were not able to help the
Palestinian Arabs defeat the Palestinian Jews, and on May 15, 1948, Arab
armies from Egypt, Transjordan, Lebanon, Syria, and Iraq invaded the newly
proclaimed State of Israel.

Israeli Foreign Policy 1948–2006

In what became known as Israel's War of Independence, the Israeli army—
thanks to higher morale, interior lines of communication, better leadership,
divisions among the Arabs, and arms from Czechoslovakia—defeated both
the invading Arab armies and the Palestinian Arabs, enlarging the area it had
been allotted under the UN partition resolution, primarily with land in the
Galilee. At the same time Egypt seized Gaza, and Transjordan (which was
soon to change its name to Jordan) seized the West Bank and East
Jerusalem—areas that had been allotted to the abortive Palestinian state. As a
result of the war, more than five hundred thousand Palestinian Arabs fled
their homes, most to escape the fighting, but approximately one hundred
thousand of them were expelled by Israel to prevent their acting as a "fifth col-
umn" behind Israeli lines in Lydda and Ramle as Israel came under attack
from Egypt and Transjordan. [5]

In the aftermath of the war, while Israel was busy resettling Jews who had
immigrated from Europe and the Arab world, security problems were upper-
most in the mind of David Ben-Gurion, who had become Israel's first prime
minister. Terrorist attacks against Israel from Egypt and Jordan led to often
massive reprisals by Israel on Egypt and Jordan, reprisals that were criticized
by the United States and Western Europe. In addition, despite abandoning its
initial position of neutrality in the NATO-USSR cold war by siding with the
United States after Soviet-backed North Korea invaded South Korea in 1950,
Israel was diplomatically isolated. The United States, under both the Truman

and Eisenhower administrations, was courting the Arab world and urging Israel not only to accept the return of hundreds of thousands of Arab refugees, but also to cede to the Arabs some of the land it controlled after its War of Independence. Israel rejected both American recommendations, fearing the security implications. Israel was also left out of the Baghdad Pact, the Anglo-American plan for an anticommunist alliance linking NATO (North Atlantic Treaty Organization) and SEATO (Southeast Asia Treaty Organization). Making matters worse for Israel was the major Soviet-Egyptian arms deal of 1955, which supplied Egypt with hundreds of bombers (along with tanks and artillery) that directly threatened Israel. Under these circumstances, Israel in 1956 joined with England and France (which had supplied some weaponry to Israel) for a tripartite attack on Egypt, Israel's role to secure the Sinai up to ten miles from the Suez Canal, and England (which had opposed Nasser's nationalization of the canal and his opposition to the Baghdad Pact) and France (which disliked Nasser because of his aid to the Algerian rebellion) to oust Nasser under the diplomatic cover of protecting international shipping through the canal. Israel defeated the Egyptian army in the Sinai, capturing or destroying large amounts of Soviet-supplied weaponry, albeit not the bombers, which had been flown abroad to escape the fighting. However, under heavy US pressure, Israel withdrew from the Sinai and Gaza, but not before a UN Expeditionary Force (UNEF) had been emplaced on Israel's borders with Egypt, to deter terrorist attacks, and at the Straits of Tiran, to ensure the freedom of Israeli shipping there (Nasser had previously closed the Straits of Tiran to Israeli shipping).[6]

Israel emerged from the 1956 Suez War with three gains. First, its military prowess served to protect Israel from the serious threat of another Arab attack for more than a decade, thus giving the Jewish state the opportunity to grow and develop and settle additional Jewish immigrants. Second, the opening of the Straits of Tiran to Israeli shipping facilitated Israel's trade with the newly emerging states of Africa and Asia. Third, the emplacement of UNEF forces sharply reduced the number of terrorist attacks against Israel from Egypt. The one negative aspect of the war for Israel was a diplomatic one: its association with the old colonial powers, England and France, which led some in the Third World to see Israel as a tool of colonialism.

The 1956–1967 period was a relatively quiet one in Israel's foreign relations, as Israel's Arab neighbors, fearful of another military encounter, seemed more intent on confronting each other than on confronting Israel. In addition, following the Iraqi revolution of July 1958, US-Israeli relations began to improve as American policymakers began to see the value of a democratic and militarily strong Israel in the volatile Middle East. During the administration of John F. Kennedy (1961–1963) the United States sold Hawk antiaircraft missiles to Israel to help protect it against the threat posed by the Egyptian bombers, although there were some serious differences between the two countries over Israel's budding nuclear program.[7]

Israel's relatively benign international situation changed radically in May 1967. Acting on erroneous information from the Soviet Union that Israel was about to attack Moscow's client state, Syria, Nasser seized the opportunity to rebuild his diminished prestige in the Arab world (Syria's defection from the Egyptian-dominated United Arab Republic in 1961 had badly hurt Nasser) by expelling the UN troops on the Egyptian-Israeli border and at the Straits of Tiran, and by signing a military alliance with Jordan, which augmented the 1966 Syrian-Egyptian alliance. Surrounded by enemies calling for its destruction, Israel launched a preemptive attack against Egypt after failing to get aid from the United States, which was bogged down in Vietnam. At the same time, it urged Jordan to stay out of the war. However, when King Hussein of Jordan responded to the Israeli request by shelling Jewish West Jerusalem from the Jordanian-controlled hills in East Jerusalem (later to be annexed by Israel), Israel struck at Jordan as well, capturing East Jerusalem and the West Bank and driving the Jordanian army back across the Jordan River. Several days later, Israel attacked Syria, seizing the Golan Heights, from which the Syrian army had regularly shelled Israeli territory.[8]

The diplomatic situation for Israel following the 1967 War was far different from that after the Suez War of 1956. Now the United States agreed with Israel that it should hold the conquered territory until a peace agreement was reached with its Arab neighbors. In addition, the administration of Lyndon Johnson, working with the United Kingdom, succeeded in November 1967 in passing UN Security Council Resolution 242, which called, as part of a peace settlement, for Israel to withdraw from "occupied territories" (not "the" or "all" occupied territories), thus implying that Israel could keep some territory to make its borders more "secure," as the UN resolution also stipulated. US-Israeli cooperation grew after the war, reaching a high point in 1970 under the Nixon administration when Israel deterred the Syrian air force from intervening in the Palestinian uprising against King Hussein of Jordan, an American ally. Following this incident, US military and economic aid to Israel grew, and during the 1973 Yom Kippur War, when an overconfident and unprepared Israel was caught by surprise by the attack from Egypt and Syria, American weaponry helped to turn the tide of the fighting in Israel's favor. In the aftermath of the war, US Secretary of State Henry Kissinger began a shuttle diplomacy that led to the partial Israeli-Egyptian agreements of Sinai I (1974) and Sinai II (1975) and set the stage for the Israeli-Egyptian peace agreement of 1979 mediated with the help of US president Jimmy Carter.[9]

US-Israeli relations remained strong under Carter's successor, Ronald Reagan, whose administration gave at least tacit support to Israel's invasion of Lebanon in 1982. The primary goal of the invasion was the destruction of the state-within-a-state that the PLO (Palestine Liberation Organization) had constructed in South Lebanon, which served as a base for launching attacks against Israel. While Israel succeeded in destroying the PLO position in South Lebanon, it was far less successful in achieving its other invasion goals, which included creating a pro-Israeli Christian-dominated government in Lebanon, destroying Syrian influence there, and convincing the Palestinians living in the West Bank and Gaza to accept the limited autonomy that Israeli prime minister Menahem Begin had offered them. In addition, Israel's reputation was sullied when its Christian allies, looking for hidden PLO operatives in the Sabra and Shatilla refugee camps, killed more than three hundred Palestinians. Heartened by the difficulties Israel was encountering in Lebanon as the Iranian-backed Hizbollah launched attacks against Israeli troops there, the Palestinians in the West Bank and Gaza rose up against Israel in December 1987 in what became known as the First Intifada. Initially, Israel did not know how to respond to the Intifada, and its heavy-handed actions eroded its position in world public opinion. The First Gulf War (1990–1991), which followed the Iraqi invasion of Kuwait, however, diverted attention from the Intifada, and PLO leader Yasser Arafat's decision to support Iraq's Saddam Hussein in the war gravely weakened the Palestinian position, not only in the West but also among the Gulf Arab states, especially Saudi Arabia.

Following the war, the Madrid Peace Conference was convened by the United States to expedite the Arab-Israeli peace process. While the conference itself did not lead to any immediate agreements, other than some private economic deals between Arabs and Israelis, the election of Labor Party leader Yitzhak Rabin as Israel's new prime minister in 1992 led to secret talks with the PLO that culminated in the Oslo I partial peace agreement of 1993, which called for mutual recognition, the end of Palestinian terrorism, and the establishment of a Palestinian Authority in Gaza (although Israeli settlements and army bases would remain there) and the city of Jericho. Oslo I was followed, despite increased incidents of Palestinian terrorism that undermined the Israeli public's confidence in the peace process, by the 1995 Oslo II agreement, which gave the Palestinian Authority both administrative and security control over the large cities on the West Bank, except for the city of Hebron. Meanwhile, Israel and Jordan signed a peace treaty in 1994, under which Jordan promised not to allow the stationing of Arab armies on its soil, and Israel promised not to expel Palestinian Arabs into Jordan.[10]

The Arab-Israeli peace process suffered a blow, however, in November 1995 when Rabin was assassinated by a Jewish religious fanatic who opposed the

Oslo agreements, and by the election in May 1996 of Likud leader Benjamin Netanyahu, who was considerably less enthusiastic about the Israeli-Palestinian peace process than Rabin had been. Nonetheless, Netanyahu signed two additional partial peace agreements with the Palestinians (Hebron in 1997 and Wye in 1998). The May 1999 elections, in which Labor leader Ehud Barak defeated Netanyahu, also brought new hope to the peace process. However, even with the mediation of US president Bill Clinton, Israel and Syria could not agree on a peace treaty, primarily because of a border dispute in the area of the Sea of Galilee. Similarly, despite Clinton's mediation efforts at Camp David in July 2000, Barak and Arafat could not reach an agreement, even though Barak offered to Arafat all of Gaza, 92 percent of the West Bank, and East Jerusalem. The subsequent outbreak of the al-Aqsa Intifada in September 2000, replete with Palestinian terrorist attacks on Israeli civilians, led in 2001 to the election of the new Likud leader, Ariel Sharon, as prime minister. Sharon, in 2002, ordered the Israeli army to reenter the Palestinian cities on the West Bank to stop the Palestinian terrorist attacks. Subsequently, he ordered the construction of a security fence between Israeli and Palestinian areas for the same purpose.

In 2004, after an unsuccessful international effort known as the "road map" (sponsored by the United States, the European Union, the UN, and Russia), calling for a cease-fire followed by a three-stage process leading to a Palestinian state, Sharon came up with a plan to unilaterally pull Israeli settlements and military bases out of Gaza, as well as Israeli settlements out of the northern West Bank, to both cement the Jewish majority in Israeli-controlled areas and give the Palestinians a chance for self-government in Gaza.[11] The plan was implemented in 2005, despite opposition by Israel's Religious Zionist community. The peace process, however, was not helped by this development. Rockets from Gaza continued to be fired into Israel, and in the January 2006 Palestinian Legislative Council elections, Hamas won the majority and formed a government on the platform of no recognition of Israel and no long-term peace with Israel. The election struck a major blow to the Israeli-Palestinian peace process. Then, in the summer of 2006, Iranian-backed Hizbollah precipitated a month-long Israeli-Lebanese war, further raising tension in the Middle East.

Israeli Politics and Society

Israel has a proportional-representation, party-list political system with a large number of political parties, because only 2 percent of the vote is needed to get a seat in the Israeli Parliament (the Knesset). With 120 seats in the Knesset, 61 are required to form a government.[12] Since no political party since

1948 has secured 61 seats, coalition governments consisting of multiple parties have been the norm. From 1996 to 2003, Israel established a separate vote for prime minister and the Knesset. Primarily because this reform gave too much power to the smaller parties, it was dropped for the 2006 elections, and the old system was reinstated.

From 1949 to 1977, the Israeli Labor Party—first under David Ben-Gurion and Moshe Sharett, and then under Levi Eshkol, Golda Meir, and Yitzhak Rabin in his first term as Israel's prime minister—dominated Israeli politics, forming all the coalitions. However, Israel's poor performance in the initial stages of the 1973 Yom Kippur War, together with a number of political scandals and the defection of numerous Labor Party members to form a new party (the Democratic Movement for Change), led to Labor's defeat in the 1977 Israeli elections and the coming to power of the Likud Party, under Menahem Begin. Following Begin's resignation in 1983 after the failures of his Lebanese war strategy had become apparent, he was succeeded by Yitzhak Shamir, who, after Shimon Peres was prime minister in a national unity government from 1984 to 1986, took over as the prime minister from 1986 to 1988.

Following the 1988 elections, Shamir headed another national unity government from 1988 to 1990. Although Likud governed alone from 1990 to 1992 under Shamir, he lost the 1992 elections to the new Labor Party leader, Yitzhak Rabin, who began the Oslo peace process with the Palestinians. Following Rabin's assassination in November 1995, Shimon Peres served as prime minister, only to be defeated by Likud leader Benjamin Netanyahu in the May 1996 elections. Netanyahu, in turn, was defeated by Labor Party leader Ehud Barak in the May 1999 elections, but Barak lost to Likud leader Ariel Sharon in the February 2001 elections as the al-Aqsa Intifada raged. Sharon overwhelmingly won the January 2003 elections, in large part because of his tough position on Palestinian terrorism. Then, because of the opposition of a number of Likud Party members to his plan for unilateral withdrawal from Gaza, in November 2005 Sharon split from Likud to form the Kadima Party, which drew members not only from Sharon's Likud Party, but also from the Labor Party, including former Labor prime minister Shimon Peres. However, in January 2006, Sharon suffered a massive stroke, which incapacitated him.

Sharon was succeeded as Kadima Party leader by Ehud Olmert, who led Kadima to a narrow election victory in March 2006. Soon after the elections, however, Olmert was confronted with a two-front war, following the kidnapping of an Israeli soldier by a Hamas-led force from Gaza in June 2006, and the kidnappings of two Israeli soldiers by Hizbollah operating from southern Lebanon in July 2006. Israel's failure to decisively win either conflict (due in part to strategic mistakes committed by Olmert),[13] coupled with a number of corruption charges against Olmert from the period before he became prime minister, gravely weakened his personal political position, although his inclusion of Avigdor Liberman's Israel Beiteinu Party in his coalition government in November 2006 did strengthen his coalition. However, Liberman was to leave the government coalition in January 2008.

From 1977 to 2005, as Israel's economy was gradually privatized, the main difference between the Labor and Likud parties was no longer over how to organize Israel economically (capitalism vs. socialism), but over the Arab-Israeli peace process, the Labor Party being more willing to make concessions to the Arabs, and especially to the Palestinians, than Likud, which advocated an aggressive program of settlement building in the West Bank. Following its formation, the Kadima Party took a centrist position between Labor and Likud on the Arab-Israeli conflict.

While security issues have dominated the Israeli scene since 1948, Israel faced a number of other challenges as 2008 dawned. These include the conflict among Orthodox, Traditional, and Secular Israeli Jews over the proper place of the Jewish religion in Israel's public life; the question as to whether Haredi (ultra-Orthodox) Jews should serve in the Israeli army; residual unhappiness among the Sephardi Jews who had immigrated to Israel from Arab countries, and who felt that they had been given second-class treatment by Israel's Ashkenazi (European Jewish) "establishment"; the success of the integration into Israeli society of Jews from the former Soviet Union and Ethiopia; growing strains between Israeli Jews and Israeli Arabs (approximately 20 percent of Israel's population) over the proper place of Arabs in a Jewish-majority society, as well as the loyalty of the Arabs to the Israeli state; and the growing gap between rich and poor in Israel, even as Israel was achieving a Western European standard of living and a per capita GNP equal to that of the United Kingdom.[14]

Within Israeli history and politics, the assassination of Israeli prime minister Yitzhak Rabin by an Israeli Jewish religious fanatic, Yigal Amir, was in many ways a turning point. Since the assassination, Israeli politics has been in turmoil, with no fewer than five different prime ministers in the following twelve years (Shimon Peres, Benjamin Netanyahu, Ehud Barak, Ariel Sharon, and Ehud Olmert). This period has also witnessed the rise and collapse of political parties such as Yisrael B'aliya, a party of Russian immigrants, and Shinui, the secularist party that, after skyrocketing from six to fifteen parliamentary seats between the 1999 and 2003 elections, disappeared entirely in 2006. There has also been a gradual estrangement of Israel's Arab minority from the country's Jewish majority, a process accelerated by the outbreak of the al-Aqsa Intifada in September 2000. The post-1995 period also witnessed the rapid privatization of the Israeli economy and an increasingly activist Israeli Supreme Court, which has played a growing role in Israeli politics.

Another major consequence of the assassination was a slowing of the peace process between Israel and both Syria and the Palestinians. While there was a temporary revival of the two peace processes under Prime Minister Ehud Barak (1999–2001), both collapsed in 2000, and attempts to revive them following the death of Palestinian leader Yasser Arafat in November 2004 have yet to meet with success.

Beyond the Arab world, while US-Israeli relations remained strong during the period following the assassination and Israel actively developed ties with Muslim Turkey and Hindu India, Israel faced a growing threat from Iran, a country many thought to be developing nuclear weapons and whose president, Mahmoud Ahmadinejad, in 2005 openly called for Israel's destruction. Compounding the threat from Iran was that country's solidifying alliance with Syria, which remained a major enemy of Israel, and its assistance to two other enemies of Israel: Hizbollah and Hamas.

Given these events, the authors of the chapters in this book have been challenged not only to explain what has happened, but also to place the events they analyze into the larger context of Israeli history.

Since the death of Rabin, there have been three right-wing prime ministers (Benjamin Netanyahu, Ariel Sharon, and Ehud Olmert) and two left-wing prime ministers (Shimon Peres and Ehud Barak); and in the twelve years since 1995, the Israeli right has controlled the office of prime minister for almost ten of the thirteen years. Ilan Peleg of Lafayette College, in Chapter 2, "The Israeli Right," traces the rise of the Israeli right since its beginnings in 1922 under Vladimir Jabotinsky. While Peleg cites the core ideological beliefs of the right, he also notes that pragmatism as well as ideological commitment was clearly demonstrated by Menahem Begin, who was willing to give up the Sinai; Netanyahu, who gave up Israel's claim to "both banks of the Jordan River"; and Sharon, who was willing to pull out of Gaza.

By contrast, in Chapter 3, "The Israeli Zionist Left," Mark Rosenblum of Queens College traces the decline of the Israeli left since 1995. In part, he argues, it was due to Rabin's misguided legacy of "fighting terrorism as if there was no peace process, and pursuing the peace process as if there was no terrorism," and in part it was due to Ehud Barak's mismanagement of both foreign policy and domestic politics during his short tenure as prime minister, although Rosenblum allots his share of blame to Yasser Arafat, whose failure to control Palestinian terrorism undercut both Rabin and Barak.

Israel's religious parties, with the exception of Shas, have been in existence since the establishment of the state. Shmuel Sandler and Aaron Kampinsky of Bar-Ilan University discuss the evolution of the religious parties since 1995 in

Chapter 4, "Israel's Religious Parties." They note the decline of Mafdal, the National Religious Party, because of its overconcentration on territorial issues: holding onto the West Bank and Gaza and proliferating settlements there. By contrast, Shas, the Sephardi ultra-Orthodox party, which emerged on Israel's national political scene only in 1984, did quite well in the post-1995 period because it sought to meet the needs of its Sephardi constituency, many of whom were not ultra-Orthodox. Using the model of consociationalism, Sandler and Kampinsky emphasize that Labor, Likud, and Kadima have all sought to include at least one religious party in their coalition governments for the sake of social harmony.

In contrast to the more mainstream Likud, Kadima, and Labor parties and also to the religious parties, Israel's Russian parties, as their name implies, get a significant amount of their support from Israel's Russian community. In Chapter 5, "Israel's Russian Parties," Vladimir (Ze'ev) Khanin of Bar-Ilan University traces the rise and fall of Natan Sharansky's Yisrael B'aliya Party as the main party of Russian immigrants. Khanin also points out that the Russian immigrants tend to split their vote between "mainstream" parties and Russian communal parties, the most recent of which is Avigdor Liberman's Israel Beiteinu Party, which received eleven Knesset seats in the 2006 elections.

While Israel's Russian parties have seen a major evolution since they first appeared on the Israeli scene, so, too, have Israel's Arab parties, as pointed out by Hillel Frisch of Bar-Ilan University in Chapter 6, "Israel's Arab Parties." Initially voting for a list affiliated with Israel's Labor Party, by the mid-1970s Israel's Arabs had shifted their vote to the Communist Party, primarily as a protest vote. By the mid-1990s, they had switched again, giving increasing support to a basically Islamist list (the UAL, or United Arab List) and to an Arab nationalist list (Balad), as well as to the Communist Party (the Democratic Front for Peace and Equality). By the 2006 elections, despite some hope for a single Arab party, the Arab votes were almost evenly divided among the UAL (four Knesset seats), the Communists (three Knesset seats), and Balad (three Knesset seats). Frisch also discusses the impact on Arab voters of such events as the al-Aqsa Intifada and the dispute over the building of a proposed mosque near the Church of Ascension in Nazareth. While noting the growing anti-Israeli radicalization of Israeli Arab elites, Frisch also emphasizes that the rank and file of Israeli Arabs, seeing the economic benefits of being citizens in the Jewish state, are not, so far at least, moving to separate themselves from Israel.

Another major change in Israeli life, although it began before Rabin's death, has been the increasing political impact of Israel's Supreme Court, as noted by Pnina Lahav of Boston College's Law School in Chapter 7, "Israel's Supreme Court." Lahav traces this development by making four major comparisons:

judicial activism versus judicial restraint; Israel as a democracy versus Israel as a Jewish state; unilateralism versus multilateralism in the context of the Arab-Israeli conflict; and catastrophe Zionism versus utopian Zionism. She concludes, however, that the Supreme Court is now under attack by the government of Ehud Olmert and that its future is unclear.

One of the major changes in the period since Rabin has been in the Israeli economy, as Ofira Seliktar of Gratz College points out in Chapter 8, "Israel's Economy." After a number of years of slowness in growth, caused in part by deepening structural problems in the Israeli economy, as well as by the al-Aqsa Intifada, in 2003 Israel embarked on a major program of economic reform. The reform included cuts in public sector salaries and transfer payments, a major privatization of government-owned public companies, and the restructuring of the Israeli capital market. The result was a sharp increase in gross national product per capita, a rise in Israeli exports, and an increase in foreign investment, making Israel, in the mind of some observers, a new "economic miracle," although Israel still has a poverty problem.

In the realm of foreign policy Israel's relations with the Palestinians are perhaps the most difficult and complicated of any of its foreign relationships. In Chapter 9, "Israel and the Palestinians," Barry Rubin of the Gloria Center argues that the failure to solve the Israeli-Palestinian conflict is primarily the responsibility of the Palestinians and, in particular, Yasser Arafat. Arafat, argues Rubin, despite being given numerous opportunities to create a Palestinian state, not only refused a series of generous offers, at Camp David II in July 2000 and in the Clinton Parameters of December 2000, but also chose to use terrorism as a tool of his negotiating strategy—a tool that backfired when Ariel Sharon was elected Israel's prime minister in February 2001 and re-elected in 2003. The result was an increase in Palestinian misery and, by June 2007, a split between Gaza and the West Bank, which were controlled by rival Palestinian factions.

While Rubin primarily blames the Palestinians for the failure to advance the peace process, David W. Lesch of Trinity University, in Chapter 10, "Israel and the Arab World," also puts a good bit of blame on Israel and the United States. Although highly critical of Palestinian suicide bombings, Lesch also feels that both Israel and the United States lost a real opportunity by failing to complete an Israeli-Syrian peace treaty in 2000. Had such a treaty been completed, Lesch speculates in an exercise in "counterfactual history," the war in Iraq and the 2006 Israel-Hizbollah conflict might never have happened.

While in the period after the assassination of Rabin Israel was preoccupied with its relations with the Palestinians, Lebanon, and Syria, successive Israeli governments also developed relations with both Turkey and India. This is the topic of Efraim Inbar of Bar-Ilan University in Chapter 11, "Israel's Strategic

Relations with Turkey and India." Building on arms sales to both Turkey and India, Israel was soon to develop strategic ties with both countries, Islam being an important factor. In the case of Turkey, Israel sees the importance of close ties with a leading Muslim state. In the case of India, Israel gains access to India's 100-million-strong Muslim community even as it cooperates with India against the threat from Muslim Pakistan. Inbar also notes that the survival of Israel's relationships with Turkey and India despite domestic changes in both countries indicates the "staying power" of the relationships.

America, both at the time of Rabin's assassination and during the twelve years following that tragic event, has remained Israel's closest ally. Robert O. Freedman of Johns Hopkins University argues in Chapter 12, "Israel and the United States," that despite occasional problems, as during Benjamin Netanyahu's prime ministership and immediately after September 11, 2001, US-Israeli relations have remained solid since 1995. In addition to providing $3 billion in military and economic aid to Israel, the United States has strongly backed Israel at the United Nations. Especially under George W. Bush, who strongly denounced Palestinian terrorism, the United States has backed the main Israeli positions in the Arab-Israeli conflict, supporting Israel's right to retaliate against terrorist attacks from any territory from which it would withdraw, and affirming that a solution to the Palestinian refugee problem had to be found in the new Palestinian state, not in the return of the refugees to Israel, thus preserving Israel as a Jewish state.

Since 1995, Israel has had to confront a number of new strategic challenges. In Chapter 13, "Existential Threats to Israel," Steven R. David of Johns Hopkins University examines a series of these potential threats. While basically ruling out the threat of attack by neighboring Arab armies and the so-called demographic threat of the Arab population in Israel, he states that Iran is currently the sole existential threat to Israel, especially since its president, Mahmoud Ahmadinejad, and some of the other top Iranian leaders seem to believe that the destruction of Israel, whatever the cost of a retaliatory Israeli strike, would pave the way for the return of the "Hidden Imam," and that against such "true believers" normal deterrence doesn't work.

While Yitzhak Rabin went down in history as the victor of the 1967 War, Ehud Olmert will probably go down in history as the man who did not win the 2006 war with Hizbollah. In Chapter 14, "Israel's 2006 War with Hizbollah: The Failure of Deterrence," Elli Lieberman of Baltimore Hebrew University argues that it was not only Olmert who was at fault for the failure to defeat Hizbollah, but also his predecessors, Ehud Barak and Ariel Sharon. Had Barak and Sharon reacted more forcefully to the limited Hizbollah attacks and incursions between 2000 and 2006, Lieberman argues, Hizbollah would never have dared to launch the type of attack it did in July 2006. Given Israel's devastating response to that attack, Lieberman asserts, Israel's deterrence posture has been restored.

In sum, the years since 1995 have been highly eventful ones for the State of Israel, and it is hoped that readers of this book will better appreciate the complexities of Israeli domestic politics and foreign policy after engaging with the varied perspectives of the contributors.

Notes

1. For a detailed analysis of the evolution of Zionism, see Walter Laqueur, *A History of Zionism* (New York: Holt, Rinehart & Winston, 1972). For excerpts from leading Zionist thinkers, see Arthur Herzberg, ed., *The Zionist Idea: A Historical Analysis and Reader* (New York: Jewish Publication Society, 1997).

2. On this point, see Barbara Tuchman, *Bible and Sword: England and Palestine from the Bronze Age to Balfour* (New York: Ballantine Books, 1984).

3. For a very readable analysis of Britain's conflicting promises during World War I, see David Fromkin, *A Peace to End All Peace* (New York: Avon Books, 1990).

4. For studies of the growth of the Jewish community in Palestine during the British Mandate, see Martin Gilbert, *Israel: A History* (New York: William Morrow, 1998), chaps. 3–8; Howard Sachar, *A History of Israel from the Rise of Zionism to Our Time*, 3rd rev. ed. (New York: Knopf, 2007), chaps. 6–11; and Tom Segev, *One Palestine Complete: Jews and Arabs under the British Mandate* (New York: Henry Holt, 2001).

5. For studies of the dynamics of the 1948–1949 war, see Gilbert, *Israel;* Sachar, *History of Israel;* and Chaim Herzog, *The Arab-Israeli Wars: War and Peace in the Middle East* (New York: Random House, 1982).

6. On these events see Steven Spiegel, *The Other Arab-Israeli Conflict: Making America's Middle East Policy, from Truman to Reagan* (Chicago: University of Chicago Press, 1985).

7. See Warren Bass, *Support Any Friend: Kennedy's Middle East and the Making of the U.S.-Israel Alliance* (New York: Oxford University Press, 2003).

8. The 1967 war is discussed in Gilbert, *Israel;* Sachar, *History of Israel;* Herzog, *Arab-Israeli Wars;* and Michael Oren, *Six Days of War: June 1967 and the Making of the Modern Middle East* (New York: Oxford University Press, 2002).

9. U.S. policy toward the Arab-Israeli conflict from 1967 to 2004 is discussed in William Quandt, *Peace Process: American Diplomacy and the Arab-Israeli Conflict since 1967,* 3rd ed. (Los Angeles: University of California Press, 2005).

10. For an insider's view of the peace process, see Dennis Ross, *The Missing Peace: The Inside Story of the Fight for Middle East Peace* (New York: Farrar, Straus, & Giroux, 2005).

11. For a study of the disengagement, see David Makovsky, *Engagement through Disengagement: Gaza and the Potential for Renewed Israeli-Palestinian Peace-Making* (Washington, DC: Washington Institute for Near East Policy, 2005).

12. For introductions to the Israeli political system, see Gregory Mahler, *Politics and Government in Israel* (New York: Rowman & Littlefield, 2004), and Don Peretz and Gideon Duron, *The Government and Politics of Israel* (Boulder, CO: Westview Press, 1997).

13. See the chapter by Elli Lieberman in this book.

14. For an introduction to the interaction of the varied elements of Israeli society, see Amos Oz, *In the Land of Israel* (New York: Harcourt Brace, 1993).

PART ONE

Israel's Domestic Politics

2

The Israeli Right

Ilan Peleg

PROMOTING THE IDEA THAT JEWS should return to Eretz Israel (Palestine) in large numbers, the Zionist movement has experienced the emergence of political factions within it from its very inception. But possibly its most important ideological split, a cleavage still existing today within the Israeli society, occurred in 1922. In that year the Zionist movement had begun to witness what might be conceptualized as a fundamental, deep-seated division between a pragmatic-moderate "Left" and an idealist-maximalist "Right."

The Left or, more accurately the Center Left, included political parties associated with the labor movement in Mandatory Palestine (1917–1948) and with centrist parties (the "bourgeoisie," or middle class). Its leaders (e.g., Chaim Arlosoroff, David Ben-Gurion, and Chaim Weizmann) believed that the emerging Arab-Jewish conflict over the land, escalating particularly after World War I, could be resolved through territorial partition of the country. The Right, associated with the personality of Vladimir (Ze'ev) Jabotinsky (1880–1940), doubted both the possibility and the desirability of any compromise solution, including partition. This fundamental division has been in existence since the 1920s, although it has changed its form through the years and was, in part, responsible for the assassination of Prime Minister Yitzhak Rabin in 1995.

In studying the Right, this chapter has several functions. The first is to review the history of the Zionist Right and, later (after 1948), the Israeli Right between its inception (in 1922), through the premiership and assassination of Rabin (November 1995) in a poisonous political atmosphere created by the Israeli Right, to the time of writing (mid-2007). Historical insight is essential for understanding the behavior of the contemporary Israeli Right. The chapter's

21

second function is to offer a detailed analysis of the fundamental ideology of the Right by pointing to the common features of its factions through several decades, commonalities that have been sustained despite numerous tactical changes (which will be pointed out in the chapter). The third function is to link the history and the ideology of the Right and to explain the overall political behavior of that political camp, especially during the last three decades. The concluding section discusses the capacity of the Right to adjust to new realities while maintaining its ideology.

The overall thesis of this chapter is that while the Right has emerged among Zionists and later Israelis as a fairly coherent ideological camp, since 1965 (that is, even before the Six Day War) it began to lose its ideological purity due to considerations of attaining and then maintaining power and responding to external political pressures. This process was further accelerated, surprisingly, under the leadership of Menahem Begin, following his ascendance to Israel's premiership (1977). This pragmatic tilt was reflected in the 1978 Camp David Accords. Begin's successors as the leaders of the Right followed his path for the most part, although some with more vigor than others; while they spoke an ideological language, they often behaved pragmatically. In other words, they adjusted to the realities on the ground. One of them, Ariel Sharon, completely broke ranks with the Right and its ideological commitments by moving ideologically to the center and, equally important, by leaving the Likud and establishing the Kadima Party (2005). At the same time, since the entire Israeli political system moved to the right, in a way that will be explained in the concluding section, the Right had to make relatively modest concessions in terms of its overall ideology. The chapter will try to assess the likely behavior of the Right in the future, as it attempts to maintain its traditional ideological purity in the face of changing political realities.

The Zionist-Israeli Right, 1922–2007

The birth of the Zionist and later the Israeli Right is directly connected to the history of Palestine (Eretz Israel) at the end of World War I and the evolution of conflict between Jews and Arabs in the land. Toward the end of the war, Palestine was conquered by the British army. While the British were committed to the establishment of a "national home for the Jewish People" in Palestine, in the language of the famous Balfour Declaration of November 2, 1917, the Arabs of Palestine and beyond resisted the rule of the new colonial power and, in particular, the implementation of the Balfour Declaration. Riots broke out in Jerusalem in 1920 and continued sporadically throughout most of the period of the British Mandate, leading occasionally to massive violence.

In June 1922, the British government published a document that indicated that the Balfour Declaration would apply only to the area west of the Jordan River, not to "Transjordan," east of the river. This position was among the most important provisions of what became known as the "Churchill White Paper," a document in which Winston Churchill, the Secretary of State for the Colonies, sought to clarify the British position on the future of the region.

The diverse reactions of Zionists to the new British policy gave birth to what could be regarded as the Zionist Right and, after 1948, the Israeli Right. The vast majority of leaders of the World Zionist Organization, including the Zionist Executive, accepted the British decision to separate Transjordan from what became the British Mandate of Palestine west of the river. One important Zionist leader, Vladimir Jabotinsky, rejected this proposal and insisted on Jewish control over all of Palestine, east and west of the Jordan River. He adopted a noncompromising, territorialist, maximalist, and militaristic approach to the evolving conflict between Arabs and Jews in the land. Thus was born the Zionist Right, a political camp that still exists.

Throughout the 1920s and 1930s, and until his death in 1940, Jabotinsky promoted persistently the demands for Jewish settlement of the East Bank (Transjordan) and the immediate establishment of a Jewish state, positions that most Zionists found unachievable. Since the Zionist leadership adopted a significantly more moderate, gradual, and conciliatory policy toward the Arabs as well as the British, Jabotinsky's relationships with other leaders, particularly those representing the socialist labor parties, grew more and more strained.

While Jabotinsky's popularity in Palestine was limited, he was more enthusiastically received in eastern Europe, especially in Poland. His nationalist message resonated with Jews who lived under pressure in a hostile, often anti-Semitic environment. One of Jabotinsky's Polish disciples was the young Menahem Begin, later his successor as the most prominent leader of the Right.

Jabotinsky acted decisively to develop a distinct rightist identity among the Zionists. In 1925 he established the Revisionist Zionist Organization, emphasizing his demand for revising (thus the name of his organization) the position of the World Zionist Organization. A decade later he completed his public break with the Zionist establishment by forming the New Zionist Organization.

The difference between the ideological Right and the pragmatic Center and Left among the Zionists was reemphasized and put on public display following the Arab revolt of 1936, an eruption of massive violence of the Arabs of Palestine against the British rulers and the Jewish Zionists in the land. While the majority of Jews and members of the Zionist movement supported negotiation with the Arabs on the basis of the partition plan proposed by Britain's Peel Commission (1937), Jabotinsky and his followers on the Right rejected partition in principle and argued for exclusive Jewish dominion on both sides of the Jordan River.

Menahem Begin, who came to dominate the Zionist Right following Jabotinsky's death, represented an even more radical right-wing ideology and action than his master.[1] On a number of occasions, Jabotinsky and Begin clashed publicly over important political and ideological matters, Begin invariably representing a more radical position. While Begin received "a solid European-style general education" in the Polish gymnasium he attended, he was exposed to a good deal of anti-Semitism among the students, an important experience in his ideological development.[2] When he was sixteen, Begin joined Betar, a Zionist organization committed to intense nationalism, discipline, and military power.[3]

Begin rose quickly within Betar, eventually becoming the leader of seventy thousand Betarists in Poland. When World War II erupted, he escaped to Vilna. Following imprisonment in the USSR, he was unexpectedly released under an agreement between the Poles and the Russians. He volunteered for the Polish army and was sent to Palestine in May 1942. In December 1943 he was discharged and immediately appointed as the commander of the Irgun Zvai Leumi (National Military Organization).

The IZL was on the far right among Zionists. Its goals were to defeat both the Arabs and the British by armed force. Reflecting the IZL's and his own philosophy, Begin titled chapter 4 of his book about this period, *The Revolt*, "We Fight, Therefore We Are."[4] Reflecting its militant approach, the IZL's emblem was a raised arm carrying a bayonet-tipped rifle over a map of Palestine in its entirety; the words *Rak Kach* ("Only Thus") were superimposed.

The IZL declared a revolt against the British administration in Palestine in early 1944. Its anti-British campaign was designed to destroy the relationship between the colonial power and moderate Jews. The leadership of the Jewish community in Palestine, the Yishuv, was alarmed; IZL's violent activities jeopardized the sympathy toward Zionism in Western public opinion, particularly in Britain and the United States.

When the war ended, IZL operations became even less restrained. They increasingly resembled the activities of Lehi, a splinter group known for its extreme radicalism.[5] While Haganah, the "official" defense force of the Yishuv, acted moderately and with limited political goals—the establishment of a Jewish state in part of Western Palestine—the IZL acted in an extreme manner in order to achieve radical goals: a Jewish state in all of Palestine, on both sides of the Jordan River.

On November 29, 1947, the General Assembly of the United Nations passed the partition resolution, dividing the land between Jews and Arabs. Although the leadership of the Yishuv and the vast majority of Jews all over the world accepted the resolution, the IZL and the Revisionists rejected the initiative. A similar position was taken publicly, when David Ben-Gurion declared the establishment of the state of Israel (May 14, 1948), the IZL swearing to "redeem" the entire land.

Yet, once the war ended, the Right found itself in the parliamentary opposition. Begin and his associates established the Herut (Freedom) Party. The birth of Herut signaled the victory of the military branch of the Revisionist movement over the civilian branch, the militants over the moderates. The platform of Herut was quite radical: a call for territorial expansion, rejection of the borders of the newly established state, and negation of any document designed to reach a compromise, including the November 1947 resolution. Herut alone remained outside the Israeli consensus in regard to the 1949 armistice agreements and borders.

Herut's radicalism was reflected in its position not only on the territorial issue but also on other matters. The 1952 political crisis in Israel over monetary reparations from Germany was indicative of Herut's mode of operation. The party organized extraparliamentary, violent opposition, with Begin directing it from above.[6]

Throughout the 1950s Herut continued to consistently support an activist foreign policy. While within Mapai, Ben-Gurion's ruling party, there were dovish and hawkish attitudes and even organized ideological camps, Herut was hawkishly univocal. It supported enthusiastically the controversial Reprisal Policy, promoted close military and political alliances with the West (especially with France), and endorsed preventive and expansionist wars.

But the behavior of Herut prevented it from gaining legitimacy within the young democracy, especially during the state's first ten to fifteen formative years. With the departure of Ben-Gurion from the scene (1963), however, the situation began to change. A political realignment occurred. In early 1965 Herut and the Liberal Party established GAHAL, an acronym for "Herut-Liberal Bloc." It was a political victory for Begin since it signaled that the respectable middle class (that is, the Liberal Party) was ready to cooperate with his ultranationalist party, as a counterbalance to the left-of-center, ruling *Ma'arach* ("Alignment").

While GAHAL lost badly the 1965 election, by starting to build political bridges to other, more moderate parties Herut was successful in blurring its own controversial image without actually giving up its long-held ideological positions. Begin remained an expansionist, annexationist zealot until the 1967 War.[7]

The 1967 conflict not only changed the entire balance of power in the Middle East, but it also gave the Israeli Right a new lease on life, an opportunity to become a politically relevant and eventually dominant political power within Israel. A process that might be called *Herutization* occurred, a process in which the moderate, liberal elements in GAHAL and beyond succumbed to the nationalist language and policy of the hard-core Right. The change was already reflected in the 1969 GAHAL electoral platform. It stated bluntly, "We will maintain the integrity of the land; Eretz Israel will never be divided again."

By the time the 1969 document was written, Begin was already an accepted member of the country's political establishment. The acute political crisis in Israel prior to the 1967 War had brought him into the government of national unity. While a member of the Levi Eshkol and Golda Meir governments, Begin created an image of moderation and reasonableness, although his position grew increasingly hawkish. Thus, he protested the official meetings of Israelis with UN mediator Gunnar Jarring[8] and argued for setting up Jewish quarters in Arab cities of the West Bank. When the Meir government decided to accept an American diplomatic initiative calling for Arab-Israeli discussions through Ambassador Jarring, Begin and his party left the government.

Out of power and in opposition again, the Right organized itself once more, this time under the banner of Likud. Interestingly, the political program of the new body was a carbon copy of Herut's traditional ideological perspective. It declared that the Jewish people had an inalienable right to all of biblical Palestine and that the Likud would not accept any Israeli withdrawal from the West Bank. The message of the new political alliance was simple: "Not an inch!"[9]

In 1977 the Likud won, unexpectedly, the Israeli election, ending more than half a century of political dominance by the labor parties. Low-income, blue-collar Israelis and Jews of non-European descent voted overwhelmingly for Likud. The election reflected the move of the Israeli Jewish public to the right as a result of the traumatic wars of 1967 and 1973. While most Likud voters might never have heard of Jabotinsky, by voting for Begin, they gave him an opportunity to implement the master's vision. Likud's 1977 electoral platform stated categorically that "Judaea and Samaria shall not be relinquished to foreign rule" and that "between the sea and the Jordan there will be Jewish sovereignty alone." This position closed the door not only on a Palestinian state but also on the return of the West Bank to Jordan. Yet it left the door open to some sort of nominal autonomy for the West Bank Palestinians.

As prime minister of Israel, Begin implemented faithfully the ideology of the Right, including the Likud, although he had to adjust it to external pressures. The cornerstone of that policy was the effort to maintain Israel's control over the West Bank and Gaza. Begin's positions before, during, and following the famous Camp David conference (September 1978) and his attitudes toward Egypt, Syria, and Lebanon form a comprehensible, logical whole only if interpreted within the fundamentalist ideological context within which he operated.

Begin's policies can clearly be divided into two periods. In the first, that of *moderation* (1977–1979), he carried out what some have perceived as "peace diplomacy," agreeing to Israeli withdrawal from the entire Sinai Peninsula and pursuing negotiations over the future of the West Bank and Gaza. During this period he adjusted his traditional ideological positions by agreeing, for example, to the concept of territorial withdrawal, possible autonomy for the inhabitants of the West Bank,[10] recognition of the "legitimate rights" of the Palestinian people (at the Camp David Accords), and so forth. In the second period, that of *radicalization* (1980–1983), a new policy emerged; it included efforts to guarantee that negotiations on Palestinian autonomy would fail and, eventually, ordering a full-fledged invasion of Lebanon.

Begin's policy in the first period led to the radicalization of the second period. "He managed the autonomy talks so that nothing could be possibly achieved," said one observer.[11] Other analysts knew, even at the time, that Begin was offering "false autonomy"[12] and that, above all, he wanted to "kill" the autonomy talks.[13] Even Begin's big concession to the Egyptians—Israeli withdrawal from the entire Sinai Peninsula—could be understood only as part of his larger, ideologically determined plan; "He was giving up the Sinai to protect himself against any eventual concession in the West Bank," testified Begin's first defense minister.[14] As predicted, the autonomy talks eventually collapsed and the government's annexationist policies through massive settlement continued unabated.

The settlement effort by the Likud government was highly successful in numerical terms. During Begin's tenure as prime minister, the number of settlements increased from 24 to 106, and the number of settlers from 3,200 persons to 28,400.[15] Yet, from a political perspective, the settlement effort was a failure. Rather than breaking the resistance of the local population to the occupation, it increased it. Moreover, the cause of the Palestinians, especially their claim to an independent state in the West Bank and Gaza, generated increased worldwide support. Much of this support came from the center of PLO (Palestine Liberation Organization) activity in Lebanon. The realization of this fact led the Begin government into its greatest blunder, the 1982 Lebanon war.

The war in Lebanon was an outgrowth of the political thinking of the Right, particularly since 1967 but in many ways since 1922. The assumption of the Right has always been that there is a place for one and only one sovereignty in

Eretz Israel, and that this sovereignty must be Jewish. Therefore, it was concluded, no real compromise, territorial or otherwise, was possible or even desirable. When the resistance to Israel's occupation persisted, Likud leaders thought that the only way to deal with it was to crush it, and that the way to crush it was to defeat the PLO in Lebanon.

The results of the Lebanon war were, however, disastrous. While the PLO was forced out of Lebanon, it was not defeated or, more important, perceived as having been defeated. In fact, its prestige grew. The war generated strong anti-Israeli feelings in Lebanon, affecting Israeli-Lebanese relations negatively even a quarter of a century later. The conflict damaged Israel's image in the world and polarized the Israeli public as never before. These one-sided consequences led eventually to Begin's sudden resignation and complete withdrawal from public life in 1983.

Menahem Begin was succeeded in office by his foreign minister, Yitzhak Shamir, a former leader of Lehi, the radical underground in Mandatory Palestine. The Lebanese debacle and the establishment of a Likud-Labor National Unity government in 1984 marked a hiatus in the power of the Right, although the settlement effort continued unabated. Moreover, in 1988 the Likud returned to power as the leading partner in the coalition. The Shamir government intensified the settlement policy, thus antagonizing Israel's chief international supporter, the United States, as well as significant segments of the Israeli public. Shamir refused even to consider an Israeli withdrawal from Gaza, a highly popular idea among the vast majority of Israelis.[16] No wonder that in the June 1992 election Likud under Shamir was defeated by the more pragmatic Labor under Yitzhak Rabin.

Yet it is essential to realize that even in decline, the Likud maintained its ideological purity. Its leaders saw the defeat as merely a temporary retreat, and they did not have any intention of bowing to either international pressures or internal demands for moving away from the idea of Greater Israel. Even the Intifada, the Arab popular rebellion against the occupation that erupted in December 1997, did not change the mind of the Likud leadership.

Following Shamir's defeat, the Likud chose Benjamin Netanyahu as its new leader. With Netanyahu's biographical background—he was raised in a Revisionist home—and known ideological positions, his elevation to the top leadership was an act of reviving the Revisionist legacy, not abandoning it.[17]

The Israeli-Palestinian agreement of September 1993—the Oslo Accord negotiated by the Labor government—was a massive blow to the Right and especially to the Likud and its newly elected leader. The Palestinians were recognized as a party to the conflict, they were promised some control over the occupied territories, and, more important, the clear although unstated implication of Oslo was that a Palestinian state ought to be established, side by side and in peace with Israel. Netanyahu and his associates in Likud's leadership attacked the agreement in the harshest possible words. In an op-ed in the *New York Times* entitled "Peace in Our Time?"—typically unable to avoid the Right's habitual Holocaust fixation—Netanyahu argued that Israel needed the West Bank for defensive purposes.[18]

Despite the endorsement of Oslo by the Israeli Knesset and the vast majority of the people, Netanyahu and the Israeli Right continued to vehemently oppose the deal. Some groups and individuals on the far right, often with the tacit encouragement of the more moderate elements within Likud, including Netanyahu himself, demonized Rabin personally. Nonetheless, when Israel signed its peace treaty with Jordan in 1994, the Right finally gave up its hope to control both sides of the Jordan.

The November 4, 1995, assassination of Rabin, committed by a right-wing religious fanatic in a political atmosphere poisoned by the Right, generated a few immediate benefits for the Israeli Right. Shimon Peres, who succeeded Rabin, had a lot less credibility than the assassinated prime minister. The assassination resulted in an early election, enabling the Likud under Netanyahu to return to power.

Netanyahu was committed to the ideological program of the Right despite the increasingly difficult circumstances confronting him, particularly the growing international commitment to and expectation of an independent Palestinian state. At the same time, the Likud prime minister understood that he would be able to achieve his goals only via different and more sophisticated tactics than his predecessors, Begin and Shamir. Therefore, when some analysts called the 1996 Israeli elections "post-ideological,"[19] it was clearly a misnomer. While he often projected a shifting and unprincipled image, Netanyahu was consistently loyal to the traditional right-wing ideology. Although Netanyahu deviated on occasion from the Right's ideology—as had Begin and Shamir—these deviations were merely tactical in nature. They were circumstantial retreats designed to maintain the Right's ideology and policy, not to undermine them.

It is clear that had Netanyahu been committed to Oslo or even an improved Oslo, as he eventually said he was (but only after Rabin's assassination), he could have pushed the peace process forward. All indications are, however, that he decided from the start to slow down the peace process if not kill it altogether. "Netanyahu's first 100 days undermined the accumulated benefits of [Israeli-Palestinian] partnership built up since the summer of 1993," noted one observer.[20] The prime minister's refusal to meet Yasser Arafat for months after his election, his approval of a few controversial projects (e.g., the Jerusalem tunnel, the Har Homa housing project, and the expansion of West Bank settlements), and his humiliating proposals to the Palestinians indicated a systematic strategy to prevent Oslo from developing into a comprehensive negotiated settlement.

In terms of the competing value systems within the Israeli body politic, it is clear that with the return of Netanyahu to power and throughout his administration (1996–1999), territorial expansion became once again more important than strengthening the state's Jewishness by withdrawal from Arab-inhabited territories. Although many observers interpreted the prime minister's behavior as mostly incompetent,[21] it was for the most part consistent with his overall political philosophy, as well as his general political strategy. While Netanyahu's actions were counterproductive in terms of promoting a peace process based on a two-state solution, they were entirely compatible with the Right's traditional commitment to exclusive Jewish control over Eretz Israel.

In some ways, Netanyahu's diplomacy could be defended as rational from the perspective of his ideological convictions. While he opposed the Oslo process from the beginning, Netanyahu could not have come out against this crucial development directly and publicly. A direct assault on Oslo would have been costly, both internally and even more so internationally.

While Netanyahu was frequently inconsistent on a tactical level, he was much more consistent on the strategic level. The signs of tactical inconsistency were many (for example, his shifting position on the Oslo Accord), but so was his commitment to slowing down the Oslo process and minimizing the chances of its leading to the establishment of an independent Palestinian state. What observers viewed as Netanyahu's "tricks"[22] were compatible with the prime minister's long-held ideological positions.

It is relatively easy to argue that in terms of Israel's international standing Netanyahu's policies damaged the country's long-term interests. First, the peace process came to an almost complete halt,[23] and consequently, Israeli-Palestinian relations returned to their old full-blown hostility. Second, the "intimate strategic coordination" with the United States, clearly on display during the administration of President Bill Clinton and Prime Minister Yitzhak Rabin, disappeared under Netanyahu.[24] Third, relationships with the moderate Arab states, especially Egypt and Jordan, quickly deteriorated once Netanyahu assumed power.

From the perspective of domestic Israeli politics, however, Netanyahu's policy on the peace process—endless negotiations without results—proved highly successful, especially from the perspective of the prime minister himself. Netanyahu was successful in maintaining the delicate balance between his own nationalist Right (the Likud), the radical Right (parties such as the National Religious Party and Tsomet), and what some observers saw as the "soft

Right," the mélange of ultra-Orthodox Jews and secular immigrants from the former Soviet Union.[25]

It is interesting to note that the right-wing government of Netanyahu collapsed eventually (1999) for the same reasons that the Begin government had collapsed in 1983 and that the Shamir government had collapsed in 1992. In all three cases, unrealistic, ideologically driven foreign policy met external pressures that were translated into internal pressures, resulting in the loss of confidence by the Israeli electorate. The right-wing governments that pursued this unrealistic foreign policy could not withstand these pressures. In the case of Netanyahu, he lost the 1999 election to Ehud Barak of Labor by an unprecedented margin.

While in opposition, the Likud chose Ariel Sharon as its leader. Sharon was an interesting and somewhat surprising choice as the leader of the Israeli Right, possibly (although not necessarily) reflecting long-term changes in that camp. Sharon had been raised in a home of Laborites; thus he was the first recognized leader of the Right who did not have a Revisionist background, with its commitment to Greater Israel and maximal territorial expansion. On the other hand, Ariel Sharon had impressive credentials of his own as a long-time leader on the Right. As an officer in the Israel Defense Forces (IDF) he had led Unit 101, the spearhead of the young country's reprisal policy in the 1950s. He had then served with distinction as high-ranking officer in both the 1967 and the 1973 wars. Most important, once Sharon left the IDF, having been passed over as chief of staff, he had engineered the establishment of the Likud, the broad right-wing coalition on which Menahem Begin eventually rode to power.

As minister within several Israeli governments, Sharon had pushed as hard as he could for the expansion of Israeli settlements in the occupied territories. He became known as the "grandfather" of the settlements. Moreover, when he became minister of defense in Begin's second government (1981), he prepared the IDF and in effect led it to the war in Lebanon (June 1982). So seventeen years later, when he became the leader of Likud and thereby the leader of the entire Israeli Right, Sharon had the image of a committed hawk and a supporter of the vast Israeli settlement project in the territories taken in the 1967 conflict.

While in opposition, Sharon was critical of Prime Minister Ehud Barak's peace policy. When this policy was on the verge of failing, following the unsuccessful Camp David II conference (July 2000), Sharon, always a great military and political tactician, decided to give it a push that turned out to be a serious body blow. Sharon used the rumors about significant concessions by Barak on the issue of eventual control over the Temple Mount to engineer his own visit to the holy site. His visit to the sensitive area on September 28, 2000, accompanied by a large number of Israeli security men, contributed markedly to the deterioration of the already tense Israeli-Palestinian relationship and led in part to the Second, or al-Aqsa, Intifada.

The disintegration of the Barak government in late 2000 led to the elections of 2001. Sharon defeated Barak easily, returning the Likud to control over the Israeli government. He was reelected, with a huge majority, in 2003. Many observers thought that the rise of Ariel Sharon signaled the victory of the Right and its domination over the political process and especially foreign policy for many years to come. But Sharon moved the government to the center of the political map, and the support of the American administration facilitated this move. Sharon indicated as early as 2002 that he supported a two-state solution to the Israeli-Palestinian conflict. His support for building a "defense fence" began the practical demarcation of a future borderline between Israel and a future Palestinian entity. Along the same line, it is interesting that Sharon, despite his right-wing, hawkish credentials and almost uninhibited support for the settlement effort, decided to withdraw all IDF forces and remove all Israeli settlements from the Gaza Strip, and also to remove four settlements from the northern West Bank.

This move, although unilateral in nature and without negotiations with the Palestinian Authority, might have reflected new realism on the part of the Right, although not the far Right and especially the religious elements within it. In moving toward a new political position, Sharon stated publicly that annexation was not in Israel's best interests. More important, he put himself in political and even physical danger in initiating the evacuation. Equally interesting, the vast majority of Israelis accepted and supported the evacuation, and the opposition was much weaker than expected. Maybe most relevant, Sharon withdrew from the Likud and established a new party, Kadima, arguing that many in Likud were simply not ready for the necessary concessions. The new party had a decidedly centrist face, and it included even some well-known left-of-center Labor politicians, such as Shimon Peres, Haim Ramon, and Dalia Itzik. Its establishment meant a fundamental realignment of the Israeli political system. Kadima signified the erosion of the traditional Left-Right division within the Israeli body politic.[26]

A brief time after the Hitmatkut, or the Israeli unilateral disengagement from Gaza in August 2005, Sharon suffered a major stroke. His political career came to an abrupt end. This event facilitated the ascendance to leadership of Ehud Olmert, a politician who had been raised in a Revisionist home but had become closely identified with what was generally perceived as the increasing moderation of the Right. It is interesting that despite his different background, Olmert's ideological convictions have been identical to those of his predecessor as prime minister, Ariel Sharon.

At the same time, it is equally important that the Likud did not cease to exist with the formation of Kadima under Ariel Sharon and Ehud Olmert. The party was taken over by its previous leader, Benjamin Netanyahu. In the March 28, 2006, election, however, Kadima and Labor, both committed to withdrawal from at least some of the occupied territories, won the plurality of seats in the Knesset, while Netanyahu's Likud sank to twelve seats, the lowest in its history.

Nevertheless, as will be explained in the final section of this chapter, it is important not to overinterpret the results of the 2006 elections as a sign of long-term moderation and the withering away of the hard-core Right. Since these elections, the government, now under the leadership of Prime Minister Ehud Olmert (Likud) and Defense Minister Amir Peretz (later replaced by Ehud Barak), got involved in the ill-fated, badly planned, and disastrously executed Lebanon war of 2006. The Lebanese entanglement, along with the victory of Hamas among the Palestinians, the rising Iranian threat, and the almost universal feeling in Israel that "there is no one to negotiate with," might still enable the traditional Right to recapture the Israeli government.

The Ideological Foundations of the Right

The long history of the Zionist Right and, after 1948, the Israeli Right raises several fundamental questions. In what ways is it useful to speak about the "Right" as a political camp? If it is a "camp," is there an identifiable, common ideology shared by its different organizations, groups, parties, and individuals? And more specifically, what are the ideological elements characterizing the ideology of the Right and how do they relate to its politics and policies? This section deals with those questions.

Some analysts believe that using the Right-Left continuum for the analysis of any political system is merely "a useful shorthand . . . to understand and order the political scene."[27] This sort of use of the designations "Right" and "Left" might help the analyst to position a political party or a person in relation to another party or person. It is *relative* in nature.

On the other hand, one might use the notion of Right and Left to designate the contents or substance of a position taken by a political party or an individual. As an *absolute concept* of this sort, the Right-Left continuum is more complicated and problematic, yet more promising than its relativistic counterpart. The absolutist concept focuses attention on the role of substantive political ideology within the political system. A political ideology is a belief system that presents a set of normative goals and identifies the means of achieving them.

This analysis is applicable to Israel in several ways. First, it has been argued by many (although their number has decreased substantially over the last few years) that Israelis are evenly divided between "Right" and "Left," particularly on the territorial issue and the future of the West Bank and Gaza. Such an argument is based on the assumption that one can intelligently and usefully place Israelis along a Right-Left continuum. Second, it has been suggested that Israel has drifted to the right since 1967. Such an observation indicates that analysts are capable of determining the ideological direction toward which the country has moved. Asher Arian believes that both arguments are borne out by the data, and his position validates the usefulness of the Left-Right conceptualization.[28]

The argument promoted in this chapter in regard to the Zionist and Israeli Right reflects both a relativist and absolutist perspective. In terms of substance, the Right has exhibited since 1922 a nationalist position with several elements (to be explored below). At the same time, the Right's position has not been by any means entirely fixed and totally stable. In looking at the Right through a relativistic lens, emphasis will be put on how right-wing parties and leaders have tended to adjust their positions in response to the positions of others in the political system and beyond (e.g., changes in the international situation). In an analysis of the absolutist nature of the Right's position, attention will be directed toward the fixed nature of the Right's ideology, its continuous substance. The interplay between the two will be emphasized in the third section of this chapter.

The Zionist and Israeli Right has taken several ideological positions that will be explored in this section:

1. Demanding maximal territorial expansion
2. Negating the outside, non-Jewish world as fundamentally hostile to Israel
3. Viewing the power of the nation as a measure of all things, a supreme value
4. Emphasizing military power as the sole instrument in the relations between nations
5. Dehumanizing Israel's opponents by using powerful historical references
6. Identifying internal Jewish adversaries as unpatriotic traitors

This six-part ideological framework made possible the revolution of 1977, that is, the ascendance of the Right as Israel's majority camp. Moreover, it gave the policies that followed when Likud was in power a measure of coherence and consistency.

While on some ideological issues the Right's position has not been entirely consistent, not clearly always distinguishable from that of more centrist elements within the Zionist movement and the Israeli Jewish public, in regard to maximal territorial expansion the Right has demonstrated remarkable consistency for more than eighty years after its emergence in 1922. The founding father of the secular Right, Ze'ev Jabotinsky, demanded that every new member of the Revisionist movement take a formal vow to support the principle of *shlemut ha'moledet* ("Greater Israel"), that is, the right of the Jewish people to Eretz Israel in its entirety (on both sides of the Jordan River). Begin continued to insist on the idea, although the establishment of the Hashemite Kingdom of Jordan, its annexation of the West Bank, and the demarcation of the Israeli-Jordanian armistice lines seemed to have made this notion irrelevant. The occupation of the West Bank and Gaza in 1967 renewed and energized the Right's territorial appetite; GAHAL and then Likud were among the strongest supporters of the incorporation of the West Bank into Israel. Their leaders, Begin, Shamir, and Netanyahu, were guided by the "territorial imperative,"[29] trying to keep as much land as possible under Israel's control.

People unaware of the strength of the Right's territorial position have often misinterpreted tactical withdrawals as strategic transformation on the part of this camp. When Begin, for example, recognized at Camp David "the legitimate rights of the Palestinian people" (September 1978), some saw this recognition as a fundamental change in the Right's historic stance on the territorial issue. Such a reading of the phrase was detached, however, from the relevant ideological as well as political context. An opposite reading would have been more accurate. Begin tried at Camp David to get the tacit agreement of the United States and Egypt to an Israeli annexation of the West Bank and Gaza in return for the Sinai. He was coerced into an acceptance of a phrase that he was vehemently opposed to.[30] At Camp David, as in other situations, Begin was ready to offer the Palestinians merely autonomy; Shamir's and Netanyahu's positions were virtually the same. That fundamental territorial position on the part of the Right has been incompatible with a peaceful settlement of the Arab-Israeli conflict. While other right-wing leaders began deviating from this orthodoxy, Sharon was the first to break away from it fundamentally.

On the part of many, although interestingly not all, Revisionists, there has been a tendency to negate the outside, non-Jewish world, and to view it as inherently hostile to Israel. Jabotinsky, the founding father of the Zionist Right, believed that the Zionist movement could greatly benefit from the support of non-Jews; in this respect he followed in the footsteps of Theodore Herzl, sharing with him a cosmopolitan attitude. Begin and Shamir, on the other hand, represented a different, neo-Revisionist (rather than Revisionist) attitude to the outside world.[31] These leaders of the post-Holocaust Right viewed the world as thoroughly anti-Jewish. Their assumption was that Israel could rely only on itself and on the Jewish communities around the world. Netanyahu fell somewhere in the middle. He argued, and possibly believed, that the world applies stricter standards of behavior to Israel than to other countries when it comes to human rights violations in the territories,[32] and on occasion he hinted that fundamental anti-Semitism was at the basis of criticism of Israel.[33]

The negation of the outside world has often been applied by the Right to the Arabs and others whom many have described as latter-day anti-Semites. The continuous Arab-Israel dispute has added to the deep sense of mistrust toward the world that dominates the Right's worldview. Since 1967 in particular, the sympathy of many to the Palestinian cause has been interpreted by the Right as simply an extension of the historic hostility of the world toward the Jews. As the most important leader of the Right, Menahem Begin frequently accused his non-Jewish critics of anti-Semitism. Thus, for example, in an October 1980 speech in the Knesset, Begin charged the French government of creating an atmosphere conducive to anti-Semitism by condemning Israeli policies.[34] This type of interpretation has emerged as the standard defense of the controversial policies of the Right over the last thirty years.

Above all else, the Israeli Right has been committed to the power and greatness of the nation. This power has been the measure of all things, a supreme value. While the labor movement among the Zionists and later Israelis has dreamed of the emergence of a model society, egalitarian and progressive, for the Revisionists and the Right in general the dream has been not merely survival but power and greatness. They have wanted to move from a condition of total insecurity to one of total security. Under neo-Revisionism, particularly in the post-Holocaust era, the dream of national greatness grew to enormous, abnormal proportions. Neo-Revisionism went through "a rapid transition from inferiority to overcompensation," a phenomenon known also among individuals.[35] Starting from the recognition of Jewish inferiority and dependence, the Right developed a dream of Jewish superiority, political grandeur, and total domination of others.[36] Jabotinsky's original message of national power, redemption, and greatness was further strengthened by the legacy of the Holocaust.

In many ways, the Israeli Right has carried out the Zionist dream to its extreme. Although Zionism was an activist ideology, its nationalist activism was most often restrained by practical considerations, such as the necessity of obtaining international support, and by cosmopolitan, Western, and humanitarian values. In the case of the Right, national power and greatness have dominated over values such as democracy and equality.

Among supporters of the Right, military power has always had a central place in conducting the relations between nations. Already, Jabotinsky was an unabashed militarist. He introduced to the public debate among Zionists the notion of the "Iron Wall," the use of force to convince the Arabs that they would never be able to defeat the Jews.[37] His writings reflect the colonial character of his era, as well as Machiavellian thinking. No wonder that the hero of his major novel is Samson, a military leader.[38] One of Jabotinsky's greatest achievements was establishing Jewish units in World War I.[39]

Begin was even more blatantly militaristic than Jabotinsky; early in his public career he demanded to shift from political to military operations against military and civilian targets despite the Yishuv's policy of restraint (*havlaga*). When Begin served as Israel's prime minister he initiated the ill-fated 1982 Lebanon War. The Netanyahu approach to international relations was similar to that of his predecessors as leaders of the Right, Begin and Jabotinsky. In his 1993 book, chapter 7 is entitled "The Wall," an allusion to an article with this title written by Jabotinsky decades before. For Netanyahu, as for Jabotinsky and Begin, peace was not a function of mutual acceptance and recognition; it was the result of deterrence and domination.

In promoting ultranationalist ideology, the Right has tended to dehumanize Israel's opponents, often by using powerful historical analogies. In doing so, most right-wingers closed off any possibility of Jewish-Arab reconciliation. Jabotinsky himself saw the Arabs of Palestine as backward people who must be defeated by the force of arms.[40] For Menahem Begin the Arabs were the latter-day bearers of the old anti-Semitic germ; he never saw them as an authentic indigenous population. Many people on the Right have referred to the Arabs as "Amalek," the hostile nation that God commanded the Israelites to annihilate. Netanyahu typically borrowed from both his predecessors. Like Begin, he refused to recognize "the force, authenticity, let alone legitimacy of Palestinian Arab nationalism."[41] Like Jabotinsky, he saw only power, in its military form, as the single important factor determining Jewish-Arab relations. As for the Palestinian problem, Netanyahu argued that Palestinians had no justified claim on the land,[42] thus negating their case entirely.

Finally, the Right has shown a systematic tendency to describe its domestic political adversaries as unpatriotic traitors, disloyal to the nation, sympathizers with Israel's enemies, and so forth. Since for the Right the nationalist program is of supreme value, effective opposition to it is likely to lead to severe criticism, actual sanctions, and even violence.

Political Adjustment and Its Limits

The Zionist Right has been a highly ideological movement from the very beginning. It split from the rest of the Zionist movement over an ideological issue: how extensive the future Jewish state should be and, in effect, whether a compromise with the Arab inhabitants of Palestine was possible and desirable. While the Right has shown a limited inclination to compromise on its ideology while in opposition, both before and after the establishment of the state of Israel, when it finally ascended to power in 1977 reality frequently forced it to deviate from its pure and often radical ideological positions. These deviations, however, were usually tactical, designed to take the Right out of one "tight spot" or another. These deviations rarely amounted to real fundamental change in the Right's long-held ideological positions. The history and ideology of the Right reviewed in the first two sections of this chapter assist us in evaluating the Right's capacity to adjust its positions.

Prior to the establishment of the state, the Right, which was in permanent opposition to the Labor-dominated majority in the Jewish community (the Yishuv) under the British Mandate, rarely deviated from its ideological positions. Its capacity as well as motivation for political adjustment was minimal or entirely nonexistent. Thus, it never even entertained the possibility of changing its stand on the territorial issue and stuck to its maximalist position during the most important, critical junctures. This was particularly clear in relation to the Right's reaction to the Peel proposal (1937) and the United Nations proposal (1947–1948) for partitioning Palestine: It rejected both, mirroring the position of most Arabs but deviating from the position of most Jews.[43]

During Israel's formative years, the Right, under the authoritarian leadership of Menahem Begin, continued to exhibit pure ideological positions on all issues. Thus, while almost all Israelis recognized the status of the 1949 armistice lines as Israel's final borders, Herut continued to believe and argue that both the Jordanian-annexed West Bank and the Hashemite kingdom of Jordan (that is, the East Bank) belonged to Israel.[44] The Right behaved ideologically on a variety of other issues, including an enthusiastic rejection of the 1952 German reparations,[45] Ben-Gurion's reprisal policy,[46] the Kastner trial,[47] and the development of close relationships with Western countries.

While in the mid-1960s the Right began to move to the center organizationally by establishing coalitions with others and attempting to broaden its base of support, there was little indication of any truly meaningful ideological change in this camp prior to the 1967 War. Thus, the hard-core Right, Herut under Begin, gained rehabilitation and legitimacy while avoiding an ideological cost of any significance. Moreover, following that eventful war, the Right, first under the banner of GAHAL and eventually under the banner of Likud, clearly placed itself among those arguing for eventual annexation of the occupied territories by Israel.

The real test for the capacity of the Right to adjust ideologically came with the ascendancy of Menahem Begin to power (May 1977). While Begin's immediate reaction indicated a continuation of the traditional ideology—he promised many more settlements and went to pray at the Wailing (Western) Wall—it soon became clear that the newly elected prime minister would need at least to adjust his tactics, if not to abandon his ideological goals, if he wanted to achieve his main political objectives. Many who hoped for or feared an immediate declaration on annexation of the West Bank ("Judea and Samaria" to Begin) and Gaza found out that Begin did not intend to act unilaterally or hastily on that important issue.[48] Even more surprising to many, the Begin government actively sought peace with Egypt and eventually got it in return for complete withdrawal from the Sinai Peninsula.

The decision to return the Sinai to Egypt ought to be looked upon, despite its enormity, as the classic example of a tactical withdrawal designed to secure important ideological and political goals. What was important to Begin was *shlemut ha'aretz*, Greater Israel. The Sinai Peninsula was never part of Eretz Israel as envisioned by the Revisionists and their leader, Ze'ev Jabotinsky. Moreover, Begin believed, justifiably as it turned out, that by returning the Sinai to Egypt he would neutralize that most powerful of all Arab countries and secure Israel's hold on the West Bank and Gaza, both parts of biblical Eretz Israel. The pressure from the United States to settle the Palestinian issue—that is, to withdraw from the West Bank—gave Begin added incentive to reach this momentous—yet, from his perspective, tactical—arrangement with Anwar Sadat.

Dealing with the Palestinian issue was inherently more difficult for the leader of the Right. His ultimate goal, the center of his ideological being, was the annexation of the West Bank and Gaza. Noting that the areas were solidly Arab in population, he acted vigorously to add as many Jews as possible to the territories. He also offered limited, personal autonomy to the Arab inhabitants of these areas. Under enormous pressure at the Camp David conference in September 1978 to make concessions on the Palestinian issue, Begin agreed to sign an agreement that recognized the "legitimate rights and just requirements of the Palestinian people." Yet, while most of the international community thought that this meant self-determination and, eventually, statehood—as recognized by the UN's 1947 partition resolution—Begin believed that his proposal for limited, personal autonomy was compatible with it.

The final proof of Begin's real ideological goals and his inherent inability to compromise on them was given when he authorized the 1982 invasion of

Lebanon. While the war was presented to the public, the Knesset, and even the cabinet as a limited operation, in fact it had far-reaching goals.[49] Begin and his associates in the right-wing government believed that by defeating the PLO in Lebanon they would be able to subdue the Palestinians in the occupied territories and convince them to quietly accept Israel's annexation.

The ideological tenacity of Begin was equally exhibited by his successor, Yitzhak Shamir. While Shamir was forced to share power with Labor following the 1984 election, he did everything he could to prevent changes in the status of the West Bank. Encouraging intense Israeli settlement in the area, he hoped to eventually annex it. Diplomatic opportunities were purposely ignored. Thus, following the eruption of the intifada, in late 1987, Labor made intense efforts, inspired by fear of Palestinian claims on the West Bank, to return the area to Jordanian control. Shamir, as Israel's prime minister, successfully blocked this initiative. Even when urged to withdraw from the Gaza Strip and thus possibly avoid defeat in the 1992 election, Shamir steadfastly refused.

The Likud return to opposition following the 1992 election revealed again the difficulty of the Right in adjusting to the new realities as reflected in the ballot box. The election of Netanyahu as Likud's leader indicated that the tough line on ideological matters would be maintained. The young leader vigorously criticized the Rabin government for the Oslo Accords (September 1993), comparing it to the sacrifice of Czechoslovakia in 1938. While some analysts argued that the Oslo agreements blurred the distinction between the two main political parties[50]—Labor and Likud—this argument is true in only a relative and limited way. The prime minister himself became a target of virtually unrestrained political attacks by the most important leaders of the Right, including Netanyahu. Only following the Rabin assassination was Netanyahu willing to accept Oslo, and his "acceptance" was, for the most part, a formality.

Netanyahu's prime ministership (1996–1999) reveals the Right's readjustment dilemma in all of its complexity. On the one hand, Netanyahu found himself under enormous pressure to move forward with negotiations on further withdrawals and thus eventual Palestinian independence (as promised in the Oslo Accords). This pressure came from the international community, including the United States, as well as the Israeli public and the Palestinians. Through a long series of maneuvers Netanyahu succeeded in avoiding large-scale withdrawals, although minor redeployments—that is, tactical retreats—were inevitable. Equally important, Netanyahu's behavior indicated that he wanted to avoid at all costs a final deal on the West Bank and Gaza. Nevertheless, following the Israeli-Jordanian peace treaty of 1994, Netanyahu had given up Jabotinsky's claim to the "East Bank" (Jordan).

Ironically, despite his ultimate commitment to the Right's ideology, which many observers did not appreciate, when Netanyahu signed the Wye Plantation agreement in 1998, his fate was sealed. Many in the hardened Right saw Netanyahu as a traitor to the cause. The Likud was soundly defeated in the elections that followed.

Likud's return to opposition, for the second time in seven years, gave yet another opportunity to observe its behavior when out of power. At this time it was led by Ariel Sharon, a retired hawkish general with a reputation for tactical brilliance, strategic errors, and relatively weak ideological convictions. While Sharon was critical of Prime Minister Barak's initiatives, the opportunity to topple the Labor government did not materialize until it was evident that the Second Intifada was under way.

Under these circumstances, Sharon did not have much difficulty in beating Barak soundly. Thus, Likud returned to power, although under a new prime minister who did not have the pedigree of his three Likud predecessors, Begin, Shamir, and Netanyahu. It is interesting that without this ideological baggage, Sharon was able to deviate on a number of critical issues from the traditional Likud positions. Thus, he adopted the idea of erecting a barrier between the West Bank and Israel, despite the opposition of some ideological hawks within his own party, who saw this act as an implicit territorial division of the West Bank. But then, in 2002, Sharon said clearly and openly that he supported Israeli withdrawal from parts of the West Bank and Gaza because it was in the best interest of the country. Finally, while refusing to talk to Arafat, Sharon decided in 2005 to initiate and implement a unilateral Israeli withdrawal from the entire Gaza Strip and from four settlements in the northern West Bank. To implement this plan, the decisive prime minister left the Likud and established a new, centrist party (Kadima).

Following Sharon's massive stroke, his deputy, Ehud Olmert, rose to power. While Olmert had a pedigree similar to Netanyahu's, he appeared loyal to the legacy of the stricken premier. On March 28, 2006, Israelis voted for the seventeenth Knesset. Kadima and Labor got the most votes, while Likud under Benjamin Netanyahu was decisively defeated. Although many thought that "the resounding defeat of the Likud and the Right in favor of the 'center' confirmed a shift in political culture away from the Greater Israel ideology and permanent preemptive war against terrorism,"[51] it is unclear that the Right was truly defeated in the long run. Thus, before being able to initiate new withdrawals from additional parts of the West Bank, Prime Minister Olmert allowed Israel to be dragged into a second large war in Lebanon. His agenda for further withdrawals was thus disrupted, and equivalently, new opportunities for the Right were opened.

In a look at contemporary Israel from a larger, longer-term perspective, it seems that in many ways the philosophy of the Israeli Right has been on the decline. It is clear that the international community as a whole is opposed to the annexation of the West Bank and that, given the demographic realities, Israel does not have sufficient political, economic, and military resources to effect such a fundamental territorial change on its own.

On the other hand, at the time of this writing, many of the characteristic psychological and ideological components of traditional right-wing thinking seem to have penetrated the Israeli political system as a whole; these components might even dominate today's system. Thus, in contemporary Israel there seems to be a set of assumptions that have traditionally governed the attitude of the Right. First, there is a deep sense of pessimism as to the possibility of any agreement with the Arabs, including the Palestinians. Second, the idea of a negotiated settlement, achieved via direct talks between the parties, has been marginalized since the ascendance of Hamas. Third, there is an almost reflexive reliance on military power, as demonstrated by the Second Lebanon War (2006). Fourth, since September 11, the 2003 Iraq war, and the ascendance of Iranian power, there is a strong sense that Israel is not only part of the "West," in confrontation with the radicalized Islamic world, but part of the Middle Eastern Pax Americana.

While each of these assumptions is easily explainable, in their totality they are sending Israel back to the dark days of 1948, this time under a set of assumptions that used to characterize the Right, a small minority at the time. A frightened nation is unlikely to make concessions that could lead to a just and stable settlement.

Notes

1. Ilan Peleg, *Begin's Foreign Policy, 1977–1983: Israel's Move to the Right* (Westport, CT: Greenwood Press, 1987), pp. 18–19.

2. Gertrude Hirshler and Lester S. Eckman, *From Freedom Fighter to Statesman: Menachem Begin* (New York: Shengold, 1979), pp. 44–45.

3. *Betar* had two meanings. First, it stood for the Hebrew acronym of "Brit (Covenant, Alliance) Yossef Trumpeldor," named after the Zionist military hero who died in Tel Hai in 1920 fighting against Arab attackers. Second, Betar was the fortress near Jerusalem where Bar-Kochba staged the final Jewish rebellion against Rome in 135 CE.

4. Menahem Begin, *The Revolt*, rev. ed. (New York: Nash, 1977).

5. Howard M. Sachar, *A History of Israel: From the Rise of Zionism to Our Time* (New York: Knopf, 1979), p. 265.

6. Thus Begin declared the reparation agreement "Chilul Hashem," the defamation of God's name, a rather strong term.

7. See, for example, his views in Menahem Begin, "Concepts and Problems in Foreign Policy," *Ha'uma*, vol. 16 (March 1966), pp. 461–487 (in Hebrew).

8. "Coalition under Strain," *Jewish Observer and Middle East Review* (May 24, 1968), pp. 5–6.

9. Hirshler and Eckman, *From Freedom Fighter,* p. 267.

10. Begin's ideas on autonomy were greatly influenced by those of Jabotinsky. See Ya'akov Shavit, "The Attitudes of the Revisionists to the Arab National Movement," *Forum* (Spring–Summer 1978), pp. 106–107. Begin was also influenced by the claims of cultural autonomy by the Jewish communities in eastern Europe in the early twentieth century (author's interview with Dr. Israel Eldad, July 7, 1986).

11. Author's interview with Abba Eban, August 8, 1985.

12. Mark Heller, "Begin's False Autonomy," *Foreign Policy,* vol. 37, no. 1 (Winter 1979–1980), pp. 111–132.

13. Ian S. Lustick, "Kill the Autonomy Talks," *Foreign Policy,* vol. 41, no. 1 (Winter 1980–1981), pp. 21–43.

14. Ezer Weizman, *The Battle for Peace* (New York: Bantam Books, 1981), p. 151.

15. Peleg, *Begin's Foreign Policy,* pp. 110–111.

16. Arie Avnery, *The Defeat: The Disintegration of Likud's Rule* (Tel-Aviv: Midot, 1993), p. 22 (in Hebrew).

17. Ilan Peleg, "The Likud under Rabin II: Between Ideological Purity and Pragmatic Readjustment," in Robert O. Freedman, ed., *Israel under Rabin* (Boulder, CO: Westview Press, 1995), pp. 143–167.

18. September 15, 1993.

19. David Makovsky, "The Country's First Post-Ideological Election," *Jerusalem Post* (May 23, 1996).

20. Adam Garfinkle, "Israel and Palestine: A Precarious Partnership," *Washington Quarterly,* vol. 20, no. 3 (1977), p. 9.

21. See, for example, Joel Marcus, "Shlumiel in the Head," *Ha'aretz* (October 7, 1997).

22. Gideon Samet, "Tricks instead of a Settlement," *Ha'aretz* (March 2, 1998).

23. Jerome Slater, "Netanyahu, a Palestinian State, and Israeli Security Reassessed," *Political Science Quarterly,* vol. 112, no. 4 (1997–1998), pp. 675–689.

24. Ze'ev Schiff, "Doubtful Victory," *Ha'aretz* (January 30, 1998).

25. Ehud Sprinzak, "Netanyahu's Safety Belt," *Foreign Affairs,* vol. 77 no. 4 (July–August 1998), pp. 18–28.

26. Jonathan Mendilow, "Party Strategy in the 2006 Elections: Kadima, Likud, and Labor," in Asher Arian and Michal Shamir, *The Election in Israel 2006* (Albany: State University of New York Press, 2007).

27. Asher Arian and Michal Shamir, "The Primarily Political Functions of the Left-Right Continuum," *Comparative Politics,* vol. 15 no. 2 (1983), pp. 139–158.

28. Asher Arian, *The Second Republic: Politics in Israel* (Chatham, NJ: Chatham House, 1998), pp. 356, 358.

29. Gad Barzilai and Ilan Peleg, "Israel and Future Borders: Assessment of a Dynamic Process," *Journal of Peace Research,* vol. 31 no. 1 (1994), pp. 59–71.

30. See, for example, Uzi Benziman, *Rosh Memshala Be'Matzor* [A Prime Minister under Siege] (Tel Aviv: Adam, 1981). Several other books describe the situation in similar terms.

31. Peleg, *Begin's Foreign Policy,* especially chap. 3.

32. Benjamin Netanyahu, *A Place among the Nations: Israel and the World* (New York: Bantam Books, 1993), pp. 170, 177, 397.

33. Ibid., pp. 397–398.

34. *New York Times* (October 14, 1980).

35. Jay Gonen, *A Psychohistory of Zionism* (New York: Mason/Charter, 1975), p. 3. While Gonen argues that Zionists in general exhibit these symptoms, it is my contention that they characterize particularly the Right.

36. See, for example, Zvi Shiloach, *Eretz Gdola Le'am Gadol: Sipuro Shel Maamin* [A Great Land for a Great Nation: The Story of a Believer] (Tel Aviv: Orpaz, 1970).

37. On this important issue, see Ian Lustick, "To Build and to Be Built By: Israel and the Hidden Logic of the Iron Wall," *Israel Studies,* vol. 1, no. 1 (Summer 1996), pp. 196–223.

38. Vladimir (Ze'ev) Jabotinsky, *Samson* (Tel Aviv: Shikmona, 1976) (in Hebrew).

39. Vladimir Jabotinsky, *The Story of the Jewish Legion* (New York: B. Ackerman, 1945).

40. Israel Kolatt, "The Zionist Movement and the Arabs," *Studies in Zionism,* vol. 5 (April 1982), pp. 129–157 (especially p. 138).

41. Shlomo Avineri, *The Making of Modern Zionism: Intellectual Origins of the Jewish State* (New York: Basic Books, 1981), p. 179.

42. Netanyahu, *A Place,* chap. 3.

43. Peleg, *Begin's Foreign Policy,* pp. 27–28.

44. Ibid., pp. 30–31.

45. Sachar, *A History,* p. 372; Hirshler and Eckman, *From Freedom Fighter,* p. 201.

46. See, for example, *Divrei Haknesset* [Knesset Record], vol. 16 (August 30, 1954), p. 2558.

47. Sachar, *A History,* p. 376.

48. One indication that Begin might be more cautious than his ideology indicated was that he appointed General Moshe Dayan, a Laborite who opposed annexation, as foreign minister.

49. Ze'ev Schiff and Ehud Ya'ari, *A War of Deception* [Milhemt Sholal] (Tel Aviv: Schocken, 1984) (in Hebrew); published in English as *Israel's Lebanon War* (New York: Simon & Schuster, 1984).

50. See, for example, Dani File and Udi Lebel, "The Post-Oslo Israeli Populist Radical Right in Comparative Perspective: Leadership, Voter Characteristics and Political Discourse," *Mediterranean Politics,* vol. 10, no. 1 (March 2005), pp. 85–97.

51. See, for example, Michel Warschawski, "The 2006 Israeli Elections: A Drive to Normalcy and Separation," *Journal of Palestine Studies,* vol. 35, no. 4 (Summer 2006), pp. 44–53.

3

After Rabin: The Malaise of the Israeli Zionist Left

Mark Rosenblum

The Wounded Dove: Electoral Debacles

THE ISRAELI ZIONIST LEFT IS NOT DEAD, but it is wounded.[1] One bottom-line measure of the severity of its political wounds can be observed at the ballot box. Between 1992 and 2007 the Israeli Left won only two out of six national elections. Its first victory, in 1992 under the tutelage of Yitzhak Rabin, amassed forty-four Knesset members, a throwback to those heady days when Mapai (the predecessor of the current Labor Party) was winning a similar number of seats in the Knesset and forming governments with other left-wing Zionist parties. In conjunction with Meretz's twelve mandates, Rabin's Labor Party created the foundation for the governing coalition of 1992 that presided over the signing and initial phases of implementing the Oslo Accords.

The second victory of the Zionist Left took place in 1999 under another would-be Labor Party "general of peace," Ehud Barak, who, as the head of a renovated Labor Party, One Israel, forged an alliance with two other small parties, Gesher (a Sephardi group associated with then foreign minister David Levy) and the Orthodox peace bloc associated with Rabbi Michael Melchior. Ehud Barak's victory was one of only three Israeli elections that involved dual ballots, one for the prime minister and the other for the Knesset. Barak was a runaway winner, crushing Benjamin Netanyahu in the separate election for the prime minister. In the parallel parliamentary election, however, his party garnered only twenty-six Knesset members, down from thirty-six seats in 1996. Meanwhile, Meretz gained a seat, breaking into double digits at ten. With only thirty-six seats between One Israel and Meretz, Barak cobbled together a broad coalition that included five other parties. However, the breadth of his government could not disguise the depth of its explosive fissures. Four parties had strong objections to Barak's peacemaking efforts, and several of them had a fundamental conflict on questions of synagogue and state as well.

This fractious "rainbow coalition" had no pot of gold at the end of its colorfully diverse spectrum of policies and priorities. Barak's personal triumph in handily winning the prime ministership was tempered by the coalition of the unwilling that he assembled.

Both of these electoral victories of the Zionist Left had their tenures in office interrupted by early elections. The first was triggered by the assassination of Rabin and Shimon Peres's attempt to ride a tailwind of sympathy votes; the second, by a collapsing peace process and disintegrating Barak government. And these were the moments from the left-wing Zionists' highlights reel of electoral triumphs.

Things would only get worse, both for Labor, which had once been the "Party of the State," and its left-wing Zionist companion party, Meretz. The 2001 national election was held less than two years after the previous one, and it was the third and last separate prime ministerial election, with the distinction of being the only one that was not accompanied by Knesset elections.[2] In a head-to-head contest, Ariel Sharon won an unprecedented landslide victory with over 64 percent of the vote, nearly double Barak's share of the ballots.

The 2003 national election returned to the tradition of a single ballot for party lists in the Knesset and continued the downward trajectory of the Zionist Left, with Labor losing seven more mandates (nineteen Knesset members remaining) and Meretz losing four seats (six Knesset members remaining). One Nation, a new workers' list, joined this potential Left bloc with three seats, leaving the Zionist Left parliamentary forces with a net loss of eight from the previous Knesset election. Under Sharon's leadership Likud had doubled its own size from the last election (to thirty-eight members of the Knesset), winning twice as many seats as Labor in this election. Labor would neither be the governing party nor lead the opposition. It would now succumb to the status of junior partner under Sharon, joining Tommy Lapid's Shinui Party (the new, assertively secular centrist party with fifteen seats), hoping to pressure Sharon to pursue his "painful compromises" in a deoccupation process that included a rerouted separation barrier that was less intrusive in the West Bank.

It can be argued that there were salutary aspects to the Labor Party's joining the Sharon government and a significant part of the Zionist Left's supporting its disengagement. With the support of the Labor Party in the government, a very reluctant wing of Meretz from the backbenches, and left-wing Zionist extraparliamentary forces led by Shalom Achshav (Peace Now) in the street, Sharon did confound many of the skeptics. He implemented his disengagement plan, removing the Israel Defense Forces (IDF) from the Gaza Strip, including the Philadelphi corridor,[3] and evacuating all of the Jewish settlers and settlements from the Gaza Strip.[4] In addition, the Zionist Left could claim that it had played an instrumental role in altering the route of the separation barrier. The projected revised line of construction would incorporate approximately 9 percent of the West Bank on the Israeli side. Sharon's initial plan would have incorporated nearly five times as much of the West Bank.

One of the nongovernmental organizations most responsible for the judicial whittling away at the Sharon government's territorial appetite in routing the barrier was (and remains in the fall of 2007) the Council for Israeli Peace and Security. This pragmatically dovish Zionist body is composed of retired Israeli generals, security experts, and intelligence officials in the Mossad and Shin Bet, many of whom are affiliated with the Labor Party. Meretz also had important representation in this security-oriented organization in the person of Shaul Arieli, a former commander in Gaza and an accomplished cartographer, who served as the key Israeli mapmaker for the Geneva Initiative in 2003. As a primary researcher for the council, he has successfully petitioned the Israeli Supreme Court to instruct the Israeli government and army to abide by the principle of proportionality in building the barrier, that is, pursuing Israeli security while minimizing hardship for the Palestinians.

These beneficial effects of the left-wing Zionist support of Sharon's disengagement policy were offset by their failure to prevail upon Sharon to coordinate Israel's withdrawal with the government of Mahmoud Abbas. From his initial landslide election in 2001 to his incapacitation in January 2006, Sharon was seemingly determined to avoid any negotiating process with the Palestinian Authority, with or without Arafat. He feared being cornered into bargaining on the radioactive permanent-status issues, with the Bush administration pressuring him to make unacceptable compromises on Jerusalem, territory, and settlements.

Sharon's unbridled unilateralism weakened President Abbas's relatively moderate Palestinian wing, which espoused the power of diplomacy, and strengthened Hamas, which claimed that only the force of arms would liberate Palestine. Sharon's success in getting out of Gaza was celebrated as a triumph by Hamas and those who supported its claim that "violence pays." Their sense of triumph was concretized with their January 2006 victory in the Palestinian Legislative Council ballot and their military seizure of power in Gaza in June 2007. Qassem rockets and mortars continued to rain down on the western Negev. Elements of the extraparliamentary Zionist Left could assume some credit for relocating the barrier closer to the Green Line (the armistice line that was agreed upon by Israel, Egypt, Jordan, Lebanon, and Syria in 1949 after Israel's War of Independence) and evacuating settlements in Gaza that enjoyed limited support within Israel. These two actions would not, however, rehabilitate their camp's security reputation, which had become hopelessly associated with an Oslo peace process that was increasingly perceived by Israelis as an unfathomable swap: "land for terror."

In retrospect—a convenient place to find wisdom—the unilateral disengagement brought grief not only to Abu Mazen, the president of the Palestinian Authority, but also in the longer run to Sharon's plan, at least as it was articulated by his most trusted aide, Dov Weissglass. In an interview with *Ha'aretz,* Weissglass suggested:

> The disengagement is actually formaldehyde that's necessary so that there will not be a political process with the Palestinians. . . . The disengagement plan makes it possible for Israel to park conveniently in an interim situation that distances us as far as possible from political pressure. . . . I found a device, in cooperation with the management of the world [i.e., the United States], to ensure there will be no stopwatch here. That there will be no timetable to implement the settlers' nightmare. I have postponed that nightmare indefinitely. Because what I effectively agreed to with the Americans was that a part of the settlements would not be dealt with at all, and the rest will not be dealt with until the Palestinians turn into Finns.[5]

The Zionist Left: Color Them Blue in Supporting Sharon's Disengagement

Labor and a large part of the Zionist Left were in the peculiar position of seeking revival in the shadow of Sharon's evacuation of Gaza in the summer of 2005. Tel Aviv, Jerusalem, and much of the rest of the country were transformed into a summer camp waging an intense politicized color war over Sharon's withdrawal and evacuation policy. Most of the settlers and those who sympathized with their plight, if not their ideology, wrapped themselves, their cars, their book bags, and other personal effects in orange ribbons in registering their opposition. Important sectors of the Zionist Left, including Ami Ayalon's One Voice supporters and Shalom Achshav, brandished slightly different variations of a blue ribbon ostensibly meant to project a pragmatic patriotic dovish support for the evacuation.

Of course, there were other colors on display in this tumultuous test of wills, including those that revealed potentially significant cleavages within the settlement community. There was a minority of messianic, violent "hilltop youth" who were prepared to spill blood, their own and that of those who came to remove them. Many of their parents and religious leaders disapproved of this red flag of the violent youthful minority. Their violent behavior crossed a line that most of the senior officials of Yesha, the Jewish settlement council of the West Bank and Gaza, feared would engender a backlash among broad sectors of the Israeli public and perhaps even delegitimize the entire settlement enterprise. The Yesha leadership was promoting a different, less militant, but determined strategy that in the metaphor of the color war might be characterized as the black-and-blue strategy. They understood that they would not be able to prevent the Sharon government's disengagement. However, they were committed to leaving a bruising mark on the body politic, which would perhaps deter a similar evacuation from the heartland of Judea and Samaria.

The elders of Yesha were also sensitive to another threatening color, one associated not with the minority of alienated, violence-prone hilltop youth, but with the majority of commercially minded settler home owners, who were receptive to the color green. Their mission was not an ideological assault on the Israeli government's policy of "ethnic cleansing," but a nervous wait for a financial compensation package that would facilitate their return to Israel proper or relocation to one of the settlement blocs around Jerusalem (Ma'ale Adumim), near Bethlehem (Gush Etzion), or in the northern West Bank (Ariel). It was presumed that these areas would be incorporated into Israel. The mainstream Zionist Left had commissioned surveys of the settlers' attitudes and had begun to pursue policy options that might attract the majority of settlers, who were driven more by the generous subsidies and lifestyle than by heritage and religious fervor.[6]

Even those in Meretz who were appalled by the unilateralism of Sharon's "disengagement" and demanded a negotiated withdrawal and evacuation (or, at least, one that was done cooperatively or in coordination with President Mahmoud Abbas and the moderate Palestinians) were marginalized by three developments: (1) the relative ease with which the evacuation was carried out; (2) the broad public support it enjoyed, including within their own camp; and (3) the perception that Sharon was potentially a positive instrument for implementing the next stage of a "secure deoccupation."

There were those on the Left who warned about the creation of a Hamastan, if Abbas and Palestinian pragmatists were not able to project themselves as the party that had negotiated the liberation of Gaza and the areas of the northern West Bank from which Israel had withdrawn. However, these warnings were often couched in a pained resignation of support for the evacuation, if not for Sharon.[7]

The specters of Sderot becoming a ghost town and the western Negev being subjected to a hail of Qassem rockets, as well as the Second Lebanon War, driving hundreds of thousands of Israelis from their homes in northern Israel for thirty-four days, were not factored into the Zionist Left's cost-benefit calculus of Israel's unilateral withdrawal from either Lebanon (June 2000) or Gaza (August 2006). From their viewpoint, getting out of Lebanon and Gaza was not only a moral imperative associated with ending occupation but also an act of enlightened self-interest. They expected that the incentive for attacking Israel from Lebanon would be radically reduced. They also envisioned that Israel's withdrawal from Gaza and an initial swath of the West Bank would begin the process of rescuing their country from its slide into a demographic and political calamity in which a Jewish minority would be trapped in a de facto binational state ravaged by civil war. By "returning home" to a smaller and more secure Israel, the Zionist Left did not expect their enemies in Lebanon and Gaza to follow them with such lethal effectiveness. They presumed that some combination of Israeli deterrence, Palestinian restraint driven by national interest in converting the Israeli withdrawal into a broader peacemaking initiative, and third-party mediation would contain the risks.

Paradoxically, the man whom the Zionist Left had historically loathed was seen as part of their insurance policy against these deadly threats. Shlomo Ben-Ami, one of the most important leftist Zionist politicians, statesmen, and academics, captured the paradox of his tentative embrace of Sharon's disengagement plan as

> the only game in town. [Sharon] the unscrupulous and ruthless man of action has finally realized the limits of force. No one who knew his personal and political history would have imagined him delivering a speech like the one he gave on the day the Knesset approved his plan. Addressing the settlers, those whom he had spoiled and cultivated for years, he said: "You have developed among you a dangerous Messianic spirit. We have no chance to survive in this part of the world that has no mercy for the weak if we persist in this path. I have learnt from my own experience that the sword alone offers no solution. We do not want to rule over millions of Palestinians who multiply every year. Israel will not survive as a democratic state if she continues being a society that occupies another nation. The withdrawal from Gaza will open the gates of a new reality."[8]

Sharon's withdrawal from Gaza did briefly open the gates to a dramatic, potentially positive new reality. His resignation in November 2005 from Likud, a party that he concluded was captive to a "dangerous messianic spirit" and prone to living by the "sword alone," created a potential historic realignment in Israeli national politics. His formation of a new centrist party—Kadima

(Forward), committed to forging a new reality and pursuing policies based on choosing demography over geography, security over settlements, and democracy over occupation—created a new centrist force that seemed a natural ally for the Zionist Left.

Sharon's journey of being born again was complete. The birthing of Kadima not only recruited many of the who's who of Likud but also attracted a number of the stalwarts of the Labor Party, including Shimon Peres, Dalia Yitzhak, and Haim Ramon. The last was an indefatigable advocate for this "big bang," who labored long and hard to deliver what he hoped would be a leftist-centrist Zionist bloc that would finally break the stalemate in Israeli politics. The Zionist Left's relationship with the man they had despised as the "butcher of Beirut" and the "godfather of settlements" now seemingly afforded them their best, if not last, chance to "liberate Israel from the occupation."

The full realization of just how dependent the Zionist Left was on their old adversary was driven home with the news of his hospitalization on December 18, 2005, for what was considered a mild stroke. For the next two weeks the Zionist Left was as consumed as the rest of the nation by the media's crash medical course on strokes, atrial septa, and cardiac catheterization procedures. The tragedy that befell Sharon on January 4, 2006, a massive hemorrhagic stroke that left him comatose, not only was a human tragedy for the prime minister and his family but was also internalized by the Zionist Left as a potentially debilitating development for their political hopes in the Knesset elections on March 28. That Sharon's personal tragedy had become their own political disability was a watershed in the electoral eclipse of the Zionist Left.

Week by week the polls indicated the slippage of Kadima without Sharon at its helm. Labor's most compelling electoral argument seemed to focus on "vote for Labor to strengthen Kadima." Campaigning on the basis of strengthening their junior partnership with a fading Kadima was as close to winning as even Labor's activists and candidates could imagine.[9] Labor seemed resigned to playing electoral horseshoes—where getting close to power was the point.

Even with Sharon incapacitated, Olmert managed to hold some of the huge lead in the polls that Sharon had built for his new party. He was able to hang onto twenty-nine mandates, and as the lead party in the thirty-first Knesset, he formed a new government to become the twelfth prime minister of Israel. A Sharon-less Kadima proceeded to build a coalition that included Labor. However, the latter, under the populist politician Amir Peretz—who became the unlikely defense minister—did no better than match Labor's last electoral performance of nineteen seats. Meretz fared even worse and lost another seat, shrinking to five mandates.

Decline, Dependency, and Electoral Instability

The plight of the Zionist Left (Labor and Meretz) is mathematically foreboding for its supporters. Since the election of Rabin, there has been an erosion of support in every election, from the high tide of fifty-six seats in 1992 to forty-three in 1996, thirty-six in 1999, twenty-five in 2003, and culminating in the current lowest level of twenty-four in 2006. In less than fifteen years, electoral support for the Zionist Left has been more than halved.

This trend is matched by other developments that are ominous for the entire electoral political system in Israel. Perhaps the most significant trend is the erosion of representation in the Knesset of the two historic major parties, Likud and Labor. Both Labor and Likud have been in a state of decline, with the exception of Likud's 2003 victory with Sharon at the helm helping his party win thirty-eight seats, doubling its representation from the previous Knesset. However, this victory was not enough to give the two parties together half the mandates. In the last elections, in 2006, the two parties accounted for only thirty-one seats in the Knesset. The decline of the two major parties has been accompanied by increasing instability. The last Israeli prime minister to serve a full term was Menahem Begin, from 1977 to 1981. The fragmented and polarized Israeli electoral system remains unstable, despite the emergence of centrist parties that tend to make dramatic entrances onto and ignominious exits from the political stage.

The Israeli Zionist Left cannot take much comfort from the systemic political electoral crisis that plagues Israel. Neither "waiting for Lefty" nor substantive electoral reform seems the likely source of deliverance. For now, the fate of the Zionist Left seems hitched to the latest manifestation of a centrist party, one that has lost its founder and hegemonic leader. It could lose Olmert, its less imposing replacement, to personal legal investigations or to the second installment of the Winograd Commission report investigating Israel's less than inspiring performance in the Second Lebanon War. In addition, demographic trends are not favorable to the Zionist Left.

The proportion of veteran Ashkenazim, who traditionally voted for leftist Zionists, has diminished, while the influence of the religious and Arab sectors has grown. While the Palestinian population of Israel has generally been presumed to be part of an electoral bloc that included the leftist Zionists, this is a tenuous assumption. Palestinian Knesset members are increasingly alienated and alienating in their public discourse with Zionist institutions, and the Zionist Left has failed to cultivate a more understanding discourse with the larger Palestinian Israeli public.[10]

The prognosis for winning the invaluable floating voter is also problematic for the Zionist Left, which will be dependent on an allied non-Left party like

Kadima to attract the Jewish "swing" vote among those of Sephardic descent, immigrants (particularly Russians), and young voters. However, it is a long shot that the Sharon-less Kadima has staying power as a governing party, much less as a party that weds security to deoccupation.

This brief introduction to the status of the post-Rabin Israeli Zionist Left has emphasized its diminished electoral strength and its growing dependence on a centrist party that has at least temporarily gutted Likud, the standard bearer for hard-line peace-and-security policies. This decreased strength and increased dependence has created a potential realignment in Israeli politics. It has also empowered the center, shifting nearly twenty mandates to a pragmatic Center-Left base that now constitutes exactly half the Knesset. However, this Israeli Center, which has swelled, not just held, in the last election, is facing a severe leadership and identity crisis. It does not appear empowered to pursue either a Zionist Left social-economic or peace-and-security agenda. In fact, both Kadima and the public mood seem to eschew the heady, monumental heydays of the Left or Right, hawks or doves. They are not drawn to past models: not to the Labor pioneers who cleared the land and built the state; not to the settler generation of Gush Emunim, the religiously observant Zionist movement that has helped to forge a de facto second Jewish state in Judea and Samaria; and finally, not to the generation that has waged a peace that seemed within reach.

These megaenterprises seem distant from the national mood that catapulted Kadima into power. Sharon's successful political acquisition of the core of Likud has tapped a national hunger for the unheroic, introverted policy of living less grandiosely, with less territory and smaller diplomatic ambitions. The leftist Zionists played on this mood in marketing their support for Sharon's disengagement as "returning home." However, they are not above returning to their past ambitious moment of peacemaking, which featured their heroic-tragic figure, Yitzhak Rabin. This journey back to the future-that-might-have-been may be motivated by sheer melancholy for a lost cause or by an attempt to reenergize activists to wage peace anew. However, in this chapter, the voyage will attempt to shed light on the electoral eclipse of the Israeli Zionist Left and a number of the key factors that may help to explain its fall from power and prospects for regaining it.

Yitzhak Rabin, the Unlikely Icon

Yitzhak Rabin is an unlikely icon for the Israeli Zionist Left. While he was a lifelong member of the Labor Party and its precursor, Mapai, there was little in his biography to anticipate his coronation as Israel's would-be general of peace. Neither his nonideological pragmatism nor his policies suggested a leftist or dovish orientation while he was prime minister from 1974 to 1977 and defense minister under Shimon Peres and Yitzhak Shamir in the period 1984–1990. The jolting tragedy of his assassination surely accounts for some of the empathetic, sentimental, and selective memorializing of a fallen prime minister. However, using the shock waves of bereavement as the explanation trivializes the primal identification of many Israelis with Rabin. They connected the adversity-failure dots—the beat down and break down with the bounce back and fight back that marked his life, a life symbolized by the possibility of a second chance of being prime minister, an opportunity seen by many as the first and only chance for peace.

Shlomo Ben-Ami, the dovish Labor Party Knesset member who worked with and closely observed all three would-be Israeli "generals of peace" (Rabin, Barak, and Sharon), characterized Rabin's connection with the Israeli public in the following terms: "No one reflected in his life what the Israelis believed was their collective biography as he did. No one expressed so well their dilemma in the transition from war to peace. His hesitations and ambiguities were theirs, his skepticism and doubts were theirs and, like him, they feared the risks involved in this leap into the future as much as they were excited by the opportunities it opened."[11]

Bridging the politically valuable terrain between Israeli security hawks and security doves, Rabin could not get comfortable, either at the beginning of his journey in waging peace with Arafat on the South Lawn of the White House on September 13, 1993, or at the end of it, at the November 4, 1995, peace rally in Tel Aviv with Shalom Achshav (Peace Now) banners fluttering around him. His reluctant handshake with Arafat was his nation's reticence. His awkwardness in trying to sing a song of peace, the words of which he was unsure of, was his nation's uncertain voice.

Rabin resonated sufficiently with the nation's electorate to lead the Labor Party back into power in 1992, ending an electoral drought that had stretched back to Golda Meir's 1973 victory. Her tenure ended in her resignation after the 1973 war in response to criticism of Israel's state of readiness. Rabin became prime minister, narrowly defeating his archrival Shimon Peres in an internal Labor Party conclave.

Whatever the nature of his connection with the Israeli public in life, his death transformed him into a martyr, and not only for Israelis. The legacy of Rabin would now become embellished, and a legend was in the making.

The assumption that the assassination of Rabin killed the Oslo peace process, or at least was a seminal event in its decline, has been embraced by serious scholars, including important Palestinian academics. Rashid Khalidi, the Palestinian-American scholar, who was a member of the Palestinian negotiating team at the Madrid Conference and beyond, argues, "Within a few years after Oslo, especially after the assassination of Yitzhak Rabin by an Israeli right-wing extremist in late 1995, negotiations between the two sides bogged down."[12] Khalil Shikaki, the director of the Palestinian Center for Policy and Survey Research in Ramallah, suggested, "Palestinian optimism regarding the negotiating process declined with the assassination of Rabin, and this will be judged as a key turning point in the collapse of Oslo."[13] Palestinian negotiators also looked wistfully on the Rabin legend as Barak assumed the prime ministership after beating Netanyahu in the 1999 elections. Their perception that Barak was "Rabin's successor" raised Palestinian expectations of a rejuvenation of Oslo.[14]

What made Rabin such a compelling and potentially effective advocate for peace was his biography, which placed him so forcefully in the hard-line camp. After all, it was Rabin who, as defense minister in January 1988, initiated a new policy instructing the Israeli Defense Forces to counter the intifada with "force, might, and beatings." These instructions included breaking the bones of Palestinian protestors to prevent them from throwing potentially lethal stones or fleeing the scene of protests. Ephraim Sneh, a former Israeli general and a medical doctor, who served as the head of the civil administration in the West Bank, quipped that Rabin had developed an "orthopedic problem with the Palestinians." It was precisely this problem that was an asset in marketing the Oslo Accords to the Israeli public, especially security hawks, who were—and are perhaps still—the most important swing constituency on foreign and defense issues.

Political ideological constituencies in Israel get the lion's share of attention, particularly the ideological hawks and ideological doves, with their dueling sound bites and street rallies. However, elections are often determined in the more fluid intersections where nonideological hawks and doves meet, searching for answers to their security concerns. They may also join the street rallies, but they possess less political certitude and a more questioning orientation, which predispose them to make situational judgments based on security-related issues. This is not to downplay the significance and the impact of those at the ends of the political spectrum, especially the ideological absolutists associated with "Greater Israel" (Eretz Yisrael Hashlema, literally, the "whole land of Israel"). This sector of Israeli politics is most closely identified with religious messianists who view the War of Independence and the Six Day War as part of the divinely ordained process that will culminate in reunifying the people of Israel, the biblical land of Israel, and the Torah of world Jewry into an organic whole. Jews are prohibited from withdrawing from any part of their providentially mandated mission. This ideological camp, espousing the "politics of not one inch," was not moved by Rabin's biography or by his security credentials. They had a higher calling. But in the 1992 election, the former chief of staff led the Labor Party back into power and the prime ministership. One of the keys to the Zionist Left's return to power was Rabin's credentials, which passed the threshold for getting security clearance from the nonideological hawkish sector of the Israeli public, which harbored real fears about their Palestinian and Arab neighbors' intentions.

Rabin's personal biography and political orientation helped to provide the Labor Party and the Zionist Left with a narrow margin of victory over Likud.[15] As a decorated warrior, former head of the IDF, and a defense minister who had ordered the breaking of Palestinian bones, he had established his credentials with his nation's security hawks. He shared their skepticism about Palestinian willingness to make peace, but he was pragmatic enough to know that Israel would have to compromise. He seemed to resonate with the national zeitgeist.

Rabin's Inheritance

As Rabin introduced his new government to the Knesset for its approval, he sounded like an untroubled prime minister brandishing a bold new message: "We must overcome the sense of isolation that has held us in thrall for almost half a century. We have to stop thinking the whole world is against us."[16] Rabin did inherit some very significant strategic and security assets that empowered him to signal a volte-face and turn away from emphasizing the Holocaust and Israel's global isolation, which had been central themes in the previous Likud governments.

A new, more hospitable international, regional, and local environment greeted Rabin. Two wars were ended, the First Gulf War and the cold war. One empire had imploded, the Soviet Union, and a new Middle East peace initiative in Madrid had spawned bilateral negotiations in Washington as well as multilateral talks in a number of other venues on hot-button regional issues such as arms control, water, trade, and the environment.

These developments were a potential boon to Israeli security, which generated a new initiative that would use the battlefield in the Gulf as a springboard to the negotiating table in Madrid. First, Yasser Arafat and the Palestine Liberation Organization (PLO) were severely weakened, and pragmatic Palestinian leaders from the West Bank, Gaza, and Jerusalem were increasingly assertive, lobbying the external leadership of the PLO to open a diplomatic track with Israel. Arafat's embrace of Saddam Hussein, who was firing Scud missiles at the Saudis, provoked retribution against him personally as well as against the organization and the Palestinian people. The PLO lost its bankers in the Gulf, and thousands of Palestinian workers lost their jobs. The drying up of the earnings they had been repatriating to the West Bank intensified the economic woes in the territories. The large and wealthy Palestinian community in the Gulf suffered grievous losses, and in Kuwait it was decimated. It suffered a double hit, first from the Iraqi invasion and subsequently at the hands of angry Kuwaitis who believed Palestinians had supported the invasion of Kuwait. The Kuwaiti Palestinian population dropped precipitously from approximately 400,000 before the war to less than 100,000 by the end of 1991.[17] This economic calamity for the Palestinians could not have come at a worse time, as the number of West Bank and Gaza residents working in Israel was reduced to half its prewar total of 150,000, in part because of the attempt to provide jobs for the massive Russian immigration and in part out of fear of terrorist attacks.

The West Bank was not only facing an economic crisis but also showing new societal strains with the intifada's "loss of direction" and an explosion of intra-Palestinian violence. In 1991 more Palestinians were killed by Palestinians (approximately 150) than by Israelis (100).[18]

Arafat was a casualty of his own blunders. Mr. Palestine remained stateless and increasingly isolated in exile. Disaffection with "Arafatocracy" was spreading among Arab leaders and former wealthy benefactors, as well as among the Palestinian everyman and Palestinian political elites.

The second potential security and diplomatic benefit to Israel was the military defanging of Saddam Hussein. He and his regime were left standing, but bloodied and less threatening on Israel's eastern front. With the military neutering of Iraq—at least, temporarily—Israel had bought time and space to consider "taking risks for peace" in the Palestinian arena.

The implosion of the Soviet Union represented a third potentially positive security development for Israel. Arafat lost an important diplomatic asset and countervailing power to the United States. This loss would only strengthen the case for a diplomatic gambit by the "inside" Palestinian leadership.

The fourth and perhaps most important security benefit Rabin inherited from the new political landscape and the collapse of the Soviet Union was the near hegemonic position of the United States, Israel's staunch ally. The prospect of a potential "new world order" whose fulcrum was Washington, D.C.—the sole superpower generating the necessary political and economic voltage to help Israel enhance its security and grow its economy—emboldened even a taciturn, undemonstrative leader like Rabin. In these new circumstances, he beseeched his nation to reach out to build new relations in a world where its allies were strong and its enemies could be held at bay.

The scene had now been set for an American-dominated effort to use the First Gulf War battlefield as a launching pad for a Middle East peace initiative that would, for the first time, begin face-to-face negotiations between Israel and the four of its immediate Arab neighbors with whom it did not have peace. However, rather than solidifying Israel's security and its relations with the United States, this new hopeful environment generated a new round of acrimony and tension with Rabin's immediate predecessor, Prime Minister Yitzhak Shamir.

Rabin's Rise to Power:
The Loan-Guarantee Saga

Yitzhak Rabin's ascent to power in 1992 emerged from a specific environment that featured an open conflict between the Bush administration and the Shamir government. The Likud and Republican administrations tangled in a brawl that has important historical and political implications. The nature and significance of this collision have alternately been distorted for partisan ends. The Israeli hard Right and their American supporters see it as symptomatic of the erstwhile American betrayal, "selling Israel down the river" and fearing more of the same. The Israeli Zionist Left and its American supporters greet it as a rescue mission "saving Israel from committing suicide through annexation," with requests to "play it again, Sam."

An examination of the 1991 loan-guarantee crisis suggests that both these fears and hopes of Uncle Sam's behavior were wildly exaggerated. As we shall see, the Bush administration's intervention in Israeli electoral politics did succeed in a messy regime change of a stalwart ally. However, Washington subsequently returned to a more private and less intrusive involvement in the Israeli-Palestinian conflict. James Baker, who was so instrumental in pressuring and confronting the Shamir government, moved from the State Department to the White House in a failed attempt to save the Bush presidency. This move caused not just a traditional momentary electoral-season diversion of attention from American engagement in the Arab-Israeli conflict. There was a return to diplomatic dormancy. William Jefferson Clinton's next seven years, with spurts of foraging for peace when the hibernation season ended, fit comfortably into this pattern of diplomatic activity. There was no secret Washington back channel that would host and facilitate Israeli-Palestinian negotiations. Oslo would become the workplace for peace, and Washington's role was scaled down as the showplace for peace on the South Lawn of the White House. The Clinton peace team did inherit the Oslo Accords, stepping gingerly around the land mines and deferring political showdowns even at the cost of diplomatic breakdowns. Its last-ditch effort to save the crumbling Oslo process via the Camp David summit and Clinton Parameters had a familiar patina of peace, but it was a belated effort at compensatory diplomacy having an aura of the noble that could not offset the neglect and rot that had overtaken the Oslo Accords.

For one brief historical period, the George H.W. Bush administration did not cautiously sidestep a political land mine. It considered the post–Gulf War environment a moment of such extraordinary opportunity for a diplomatic breakthrough that it was prepared for a political showdown with a resolute ally, Israel, and its formidable American supporters. Spearheaded by two national umbrella bodies, the American Israel Public Affairs Committee and the Conference of Presidents of Major American Jewish Organizations, a thousand American Jewish leaders were preparing to descend on Congress in a "crusade" to save Israel from President Bush's "threatening ultimatum." The collision between the Shamir government (and the American "Jewish Lobby") and the Bush administration was an unlikely vehicle for the leftist Zionists' ride back into power after a fifteen-year hiatus.[19]

In 1991, the Israeli government under Prime Minister Yitzhak Shamir requested $10 billion in American loan guarantees over the next five years. That amount would have allowed Israel to borrow significant sums of money at much lower interest rates and help the country absorb over one million new immigrants from the Soviet Union. Neither President Bush nor Secretary of State James Baker was prepared to see any of this money spent beyond the Green Line. But neither did they want a showdown on the issue of settlements when they had bigger fish to fry at the moment: getting Shamir to accept the American terms for participation in the International Peace Conference in Madrid. Shamir rejected the American approach on settlements, and the Bush administration postponed its decision on the loan guarantees until January 1992 (two months after the Madrid Conference and the initiation of bilateral talks), when congressional leaders entered the fray, exploring possible compromises. While Shamir did subsequently agree to participate in the Madrid Conference, the unresolved loan-guarantee–settlement-freeze dispute began to bump up against the Israeli and American elections. With Israeli elections scheduled first—in June 1992—pressure mounted to see who was going to blink first and confront a potential domestic political backlash.

Neither blinked. In late January 1992, Shamir made it clear that there was no wiggle room for a compromise. Jewish settlements were sacrosanct. President Bush, in turn, decided to offer the full $10-billion loan-guarantee package, but with a dollar-for-dollar reduction for every dollar the Israelis spent on settlements. President Bush understood that Shamir would likely reject this offer, both because he was firmly in the camp of the ideological absolutists of Greater Israel and because his annexationist electoral base was already criticizing him as elections approached. This showdown on the loan guarantees and Jewish settlements was an important factor in the election of Yitzhak Rabin, and it was used consciously to this end by President Bush and James Baker.

Dennis Ross, the Middle East envoy and the chief peace negotiator in the presidencies of George H.W. Bush and Bill Clinton, was involved in the details of this backstage drama that helped Rabin win the role of leading man. Ross preferred—and he was initially authorized to negotiate—a compromise. Israel would receive a one-year $2-billion loan guarantee. In exchange, the Israeli government would divulge to the United States the level of its expenditures on settlements prior to receiving the loan guarantees. This agreement would supposedly allow the United States to determine if Israeli expenditures on settlements had increased after the provision of the loan guarantees. Ross actually negotiated this preferred option of his in 1990 for a much smaller loan guarantee of $400 million. Shamir subsequently reneged on the terms of the agreement.[20]

This brief summary of the loan-guarantee crisis is strategically important for Left Zionists. It suggests a second key variable in explaining their rise to power. Besides having a standard bearer who had security clearance, the Left benefited from US intervention. The Bush administration had demonstrated the power of American engagement in influencing the outcome of the Israeli elections and, ultimately, Israeli peace and security policies.

The case of the American loan-guarantees showdown is also significant because it reveals some key lessons on the specific circumstances that propelled the Bush administration to engage in such a high-stakes public diplomatic gambit. The Bush administration not only could have deferred the loan-guarantee showdown, which it did for nearly five months, but could also have simply dropped it altogether as too hot to handle. After all, popular wisdom has it that nothing good can come of publicly challenging the prime minister of Israel. This is particularly true in an electoral season and especially when the confrontation entails an issue that is central to the prime minister's ideology and is a core issue for his political base.

Why then did Bush and Baker persist in what they presumed would be a nasty and noisy collision with Shamir? Dennis Ross has suggested that the reason was both principle and politics. The principle was that both men firmly believed the Jewish settlement activity was part of the problem and the primary tool used by Shamir and Likud to render territorial compromise moot and the conflict unmanageable. Without a territorial compromise and conflict management, American strategic interests were imperiled. The politics entailed several considerations. First, once the president had been persuaded to defer his showdown with Shamir for more than four months, beginning in February, the loan-guarantee issue had become inextricably entangled in the Israeli electoral season. Second, according to Ross, "Baker was determined not to do anything that might help Shamir. Providing the loan guarantees would show that he could have settlement activity and still get our support. There would be no cost to him and he could use that in the election."[21] Baker's message was clear: Shamir had to pay a price for his settlements policy. The price was helping "the other Yitzhak."[22]

Ross offers one last political insight into why the Israelis wanted "the other Yitzhak." Rabin represented a "promise" of peace not just to the Zionist Left. He also embodied the "promise" of peace for the Bush administration—sufficiently so that Bush was prepared, as we have seen in the loan-guarantee showdown, to directly and publicly break with an Israeli prime minister during an election cycle. This American intervention and the election of Rabin were joined almost symbiotically as part of a double legend. Rabin was cast as the prince of peace and the Americans as the deus ex machina. The truth was much more modest and disappointing for the Zionist Left. Rabin did represent a breakthrough of sorts, but he also carried the seeds for the breakdown that materialized. The Bush administration played a decisive role in this one moment, but it was more an aberration than a pattern for subsequent American policy.

There was some potential affinity between the leftist Zionists' peace agenda and American diplomatic intervention in the Arab-Israeli arena. The Israeli Zionist Left can take solace from the natural advantage it seems to enjoy over annexationist and hard-line Israeli governments when it comes to America's formal policies and its articulated interests on issues of Jewish settlements and the occupation. However, this general congruence of preferences and values does not necessarily translate into a strong US connection. In fact, the case of the loan guarantees suggests that the expenditure of a great deal of diplomatic energy requires a specific combination of variables that the US administration construes as "ripeness." It also suggests that the change from ripe to rotten happens with seasonal regularity. Sustaining American peacemaking efforts for any length of time is a dubious proposition. In a time of bountiful harvest Washington may pick the low-hanging fruit and occasionally make a difference in the orchard.

Passing the Ripeness Test

The historical juncture of the post–Gulf War environment in which the Bush Administration initiated both the Madrid Peace Conference (which spawned four bilateral and a series of multilateral working groups) and the potentially historic change in leadership in Israel elicited an American intervention—one that made a difference and breathed new life into the Israeli Zionist Left. However, even a cursory summary of the specific variables that constituted the "ripeness" that the Americans required before intervening in the loan-guarantee issue highlights the difficulties of depending on American intervention.

Shamir, Mr. "Stall-mate"

The potential political cost to an American president of openly colliding with an Israeli government is so steep that it takes a very significant pattern of grievance to elicit the kind of showdown that occurred in the loan-guarantees issue. Shamir provided that pattern of grievance. No Israeli prime minister since Shamir has proven as intransigent, ideologically hawkish, and openly flaunting of a policy of "stall-mate." Prime Minister Shamir was brazenly obstructionist in his commitment to Greater Israel. There was remarkably little subtlety in his attempt to disguise his intentions. The few important acts of statesmanship of his tenure as prime minister, such as his steely discipline in not allowing Saddam Hussein to lure him into the First Gulf War, were trumped by his steadfastness in blocking progress on the diplomatic front. In case there was any doubt of his intentions, he confirmed the most egregious claims made against him. In an interview with the Israeli press after his defeat by Rabin he is quoted as saying, "If I had been reelected, I would have continued negotiations on Palestinian autonomy for ten years, and in that time half a million Israelis would have settled on the West Bank."[23] In his book *The Missing Peace,* Dennis Ross argues that it was the presence of the indefatigable obstructionist, Prime Minster Shamir, that played a key role in creating a new positive dynamic. "In no small part there emerged an increasingly credible peace camp in Israel because Shamir was not willing to give up the right-wing agenda, and the Israeli public saw the cost of this, in terms of both Israel's relationship with the United States and the possibility of peace."[24]

Rabin, the "Other Yitzhak"

Shamir's intractable obstructionism might have been insufferable, but without a viable alternative, the Bush administration might have had to go on suffering. However, as Dennis Ross has testified, the administration perceived that it had an alternative—Rabin—and that he was electable. His security credentials, pragmatic orientation, and governing experience had all the makings of Israel's next prime minister.

The Israeli Electorate's Choice of the World, Not Shamir's World

The Bush administration had impeccable timing. By deferring the loan-guarantee showdown with Shamir in January 1991 (Bush was focusing on getting Shamir to accept the terms for attending the Madrid Conference and did not want to create another contentious issue), Bush and Baker had intruded on the Israeli electoral season and created a wedge issue that would compromise Shamir's candidacy for many centrists and security hawks, for whom misman-agement of Israel's fundamental relationship with America was unacceptable. The wedge issue was not just a settlement freeze (which Shamir rejected) nor was it only the $10 billion in loan guarantees (which he abandoned). (He had originally requested it to help facilitate the ingathering of the massive immigra-tion from the Soviet Union, with its surging electoral clout.) The wedge issue included Israel's relationship with the United States. Shamir was saying no to the United States at the height of its prestige and influence, which some have characterized as the "American Era" in the Middle East.[25] President Bush, not known for ambitious vision ("the vision thing"), had called for a "new world order." Shamir's world revolved around expanding Jewish settlements and Greater Israel. One can speculate that in his heartfelt opposition to both territo-rial compromise and Bush's demand for a settlement freeze, Shamir might have calculated that he would derive some benefit from a backlash against the dic-tates of Uncle Sam. It may have rallied his ideological base and strengthened his position within his party. However, this raw and public dispute with the presi-dent of the United States would be decided not in a Likud caucus but in a gen-eral election, where running to the center was not only an American condition for victory. If Shamir was counting on the "American Jewish lobby" to dissuade Bush and Baker from linking the loan guarantees to Jewish settlements in the West Bank and Gaza, he was in for a surprise. There were limits to the "lobby's" power. Those limits were reached on this issue.

Shamir's failure to manage his nation's lifeline relationship with the United States left the swing voters to choose between "Shamir's world" of Eretz Yis-rael Hashlema and expansive Jewish settlements versus the world of prag-matic realities in which the global superpower ally was offering $10 billion to help cope with Israel's massive Russian immigration.

Israel's Partner for Peace

In *The Missing Peace,* Dennis Ross argues, "It was not just the loan guarantees that had done Shamir in. It was also that Shamir made a basic miscalculation:

when the Israeli public believes they have a partner in peace, they want a government that is capable of negotiating peace. . . . In 1992, the Israeli public,
post-Madrid, believed that there was an opportunity for peace and they
wanted a government capable of pursuing it. A Rabin-led government certainly seemed to promise this."[26] Ross also presents the inverse dynamic, in
which the Israeli public perceives there is no partner, and security is the para-
mount issue. In this environment the Israelis "will vote for those who will
show the Arabs the consequences of not being partners—and will vote against
those they deem 'soft' toward Israel's neighbors."[27] In Ross's view the Israeli
public perceived that they now had negotiating partners. The Israeli Jewish
public was moving in the same direction as Rabin: "What can we do? Peace
you don't make with friends, but with very unsympathetic enemies. I won't
try to make the PLO look good. It was an enemy, it remains an enemy, but negotiations must be with enemies."[28] Rabin's cold, analytical logic was warming
him to the necessity of negotiating with the PLO. However, he was not yet
ready to break the taboo of negotiating directly with the PLO. The partners
Ross and the Israeli public seemingly had in mind were the "inside" West
Bank and Gaza Palestinians, who so ably represented the Palestinians at
Madrid: Dr. Haider Abdel Shafi, Ghassan Khatieb, and Faisal Husseini. The
last was the son of Abd al-Kader al-Husseini, the charismatic Palestinian
leader who had been killed in April 1948 in a fierce battle at the strategic village of al-Qastal on the road to Jerusalem. Rabin encouraged the Americans
to add Husseini as the head of the delegation in the hope of strengthening the
"inside" representatives so that they might yet become an alternative to Arafat
and the PLO. This hope would prove to be illusory, not just because Arafat
continued to assert his control over the delegation. More interesting, the "inside" insisted on negotiating the fundamental permanent-status issues,
whereas Arafat would subsequently agree to defer them.

This brief and selective overview of the electoral plight of the Israeli Zionist
Left over the last decade and a half has highlighted two important historical
developments: the pre-Rabin loan-guarantee showdown between the Shamir
government and the Bush White House and the Sharon government's unilateral disengagement from Gaza plus a notch of the northern West Bank. The
first event, a pre-Rabin moment, focused on the circumstances that catapulted the Zionist Left back into power. The second, a Sharon postdisengage-
ment moment, represented the culmination of the political and electoral
decline of the Zionist Left. Together these two developments represent the
bookends of an era that was launched with the promise of waging peace under a dovish Israeli government. It concluded with the continuing peril of
rocket and missile attacks on Israel's home front following the unilateral
withdrawal from Gaza and the inconclusive Second Lebanon War. The Labor

Party, the standard bearer of the Zionist Left, was the culpable junior partner in this pair of policy boomerangs, which enhanced Israel's quest neither for security nor for peace. These adventures represented a long fall from grace and disillusioned many Israelis who had once had high hopes for peace and security that were associated with the Rabin-led leftist Zionist government.

Rabin: The Tainted Icon

The Rabin model of success for the Zionist Left is, however, doubly problematic. First, his rise to power was made possible by a rare confluence of factors that will be exceedingly difficult to replicate. They included a politically vulnerable incumbent prime minister with uncompromising ideological policies that were in conflict with both the interests of an American administration and the values of the Israeli public; an electable alternative national candidate with the untainted security credentials that were necessary to effectively market the "painful compromises" associated with substantive peace negotiations; and finally, a viable Palestinian partner.

The second problem with the Rabin precedent is that it failed. His security clearance with the Israeli electorate was only for taking off, and his flight was freighted with trouble long before the tragic crash landing. A double tragic paradox haunted this would-be general of peace. He was as unable to secure his own life as he was to cope with the Palestinian terrorism that ravaged the Oslo peace process. While terrorism was a general Israeli problem, the suicide terrorist stalked the Israeli Left government with strategic specificity.

Hamas and Islamic Jihad were particularly threatened by the prospect of negotiating breakthroughs that could lead to recognition of and coexistence with the state of Israel. Their conception of Greater Palestine is driven by a religiously absolutist theology that considers it blasphemous to cede any part of Islamic Palestine, from the Mediterranean Sea to the Jordan River. The charter of the Islamic Resistance Movement (Hamas) unequivocally prohibits yielding any land and asserts jihad (emphasizing only its martial component) as the inevitable and sole means of retrieving Palestine. Both the goal (redeeming Palestine in its entirety) and the means (only through force of arms) are expressly linked to religious faith. Hamas's charter asserts that to forgo either part of Palestine or armed struggle is tantamount to surrendering part of Islam.[29]

This ideological dimension of Hamas, which reeks of politicidal and genocidal ambitions vis-à-vis Israelis, is one of a pair of its strategic commitments. The other is its social movement, which is central to Hamas's identity. Hamas's declared doctrine and long-term vision, which revolve around absolutist goals and violent means, are uncomfortably coupled with the immediate, pragmatic

daily mission of providing education, health, and welfare services to its beleaguered traditional base of refugees and the urban poor. This latter mission entails not ideological purity and military jihad but pragmatic adjustments and
medical clinics. These two impulses of Hamas often pull the movement in different directions, not just the social versus the martial, but also, geographically,
the "inside" versus the "outside."

The second duality, the "inside" Palestinians (the West Bank and Gaza
Strip) and the "outside" Palestinians (headquartered at different times in
Springfield, Virginia; Amman; London; and Damascus), also exhibited dueling characteristics that would frustrate Rabin and help stain his security
persona. The "inside" was riveted on local community services and activities
in the mosques, schools, and other social settings geared to cope with the
daily challenges of the Israeli occupation. For them the *da'wa,* or the Is-
lamization of the community via religious instruction and social mobilization at the grass roots, was a priority. In contrast, the "outside" leadership
was animated by a "vision of political Islamism . . . a revolution from
above."[30]

The diaspora Hamas gained in influence with the consolidation of two ex-
ternally based institutions, the religious Advisory Council (Majlis shura) and
the Political Bureau. Increasingly, the Political Bureau enhanced its power
through the collection of significant funds and regional and global contacts
with the broader Islamic world, including with Iran and Hizbollah. It also cul-
tivated close relationships with branches of the newly formed military arm of
Hamas, 'Izz al-Din al-Qassam. In July 1992, a month after the election of Rabin, the Hamas leadership in the United States sent a representative with
funds, a list of activists to contact, and directives for coordinating military activities between Gaza and the West Bank.

Rabin and Israeli security officials were increasingly concerned about the
growing terrorist threat and the threatening regional alliances that Hamas was
consolidating. Iran had committed itself to support Hamas politically, finan-
cially, and militarily in an effort to scuttle the nascent peace process. Israeli
scholars Shaul Mishal and Avram Sela argue, "It was this agreement that
spurred Hamas to escalate its military operations against Israel—manifested
in the murder of an Israeli policeman—in an attempt to derail the peace
process."[31] The Israeli crackdown on Hamas in the territories; the arrest in
1989 of Hamas's leader, Sheikh Ahmed Yasin, in Gaza; and the mass arrest and
deportation of 415 Hamas (as well as Islamic Jihad) activists in retaliation for
the December 1992 murder of the Israeli policeman, Nachshon Wachsman—
all presented yet another opportunity for the external forces of Hamas to assert themselves.

Rabin's response to the kidnapping and killing of Nachshon Wachsman represented an early test of his management of the security portfolio. It was a test that Hamas would ace and Rabin perform poorly on. His deportation backfired. First, it changed the conversation from the murder of the Israeli policeman to the presumed Israeli culpability in what was perceived as an egregious violation of Palestinian human rights. Second, it rescued Hamas from a very problematic situation. Hamas had just negotiated a tenuous truce with Fatah following internecine violence that appeared on the brink of escalating into a civil war. The ideological cleavages and political competition had not been mediated, and the relationship had "reached its lowest ebb as Arafat's attacks on Hamas became more vehement and humiliating."[32] The next round of a combat between Fatah and Hamas seemed to be in the offing as Arafat likened Hamas to a "Zulu tribe." Arafat was scornfully comparing Hamas to the Inkata movement in South Africa, which had refused to submit to the authority of Nelson Mandela and the African National Congress during talks with Frederick de Klerk's white government. Arafat's bravado was short-lived. He was no Nelson Mandela under any circumstances, and Hamas was looking more and more like an emerging alternative to Fatah than like a marginalized "Zulu tribe."

Chinks had also begun to show in Rabin's security armor. With one policy act, Rabin had turned the issue of Hamas into a human rights issue, transformed Hamas and the deportees into national heroes, and had made the Israelis villains. Hamas and its fighters would now become worthy allies of important elements within Fatah.

For the first time since the intifada began in 1987, the PLO and Hamas issued a joint leaflet. More ominously, this was followed by an ad hoc agreement between the battalions of 'Izz al-Din al-Qassam of Hamas, the Fatah Hawks, and the PFLP's (Popular Front for the Liberation of Palestine) Red Eagles to cooperate in military operations against Israel. Rabin's early security move to exile his problems was bold. Whether it was wise was less clear. Rabin had seemingly imported even bigger troubles. Shaul Mishal and Avraham Sela characterize Rabin's deportation of the 415 Islamic activists as

> a milestone in Hamas's decision to use car bombs and suicide attacks as a major *modus operandi* against Israel. Shortly thereafter, Hamas leaders in Amman instructed its military activists to carry out two attacks, one by a car bomb, as a gesture to the deportees. Hamas's escalated military activity was a direct result of the presence of the deportees for almost a year in south Lebanon, which provided the Palestinian Islamists an opportunity to learn about Hizbollah's experience in fighting the Israelis, the effect of suicide attacks, and the construction of car bombs. . . . Thus it

was no coincidence that Hamas's first suicide operation was carried out after the deportees returned to the occupied territories.[33]

During Rabin's first year Hamas discovered the exposed Achilles' heel of the Oslo Accords: Israeli security versus the Palestinian economy. Terrorist attacks that were successful in inflicting high casualties on Israeli civilians were certain to trigger retaliatory Israeli collective punishment, particularly in the economic sphere. Israel could be counted on to seal off the West Bank and Gaza from Israel, denying access to Palestinian workers and products, and discrediting Fatah and the Palestinian Authority. Hamas had honed an insidiously effective means of simultaneously undermining the peace process, delegitimizing its secular nationalist opponents, and bleeding the Israeli public. The suicide terrorist attacks represented more than a series of personal and familial tragedies. They were a strategic threat to peacemaking, and they triggered a deadly dynamic. It began with a mobilization of the ideological hawks on both sides in a mutually reinforcing campaign of incitement and violence against the Oslo Accords and metastasized to both the Israeli and Palestinian streets, sowing fear in Ramat Gan and increasing poverty in Jubalya.

Rabin's peacemaking efforts would now confront a problem for which he had no answer, save the determined commitment to "fight terrorism as if there was no peace process and pursue the peace process as if there was no terrorism." The problem was that Rabin did not necessarily have a reliable partner for either the battle against terror or waging peace. More a sound bite than a sound policy, this dictum caused Rabin to slowly but surely lose altitude with no safe landing in sight.

Rabin's failings on the security front were symbolized, not summarized, by the December 1992 deportations. The grisly murder of Nachshon Wachsman was followed by a series of escalating attacks, including suicide terrorism. The violence had reached unprecedented levels. Israeli scholar Benny Morris claims, "The 1994–96 period was the heyday of the suicide bombers."[34] Tragically, worse was yet to come in March 2002, a year after Morris's book was published. Shlomo Ben-Ami argues that "terrorism undermined the legitimacy and the moral foundations of the peace process" during Rabin's tenure; "Rabin was marching to his political demise."[35] While "the heyday of suicide terrorism" extended into the post-Rabin era, its ravaging effects on the embryonic peace and the people of Israel—two-thirds of whom had supported the Oslo Accords in the fall of 1993—was manifest long before his assassination.

Rabin may have courageously wanted "to fight terrorism as if there was no peace process and pursue the peace process as if there was no terrorism." However, this formula lacked the necessary personal chemistry between the two principals, Arafat and Rabin, and the laboratory conditions were a petri dish for conflict, not conciliation. In addition to Arafat's and Rabin's divergent views of Oslo's final destination and the speed with which they wanted to travel, they held incompatible security conceptions. Rabin presumed that Arafat had the legitimacy to rein in Palestinian violence that the Israelis could never exercise. Arafat disdainfully dismissed this as a degrading presumption that the Palestinian Authority was a subcontractor for Israeli security.

Arafat did have a few red lines that he might have been persuaded not to let Hamas cross in its use of violence. He was prepared to crack down on Hamas, but only in specific and limited circumstances. If it was demonstrated that Hamas had attacked Israel from the territory under the jurisdiction of the Palestinian Authority (PA), Arafat might be moved to act, but only if Rabin threatened to halt Israel's withdrawal from additional territory or stop the devolution of its control to the PA. This meant that Arafat was, at the very least, implicitly giving an amber light to Palestinian terrorism that originated from Israeli-controlled territory. In these circumstances Rabin's formulaically compartmentalized commitment to simultaneously fight terror and wage peace would leave his narrow majority government in desperate straits. Terrorism and peace were not only an odd couple, but an impossible one.

Arafat's permissive approach to terrorism included phantasmal claims that blamed Israeli agents even as Hamas and the Islamic Jihad were assuming responsibility for these attacks. Rabin's security shield had fallen, and his would-be partner had been delegitimized: The Americans were only episodically engaged and never willing to seriously monitor and adjudicate the mutual obligations that had collapsed into a blame game. And the Israeli public was restless; half were prepared to vote for Netanyahu. The factors that combined to catapult Rabin into the premiership had recoalesced to bring him down politically by the summer of 1995. Itamar Rabinovich, the notable Israeli scholar who served under Rabin as the chief negotiator with Syria and as ambassador to the United States, provides a detailed survey of the evidence that "the peace process which [Rabin] had launched was already receding" before his assassination.[36] Shlomo Ben-Ami takes an even more grave view of the status of the peace process under Rabin. "The truth of the matter was. . . that by the time Rabin was murdered the peace process was, for all practical purposes, in a state of political coma."[37]

Rabin's striking reversal in fortune was attributable not only to Arafat's complicity with terrorism and an insufficiently involved US administration. Dennis Ross, not a fan of Arafat's and not often accused of gratuitous criticism of Israeli policies or behavior, identified a nefarious linkage between Arafat's tolerating, if not condoning, terrorism and the expansion of Jewish settlements in the West Bank and Gaza. The context for Ross's comment was the aftermath of a January 22, 1995, suicide bombing in the Israeli town of Beit Lit, in which twenty-two Israelis were killed. While Rabin continued to declare that he was going to fight terror as if there was no peace process and to pursue peace as if there were no terror, he also insisted that real pressure had to be put on Arafat to arrest and punish the killers. In February 1995, Rabin reported that Arafat was finally acting against terror. It was on the heels of this improved security performance of the PA that the Americans were trying to consolidate a broader initiative against terrorism with specific commitments from Arafat, while the Israelis would simultaneously agree to try to expedite the Oslo II Interim Agreement by July 1, 1995. In this momentarily hopeful environment, Ross offers his commentary:

> Yet Israeli settlement activity was expanding, not contracting, in the West Bank and Gaza, threatening to undermine our efforts. The Palestinians saw the new settlements as a sign that the negotiations would not stop Israel from taking land Palestinians considered to be theirs—grist for extremists, which inevitably weakened the PA and Arafat. Arafat himself would rarely raise the issue, leaving it to his deputies. It was as if he felt he had an implicit deal with Rabin: "you don't push me beyond where I can go with my opponents and I won't push you beyond where you can go with your settler constituency." It was a rare instance of diplomatic subtlety.[38]

There are half a dozen eye-opening insights imbedded in Ross's observations. They are essential to understanding how Rabin's government, as well as the Clinton administration, was complicit in the unraveling of Oslo and was part of the pattern of failure that plagued the Rabin government and all the subsequent Israeli and American governments. First there is a direct acknowledgment, often repeated in Ross's memoirs, of the expansion of Jewish settlements under all Israeli governments, including those of Rabin, Peres, and Barak. Second, this expansion threatened to undermine the Clinton administration's peacemaking efforts. Third, this settlement expansion was inexorably leading to greater and greater Israeli control over land whose status was supposed to be determined at the negotiating table. Fourth, this settlement expansion strengthened the Palestinian extremists, who eschewed negotiations and weakened the PA and Arafat. Fifth, it led Arafat to believe that he had a de facto deal with Rabin not to directly confront their most contentious domestic constituencies: The Jewish settlements would expand, and Hamas and the Islamic Jihad would remain relatively free to spread their violence. In his concluding punch line, Ross characterizes this feeling that Arafat had regarding an "implicit deal" with Rabin as "a rare instance of [Arafat's] diplomatic subtlety." This last comment by Ross sounds blissfully dismissive of the perilous message that he communicates in the rest of his analysis. Ross provides a less dismissive and more sober clarification at the bottom of the page following an asterisk: "While tactically useful, this complicit bargain was strategically damaging. Israeli settlement activity convinced Palestinians over time that the process was a sham, and gave Arafat, at least in his mind, an excuse not to fulfill his responsibilities on security."[39]

Dennis Ross and the Clinton administration seemingly had a clear understanding of this deadly dynamic between Palestinian violence and Jewish settlements. One does not have to stretch the parallel by claiming a moral equivalency. Building Jewish settlements was as strategically dangerous as Ross implies, but it was not the same as blowing up buses packed with innocent civilians. This combustible interaction was not treated with sufficient energy or urgency in Washington. American presidents deferred to Israeli prime ministers, particularly when they seemed prepared to "make painful compromises for peace." Both Bush and Clinton were relieved that "the other Yitzhak" was the prime minister, just as Clinton exhaled with pleasure when Barak replaced Netanyahu. George W. Bush was equally anxious to saddle up with Sharon in the post–9/11 world, where security came first. Save for an exceptional moment in 1992, there had been bipartisan agreement not to disturb America's relationship with Israel over the issue of settlements.

Hence, the American $10-billion loan-guarantee offer that was denied Shamir was extended to Rabin. The settlement freeze was restricted to new building, and approximately ten thousand housing units that had already been started were exempted. The number of Jewish settlers in the West Bank and Gaza nearly doubled from the signing of the Declaration of Principles in September 1993 to the Camp David II Summit in July 2000. The number has continued to grow, with a spin-off enterprise of over one hundred "outposts"—settlements that are unauthorized and illegal under Israeli law.

Ross's comments are a severe rebuke to his own government's policies as well as Israel's. The Zionist Left governments of Rabin and Barak were complicit in allowing Jewish settlements to drive Israel's legitimate security considerations in a direction that would literally build hundreds of roadblocks to reaching peace and enhancing Israel's security. Security was seen through the prism of settlements. The necessity of defending and servicing a far-flung network of Jewish communities and supportive infrastructures has made a territorially viable and contiguous Palestinian state increasingly problematic.

When Barak explored a permanent status agreement with the Palestinians via the Stockholm Talks, Camp David II, the Clinton Parameters, and Taba, cartographic possibilities were restricted by settlement realities. While Barak and President Clinton discussed territorial swaps and accommodating 80 percent of the Jewish settlers with relatively modest annexations (a 9 percent "offer" at Camp David and as low as 3 percent in the Clinton Parameters), the settlers and their powerful parliamentary allies were on the move, stripping away support for Barak's government. Reports in Israel of his supposed growing concessions led to an ever-shrinking government. His broad coalition of seventy-three Knesset members collapsed to thirty. Shas, the National Religious Party, and Natan Sharansky, weary of the magnitude of Barak's concessions, bolted from the government. While Barak managed to hang on for a few more months, peace and Israelis were increasingly under fire as the Palestinian al-Aqsa Intifada ushered in a long, dark period of murder and mayhem. *Peace* and *partners* were now words associated with some bygone era. The pop star Shakira's lament "disillusion takes what illusion gives" resonated with an increasingly large number of Israelis and the Zionist Left.

Settlements were not the only major stumbling block in this all-or-nothing reach for negotiating an Israeli-Palestinian permanent-status agreement. Arafat's passivity and duplicity in the negotiations and his complicity with violence were also critical factors. American mismanagement and responsibility for the failure at Camp David have been understated in the cottage industry that has emerged trying to analyze "what went wrong." Poor timing, with parties out of sync and governments with one foot out the door (Clinton's second term was expiring and Barak's first term was coming to a premature end), made this an unpromising moment for such a sweeping diplomatic gambit. All of these factors and many others are part of the tragedy of the failed peace negotiations at the beginning of the century. However, expansion of Jewish settlements and the policies of both Left Zionist governments and American administrations have been permissive, negligent, and, in the words of Dennis Ross, part of a "strategically destructive" dynamic of settlements and terrorism.

Barak had not only lost his office. The Zionist Left had lost its way, disillusioned and wondering if the quest for peace and partners was not just elusive but an illusion. The settlements were real and had seemingly already created a two-state solution—but not the one the Left expected: the state of Israel and the de facto state of Judea and Samaria.

The Israeli Zionist Left is suffering from the post-Rabin blues not only in the romantic sense, of longing for the good old days. The good old days have left a pernicious legacy: a pair of SOSs whose urgency has been ignored by the governments of the Israeli Zionist Left, successive American administrations, and the weak and territorially divided Palestinian Authority. The Israeli SOS (security over settlements) and the Palestinian SOS (sovereignty over suicide) await an answer that neither Rabin nor any other of the Zionist Left leaders or parties have succeeded in providing.

Can the sheer peril of the times, with frail and flailing governments in Jerusalem, Ramallah, and Washington, along with "six long wars"[40] in the Middle East that threaten regional and global stability, security, and economy, create a new negotiating moment? The ideas of the Israeli Zionist Left remain in play, perhaps even in shaping the future. Their legacy is a template for Israeli-Palestinian peace: a two-state solution that resembles the Clinton Parameters. This possibility represents the proverbial "light at the end of the tunnel." The problem is that the tunnel has been obliterated. At the moment, the diplomatic engineers look outmatched in their efforts at reconstruction. Nevertheless, one can already see the scaffolding of a new initiative that may yet reengage the Israeli Zionist Left.

There may be life after the post-Rabin blues. However, the Zionist Left has not escaped its past. Ehud Barak has rehabilitated himself as the head of the Labor Party and the minister of defense. He has politically positioned himself, at least tactically, to the right of "the other Ehud," Prime Minister Olmert. The immediate future of leftist Zionism, particularly in the political electoral arena, seems dependent on how the relationship between the two Ehuds and their parties evolve. And given Israel's political instability, it is never too early to anticipate national elections. They are part of the scaffolding that will determine whether any new peace initiative can answer the dual SOSs and rebuild the tunnel that leads to the light at its end.

Notes

1. The Israeli Zionist Left is a slippery and contentious category. Its meaning may vary according to one's definitions of and perspective on the meaning of the words *left* and *Zionist*. In this chapter, I am referring primarily to the two political parties Labor and Meretz, both of which have won electoral representation in the Israeli parliament (the Knesset) from 1992 to the present. Both parties attach a priority to living in a Jewish and democratic state that strives for greater domestic, social, and economic equity as well as a secure and comprehensive peace with its Arab and Palestinian neighbors. The Palestinians are the focus of a variety of initiatives that have evolved in support of a final two-state agreement roughly based on US president Bill Clinton's parameters presented to the Israelis and Palestinians in December 2000. Incomplete and imperfect as they are, Clinton's parameters remain a plausible rendition of the Israeli Zionist Left's vision of peace and security, which is

to be the focus of this chapter. Prime Minister Barak accepted Clinton's parameters even though they did not meet all of his demands on security, on territory, or, especially, on Jerusalem. It goes without saying that both Labor and Meretz have members with a significant range of opinions and have seen an evolution of their policies, whether in power or in opposition.

2. Until 1996 Israelis cast a single ballot for a political party. The leader of the party that won the most votes was traditionally selected by the president to form a new government. There was no separate election for choosing the prime minister. The next three elections—1996, 1999, and 2001—entailed direct election of the prime minister. The first two of these elections were based on simultaneous separate ballots: one for seats in the Knesset and one for the prime minister.

3. The Philadelphi Corridor is a narrow band of territory between the Gaza Strip and Egypt.

4. The disengagement also included an evacuation of four settlements in the northern West Bank.

5. Dov Weissglass interview with Ari Shavit, "The Big Freeze," *Ha'aretz* (October 8, 2004).

6. Shalom Achshav sponsored several surveys indicating the existence of a pragmatic majority of nonideological Jewish settlers who were prepared to accept a fair buyout. Members of the Labor Party and Meretz also began to explore the possibilities for implementing such a plan.

7. See Shlomo Ben-Ami and his own pained judgments about the wisdom of supporting Sharon's disengagement plan, *Scars of War, Wounds of Peace, The Israeli-Arab Tragedy* (New York: Oxford University Press, 2006), pp. 305–311.

8. Ibid., p. 308.

9. Interview with Yariv Oppenheimer, the director of Shalom Achshav and a Labor Party candidate for the Knesset, January 10, 2006.

10. A leading Israeli general who was intimately associated with Sharon's "consolidation-disengagement" plan lamented that the Israeli political class is not yet sure whether the Palestinian residents of Israel should really be welcomed as permanent citizens of the state of Israel.

11. Ben-Ami, *Scars of War*, p. 235.

12. Rashid Khalidi, *Resurrecting Empire, Western Footprints and America's Perilous Path in the Middle East* (Boston: Beacon Press, 2004), p. 115.

13. Lecture at Queens College, Flushing, NY, November 8, 2005.

14. Gilead Sher, *The Israeli-Palestinian Peace Negotiations, 1999–2001* (London: Routledge, 2006).

15. The left wing of the Labor Party and its young guard understood they had significant differences with Rabin and many of the "Abu's" of their party. Nevertheless, they saw it as their victory as well, but one that was decidedly an uphill struggle, not only within their nation but also within their party. In an emotional, euphoric gathering at the Jerusalem home of Roberta Fahn and her husband, Stuart Schoffman, shortly after the election, on June 25, 1992, the Left Knesset members of Labor and Meretz exhorted the cheering crowd of their Israeli supporters and the American guests mingled with them to be steadfast. This was the Left's and the peace camp's moment. Avrum Burg, the young, charismatic, and ambitious Orthodox Labor Knesset member, reminded them that the Israeli Zionist peace camp could not be complacent or compliant. Neither they personally nor their parties (Labor and Meretz) could be allowed to be seduced by position and power. He ended with a plea to the Israeli peace camp to "hold our feet to the fire. Don't give us a pass. Don't be hesitant to go to the streets and criticize us. We will need your pressure even if we ask for your patience."

16. Cited in Myron J. Aronoff, "Labor during Fifty Years of Israeli Politics," in Robert O. Freedman, ed., *Israel's First Fifty Years* (Gainesville: University of Florida Press, 2000), p. 125.

17. For more information about the fate of the Palestinian community in Kuwait during and after the First Gulf War, see Ann Mosley Lesch, "Palestinians in Kuwait," *Journal of Palestine Studies*, vol. 80 (Summer 1991), pp. 42–54.

18. Mark Tessler, *A History of the Israeli-Palestinian Conflict* (Bloomington: Indiana University Press, 1994).

19. The Labor Party was part of a national unity government with Likud from 1984 to 1988; it included an agreement to rotate the office of the prime minister, with Shimon Peres holding that office for the Labor Party from 1984 to 1986.

20. Ross has corroborated this story as well as the Bush administration's motivations and positions in the management of its conflict with Prime Minister Shamir on the loan-guarantee saga. He is also one of the sources of my claims regarding the consequences of this imbroglio, including the election of Rabin. Dennis Ross, *The Missing Peace: The Inside Story of the Fight for Middle East Peace* (New York: Farrar, Strauss & Giroux, 2004), pp. 82–85. Also see William B. Quandt, *Peace*

Process: American Diplomacy and the Arab-Israeli Conflict since 1967 (Washington, DC: Brookings Institution, 2001), pp. 306–317.

21. Ross, *The Missing Peace,* p. 83.

22. Following Rabin's seemingly unpleasant meeting with Secretary of State Baker on the prime minister's first visit to Washington, Rabin complained to Dennis Ross that "he should tell the Secretary that he is dealing with a different Yitzhak now." Ross, *The Missing Peace,* p. 89.

23. This interview appeared in the Israeli newspaper *Ma'ariv* on June 28, 1992. Shamir's office subsequently suggested that the prime minister had been misunderstood. He had meant only to suggest that final status negotiations could last ten years. *Mideast Mirror* (June 30, 1992), p. 8; *Le Figaro* (May 26, 1992), p. 193.

24. Ross, *The Missing Peace,* p. 82.

25. Richard Haass, "The New Middle East," *Newsweek International* (January 8, 2007).

26. Ross, *The Missing Peace,* pp. 84–85.

27. Ibid., p. 84.

28. Ibid., p. 92.

29. The Charter of the Islamic Resistance Movement (Hamas). See chapter 1, article 7, and chapter 3, articles 11–13. While there is no official English version of the charter, a full English version, which is strongly preferred, can be found in Shaul Mishal and Avraham Sela, *The Palestinian Hamas: Vision, Violence and Coexistence* (New York: Columbia University Press, 2006), pp. 175–199.

30. Ibid., p. 161.

31. Ibid., p. 97.

32. Ibid., p. 96.

33. Ibid., p. 66.

34. Benny Morris, *Righteous Victims: A History of the Zionist-Arab Conflict, 1881–2001* (New York: Vintage Books, 2001), p. 626.

35. Ben-Ami, *Scars of War,* p. 216.

36. Itamar Rabinovich, *Waging Peace: Israel and the Arabs 1948–2003* (Princeton, NJ: Princeton University Press, 2004), pp. 67–70.

37. Ben-Ami, *Scars of War,* p. 235.

38. Ross, *The Missing Peace,* p. 195.

39. Ibid., p. 195.

40. A term used by Middle East expert Anthony Cordesman, who was referring to the wars in Iraq and Afghanistan, the conflict in Lebanon and between Israelis and Palestinians, the global war on terrorism, and the struggle to prevent Iran from acquiring nuclear weapons.

4

Israel's Religious Parties

Shmuel Sandler and Aaron Kampinsky

ISRAEL'S POLITICAL SYSTEM has undergone far-reaching transformations since the mid-1990s. On the formal level, direct elections for prime minister were adopted in the 1996, 1999, and 2001 elections and then canceled; the leader that could put together a majority coalition once again became the head of government. On a structural level there have also been significant transformations: From a two-bloc political system, the Knesset was split into medium-sized parties that threatened the supremacy of the two traditional large parties, the Likud and Labor. The peak of this trend was the establishment of the centrist party Kadima by Prime Minister Ariel Sharon at the end of 2005. The party's success in the 2006 elections, under the leadership of Ehud Olmert, marked the first time in Israeli history when a centrist party succeeded in wresting power from the two traditional ruling parties.

The religious parties were not unaffected by these transformations. Since the late 1980s, the ultra-Orthodox parties, Shas and United Torah Judaism, have amassed significant power and seen their strength grow steadily. The balance of power in the religious camp has shifted. The National Religious Party (NRP; *Mafdal* in Hebrew), which had always represented state orientation and integration into Israeli society, was pushed aside and became a small party almost always outside the government. On the other hand, Shas, the ultra-Orthodox Sephardic party, grew to be a medium-sized party that participated in most governments. To this day, the NRP must struggle for the votes of any national religious voters who consider giving their vote to religious parties like Shas or to secular right-wing parties.

In light of these changes, it is worth examining the relationship between the ruling parties and the religious parties from 1996 to the present. We shall compare their performance with two other important periods in Israeli electoral history. The first era stretches from the founding of the state to the revolution of 1977, during which the Labor Party (or its ideological predecessor, Mapai) held power. In this period there was a full partnership (except for short phases) between Labor and the NRP, while the ultra-Orthodox Agudat Yisrael remained in the opposition. This relationship came to be known as the *historic alliance*. The second period is that of the Likud Party's supremacy, in which the NRP participated in both the regular majority and the national unity governments (1984–1990). During this period all the religious parties were members of the coalition and were full partners in the government. The period of the Yitzhak Rabin and Shimon Peres governments (1992–1996) was in many ways an interim period, in which the religious parties were in the opposition for the first time, aside from a limited period during which Shas was in the government.[1]

The ruling party's interactions with the religious parties reflect, among other things, the system of relations between religion and state in Israel. In this chapter we shall argue that although Israeli politics might seem to be moving toward a politics of "constant crisis" in the relations between religion and state, the traditional patterns of regulation, as expressed in the relationship between the various ruling parties and their religious counterparts, have been preserved. Yet, unlike in the past, ultra-Orthodox parties are, to a large extent, assuming the NRP's historical role.

As opposed to the contemporary NRP, which since 1977 has also had matters of foreign policy and security on its agenda, the ultra-Orthodox parties tend to focus primarily on socioeconomic issues. It will be our argument that an important reason for these parties' success in securing arrangements with the ruling parties is their relative neutrality on questions of foreign policy and of security, including the question of the future of the territories acquired in 1967. Ruling parties want room to maneuver in the areas of foreign and security policy, without restrictions from their partners in the coalition. This is one of the main reasons why David Ben-Gurion preferred to include the NRP and the Progressive Party in the coalitions that he led. The two parties agreed with him on matters of foreign affairs and, particularly, on the question of international orientation. By contrast, in 2001, Ariel Sharon, at the outset of his government, did not bring the NRP, closest to him on settlement policies, into his government. The special relations between the ruling party and the NRP, even when the former was Likud, continued as long as the religious party did not venture into matters of foreign policy. Today, as mentioned above, the ultra-Orthodox parties, by consenting to a minor role in determining foreign policy, are gradually taking over part of the NRP's traditional role.

This chapter comprises three sections. The first discusses the theoretical framework suggested by the Dutch scholar Arend Lijphart: consociational (arrangement) democracy and its possible manifestation in Israeli politics. The second part discusses the political history of each of the three religious parties: the NRP, Shas, and United Torah Judaism (UTJ), with a focus on the Oslo and post-Oslo periods. The third section discusses the reasons why "accommodation politics" has been maintained despite the ongoing crises in the relationship between religion and state.

Theoretical Framework:
The Consociational Model

Arend Lijphart's consociational model aims to explain how deeply divided states manage to maintain their stability. His principles are based on the political functioning of state elites, which manage to attain arrangements and understandings that disarm the potential land mines. The principles of the model are[2]

1. Avoidance of conflict resolution. In a situation of deep disagreements within the society, attempts at conflict resolution may damage the government's stability. Therefore, avoiding a clear resolution enables each camp to feel that it has "won."
2. Avoidance of activating the majority principle to achieve a resolution. As it follows from the first principle, decision by majority does not always yield stability. Sometimes, it is avoiding the legitimate use of the majority principle that can lessen societal rifts.
3. Mutual recognition of red lines and right of veto. Both sides in a disagreement understand that sometimes crossing a red line would be unbearable to them and would be considered an assault on their most basic values. Therefore the camps' representatives are given a right of veto in matters deemed essential.
4. Autonomy for the various camps in well-defined areas. Despite the accommodation in the political system between the rival camps, common in the public domain, it is necessary, according to this model, to grant autonomy to the various camps in well-defined areas—in which each group determines its way of life and values.

Deep disputes in society are a recipe for political instability and in severe cases can lead to a collapse of the state. One must differentiate between two levels of these deep disagreements: the national and the sectoral. A rift on the national level relates to the question of the character of the state and the society. Each side struggles to leave its mark on the identity of the state. When the clash is between sectors, the struggle is over the right of each camp to preserve its distinctiveness and identity. It is commonly held that a rift between societal segments can be solved more easily, because each camp's goal is no more than to preserve its individuality and identity. By contrast, on the national plane each camp wishes to impinge on society as a whole. This desire can cause the outbreak and widening of the rift and make solving it very difficult. A struggle over foreign policy could belong to the national disagreement category.

A recognition of the consociational model as applicable as early as the prestate era in Israel has been proposed by Dan Horowitz and Moshe Lissak. They argue that the political and social arrangements of the prestate period can explain the basic stability achieved by the Jewish community in Israel even before the state was established in 1948.[3] But the scholar considered most prominent in applying the consensual framework to religious-secular relations is Eliezer Don-Yehiya. Don-Yehiya argued that "accommodation politics" patterns could successfully explain the relative stability in Israel's political regime during the first decades of statehood.[4] These arrangements were especially prominent during the reign of the historic Mapai Party. Thus, for example, educational denominations[5] (the state or state-religious systems), who is a Jew,[6] the Law of Times of Work and Rest,[7] and other laws on matters of religion and state were regulated according to the consociational model.

In contrast to the widespread acceptance of the idea that the principle of accommodation politics held true during the State of Israel's first generation, the question of its continued relevance is highly debated. Asher Cohen and Baruch Susser argue repeatedly that on those major topics in which accords were reached between the religious and secular camps, an opposite trend is discernible today. Thus, for example, the question of the degree of Sabbath observance by the state was agreed upon in the first generation with the Law of Times of Work and Rest. In the present day, however, the subject is fiercely disputed, as evidenced by the struggle over opening businesses and malls on the Sabbath. Similarly, on collective identity, in the past, parties on both sides of the issue had come to agreements on the question of who is a Jew. Today the previously accepted Orthodox monopoly is breaking down, and the Reform and Conservative movements are slowly managing to attain official recognition.[8] Don-Yehiya disputes this overall claim, arguing that the existence of crises does not necessarily indicate a state of "crisis politics." Rather, despite cracks that have been forming in religion-state relations, both sides of the equation—the religious and the secular—still prefer to maintain the accepted patterns of accommodation.[9] The following section demonstrates how this tendency has developed over the last decade. To clarify the matter, we examine the history of the religious parties since the murder of Prime Minister Rabin in 1995.

The Religious Parties in Israeli Politics

The National Religious Party

The NRP, the heir to the Mizrahi and Hapoel Hamizrahi Parties, has been representing the Religious Zionist camp since 1956. After the initial period known as the historic alliance, during which the NRP joined governments led by Labor and its ideological predecessors, the NRP has, since 1977, tended to join right-wing governments. Over the years, preoccupation with the future of Judaea, Samaria, and the Gaza Strip increased significantly among the National Religious public, and it was in the vanguard of the settlement movement once the Likud came to power.[10]

At the same time, a public debate began within the National Religious camp about the role national issues should play in the agenda of the NRP. Some argued that the camp should continue to focus on the areas of religion and state as it had done in the past. In any case, since 1977 the NRP has generally been a solid ally of the Likud and other right-wing parties. They have been unwilling to join governments led only by the Labor Party, its historical ally. This unwillingness completed the political-ideological shift that had begun in the 1970s. Not only did the historical alliance evaporate, but religious Zionism actually found itself spearheading the opposition to the Labor Party's camp.[11]

And indeed, the Rabin and Peres governments (1992–1996) placed the NRP in a political reality that it had never known before. For the first time in almost twenty years, the NRP found itself in the opposition. During this period, religious Zionism encountered many crises. The first was the signing of the Oslo Accords, which led to the evacuation of the major Palestinian cities in Judea and Samaria (the West Bank) and the entrance of the Palestine Liberation Organization (PLO) leadership into Gaza and the West Bank. Debates over the wisdom and likely consequences of these moves created a rift among the National Religious public. At that time there was little talk of evacuating settlements, but even raising the prospect constituted a bad omen. Second, the murder of Prime Minister Rabin by a religious man led to a frenzy surrounding religious Zionism. The Israeli left wing accused the National Religious camp and its rabbis of inciting the public against Rabin and his government, agitation that, the Left claimed, ultimately led to his murder.

A counterreaction to the accusations against religious Zionism was the impressive achievement of the NRP in the 1996 elections. The party earned nine seats. In the Benjamin Netanyahu government formed after these elections, the NRP was given important ministries and a great deal of influence. Zevulun Hammer was appointed deputy prime minister and minister of education, and Rabbi Yitzhak Levi was made minister of transportation.[12]

In the 1999 elections, the NRP saw its power reduced to five seats. One reason for the decline was a split led by right-wing leaders Zvi Hendel and Hanan Porat, who claimed that they had been pushed out of realistic places, that would have ensured their winning Knesset seats on the NRP's election list. In these elections the Labor Party's Ehud Barak defeated then prime minister Netanyahu. Following his election promise to be "everybody's prime minister," Barak aspired to renew the historical alliance between the Labor Party and the Religious Zionist camp, and to continue the politics of accommodation on issues of religion and state. In addition, he hoped to heal the real divide that had emerged in the wake of the Rabin assassination. It was apparently the same logic that motivated the NRP to join a Labor-led government. However, loyal to its ideology, the NRP insisted that it would sit in Barak's government only as long as settlements were not evacuated. In other words, the arrangement did not include foreign policy.

Even though the NRP was the first party to sign a coalition agreement with Labor and the party's new chairman, Rabbi Yitzhak Levi, was appointed minister of housing, the sharp disagreement between the two parties on the future of the territories could not be deferred indefinitely. The coalition crisis broke out in the summer of 2000, following Prime Minister Barak's journey to the Camp David Summit and his announcement that he would agree to far-reaching concessions in order to achieve a permanent agreement with the Palestinians. Consequently, the NRP left the government. It is significant that the other religious parties, Shas and Agudat Yisrael, followed. One can assume that the religious and ultra-Orthodox leaders felt the atmosphere in the religious public at large. It seems that on this matter, the public was leaning in the right-wing nationalist direction even more than its leadership. The NRP's position corresponded with the new approach that surfaced in the wake of the Six Day War. Consequently, it could not share power with a government ready to implement territorial concessions in Gaza or the West Bank.

The Barak government reached its end in early 2001. In special elections for prime minister, Barak was defeated by Ariel Sharon of the Likud. Significantly, despite being the Likud's natural partner, the NRP found itself outside the coalition following unsuccessful negotiations. Having no choice, the NRP remained in the opposition, although it did not contest the basic policy outlines of the Sharon government—which also included Labor, Shas, United

Torah Judaism, and Yisrael B'aliya. The NRP was redundant (and maybe too ideological) for Ariel Sharon. In religious matters he preferred to work with other parties that could fill the Mafdal's historical role. In 2002, after an unprecedented wave of terrorist attacks, the Sharon government decided to embark on the large-scale military operation known as *Homat Magen* (Defensive Wall). During the operation the NRP joined Sharon's government, though not before the chairman of the party, Rabbi Yitzhak Levi, ceded his place to Brigadier General (Reserves)) Effi Eitam. Both were appointed as ministers without portfolio in the government, and after the National Union Party left the coalition, they became, respectively, ministers of tourism and of infrastructure.

In the 2003 elections, which were held again according to the old electoral system, without direct elections for prime minister, the Likud, led by Sharon, reached an extraordinary achievement: thirty-eight seats in the Knesset. In an effort not to repeat its previous mistakes, the NRP entered the government. However, for the first time since 1977, it joined without the ultra-Orthodox parties. Even more significant was its joining a government in which the other partner was the secularist Shinui Party headed by Tommy Lapid, who had led it to the astounding success of fifteen seats. The NRP's position signaled a return to its dominant days as the only religious party in the coalition. Asher Cohen, loyal to his paradigm of the politics of accommodation within a crisis, aptly defined the government that was formed after these elections as "an accommodation government in a crisis Knesset."[13] This terminology reflects the NRP's politics-of-accommodation priorities, as it believed that in a government headed by Sharon the evacuation of settlements would not be on the agenda. Hence, under such circumstances, the hidden agenda of the NRP was to rebuild itself as the party that represented the religious needs of the Jewish state.

The political reality turned out, however, to be quite different. Sharon's announcement of his intent to implement the disengagement plan in Gaza and northern Samaria (the northern part of the West Bank) put the NRP right back into the dilemma it had expected to escape. The party's new leader, Effi Eitam, demanded that it quit the government. Others among the party's leadership feared that by doing so the party would revert to positioning itself as a single-issue ideological party concerned only with the land of Israel, while forfeiting to its competitors the representation of religious interests. The result was a split in the party. Eitam and Rabbi Levi founded a party called Religious Zionism and joined the National Union Party, which also quit Sharon's coalition. The NRP's representatives, now four in number, formally remained in the government in order to try to influence Sharon not to withdraw from the Gaza Strip. They failed, and they left the coalition as well on the eve of the implementation of the disengagement plan in the summer of 2005.

The fear that voters would punish the party for not leaving the Sharon government earlier led the NRP to unite with the National Union Party in the 2006 elections. This was a historic step: since the unification of Hamizrachi and Hapo'el Hamizrachi in the mid-1950s, the NRP had always run independent of any partners. Nine members of this joint election list won seats in the Knesset, only three of them representatives of the NRP.

In truth, what symbolized more than anything else the political pattern in which Religious Zionism had found itself since 1992 was its irrelevance in government. After the 2006 elections it remained in the opposition, for ideological reasons: Prime Minister Ehud Olmert announced the Hitkansut (Convergence) plan, which meant unilateral evacuation of settlements positioned deep in Judea and Samaria (the West Bank), a move, of course, unacceptable to the NRP. Even after the plan was shelved following the Second Lebanon War, basic disagreements were still evident between the NRP and the Olmert government on questions of foreign policy. With Shas filling the traditional role of the NRP, there was no need for Olmert to pull the NRP into the government.

A summary of the NRP's voyage through Israeli governments shows that since 1977 the foreign policy agenda has taken up most of the party's attention, no less and probably even more than matters of religion and state. For this reason, joining Likud governments came naturally to the NRP, while joining Labor Party governments was problematic. Even when the NRP joined Barak's government in 1999, it was very clear that any move in the direction of territorial concessions in the land of Israel would result in its secession. Loyal to its new ideological commitments and to its voters even under Sharon, it quit the coalition immediately before the implementation of the disengagement plan. Today the ruling party—Kadima—has found in Shas a more convenient partner for maintaining the politics of accommodation. In turn, Religious Zionism continues to lose political power.

Shas

The party Shas appeared in the early 1980s. The link between ethnicity and religion had already emerged earlier with the split in the NRP in 1981 and the appearance of the Sephardic Movement for Israel's Tradition (TAMI) Party. Consequently, the linkage between ethnic politics and religion surfaced as an important issue in Israeli politics.[14] Shas, which first ran for the Knesset in the 1984 elections, articulated the ethnic aspect that had previously been largely hidden in Israeli politics, especially in the religious sphere.[15] Yoav Peled gives this turn a theoretical explanation. He claims that Shas's success derives from the inferior education of the lower class it represents; in other words, the lower class of Shas's potential target audience gives Shas its political power. Peled bases his argument on the "model of cultural division of labor."[16] This argument is strengthened by the research work of Riki Tessler,[17] although Anat Feldman's work also emphasizes Shas's community-oriented aspect.[18]

Shas was a full partner in Israeli governments headed by Shimon Peres and Yitzhak Shamir and even played a considerable part in the failed so-called smelly exercise of March 1990, which aimed at forming a new government headed by Peres. Shas's leadership, both spiritual, through Rabbi Ovadia Yosef, and political, understood that portraying a flexible line in foreign policy would give it an advantage over the NRP, which was ideologically committed to the land of Israel. Despite the gap between Shas's more hawkish voting base and its leadership, the pivotal position of Rabbi Ovadia Yosef and his overwhelming influence allowed the leadership to make use of this flexibility to a certain degree. Indeed, in 1992, Shas was the only religious party to join Rabin's government. However, Shas ultimately quit that government as a result of the implementation of the Oslo Accords and the consequent pressure from its religious-ethnic public. The political reality of Shas as the only religious party in the coalition would repeat itself after the 2006 elections, in Ehud Olmert's government.

The 1996 elections, in which Benjamin Netanyahu was elected prime minister, defeating Peres, also returned political power to the religious parties, despite accusations of responsibility for the Rabin assassination. Gideon Doron attributes this return to power to a "search for identity" in secular Israeli society. He argues that in these elections, Shas especially provided "a return to values, a return to the Torah and a return to the feeling of purpose."[19] Despite the surfacing of corruption charges against its leaders, Shas significantly increased its power, won ten Knesset seats, and became for the first time the largest religious party. In the Netanyahu government, it held the ministry of internal affairs and the labor and welfare ministry. Internal affairs had always been the ministry that the classic NRP had demanded. In addition to the ability to control the distribution of funds to the municipalities, via this ministry, the religious parties could control and determine the conditions of the registration of immigrants to Israel as Jews.

The 1999 elections and the election of Ehud Barak as prime minister were an important turning point for Shas. Following a campaign in which Arie Deri, the party's political leader, responded to corruption allegations by claiming to be the victim of an antagonistic Ashkenazi secular elite, Shas reached a new high of seventeen seats in the Knesset. At the same time, its relative weight declined considerably within the Barak government. While joining the government, it had to relinquish the internal affairs ministry in favor of Natan Sharansky from the Yisrael B'aliya Party and make do with ministries of lesser importance, such as infrastructure and health. Unlike in the past, it was no longer the ruling party's favorite. However, the mere fact of Shas's inclusion in the government was striking. Barak insisted on bringing Shas in despite the pressure from Labor supporters who opposed this move because of the corruption accusations against Deri.

Following Barak's trip in the summer of 2000 to the Camp David Summit and his announcement of Israel's willingness to make far-reaching concessions to Yasser Arafat, grassroot pressures forced Shas to again follow the other religious parties and quit the coalition. Shas's status was restored when it received the internal affairs portfolio in the Sharon government following the special elections for prime minister. The political reality in which the NRP stayed outside the government did not bother Shas and, in a large measure, worked in its favor.

Shas's role in the special elections for prime minister was pivotal, as it objected to Knesset elections so as not to risk its 1999 electoral accomplishment of seventeen seats. With only nineteen seats Netanyahu decided not to run for prime minister, as he was concerned about the consequences of being a premier without a powerful party behind him. Thus the way was opened for Sharon to contest Barak for the job. Netanyahu has yet to recover and has so far not returned to the chief executive's office.

A low point in Shas's political career was the 2003 elections. First, its power declined from seventeen seats to a mere eleven. Then Prime Minister Sharon decided to form a government with the antireligious Shinui Party and the NRP, thus leaving Shas out of the government. For almost four years, Shas was in the opposition, all the while aiming sharp criticism at the NRP for being an accomplice to the severe damage inflicted on ultra-Orthodox society by Shinui's agenda. One of the main issues on the agenda at the time was the cutback in child stipends, advanced by Shinui as part of the economic recovery plan led by Finance Minister Netanyahu.

Shas returned to the government after the 2006 elections (in which it won twelve seats). It was given the ministry of industry, trade, and labor and the ministry of communications in the Olmert government, but not the internal affairs ministry. On the surface Shas's return seemed a poor accomplishment, but in reality the coalition agreement covered areas of importance to Shas. In September 2006, Shas's Meshulam Nahari was nominated as a minister in the finance office in charge of education and welfare. With time he in effect controlled the areas of education excluded from the ministry of education headed by Yael (Yuli) Tamir from Labor.[20] Yitzhak Cohen was nominated as minister in the prime minister's office in charge of religious affairs.[21] The ministry of religious affairs, which had been abolished during the Sharon government as part of the Shinui anticlerical coalition, was thus reinstituted informally in the prime minister's office. This ministry, which had controlled religious services via the religious councils, had been the domain of the NRP and was now under the control of Shas. Again, as in Rabin's coalition, Shas was the only religious party in the government. In short, political reality shows that when Shas, like the NRP during its heyday, can join the government, it is willing to do so not only without the NRP but even without United Torah Judaism. From the point of view of the secular ruling party, including Shas not only provides support within the Knesset but also works to reduce religious-secular tensions.

But Shas represents an additional dimension as well: It continually places emphasis on the social welfare policies of the state. As a party representing the weaker strata of the population, it sees itself as socially oriented in the full sense of the phrase, beyond its agenda in the areas of religion and state. Unlike the NRP's, many of its accomplishments are of a social nature and have less to do with matters of foreign affairs or security. Shas's uniqueness lies in its being defined as a "periphery in the heart of the center," in the words of Asher Cohen.[22] On the one hand, it is a partner in most of Israel's governments and thus is considered part of "the center," but on the other, it is still considered a "periphery party" representing both the social and the geographic margins. As a party building an independent educational infrastructure, Shas is erecting a shield against the penetration of secular values into its educational system. Participation in the government also means the distribution of funds to Shas's institutions. By combining the social and the religious dimensions and by abstaining from controversial foreign policy issues, the party succeeds in mobilizing the discontented. This success comes in addition to filling the traditional role of the NRP and keeping the politics of accommodation alive.

United Torah Judaism

United Torah Judaism comprises two factions that make up the Ashkenazi ultra-Orthodox camp: Agudat Yisrael, which mostly represents Hassidim (followers of the pietist Hassidic movement established at the end of the eighteenth century), and Degel Hatorah, which represents the Lita'im (Lithuanians), namely, the heads of rabbinical colleges originally diametrically opposed to the Hassidic movement. Until the eleventh Knesset, Agudat Yisrael represented both camps, but in the 1988 elections there was a split, after which Degel Hatorah was established under the leadership of Rabbi Eliezer Shach.

In the 1992 elections, United Torah Judaism ran for the first time representing both camps. In the Rabin government established after these elections, the UTJ was outside the coalition, although the labor and welfare ministry was reserved for it for a long time. Ultimately it was decided that the UTJ would remain in the opposition, so it was harder for Shas to be alone in the Rabin government. The fact that the minister of education was Shulamit Aloni (a human rights activist prominent in her fight against the religious establishment) did not make things easier. Rabin's decision to force Aloni to resign and replace her with Professor Amnon Rubinstein also indicated the limits of straining relations with the religious public.

After the 1996 elections, United Torah Judaism joined the coalition headed by the Likud. As was traditional, it was given the position of head of the Knesset's finance committee, as well as the post of deputy minister of ministries such as housing (important to large families).[23] All the religious parties, as mentioned above, were part of this government. In the Barak government established in 1999, UTJ was again in the coalition, but with no official positions. Like the other religious parties, it quit the coalition around the time of the Camp David Summit, when it became known that the division of Jerusalem was being discussed. Here again, it seems that the ultra-Orthodox public dictated policy. The dangers that the Old City might be divided, that it would become more difficult for Jews to reach the Western Wall, and that the Cave of the Patriarchs might be handed over to Muslims were factors that motivated a non-Zionist religious party like UTJ to play some role on foreign policy issues.

After the 2001 elections, in which Ariel Sharon was elected prime minister, United Torah Judaism joined the coalition and was given the post of chair of the finance committee. This post has always been very important to ultra-Orthodox Jewry because, through it, allotments of finances to its educational institutions can be secured, by circumvention of the ministry of education. And indeed, the need to secure funds hurt UTJ's chances of being included in the government once the state entered an economic crisis during the intifada. The 2003 elections, after which a Likud government was established with Shinui and the NRP, were bad news for the ultra-Orthodox camp, both Shas and UTJ. During this period these parties were forced to look on with hungry eyes as child stipends were drastically cut back and financial support of their institutions was reduced.

During the Olmert government, United Torah Judaism remained in the opposition. In the first year there was an attempt to include it in the coalition, and it was even agreed that Knesset member Yakov Litzman would be chair of the finance committee. But United Torah Judaism was forced to stay in the opposition after its coalition demands in the matter of child stipends failed to be met.[24] The Olmert government has made continuous efforts to attract at least the two representatives of Degel Hatorah (the Lita'i faction), Avraham Ravitz and Moshe Gafni, in order to strengthen the coalition.[25] An additional two members of the Knesset in the coalition would enable the government to function even if the Labor Party were to leave. But with Shas in the coalition, UTJ did not feel obliged to compromise on its financial demands and so chose to remain outside.

The uniqueness of United Torah Judaism lies in its constant preoccupation with the matter of subsidies to large families. Since Netanyahu's term as minister of finance (2003–2005), and even before, the ultra-Orthodox camp has been preoccupied with the setback in financial support to large families and rabbinical students. This camp has been much less concerned about matters of religion and state. And yet, what separates UTJ from Shas is its target population. Shas appeals to wide audiences, traditional and religious alike, while United Torah Judaism continues to work only for the ultra-Orthodox camp. From the point of view of accommodation politics, Shas has more of an obligation to advance political arrangements with the ruling party than does its Ashkenazi counterpart. For a homogeneous party like UTJ, as far as non-Zionism and ultra-Orthodoxy are concerned, membership in the coalition is less essential: It can satisfy its religious needs via ad hoc understandings.

The Partnership between Secular and Religious Parties

One salient feature of Israeli politics is that to this day no government has completed its term in power without the presence of a religious party. On the other hand, since the establishment of the state, there have been many cases of religious parties' quitting the coalition over a crisis in the relations between religion and state. How do we explain the continued participation of the religious parties in the various coalitions, under both left- and right-wing and even centrist parties? While we accept the consociational rationale, it is essential that we also examine the political rationale that accompanies it. We start with the proximate cause: the need of the governing coalition to control the Knesset.

Coalition Necessity

In this context one must differentiate between the character of a partnership with the Likud and the character of a partnership with the Labor Party. In the case of the Likud, the source of the religious parties' power seems to be inherent. The Likud's basis of political power is the traditional sector of society, which sees the Likud as its natural camp. Many in the NRP and Shas constituencies vote for Likud. Therefore the partnership with the religious parties seems natural, although there is still the technical need to create a majority in the Knesset. The partnership with the Labor Party is of a different character because religious parties are usually not an integral part of the left-wing camp. It is here that the fact stands out that even after the collapse of the historic alliance, left-wing governments were careful to have at least one religious party in their midst. It may be that including the religious parties stems from the need to thicken the coalition and establish its strength, or perhaps from a need to create a sense of unity and consensus among the people. Even if the second reason is assumed to be more accurate, it is still interesting that the ruling parties tend to claim that the electoral reason is primary in their coalition partnerships with the religious parties. Perhaps it is difficult for a secular Zionist party to proclaim that it needs a religious party to preserve the Jewish heritage; it is more natural to present the inclusion of a religious party as a concession for coalition reasons.

Political and Security Matters on the Agenda

One of the main contributions to the success of a society functioning on a consociational model is an existential threat to the state. The assumption is that constant preoccupation with the state's security makes the social rifts that threaten the state's cohesiveness dimmer and less immediate. The Israeli security situation surely fits this description. Since its establishment, the state has faced existential foreign and security threats, which have repressed disagreements in other areas, which are perceived as secondary. Questions of religion and state belong to this second realm. Courtship by the big parties of the religious ones is hence justifiable. The religious parties' basic demands in the area of the religious status quo or the allocation of sectoral resources are seen as legitimate, and the big parties' approach is always backed up by the basic argument that there is no sense in fighting now over what can be deferred. But here we find another phenomenon: Ruling parties tend not to include small parties in matters of national security. Indeed, the NRP's demands in the religious realm were more easily met than its demands in matters of foreign policy. Once the NRP began to develop a foreign policy agenda, its place even in Likud-led governments was no longer ensured.

The Balance between the Large Camps

The big parties that fight for control of the government wish to form as large a coalition as possible to secure an imposing majority in the Knesset. Neither camp can afford to pass up the votes of religious and traditional voters, who do not necessarily vote for religious parties but who still want the state to have a religious character. Therefore a potential alliance with the religious parties is perceived as legitimate. If ever a party decided to challenge its rival's willingness to sit with the religious parties, the accused party might endanger its pool of religious and traditional votes by being perceived as antireligious. In this context one might note that the platforms of Likud, Labor, and Kadima all devote considerable space to questions of religion and state and to relations between religious and secular groups. Furthermore, all three proclaim their support for the continued religious status-quo principle and for open channels between religious and secular people. In contrast, a party like Shinui, which did not view itself as competing for the leadership of the government, but only as a participant, could afford to recruit votes by presenting an anticlerical platform.

Integration and Seclusion in the Religious Camp

The religious camp has oscillated between two tendencies: on the one hand, seclusion from the secular camp (as expressed mainly by the ultra-Orthodox) and, on the other hand, a trend of openness and integration with the secular world (as exemplified usually by the religious Zionists). One of this chapter's authors, in making the distinction between integrationist and exclusionist religious parties, estimated that the tendency toward inclusion in Israeli society among the NRP constituency led about half of those who deserted the NRP in the 1981 elections to vote for the secular right-wing parties Likud and HaTehia (Renaissance). The other half went to TAMI.[26] This dilemma has always been part of the NRP and of the National Religious public. But it also explains the ruling parties' need to adopt tradition-oriented programs: They recognize in religious society the tendencies toward integration, and they act in the political arena to recruit religious votes in their favor. The heads of these parties do so through electoral and political actions. The Likud rewarded the NRP with portfolios beyond its relative strength, particularly by giving the ministry of education to Zevulun Hammer whenever possible. The Labor Party integrated Meimad, a small liberal religious party, into its ranks. Its leader, Rabbi Michael Melchior, was given a realistic place on the party's election list, probably beyond the number of votes that he personally brought to the Labor Party. This pattern explains the paradox of the NRP's diminishing electoral power, just as its young generation has become the most prominent sector in the army and is starting to gain access to the media, while the sectoral parties, Shas and United Torah Judaism, are increasing in power.

Tolerance toward the Religious Public: Multicultural Trends

A trend that has started to develop over the last few years and that may affect the texture of relations between religion and state is the model of multiculturalism. Over the last few years there has been a growing tendency to view the peripheral camps in the state as legitimate forces that have a right to exist in the wide panorama of compound societies. In contrast to the famous melting-pot approach, formulated by Ben-Gurion, today the desire to maintain a distinct group's cultural uniqueness is perceived as positive. The extreme version is argued in Yossi Yona and Yehuda Shenhav's *What Is Multi-culturalism? On the Politics of Difference in Israel.*[27] The main argument in this book is that each distinct group should be given equal cultural status, with no cultural preference given to a main group. To be sure, the authors' conclusion is that the state of Israel should be "a state of all its citizens" rather than a Jewish state, an approach unacceptable to much of the Jewish majority. Nevertheless, their approach shows the buds of the legitimacy granted to the needs of the religious and ultra-Orthodox camps in Israel. According to Lijphart's model as well, preserving the various groups' distinctions has great importance. Assisting in the inclusion of the religious parties in Israeli governments is thus an appreciation of the right to societal autonomy, which is perceived today as increasingly legitimate, although there is a clash here with the demand that Israel be a Jewish state—a demand that grants superiority to a certain cultural group.

Conclusion

Throughout the years during which the "historic alliance" continued between the Labor Party and the NRP, the religious camp attained many achievements on religious issues and in matters pertaining to the state's Jewish character.[28] In the era of the Likud's reign, influence among the religious parties in the government passed largely to the ultra-Orthodox camps. It was in this period that significant fissures began to appear in the relations between religion and state. Changes in the doctrines of Religious Zionism toward a greater emphasis on foreign policy played a major role in the NRP's losing its lead among the religious parties in national politics. Nevertheless, the basic model of accommodation politics was preserved.

On the one hand, one could claim that the ultra-Orthodox parties' participation in Israel's governments is an expression of "crisis politics" because their function is different from that of the NRP in previous coalitions. Unlike the NRP, the ultra-Orthodox parties adopt an aggressive and uncompromising stand on religious matters, taking such actions as employing inspectors in entertainment centers to check if they operate on the Sabbath.[29] Yet the fact that accommodation has been achieved with the religious parties does indeed reinforce the thesis that accommodation politics is still alive and well. Another trend that stands out is the ruling parties' making sure to include a religious party at least at the outset of each new government.

On the other hand, as mentioned above, we must not ignore the changes in the behavior of the religious parties. The NRP, which until the 1970s concerned itself mainly with matters of religion and state, became more and more concerned about the opposition to territorial compromise and about expanding settlement in Judea, Samaria, and Gaza. The ultra-Orthodox parties, which had refrained in the past from cooperating with Israel's governments, changed their approach and demonstrated concern about matters of religion and state.

The ultra-Orthodox parties direct their main efforts to securing resources for their communities, in addition to their fight for the state's Jewish character. United Torah Judaism has turned the matter of children's stipends into its flagship issue, while Shas is increasing its activities in social and economic areas. In the past, questions of class were not salient for religious parties, but Shas is changing this stance.[30] The NRP is also trying to create the image of a social-welfare-oriented party, but it is not perceived as one by the public. It is still seen, whether correctly or not, as a party concerned mainly about the land of Israel. This perceived concern has damaged the party badly. In the political realm, it is forced to compete with parties that are more attractive because they are more capable of becoming ruling parties. Many National Religious voters who are fairly involved in Israeli society prefer a mixed religious-secular party. In contrast, the sectoral voter who prefers to vote for a single-issue religious or ethnic party will vote for one of the ultra-Orthodox parties.

Be that as it may, despite far-reaching changes in the Israeli political map and deep differences between the various religious parties, our discussion shows that the consensual paradigm in matters of religion and state is still maintained as an overarching pattern in Israeli society. This pattern continues a trend first established in the prestate period. The ruling parties are in no rush, today as before, to give up on the alliance with at least one of the religious parties. It does not appear that this tendency will change in the near future.

Notes

1. Shmuel Sandler, "Rabin and the Religious Parties: The Limits of Power Sharing," in Robert O. Freedman, ed., *Israel Under Rabin* (Boulder, CO: Westview Press, 1995).

2. Arend Lijphart, "Consociational Democracy," *World Politics*, vol. 21, no. 2 (1969), pp. 207–225; Arend Lijphart, *The Politics of Accommodation*, (Berkeley and Los Angeles: University of California Press, 1968).

3. Dan Horowitz and Moshe Lissak, *Mayyishuv Lemedina* [From Yishuv to State] (Tel Aviv: Am Oved, 1977), p. 210 (in Hebrew).

4. Eliezer Don-Yehiya, "Religion and Coalition: The National Religious Party and Coalition Formation in Israel," in Asher Arian, ed., *The Elections in Israel—1973* (Jerusalem: Academic Press, 1975), pp. 255–284.

5. Eliezer Don-Yehiya, *Shituf Vekonflikt beyn Machanot Politiyim—Hamachane Hadati Utnu'at Ha'avoda Umashber Hachinuch Beyisrael* [Cooperation and Conflict among Political Camps—The Religious Camp and the Labor Movement and the Crisis of Education in Israel] (PhD thesis, Jerusalem, Hebrew University, 1977).

6. Eliezer Don-Yehiya, "Dat, Zehut Le'umit Upolitika: Hamashber Bish'elat 'Mihu Yehudi'—1958" [Religion, National Identity and Politics: The Crisis over the Question of Who Is a Jew—1958], in Mordechai Bar-On and Zvi Zameret, eds., *Shney Evrey Hagesher—Dat Umedina Bereshit Darka shel Yisrael* [Both Sides of the Fence—Religion and State at the Beginning of the State of Israel] (Jerusalem: Yad Ben-Zvi, 2002), pp. 88–143.

7. Asher Cohen, "Halacha Umedina, Da'at Torah Upolotika—Zikot Gomlin Beyn Manhigut Datit Lepolitit Bamiflagot Hadatiyot" [Halacha and State, Torah Decree and Politics—Interrelations between Religious and Political Leadership in the Religious Parties], in Mordechai Bar-On and Zvi Zameret, eds., *Shney Evrey Hagesher—Dat Umedina Bereshit Darka shel Yisrael* [Both Sides of the Fence—Religion and State at the Beginning of the

State of Israel] (Jerusalem: Yad Ben-Zvi, 2002), pp. 350–363.

8. Asher Cohen and Baruch Susser, *Mehashlama Lehaslama—Hashesa Hadati-Chiloni Befetach Hame'a ha–21* [From Reconciliation to Escalation—The Religious-Secular Rift at the Dawn of the 21st Century] (Tel Aviv: Schocken, 2003), mainly chap. 6.

9. Eliezar Don-Yehiya, *Hapolitika shel Hahasdara—Yishuv Sichsuchim Benos'ey Dat Beyisrael* [The Politics of Regulation—Conflict Settlement on Religious Questions in Israel] (Jerusalem: Floersheimer Institute for Policy Studies, 1997).

10. Shmuel Sandler, *The State of Israel, the Land of Israel, the Statist and Ethnonational Dimensions of Foreign Policy* (Westport, CT: Greenwood Press, 1994), pp. 150–157.

11. Daniel J. Elazar and Shmuel Sandler, "The Two-Bloc System—A New Development in Israeli Politics," in Daniel J. Elazar and Shmuel Sandler, eds., *Israel's Odd Couple: The 1984 Knesset Elections and the National Unity Government* (Detroit, MI: Wayne State University Press, 1990), pp. 11–24.

12. After Hammer died in 1998, Rabbi Levi was appointed minister of education, and Knesset member Shaul Yahalom became minister of transportation.

13. Asher Cohen, "Hazionut Hadatit Vehamafdal Bivchirot 2003: She'ifa Lemifleget Machane Lenochach Etgarey Hapilug Hadati, Ha'adati Vehapoliti" [Religious Zionism and the Mafdal in the 2003 Elections: Aspiration for a Camp Party in Face of the Challenges of the Religious, Ethnic, and Political Rift], in *Habchirot Beyisrael—2003* (Jerusalem: Israel Democracy Institute, 2004), pp. 277–310.

14. Hannah Herzog, "Midway between Political and Cultural Ethnicity: An Analysis of the 'Ethnic Lists' in the 1984 Elections," in Daniel J. Elazar and Shmuel Sandler, eds., *Israel's Odd Couple: The 1984 Knesset Elections and the National Unity Government* (Detroit, MI: Wayne State University Press, 1990), pp. 87–118; Eliezer Don-Yehiya, "Datiyut

Ve'adatiyut Bapolitika Hayisre'elit—Hami-flagot Hadatiyot Vehabchirot Lakneset ha–12" [Religiosity and Ethnicity in Israeli Politics—The Religious Parties and the Elections to the 12th Knesset), *Medina, Mimshal Viyachasim Beynle'umiyim* [State, Government and International Relations], vol. 32 (1990), pp. 11–54.

15. Asher Arian, *Politika Umishtar Beyisra'el* [Politics and Government in Israel] (Tel Aviv: Zmora Bitan, 1985), p. 153.

16. Yaov Peled, "Hatslachata He'elektoralit Hamitmashechet shel Shas: Nituach al pi Model Chalukat Ha'avoda Hatarbutit" [Shas's Electoral Success: An Analysis According to the Model of the Cultural Division of Labor], in *Habchirot Beyisra'el—1999* [The Elections in Israel—1999] (Jerusalem: Israel Democracy Institute, 2000), pp. 137–169.

17. Riki Tessler, *Beshem Hashem: Shas Ve-hamahapecha Hadatit* [In the Name of God: Shas and the Religious Revolution] (Jerusalem: Keter, 2003).

18. Anat Feldman, *Gormim Bitsmichat Mi-flaga—Shas* [Factors in the Growth of a Party—Shas] (PhD thesis, Ramat Gan, Israel, Bar-Ilan University, 2002).

19. Gideon Doron, "Dat Vehapolitika shel Hahachlala: Hatslachat Hamiflagot Hacha-rediyot" [Religion and the Politics of Generalization: The Success of the Ultra-Orthodox Parties], *Habchirot beyisra'el—2003* (Jerusalem: Israel Democracy Institute, 2003), p. 102. During these elections, Shas gave out amulets to its voters, an action that was ultimately disqualified by the Supreme Court as an election bribe. See Menachem Rahat, *Shas: Haru'ach Vehako'ach* [Shas: The Spirit and the Power] (Bnei Brak, Israel: Alpha Tikshoret, 1998).

20. Moti Basok, *Ha'aretz* (September 27, 2006).

21. Yair Ettinger, *Ha'aretz* (April 28, 2006).

22. Asher Cohen, "Shas—Periferya Belev Hamerkaz" [Shas—Periphery in the Heart of the Mainstream], in *Shas–Habetim Tarbu-tiyim Vera'ayoniyim* (Tel Aviv: Am Oved, 2006), pp.. 327–350.

23. This has been Agudat Yisrael's policy since the early days of the state: not to accept positions as ministers so as not to accept responsibility for the secular Zionist government's decisions.

24. *Ha'aretz* (May 10, 2006).

25. *Ha'aretz* (September 5, 2007).

26. Shmuel Sandler, "The Religious Parties," in Howard R Penniman and Daniel J. Elazar, eds., *Israel at the Polls, 1981* (Bloomington: Indiana University Press, 1986), pp. 105–127.

27. Yossi Yona and Yehuda Shenhav, *Rav Tarbutiyut Mahi? Al Hapolitika shel Hashonut Beyisra'el* [What Is Multi-culturalism? On the Politics of Difference in Israel] (Tel Aviv: Bavel, 2005). This tendency is prominent in the work of Knesset member Shelly Yaci-movich; see interview with her, *Ha'aretz* (September 9, 2006).

28. Dvora Hacohen, "Habrit Hahistorit—Beyn Ideologia Lepolitika" [The Historical Alliance—Between Ideology and Politics), in *Beyn Masoret Lachidush* [Between Tradition and Renovation] (Ramat Gan, Israel: Bar-Ilan Press, 2005), pp. 259–296.

29. For more, see Asher Cohen, "Shas Vehashesa Hadati-Chiloni" [Shas and the Religious-Secular Rift], in *Shas—Etgar Hay-isre'eliyut* [Shas—The Challenge of Israeli-ness] (Tel Aviv: Yedioth Aharonot and Sifrei Chemed, 2001), pp. 75–101.

30. Giora Goldberg, *Hamiflagot Beyisrael—Mimiflagot Hamon Lemiflagot Electoralliyot* [The Parties in Israel—From Mass Parties to Electoral Parties] (Tel Aviv: Ramot, 1992), p. 59.

5

Israel's "Russian" Parties

Vladimir (Ze'ev) Khanin

THE ESTABLISHMENT OF INDEPENDENT "Russian" Jewish community politics in Israel in the mid-1990s, including the political movements that were established by the former Soviet Union (FSU) immigrants, may be seen as one of the most important elements of the social and political legacy of the Rabin era. The new immigrants from the USSR and the Commonwealth of Independent States (CIS) changed dramatically the political landscape of Israel, which before had seemed to be composed primarily of the Labor Party, Likud, and the religious and Arab parties.[1]

The voting behavior of the Russian immigrants was critical in the electoral success of the Labor Party in 1992, in the victory of Likud leader Benjamin Netanyahu during direct prime ministerial elections in 1996, and in the comeback of the Labor Party–led One Israel bloc and its leader, Ehud Barak. The new immigrant vote was also significant in the 2001 election of Ariel Sharon as prime minister, as well as the unprecedented victory of his Likud Party in the 2003 elections. The support of Russian-speaking Israelis was again critical during the 2006 electoral campaign. Finally, because Ariel Sharon's attempt to establish a strong party of power in the center of the Israeli political spectrum looks unsuccessful, and Israel's political system is apparently returning to the classical competition between the two leading parties (Labor and Likud), the twenty- to twenty-two-parliamentary-seat potential of the USSR/CIS immigrants becomes critical, and even decisive, for any aspirant to the prime minister's office.

The 1990s as well as the beginning of the twenty-first century witnessed the formation, within the Israeli political spectrum, of new Russian-speaking groups, which are now in the process of developing their status vis-à-vis the traditional Israeli political establishment. However, even though the new immigrants' voting behavior is among the best studied issues in Israeli sociology, pollsters and sociologists repeatedly fail to accurately predict the results of the "Russian" immigrant vote. One can assume that the reason is their inadequate understanding of the political culture of the FSU Jews in Israel, including the phenomenon of Russian sectarian parties and movements. In turn, this misunderstanding is often a result of three assumptions about the Russian immigrants: First, the political behavior of FSU immigrants and, especially, the fact that many of them opted to vote for Russian communal political movements are part of their Soviet cultural and political legacy. Second, all the Russians are rightists. And third, a ballot cast by an FSU immigrant is always a protest vote. All three assumptions are incorrect, which this chapter will try to prove.

The "Russian" Community in Israel

The model of political behavior of the FSU immigrants in Israel stabilized in the second half of the 1990s, and since then the community has been almost equally split between the mainstream and the Russian immigrant parties. Due to intracommunal cleavage, it is customary to distinguish also between two almost equal subgroups among Russian immigrants: The first subgroup's vote is based on the hope that a solution can be found for its socioeconomic distress (housing, employment, welfare, etc.), while the members of the second subgroup vote in accordance with their ideological views, such as foreign-policy/security problems and the national identity of the Israeli state.[2] The nationalist group is better represented among the electorate of the mainstream Israeli parties, while the social-welfare-oriented more often vote for their "own" community movements. The results of the past decade's election campaign surveys indicate that the Russian vote covers nearly the entire political spectrum. While 12–15 percent (two or three Knesset seats) identify with the leftist camp, 25 percent (five or six seats) consider themselves rightists, and the remainder, which corresponds to twelve seats, is distributed over the political map, each group's having internal characteristics that divide it into subgroups. For instance, there is no consensus among Russian voters on the Arab-Israeli dispute. Similarly, the differences between religious and secular Russians determine their attitude toward religion-and-state issues. Russians are also divided into Ashkenazim (immigrants from the Baltic states, Russia, and Ukraine) and Sephardim (immigrants from the Caucasian and Central

Asian republics). Again, each of these subgroups, in different proportions, divides its sympathies between various sectarian and mainstream parties.[3]

Out of the general number of twenty to twenty-two Knesset seats, to which the Israeli Russian Jewish vote corresponds, from three to five constantly go to the parties that do not make any specific reference to the FSU *olim* (Jewish immigrants to Israel) in their platforms. This vote is divided between the Left (Labor, Meretz, and other, immigrants', left-of-center parties) and the Right (Likud, National Union, Mafdal, and other parties to the right of Likud), as well as some non-Russian sectarian parties. Thus, for example, Sephardic Russians from the FSU's Central Asian and Caucasian republics often tend to vote for the Sephardic traditionalist party Shas, eschewing "immigrant" parties. All this corresponds to the number of those Russian-speaking *olim* (12–15 percent) who, according to the polls, believe that the community has no need to have its own political institutions, organizations, and movements, and who think that the existing mainstream parties represent national interests, including Israeli Russian interests, satisfactorily.

However, the overwhelming majority of the FSU immigrants prefer two other options: either a Russian sectarian party or a mainstream movement with a strong immigrant wing. Such a distribution was clearly reflected in the results of the three recent Israeli elections.[4]

Factors of Political Institutionalization

Separate Russian parties in Israel are a relatively recent phenomenon: In the 1970s, 1980s, and early 1990s, FSU immigrants preferred, despite their growing share of the Israeli electorate, to vote for the mainstream parties. Russian immigrant lists that were established before the 1977, 1981, and 1984 elections were unable to overcome the then 1 percent electoral threshold even though the electoral potential of the FSU Jewish immigrants at that time corresponded to at least four Knesset seats. The same trend continued after the "great exodus" of the Soviet Jews to Israel that started in 1989. On the eve of the 1992 elections, which brought to power Yitzhak Rabin's government, three parties demanded the right to speak on behalf of the Russian immigrant community: the right-of-center Democracy and Aliya (DA) Party, the left-of-center Movement for Israeli Renewal (TALI), and the centrist Olim and Pensioners list. It is indicative that even at that time those FSU immigrants who chose to vote for their own community party were unable to unite under one political umbrella and split over the same ideological issues as had all of Israeli society. However, even if all the votes received by these three parties had been combined, they would not have been enough to pass through the electoral threshold to elect a Knesset member. The overwhelming majority of the new *olim* supported Labor, Likud, and the other Israeli mainstream parties.

Just four years later, in May 1996, about 50 percent of Russian-speaking Israelis voted for immigrant sectarian parties, first of all, Natan Sharansky's Yisrael B'aliya (IBA; Israel on the Rise), which won seven seats and thus became the great surprise of these elections. As was mentioned, from this time on, from 45 to 55 percent of FSU immigrants consistently voted for their "own" parties. Thus, the FSU immigrants entered the Rabin era with the intention to integrate socially and politically into the Israeli environment and went out of it with an idea of sectarian political institutions as an unavoidable need for the Russian community in Israel. Why did this happen? To answer this question, one should take into account several factors.[5]

First was the unprecedented growth of the numbers of the FSU immigrants in Israel. This factor first became significant in political demography terms in 1994–1995, when new Russian-speaking immigrants for the first time reached a 10 percent share in the Israeli population and even more in the electorate because of their relatively mature ages. In general, according to official data, over 970,000 former Soviet Jews and their family members made *aliya* (immigration) to Israel between 1989 and mid-2007.[6] The political weight of these groups, which at the moment constitute about 16 percent of the Israeli electorate, corresponds to approximately twenty to twenty-two seats in the Knesset.

To these numbers one should add the more than 170,000 former Soviet Jews who emigrated to Israel between 1969 and 1988. Though many of these people do not define themselves as Russian, others have responded positively to the creation of a new immigrant community infrastructure. For example, some experts observe a movement toward "revived Russification" among certain segments of the veteran immigrants from the USSR, including a revival of their cultural, behavioral, and consumption habits.[7]

It is the *aliya* of the 1990s, however, whom Israeli Russian-speaking leaders see as a natural source for their political support. This fact was openly acknowledged by Natan Sharansky, once the central and still a very influential leader on the Israeli Russian street, and formerly a prominent USSR human rights activist imprisoned in the Soviet Union for his Zionist activities, whose political career in Israel includes several ministerial positions. On one occasion, Sharansky frankly admitted that "the best way to become a government minister in Israel is to bring your voters with you to the country."[8]

A second major factor in the change in Russian voting attitudes was an increased Israeli acceptance of multiculturalism and social heterogeneity. The legitimization of this idea came with the mass *aliya* from the USSR/CIS in the 1990s, the formalization of new immigrant institutions, and the recognition of the Russian-Jewish identity in the country. This phenomenon was noted by Anna Isakova, adviser to former prime minister Ehud Barak on *aliya* and immigrant absorption, and a member of the government task force on the development of Israeli culture. According to Isakova, "There are a million immigrants from the Former Soviet Union, and that fact cannot be ignored. . . . A large cultural group creates a substantial cultural strata [*sic*] with many creative people who demand national recognition and undoubtedly have every right to get it."[9]

The third factor promoting the political advancement and influence of the Russian-speaking community was the system of separate voting for prime minister and Knesset members, first implemented in 1996. This system forced each candidate for prime minister to seek the support of sectarian leaders in exchange for those leaders' support in their communities. The abolition of the direct prime minister's elections in 2002 and the return to the system of pure parliamentarianism did not undermine the sectarian political structures, including the Russian ones. As one can observe, immigrant movements, as well as other communal-sectarian structures, became too strong in the recent decade and cannot again be replaced very easily by the nationwide elites.[10] The trend was obvious in the latest elections. The idea of the "new sociologists" that Israeli multicultural and postindustrial tribal society lost every difference between nationwide collective and sectarian values and interests is simply wrong.[11] One may observe that acknowledged sectarian (communal, ethnic, etc.) representatives compose about half of the current (seventeenth) Knesset, elected in 2006.

Finally, the rapid development of an institutional, social, and economic infrastructure in the Russian-speaking community during the 1990s also played a significant role. The establishment of this infrastructure was promoted by the government policy of direct absorption of new immigrants adopted at the end of the 1980s. This policy sent immigrants to reside in established Israeli communities rather than separate absorption centers, and its success was primarily due to the development of the intellectual, economic, and social resources of the immigrants.

Thus, by the mid-1990s, there were various community-owned self-help institutions and organizations. About three hundred such associations of new immigrants from the USSR/CIS received formal recognition in 1996–1997. They included: various clubs; educational institutions, including a unique system of schools for gifted children called *Mofet*; theaters; cultural, veterans', and youth groups; student unions; and professional and creative workers' unions (for teachers, academics, engineers, writers, film producers, and the like). To this list, one can add numerous newspapers and other mass media, welfare structures, and the Russian business sector. The latter includes hundreds of shops and supermarkets; Russian restaurants; medical, consulting, and law services; and construction and tourist firms. According to some data, these entities at one time provided jobs for about a quarter of the new FSU immigrants.[12] They also promoted a more autonomous view of many Russian speakers in regard to social and political issues and thus supported the relevant elements of the communal political infrastructure.

The Age of Sectarian Parties, 1995–2003

In the next stage, many immigrants found it logical to create their own political movement. However, the creation of an adequate form for this movement was a subject of discussion and confrontation between various factions of the Israeli Russian elite. One group tried to construct, with a limited degree of success, Russian branches in the Labor, Likud, National Religious, and other nationwide parties; others favored the creation of Russian sectarian parties.

The popularity of the second trend among Russian-speaking Israelis at the end of the Rabin era was due to two factors. The first was the arrival in Israel of a new generation of the Russian Jewish political elite, who had witnessed an explosion of political ethnicity under the last Soviet leader, Mikhail Gorbachev. They had also participated in the revival of organized Jewish life in the late USSR and some of the post-Soviet states, including the establishment of Jewish communities and their cultural, educational, welfare, and political organizations. Despite their strong Zionist aspirations, they had nothing against implementing this revival in the FSU. The second factor was the unprecedented campaign of blackening the FSU immigrants by the Israeli media in the first part of the 1990s, which created a feeling of injured community pride in many Russian-speaking Israelis and deep disappointment in the veteran elites and their parties.[13]

A center for the Russian political movement was provided by the Zionist Forum of Soviet Jewry, founded by Natan Sharansky in 1988 in order to support veterans of the Zionist movement. In 1992–1993, the Zionist Forum was restructured into an umbrella organization, opened a network of branches, and included many immigrant organizations as its affiliated members. Thus was created the framework for the future party. In early 1995, the political movement called Yisrael B'aliya (meaning both "Israel on the Rise" or "Israel in Ascent" and "Israel for *Aliya*") was established. The movement was transformed into a political party at its founding conference in Jerusalem on March 17, 1996. The conference adopted a basic document (the Statute and Mission Statement of Yisrael B'aliya); elected the party leader, Natan Sharansky; and formed a list of candidates for the 1996 Knesset elections.[14]

The success of Yisrael B'aliya was promoted by a favorable political situation in Israel on the eve of the 1996 elections, including the impact of the new system of separate voting for the prime minister and for Knesset members. Thus the electoral debut of Yisrael B'aliya in 1996 was very successful, gaining some 175,000 votes and winning seven Knesset seats. Natan Sharansky became minister of trade and industry, and Yuli Edelstein was minister of immigrant absorption in Benjamin Netanyahu's 1996 government. The 1998 municipal elections also brought Yisrael B'aliya representatives into the governments of many important municipalities. In 1999 the party won 172,000 votes and six Knesset seats. In Ehud Barak's 1999 government, Sharansky was minister of the interior, and another IBA Knesset member, the Russian immigrant Marina Solodkin, was deputy minister of absorption. After moving to the opposition in the summer of 2000 due to a strong disagreement with Ehud Barak's policy of concessions to the Palestinians, Yisrael B'aliya returned to the ruling coalition following Ariel Sharon's victory in the February 2001 elections. In the new government Sharansky became vice prime minister and minister of construction, and Yuli Edelstein again headed the ministry of immigrant absorption.

Similar to popular front movements in the USSR during Gorbachev's *perestroika,* which were more united against the common communist enemy than by common ideological and social principles, the Yisrael B'aliya party tried to speak on behalf of all Israelis of Russian origin. Thus, in the spirit of the party's official centrist ideology, it sought to keep a balance in its approach (or even abstain where possible) on certain issues such as the Israeli-Arab conflict and secular-religious relations. This position was especially obvious during the party's first term in the Knesset and in the government. Yet the party was unable to avoid internal ideological and personality conflicts, which resulted in the secession of various factions and the formation of the new Russian political parties.

In the winter of 1999, a large group of right-wing members, headed by Yuri Stern and Michael Nudelman, left the party. The reason was their dissatisfaction with Israeli government concessions to the Palestinian Arabs during the Wye Plantation summit, as well as a personality conflict with Natan Sharansky and Yuli Edelstein, the party's central committee chairman. After leaving the Yisrael B'aliya Party, Stern and Nudelman's faction joined another Russian party, Israel Beiteinu (Israel Our Home). This party was founded shortly before Stern and Nudelman's departure from the IBA, by the former director general of the prime minister's office, Avigdor Liberman, himself a veteran immigrant from the USSR.

The core of this new organization was created by a large group of Russian-speaking former members of Likud who were disappointed in the Wye agreement, and in the ignoring of their demands by the Likud leadership. In addition, a number of independent Russian candidates who were independent of the IBA appeared in the November 1998 municipal elections, much to the unhappiness of the Yisrael B'aliya leaders. Liberman was also supported by a group of former Zionist activists in the Soviet Union, who were disappointed by their marginalization in Israeli Russian politics and by what they saw as Soviet-style democratic centralism (strict control from the top, with the facade of democratic procedures) in Yisrael B'aliya. Another important factor was that Avigdor Liberman started his political campaign with an unprecedented attack on members of the Israeli establishment, whom he called "oligarchs." Liberman's attack on the "oligarchs" triggered a huge wave of pro-Liberman solidarity among many Israelis of non-FSU origin and was attractive to many Russian immigrants of both waves who did not want to vote for a clearly ethnic party such as Yisrael B'aliya.

Thus, in the 1999 elections, the Israel Beiteinu Party received more than eighty-two thousand votes and four Knesset seats. After the elections, Israel Beiteinu formed a joint parliamentary faction with the right-wing National Union Party and thus became one of the leading forces in opposition to Ehud Barak's center-leftist government. After the February 2001 prime ministerial elections, which were won by the candidate of the national (i.e., right-wing) camp, Ariel Sharon, Israel Beiteinu received key portfolios in the new ruling coalition. Avigdor Liberman became minister of national infrastructure, and Yuri Stern became a deputy minister in the prime minister's office.

Another secessionist group, mainly representing the left-wing and anti-clerical faction, left Yisrael B'aliya shortly after the 1999 elections. In July 1999, Knesset members Roman Bronfman, a veteran immigrant, and Alex Zinker, a new immigrant, left the party to form the Mahar (Tomorrow) parliamentary faction, which two weeks later was transformed into the Habehira Hademocratit (Democratic Choice) Party. The reason for that step was Bronfman's and Zinker's disagreement with the IBA's decision to join the government coalition together with ultra-Orthodox religious parties, as well as personal disputes with Natan Sharansky and Yuli Edelstein. (According to internal sources, Roman Bronfman, who as head of Yisrael B'aliya's election headquarters in 1999 played a key role in the mobilization of the party's support for Ehud Barak, had expected to get a position in the Barak government. Barak, however, agreed with Sharansky's decision to give this position to Yuli Edelstein).

In addition to these three parties, other political organizations were founded by different waves of immigrants from the USSR/CIS in the 1990s. In 1996, one such party was Efraim Fainblum's Aliya Party. Another was "For Unity and Dignity of Aliya," led by Efraim Gur, representing Jewish immigrants from Georgia. In 1996, these two parties created a common electoral bloc, which received twenty-two thousand votes but was unable to pass the 1.5 percent electoral threshold. Among the parties that challenged Yisrael B'aliya and Israel Beiteinu in 1999 were Tikva (Hope, or *Nadezhda* in Russian), and Lev Olim Lemaan Yisrael (LOMI; Heart of Immigrants for Israel) which identified itself as a movement of "Russian-speaking Sephardi Jews" and tried to speak on behalf of immigrants from Central Asia and the Caucasus. None of these groups was able to pass the 1.5 percent electoral barrier and had to put off their political ambitions to the future.[15]

Thus the landscape of Israeli Russian party politics in 1996–2003 involved the community centrist Yisrael B'aliya, the right-wing and market-oriented Israel Beiteinu, and the social leftist Habehira Hademocratit. Together with the Russian sections of the Israeli mainstream parties, these movements reflected the whole spectrum of opinions and cleavages within Russian Jewish society in Israel that was concerned with both nationwide and specific community issues.

Russian Parties with the Israeli Accent: 2004 and Beyond

By 2003, however, many believed that the game of Russian party politics in Israel was about to be over. The centrist Yisrael B'aliya Party of Natan Sharansky, previously the leading political force in the community, received only two Knesset seats in 2003, as opposed to seven in 1996 and six in 1999. Two other Russian parties—the right-wing Israel Beiteinu and the left-wing Habehira Hademocratit—participated in the 2003 elections as parts of ideological blocs: the National Union bloc and Meretz. After the elections, with the appending of the shrunken faction of Yisrael B'aliya to the Likud, no Russian immigrant party was left in Israeli politics, not counting petty subcommunal organizations (such as the Bukharan and Caucasian Jewish and the ethnic Russian movements), which, together, gained less than 1 percent of the FSU immigrant vote.

However, the expectations of those who believed that Israeli Russians were not Russians anymore but had already dispersed into the native Israeli social and political environment, and of those who believed that the nationwide mainstream parties would meet the needs and demands of the FSU immigrants more effectively than the sectarian movements, were soon to collapse.[16] A year after the 2003 general elections, Russian-speaking Israelis renewed their interest in effective communal representation and in a Russian Jewish lobby in national politics. In turn, this interest stimulated a new round of activities by various factions of the Russian immigrant elite, both the old guard politicians of the 1990s and the municipal leaders and grassroot activists, as well as the new generation of the community's politicians.

The most effective model for re-creating the sectarian political structure was suggested by the politicians of Avigdor Liberman's camp, deeply disappointed by their experience in the mainstream Ihud Leumi (National Union) bloc. As one can guess, Liberman took a lesson from the collapse of Yisrael B'aliya as well as from his own negative experience in the 2003 elections. Of the seven seats that the National Union–Israel Beiteinu bloc had received that year, more than five had been obtained from the Russian community due to the participation of Israel Beiteinu (IB) in the bloc; however, the IB members, due to the coalition agreement, had only three seats in the united parliamentary faction. That was a good reason to believe that paying indigenous partners with Russian votes just for the status of an all-Israeli organization was an unprofitable political investment.[17] As for Yisrael B'aliya, this formerly Russian-community consensus party had showed itself in 2003 as not right-wing enough for its ideological electorate and not Russian enough for the social-welfare-oriented, and it had received only two seats—three times fewer than in 1996 and 1999—and, as mentioned earlier, shortly afterward joined Likud and disappeared from the Israeli political map.[18]

In light of these experiences, Liberman decided to give up his previous image of an "all-Israeli right-wing party," most of the electorate of which was coincidentally Russian-speaking, and switched to the much more profitable concept of a "Russian party with an Israeli accent." As early as 2003 and 2004 Israel Beiteinu had conducted its own campaign during municipal elections, independent of other parts of the Ihud Leumi Party (Tkuma and Moledet), and had attracted many former activists of the dispersed Yisrael B'aliya. The relative success of this campaign pushed Liberman to take further steps. In November 2004 he finally parted company with the National Union Party and proclaimed his organization to be the only party that represented the Russian-speaking community in Israel.

At the end of the day, IB did succeed in becoming an umbrella for most of the ideological right, the socially oriented (center), and the left wings of that part of the Russian community who normally prefer to vote for a Russian sectarian party. Initiators of the other Russian political projects were late to recognize the newly opened niche of community politics and were therefore unable to make any challenge to IB. Thus Roman Bronfman, the leader of the third Russian party of the 1990s generation, Habehira Hademokratit, decided in September 2005 to part company with Meretz and to run in the next elections as an independent candidate, but at the peak of the campaign he reconsidered his chances and dropped out of the race.

At the end of 2004 and in 2005, several other groups and politicians demonstrated their ambitions to inherit the electoral legacy of Yisrael B'aliya. They were Ya'akov Kedmi, former noted activist in the USSR underground Zionist movement and later director of Nativ (the Israeli government's Liaison Bureau for East European Jewry); the "With You and for You" movement (an obvious allusion to the 2003 electoral slogan of Yisrael B'aliya) of the one-and-a-half generation of Russian Jewish immigrants in Israel;[19] Knesset member Professor Michael Nudelman, who had left the IB faction in September 2004; and a noted Russian Israeli philanthropist and businessman, Arkady Gaydamak. In the autumn of 2005 Nudelman proclaimed his wish to run in the election at the head of his Aliya Party; on November 25, 2005, Gaydamak announced his intention to create a party based on the World Beitar Movement, which he chaired at that time. Initiators of all these socially centrist projects used similar collections of welfare and civic slogans that had previously been used by the Russian community's centrist political organizations, as well as the sectarian slogans used by the Yisrael B'aliya Party and also by the mainstream Shinui Party. However, none of these candidates actually stood in the elections independently. Kedmi never really realized his intention even to create a party. "With You and for You" leaders in December 2005 joined the mainstream left-of-center Tafnit list of candidates of Uzi Dayan, which did not pass the new 2 percent electoral threshold. Sharon, grateful to Nudelman for support of his disengagement plan, allocated him a place on the Kadima list of candidates, and Gaydamak reserved his political ambitions for the future.

Thus IB became the only party able to portray itself as an all-community movement, since it was clear that the two subcommunal lists of candidates—that of the Russian Sephardic party Lev Leolim and that of the ethnic Russian party Leeder—would be unable to mount any challenge to Israel Beiteinu.[20] Thus that half of Israel's Russian speakers who had normally supported the sectarian party had no choice other than Israel Beiteinu. So in the March 2006 elections, IB got eleven seats, including at least nine (of twenty) from the Russian-speaking sector. Five or six of this nine came from the former IBA voters, who, in the three years that had passed after the 2003 elections, had had enough time and opportunity to be disappointed by the lists of candidates from the mainstream, such as Likud and especially Shinui. To gain this electorate, both during and after the electoral campaign for the seventeenth Knesset, the IB leaders, in contrast to their traditional liberal market-oriented platform, made a few social-welfare-oriented declarations.

In spite of moving primarily to the community square, Israel Beiteinu currently continues to position itself as both a sectarian and a mainstream party.

On the one hand, IB still seeks to preserve its Russian-community-consensus-party status, which in previous years belonged to Yisrael B'aliya. Thus the major dilemma that Liberman faces today is how to capitalize effectively on the communal solidarity vote and not simultaneously lose the party's ideological electorate. This dilemma means, in practical terms, finding an adequate balance between various party factions that have different views on the Arab-Israeli conflict, secular-religious relations, economic welfare policy, and other issues critical to Israeli society and not following the example of the now defunct centrist parties of the past: the Russian IBA and the mainstream Shinui.

The first symptoms of possible cleavages came very early: The IB electorate expressed different reactions to the lack of success in negotiations in joining the first Olmert government. While the social-centrist half of Liberman's electorate remained disappointed because the party did not get ministerial posts and thus would be unable to realize the demands of this group, a number of ideologically oriented party voters were unhappy because Liberman had considered joining the disengagement coalition at all. And the same circles became severe critics of Liberman when he finally joined the Olmert government after the Second Lebanon War, thus, as many believe, saving the governing coalition from collapse and postponing early elections.

The reasons for Liberman's widely criticized step are obvious. They came from the second dimension of the IB—its role as a mainstream party, which had replaced Shinui in the centrist party niche. However, in contrast to Shinui, IB recruited most of its electoral resources from the center-right, rather than the center-left, segment of the Israeli political spectrum. Furthermore, considering the limited prospects for any centrist party in Israel, which normally captures a narrow niche between the left-of-center Labor and the right-of-center Likud, for not more than one or two Knesset seats, Liberman's real aim was not to make a "new Shinui" out of IB, but to replace Kadima as the party of power. This ambition was impossible without a maximum gain in the "moderate" electorate, estimated as controlling between thirty and forty Knesset seats (including those held by members of the moderate factions of Labor and Likud, some of whom in 2006 supported either Kadima or the Pensioners' Party). Trying to reach this goal while staying in the opposition Liberman considered counterproductive. It was equally important to meet the civic and welfare demands of the former Yisrael B'aliya voters, a tactic critical to the preservation of the sympathies of this group, which, as mentioned above, had given Liberman about half his Knesset seats in 2006.

The IB leaders believe that the risks of this maneuvering may be bearable, since the potential losses among the right-wing Liberman supporters will be largely overcome through new gains among the moderate electorate. The results have been ambivalent. According to various opinion polls in 2007, the

IB's support has never really dropped below ten seats, proportional to the current size of the IB faction.[21] The share of Hebrew-speaking supporters of IB has jumped from 10–15 percent to about 30 percent, but with an apparent loss of the former Kadima supporters. This jump might show a successful move toward becoming the first Russian mainstream party. However, it is not enough of a jump to allow IB to pretend that it is about to become the party of power. On the other hand, it looks as if Liberman's camp, regardless of his floating toward the center, still preserves most of its strong rightist, and market-oriented, core and, as well, enjoys the sympathies of the Russian speakers who prefer, in any event, to vote for the Russian community party.

The Gaydamak Phenomenon

However, one cannot guarantee these votes for Liberman. At least some of these former Yisrael B'aliya seats may go to a Russian party that will position itself as socially centrist. A few candidates for this position, impressed by the IB success in 2006, are already observable.

One of these possible candidates is Sharansky's former close associate, Marina Solodkin (Solodkina), number six on the list of candidates that Kadima ran in the 2006 elections, who, despite promises, did not become absorption minister in Olmert's government, and who moved, with two other Russian Kadima Knesset members, Ze'ev Elkin and Michael Nudelman, into internal opposition to Olmert inside the ruling party.[22]

In fact, in May 2006, Solodkin had already called for the re-creation of Yisrael B'aliya as an independent organization that might not only depend on current Russian Kadima electees but also gain the support of the former IBA electorate, which in 2006 backed Liberman's Israel Beiteinu. There are rumors that such a party will be created on the basis of Nudelman's *aliya* movement. According to internal sources, however, oppositionist Russian Kadima members in the Knesset prefer joining the IB list of candidates over running separately.

The election of Ehud Barak as the chair of the Labor Party may become a new window of opportunity for his close friend and political associate Ya'akov Kedmi. Observers believe that Kedmi might become the leader of the new Russian wing or even of an immigrant satellite party, affiliated with Labor, with the aim of targeting social centrist factions of the Russian community.

Finally, Israeli Russian philanthropist and billionaire Arkady Gaydamak has also renewed his political ambitions. Gaydamak moved into the focus of public attention when, during the Second Lebanon War, he organized and financed the evacuation into the central areas of Israel of thousands of northern Israelis who had become targets of Hizbollah missiles. He then chose to convert his public popularity into political capital. In February 2007

Gaydamak announced the creation of the Tsedek Hevraty (Tsah, or the Social Justice Movement) which, four months later, on June 12, 2007, was officially transformed into a political party.

Like Liberman's "renewed" Israel Beiteinu Party, the new movement evidently belongs to the new generation of "Russian parties with an Israeli accent"; in contrast to IB, however, Gaydamak is positioning himself left of center, rather than in the moderate-right section of Israeli politics. According to its draft manifesto, Gaydamak's party has a clear social orientation. Thus the major Gaydamak appeal will be to economically disadvantaged groups of Russian immigrants (especially welfare allowance holders and immigrants who are recent newcomers), as well as to other peripheral groups in Israeli society. However, in an interview with the Israeli Russian TV channel, Gaydamak remarked that the Sephardic electorate will be his first priority, then Orthodox Jews, and only after that Russian immigrants.[23] In other interviews he has also promised to consider the needs of Israeli Arabs, Druze and Bedouin.

On the other hand, like leaders of other centrist one-issue parties, Gaydamak constantly makes contradictory proclamations. In an interview Gaydamak noted that according to his political worldview, he is left-wing concerning social security issues, a centrist in foreign policy and the struggle for peace, and on the "extreme right" on economic policy questions.[24] On another occasion, he proclaimed his devotion to the idea of "an equality and coexistence with Israeli Arabs, and also with the Palestinians."[25]

All these contradictory views, together with his controversial image as an oligarch, may easily destroy his party—if not now, then in the near future. On the other hand, according to polls, his movement, at the beginning, was able to capture about a third of Liberman's IB electorate as well as a number of former Kadima voters.[26] Many observers also believe that Gaydamak will be able to accumulate some of the protest potential of both Russians and some other groups, including those who are dissatisfied with the Israeli political system as a whole. In particular, he could enter the current political niche of the Pensioners' Party, whose chance of meeting the electoral threshold again does not appear to be strong.

Conclusions and Prospects

Although the Russian component of Israeli party politics is still developing, a few conclusions can be drawn from the Russian political experience between 1995 and 2007.

First, it is clear that Israel's Russian sectarian party politics, although FSU immigrants do preserve some elements of the political culture of their countries of origin, is much more a result of the Israeli experience than a Soviet legacy.

Second, Russian parties represent in the political sphere three basic models of integration into Israel. The first is "assimilation"—a total integration into the Israeli cultural environment. The second is isolation, that is, the formation of isolated Russian Jewish and ethnic Russian cultural enclaves at the periphery of society. The third is integration without acculturation, that is, integration into the host society's culture while simultaneously preserving the culture of the country and community of origin. In the 1990s these three trends were represented by Israel Beiteinu, Habehira Hademocratit, and Yisrael B'aliya, respectively. The current trend is the creation of Russian nonsectarian parties, or "Russian parties with an Israeli accent," which represent a new type of Israeli-Russian Jewish identity, as part of contemporary postmodern and multicultural Israeli society.

Third, the independent community parties will continue to dominate the political aspirations and interests of most FSU immigrants in Israel. However, two other options—attempts to use the influence and machinery of the mainstream parties in the interests of the immigrant community, and the creation of acknowledged Russian wings of the leading nationwide parties—will also be available.

Fourth, it looks as if every Russian party in Israel follows the same model: It starts as a social and political protest movement on the pattern first suggested by the German Jewish immigrants' Aliya Hadasha (New Immigration) Party of the 1940s.[27] It reaches the peak of its position as the party of communal consensus and then, due to internal ideological and personality contradictions, gradually loses the social-democratic center-left-wing and conservative right-wing factions, which the imitators of new Russian political projects try to unite under their own umbrellas. That pattern first happened when the IB challenged the IBA, and new aspirants for community power will now try to challenge the IB.

Naturally, the situation remains fluid, and much will change before the next elections. However, one way or another, there is no doubt that the niche of Russian communal party politics, first opened in the mid-1990s, will remain very important.

Notes

1. See, for instance, Marcia Drezon-Tepler, *Interest Groups and Political Change in Israel* (New York: State University of New York Press, 1990), pp. 225–254; Asher Arian, *The Second Republic: Politics in Israel* (Chatham, NJ: Chatham House, 1998); and Daniel Elazar and Shmuel Sandler, "The Battle over Jewishness and Zionism in the Post-modern Era," in D. Elazar and S. Sandler, *Israel at the Polls, 1996* (London: Frank Cass, 1998), pp. 1–32.

2. See Eliezer Feldman, *Russian Israel: Between Two Polls* (Moscow: Market DC, 2003), pp. 101–124 (in Russian).

3. For the analyses of this split, see Vladimir (Ze'ev) Khanin, "The Jewish Right of Return: Reflections on the Mass Immigration to Israel from the Former Soviet Union," in Ian Lustick and Ann Lesch, eds., *Exile and Return: Predicaments of Palestinian Arabs and Jews* (Philadelphia: University of Pennsylvania Press, 2005), pp. 183–203.

4. See Vladimir Ze'ev Khanin, "The Israeli 'Russian' Community and Immigrant Party Politics in the 2003 Elections," *Israel Affairs* (London), vol. 10, nos. 1–2 (Summer 2004), pp. 146–180; and Vladimir (Ze'ev) Khanin, "Revival of 'Russian' Politics in Israel: The Case of the 2006 Elections," *Israel Affairs* (London), vol. 13, no. 2 (April 2007), pp. 346–367.

5. For a detailed discussion of these factors see Vladimir (Ze'ev) Khanin, *The "Russians" and Power in the State of Israel: The Establishment of the USSR/CIS Immigrant Community and Its Impact on the Political Structure of the Country* (Moscow: Institute for Israel and Middle Eastern Studies, 2004), pp. 27–38 (in Russian).

6. Official Data, Israeli Ministry of Immigrant Absorption, and the Jewish Agency, May 2007.

7. Eliezer Feldman, "'Pragmatic Isolation' of the FSU Immigrants in Israel," paper presented at the international conference "Russian-speaking Jewry in Global Perspective: Assimilation, Integration and Community-Building," Bar-Ilan University, Ramat-Gan, Israel, June 14–16, 2004.

8. Address to the Second International Conference on Personal Absorption of Jewish Immigrants (Repatriates) from the Former USSR, Herzliya, Israel November 1999.

9. Anna Isakova, "Izrail'skaya cul'tura XXI veka: kuda I kak?" [Israeli Culture of the 21st Century: Which Way Ahead?"], *Vesti-Okna* (February 17, 2000), p. 24.

10. Shmuel Sandler and Jonathan Rynhold, "Introduction," in S. Sandler, B. Mollow, and J. Rynhold, eds., *Israel at the Polls, 2003* (London: Routledge, 2004). On the impact of the "separate vote" system on the political success of Israeli Russian parties in 1996 and 1999, see Edith Rogovin Frankel, "The 'Russian' Vote in the 1996 Israeli Elections," *East European Jewish Affairs*, vol. 26, no. 1 (1996), pp. 9–16; Etta Bick, "Sectarian Party Politics in Israel: The Case of Yisrael B'aliya, the Russian Immigrant Party," in Daniel J. Elazar and Shmuel Sandler (eds.), *Israel at the Polls 1996* (London: Frank Cass, 1998), pp. 129–133; and Vladimir Khanin, "Israeli 'Russian' Parties, and the New Immigrant Vote," in D. Elazar and B. Mollow, eds., *Israel at the Polls, 1999* (London: Frank Cass, 2001), pp. 101–134.

11. See, for instance, Baruch Kimmerling, "State Building, State Autonomy, and the Identity of Society—The Case of Israel," *Journal of Historical Sociology*, vol. 6, no. 4 (1993), pp. 396–429.

12. Larissa Remennick, "Transnational Community in the Making: Russian-Jewish Immigrants of the 1990s in Israel," *Journal of Ethnic and Migration Studies*, vol. 28, no. 3 (July 2002), pp. 515–530; Sarit Cohen-Gildner and M. Daniele Paserman, *The Dynamic Impact of Immigration on Natives' Labor Market Outcomes: Evidence from Israel* (London Center for Economic Policy Research, 2005).

13. Ze'ev Khanin, "The New Russian-Speaking Elite in Israel," in E. Ben Rafael, Y. Steinberg, et al., eds., *New Elites in Israel* (Jerusalem: Bialik Institute, 2007), pp. 377–393 (in Hebrew). In contrast to the common impression of the majority of FSU *olim* as educated, industrious, and highly motivated new citizens,

some interest groups in the middle class and the ruling strata, due to growing competition with new immigrants in the qualified labor market, preferred to call them the "community of Mafioso," or "*aliya* of social cases," as it was described by Moshe Shahal and Ora Namir, at that time Labor Party ministers of police and labor and welfare, respectively. This attitude created "injured community pride" among many Russian-speaking Israelis.

14. For a detailed history of the Israeli Russian parties of the 1990s, see Vladimir (Ze'ev) Khanin, "The New Russian Jewish Diaspora and 'Russian' Party Politics in Israel," *Nationalism and Ethnic Politics*, vol. 8, no 4 (December 2002), pp. 54–81. See also Dina Seigel, *The Great Immigration: Russian Jews in Israel* (New York and Oxford: Berghan Books, 1998), pp. 160–174.

15. See Vladimir (Ze'ev) Khanin, "Israeli 'Russian' Parties and the New Immigrant Vote," in D. Elazar and B. Mollow, eds., *Israel at the Polls, 1999* (London: Frank Cass, 2001), pp. 101–134.

16. For detailed analyses of these factors, see Vladimir (Ze'ev) Khanin, "Russian Parties in Israel: The Second Edition?" *Modern Middle East*, vol. 25 (2006), pp. 89–110 (in Russian), and Khanin, "Revival of 'Russian' Politics," pp. 347–453.

17. Vladimir (Ze'ev) Khanin, *The "Russians" and Power in the State of Israel: The Establishment of the USSR/CIS Immigrant Community and Its Impact on the Political Structure of the Country* (Moscow: Institute for Israel and Middle Eastern Studies, 2004), pp. 247–250 (in Russian). This conclusion was also confirmed by the Israel Beiteinu chairman Avigdor Liberman and the late Knesset member Dr. Yuri Stern in a series of personal interviews with the author in 2004 and 2005.

18. Vladimir (Ze'ev) Khanin, "The Israeli 'Russian' Community and Immigrant Party Politics in the 2003 Elections," *Israel Affairs* (London), vol. 10, nos. 1–2 (Summer 2004), pp. 146–180.

19. On the phenomenon of the "one-and-a-half generation" of Russian Jewish immigrant youth in Israel, see Eliezer Feldman, "Cross-Culture Factors of the Political Communication Strategies of the 'One-and-a-Half Generation' of Israeli Russian-Speaking Youth," paper presented at the international conference "Russian-Speaking Jewry in Global Perspective Power, Politics and Community," Bar-Ilan University, Ramat Gan, Israel, October 17–19, 2006, and Marina Niznik, "The Dilemma of Russian-Born Adolescents in Israel," in E. Ben Rafael, Y. Gorny, and Y. Ro'i, eds., *Contemporary Jewries: Convergence and Divergence* (Leiden/Boston: Brill, 2003), pp. 235–252. These terms are used in regard to those who immigrated from ages ten to eighteen. In the first years after their immigration, they normally demonstrate a positive language, cultural, and economic integration into local society but at the same time often preserve their parents' generation's social and cultural agenda and value system in a much stronger way than their younger "brothers and sisters." This attitude often includes the feelings of a "glass ceiling" that exists in Israeli society vis-à-vis the "outsiders." In the specific Israeli case, a substantial part of this generation also accepts their belonging to a local million-strong and relatively successful Russian immigrant community as a positive value, an attitude that may affect their political behavior and sharpen their demands vis-à-vis the Israeli establishment.

20. The showing of the Russian Sephardic party Lev Leolim, founded in 1999, as well as the candidate list of "ethnic Russians in Israel," which first announced itself in 2003 as the Israeli branch of the Russian Federation's Liberal Democratic Party of Vladimir Zhirinovsky, was very modest; in 2006 they gained 1,785 and 580 votes, respectively—even fewer than during their electoral debuts (about 6,000 and 700 votes, respectively).

21. See, for instance, the Smith Institute Israeli public opinion polls for Channel 2 of the Voice of Israel radio, January, February, and August, 2007, http://bet.iba.org.il/.

22. Author's interviews with Knesset members Ze'ev Elkin, Dr. Marina Solodkin, and Professor Michael Nudelman in February, May, June, and July 2007, and Lily Galili, "Kadima Aims to Gain Support of

Russian-Speaking Constituency," *Ha'aretz* (August 8, 2007).

23. Quoted by Channel 9 of Israeli TV, June 11, 2007, and *Jerusalem Post* (July 12, 2007).

24. *Globus* (Tel-Aviv) (February 14, 2007).

25. Lily Galii, "Gaydamak Completes Manifesto for His Future Center-Right Party," *Ha'aretz* (March 21, 2007).

26. Dahav Institute Poll for *Yedioth Ahronot* newspaper, November 11, 2006.

27. On Aliya Hadasha (The New Immigration) Party, see Rakefet Sela-Shiffy, "Integration through Distinction: German-Jewish Immigrants, the Legal Profession and Patterns of Bourgeois Culture in British-Ruled Jewish Palestine," *Journal of Historical Sociology,* vol. 19, no. 1 (March 2006), pp. 34–59.

6

Israel's Arab Parties

Hillel Frisch

WHILE THE ASSASSINATION of Israel's prime minister Yitzhak Rabin had major implications for the Arab-Israeli peace process, dates like 1977 and 1988 are far more important for assessing the relations between Israel and its Arab citizens. Briefly, for the first time in the history of the state, a protest organized by a political party and nascent countrywide organizations ended in bloodshed on March 30, 1976. Six Israeli Arab citizens were killed in confrontations with the police. They were protesting land appropriation for public purposes. A year later, the party that had organized the protest against the expropriation of land in the Shaknin, Arrabeh, and Dir Hana areas in northern Galilee was rewarded for its efforts when half the Arab electorate cast its vote for the Democratic Front for Peace and Equality (DFPE) in the general elections of 1977.

Within eleven years two more (predominantly) Arab parties, the Progressive List for Peace (PLP) and 'Abd al-Wahhab Darawsha's newly formed Arab Democratic Party (ADP), had joined the electoral fray. In the 1988 general elections these three parties secured 58.3 percent of the Arab vote.[1] The PLP was formed in 1984 by Muhammad Mi'ari, a founding member of the Al-Ard Pan-Arab Party, which had been banned in the early 1960s. The PLP became closely identified with the Palestine Liberation Organization (PLO) mainstream.[2] The third party emerged in a moment of intifada enthusiasm, when 'Abd al-Wahhab Darawsha, a former Labor member of the Knesset, formed the ADP in April 1988. In the aftermath of the 1989 municipal elections, a fourth possibility emerged as Islamic Movement candidates successfully contested in mayoral elections in three major Arab towns.

Rabin's Assassination: A Watershed

Ostensibly, voting patterns, except for temporary aberrations, seemed to have confirmed forecasts of increasingly salient radicalization, especially after the outbreak of the First Intifada. Oddly, in the first general elections *after* the assassination of a prime minister who had promoted Israeli-Arab affairs more than any of his predecessors, elections held in 1996 demonstrated how much more complex the picture truly was. On the one hand, former radical groups at opposite poles of the ideological spectrum decided for the first time to contest in Israel's national elections—apparently a demonstration that Israeli Arabs were increasingly working within the system. Exercising the right to vote is typically perceived as a form of recognition of the state.

In these elections, the radical left-wing Abna al-Balad (Sons of the Village) and an offshoot, Al Ansar, both of which for over twenty years had vitriolically denounced participation in the "Zionist" elections, entered a coalition between the DFPE and Balad, the National Democratic Alliance (NDA). The latter had been founded by Azmi Bishara, an Israeli Palestinian, a former professor of philosophy at Birzeit University, who has long championed "a state for all Israel's citizens" and, in lieu of that, recognition of Israel's Arabs as a national minority. He had also expressed serious reservations regarding the Oslo agreement. Culturally, he has vowed to combat what he termed the "Israelization" *(Asrala)* of Israel's Arabs, forming a movement in 1992 that championed these causes.[3] On the other side of the spectrum, a major segment of the Islamic Association, led by the movement's founder, Sheikh 'Abd Allah Nimr Darwish, entered into a coalition with the ADP to form the United Arab List (UAL).

Having participated in the elections, these groups had helped to incorporate all major ideological trends in the Arab sector into the wider political arena, and to encourage most of Israel's by-now-politicized Arab population to fulfill one of the most important civic duties: the act of voting. It was little wonder that for the first time in twenty years, the rate of participation among the Arab population increased dramatically from 68.3 percent in 1992 to 77 percent in 1996, the highest participation rate in nearly thirty years. This rate may not have been quite as high as the Jewish participation rate in these elections, but it did equal the Jewish average in the past three elections.

Whereas the Arab participation suggested an acceptance of the Israeli political system, the changes in the party platforms of the two major Arab winners in the 1996 elections indicated radicalization. Coalition building with more radical groups was bound to radicalize party platforms. A comparison between the DFPE platform in 1992 and the platform of the DFPE-Balad coalition in 1996 shows far more difference than such a comparison for the UAL.

This discrepancy may be due to the intellectual stature of 'Azmi Bishara, one of the leaders of the major group to enter into the coalition with the DFPE. Bishara's concepts found their way into the joint campaign platform just as Bishara made his way into the Knesset.[4] The following was taken from the introduction of the coalition's platform:

> The cooperation between "The Front" [the DFPE] and the Alliance [Balad] is based on a common political and social program that is epitomized by the incessant struggle to realize the just, comprehensive, and enduring Israeli-Palestinian and Israeli-Arab peace, to make the state of Israel democratic and a [state] for all its citizens, to ensure complete national and civil equality for the citizens of Israel, Jews as well as Arabs . . . by the struggle for recognition of the Arabs who are citizens of Israel as a national minority.[5]

Elsewhere in the program, in a section entitled "The State of Israel and the Equality of Arab Citizens," there was an even more explicit call to transform the Jewish state into a "state for all its citizens":

> In order that Israel become a democratic state and a state for all its citizens, we shall fight for the abolition of discrimination and national suppression on all levels and to ensure complete equality for the Arab citizens in such a way that the laws of the state and its symbols, including the flag and the "national" anthem, will conform to these principles.[6]

These statements were fraught with tension; the aspiration to make "the state of Israel democratic and a state for all its citizens" is a liberal sentiment, which treats individuals as citizens irrespective of their ethnicity. Simultaneously, these political coalitions felt that the search for equality must also take into account the collective identity of the Arab Palestinian minority. This tension between liberalism and collective minority identity is hardly novel, as it characterizes Israel's declaration of independence as well.[7] Recognition of Israeli Arabs as a national minority, the DFPE claimed, would go some way toward creating equality among Israel's Arab and Jewish citizens.

Though the Arab electorate had radicalized since 1996, as we shall see the trend was hardly noticeable in the 1999 elections, in which Israeli Arabs voted in remarkably similar fashion to how they had voted in the elections held three years previously. Once again, Arabs proved, in their strategic vote for the prime minister of their choice, to be the segment of Israel's voting public most loyal to the left-wing candidate; 94.3 percent of Arab voters voted for Ehud Barak. Once again, they proved to favor parties whose ethnonational identity was beyond dispute. Of those 69.8 percent of Arab voters who voted for the non-Zionist Arab or predominantly Arab parties, 31.1 percent voted for the UAL, compared to 25.6 percent in 1996, and 16.7 percent for Balad, which in the previous elections had run as a coalition partner with the DFPE. The UAL, an alliance between the nationalist Arab Democratic Party and the southern branch of the Islamic Association, increased its representation in the Knesset from four to five seats, the DFPE managed to hold onto its three seats, and Balad, which ran alone for the first time, managed to secure two seats.[8] This was the highest percentage of the Arab vote that these three parties had ever drawn.

Participation was as high as in the previous elections—339,164 Arabs—but significantly lower than the projections; that is, 70 percent of the eligible voters (excluding mixed towns, where Arab voting patterns are hard to assess) cast their votes.[9] Arabs accounted for only 12.1 percent of the eligible vote, less than their share of all eligible voters.[10] Ten Arabs (including Druze) were elected to the Knesset, compared to eleven members in the previous term, a figure significantly lower than the Arab proportion in the population, and substantially lower than the actual participation rates of Arabs would warrant.

Barak's Tenure in Office as a Watershed

There was, however, great disappointment in Prime Minister Barak, whom the Arabs had backed and whom Arab voters came to feel resembled his predecessor, Benjamin Netanyahu, rather than Yitzhak Rabin, the Labor prime minister before him. From the beginning of Barak's administration, the Arabs were miffed by his policy of denying Arab parties the chance of joining the governing coalition. Israel's Arab citizens expressed their disillusionment with the system both violently and at the voting booth.

In late September and early October 2000, Israel's Arab citizens participated in acts of violence on an unprecedented scale, presumably because of Ariel Sharon's much-publicized visit to the Temple Mount. Unlike previous violent events, this rioting took place in numerous localities simultaneously, from Rahat in the south to Sahnin in northern Galilee, for five continuous days. By contrast, the Land Day of March 1976, which marked the most violent event before the outbreak of violence in 2000, took place in three localities in northern Galilee alone and lasted only one day. There were other significant differences as well. On Land Day, Arab protestors confronted security personnel only. In 2000, the violence was directed against Israeli Jewish citizens who had the misfortune of using the roads that passed near Arab villages and towns. The differences were also reflected in the number of Arabs killed: thirteen compared to six. Nor can one deny the relatively long-lasting effects of the violence in 2000. Arabs were convinced years after the outbreak of the violence that Jews continued to unofficially boycott Arab restaurants and commercial services; the Jews, when interviewed, cited the fear of feeling insecure in Arab localities.

The Arabs expressed their disappointment at the polling booth as well in February 2001, six months into the wave of violence between Israel and the Palestinians. The Arab electorate, with the full support of the Arab parties, effectively boycotted the elections for the post of prime minister, which Ariel Sharon won by a landslide against incumbent Ehud Barak.[11] Less than 20 percent of eligible Arab voters turned up at the polling booths; in some villages and towns, such as Sahnin and Arrabeh, voter participation was 1 percent or less.[12] Many perceived the boycott as an ominous indication that Israel's Palestinian citizens were finally exiting the Israeli system.

Nothing so dramatic occurred, yet if one searches for a date reflecting a watershed—the final break between a center-left-wing or left-wing Zionist party and the Arab electorate—it occurred not after the assassination of Rabin, but after Barak's failure to improve on Rabin's performance regarding Israel's Arab citizens. In the 2003 elections, for the first time since the establishment of the state, no Arab Knesset members represented Zionist parties on the Left, partially because of the massive defeat of both parties (Labor and Meretz) in the elections. This lack of representation was also an indication of how marginal Arab politicians remained in the Zionist Left parties.

The same dichotomizing trend prevailed for the first time on the Arab side; the predominantly Arab DFPE placed no Jewish candidate in a realistic slot to replace a veteran Jewish Knesset member. Again, this eventuality was partially circumstantial rather than deliberate.[13] The two Druze members of the Knesset, Ayyub al-Qara and Majli Wahaba of the Likud, were former senior officers in the Israeli Defense Forces and therefore hardly representative of Arabs as a whole. But these ominous signs did not last long. In 2006, two Labor Arabs were elected to the Knesset, as was a Jewish candidate from the DFPE.

The reduced voting turnout may also have been partially a response to calls by extraparliamentary movements to boycott the elections. Though both the Jewish and Arab participation rates were lower, the reduction was far more marked among the Arabs: a drop from 70 to 62 percent in the Arab sector compared to a drop from 80 to 73 percent in the Jewish sector. Some of the drop could be attributed to voter fatigue from participating in five national election campaigns in just over a decade, but some was no doubt due to the campaign that the Islamic Movement, the Abna al-Balad, and other groups waged against participation in the elections. Moreover, Balad's relative success—increasing its share of the Arab votes from 16.7 percent in the 1999 elections, when it had run for the first time alone, to 22 percent—also indicated radicalization. Balad ranked second after the DFPE in its ability to attract Arab votes.

The Arab Political Parties:
From Fragmentation to Consolidation?

By the mid-1990s any expectation based on the outcome of the 1977 elections that political radicalism would lead to political homogenization among the Israeli Arabs had disappeared. In the 1973 elections, the Labor Party and its affiliates won 56.9 percent of the Arab vote and the Israeli Communist Party, Rakah, 28.9 percent. By contrast, in 1977, the DFPE (dominated by Rakah) won 50.1 percent of the votes, and the Labor Alignment and its affiliated parties garnered 27 percent. It seemed that a united Arab party was just around the corner. Instead, the vote was being increasingly split among three parties—the DFPE, the PLP, and the ADP—even though in terms of party platforms regarding the state, homogenization had indeed prevailed.

The parties suffered from deep ideological and personal rivalries, to the extent that they often refused to agree over the leftover votes that are normally divided among parties following an election to ensure that they are not wasted.[14] The electoral price they paid for their incessant feuding was substantial. In the 1988 elections, all three parties received more votes than seats: The PLP won 1.8 percent of the total Israeli vote and thus got only one Knesset seat; the DFPE won 4.5 percent and got four seats; and the ADP got less than 1.5 percent of the vote and one seat. Thus almost one-quarter of the votes cast for the three nationalist parties was wasted in terms of securing a larger total of Knesset seats.[15]

Fragmentation became an even more pervasive and pernicious phenomenon in subsequent years. In the 1996 elections, the most serious threat to Arab unity came from Ahmad Tibi, an Israeli Arab physician who served as an adviser to Yasser Arafat and as one of his major spokesmen in the Israeli media. Tibi's decision to run in the election also reflected badly on the ability of the Arab sector to create strong political parties. He was the third "personality" to form a one-man party, the Arab Movement for Change (AMC), in the space of twelve years. Even worse, he decided to run in the election after Mi'ari's PLP had already accepted defeat. (In the 1992 general elections, the PLP had even failed to pass the minimum threshold of 1.5 percent of the total Israeli vote required to gain any representation in the Knesset.) Nor did the ADP's chances seem much brighter in 1996. Tibi's campaign, it was feared, would destroy the ADP's chances of passing the 1.5 percent threshold, and without any assurance that Tibi's bid would be any more successful. All attempts by prominent intermediaries in the Higher Follow-Up Committee for Arab Affairs—the countrywide leadership composed of all Arab Knesset members and the mayors of the major Arab towns—to bring Tibi and Darawsha together failed completely.[16] The ADP was also being hurt by the religious rightists. 'Atif Al-Khatib, a former member of the Islamic Movement who had fallen out with Kemal Khatib, the head of the local Islamic Movement, formed the Arab Islamic Bloc in January 1996. To make matters worse, Khatib received the endorsement of Abdullah Nimr Darwish, who headed the moderate wing within the Islamic Movement.[17] The ADP had enjoyed Darwish's tacit support in the past and thus could now expect to lose votes. The Left, as already noted, was even more fragmented. Members of Abna al-Balad and former members of the PLP both officially ran in the elections.[18]

Darwish's decision to contest in the elections changed the dynamics on the Right dramatically. Darawsha knew from previous elections that Darwish's support was indispensable, and especially in the 1996 election campaign, when he faced Tibi, the other bidder for an alliance with Darwish.[19] To secure his alliance with Darwish, Darawsha was ready to make an unprecedented move in Arab Palestinian politics: to resign the chairmanship of the newly formed UAL list of candidates and assume the second slot on the list.[20]

All previous attempts to bring Darawsha and Mi'ari together in past elections, and Darawsha and Tibi together in the 1996 election campaign, had floundered on Darawsha's insistence on keeping the chairmanship of the UAL.[21] Now Darawsha yielded to two people: to 'Abd al-Malik Dahamsha, a political novice, a member of no great standing in the Islamic Movement, a lawyer, and a former prisoner convicted of membership in Fatah in 1971 before becoming devout, and to Taleeb al-Sanaa, an incumbent Knesset member, a lawyer, and a member of a prominent Bedouin tribe in the northern Negev. Al-Sanaa was crucial to Darawsha for his ability to draw votes among the Bedouin.[22] The ADP had secured 35.1 percent of the vote of the Bedouins in the 1992 elections, more than double the percentage of votes the party had drawn from the Arab sector as a whole. By 1996, the ADP's share of the Bedouin vote jumped to 64.3 percent, indicating that the alliance with the Islamic Movement also attracted votes. The recent spread of fundamentalist sentiment among the Bedouins had been observed in Jordan, Kuwait, and Bahrain as well.

But there was also a price to forming an electoral coalition with the Islamic Movement. Darwish's endorsement of the newly formed UAL caused a rupture within the Islamic Movement, particularly between Darwish and his adherents, and Ra'id Salah and Sheikh Kemal al-Khatib of the Arab town of Kafr Kanna, who formed the Northern Islamic Movement. Salah is the mayor of

Umm al-Fahum, the largest wholly Muslim town in Israel, situated on the former Green Line that separated Israel from the West Bank.[23] The ten Arab Fragmentation peaked in 2001, following the split in the UAL. The ten Arab members of the Knesset at the time belonged to no fewer than eight parties and lists of candidates represented in the Knesset. Arithmetically, this split works out to a fragmentation rate ten times higher than that found among the Jewish parties. Even in 2003, when only four Arab candidate lists vied in the elections, and two parties, the DFPE and the AMC, succeeded in reaching a surplus vote agreement, no party secured more than 24 percent of the Arab vote. In short, the dream of a united Arab party remained as improbable in 2003 as when it had first been voiced in the late 1970s.

Fragmentation raises one of the weightiest questions regarding the study of Arab politics in general, namely, whether politics in the Arab world can ever transcend the politics of personality (one-man political parties) and create in its stead parties based on aggregated interests.

The answer is yes, at least in Israel, as the last two elections proved. The DFPE and Balad had already developed an ideologically oriented constituency in the 2003 elections. They have coherent ideologies, a consistent platform, more-or-less permanent press organs, and a following that transcends subgroups based on religious identity or very narrow geographic confines.

Ideological and institutional consolidation became even more marked in the 2006 elections, as the UAL, allying itself with Tibi's AMC, secured four Knesset seats, thus recovering from the blows of the previous elections, in which it had secured only two seats. Despite low, though hardly exceptionally low, Arab voting participation in the national elections, the three Arab political parties passed the newly raised 2 percent voting threshold and succeeded in placing ten members in the Knesset. The UAL-AMC showed the strongest performance by drawing 94,786 of the Arab votes; the DFPE won 86,092 of the votes to secure three seats; and Balad, 72,066 votes and three seats, securing the third seat in a surplus-vote agreement with the DFPE.[24] Ironically, just as Arab politics was consolidating into three distinctive parties, the Israeli Jewish political arena began showing signs of increased fragmentation, as Ariel Sharon split the Likud Party to form the Kadima Party.

With Sheikh Ibrahim Sarsur at the UAL-AMC helm and another sheikh, Abbas Zakur, fourth on the candidate list, the UAL-AMC clearly presented a religious-traditional alternative to the more secular and socially oriented DFPE and the nationalist Balad. Sarsur is the leader of the Islamic Movement (southern branch) that in 1996 had decided to contest in the Knesset elections, a decision that had led to the historic split within the Islamic Movement. Sarsur won the internal UAL party primary against the incumbent leader, 'Abd al-Malik Dahamsha, in a contest over the leadership of the party—a rare event in

Arab institutions, where leadership is often viewed as a lifelong position. This contest was one more indication that the party had come of age.[25]

Nevertheless, the geographic and social distribution of the party's leadership was certainly an advantage. Al-Sanaa continued to draw most of the southern Bedouin vote, while Sarsur, who was from Kafr Kanna in Israel's Arab Triangle along the Green Line, succeeded in doing much the same in the concentration of the Arab population in the middle of the country. The party remains weak in the Galilee, where the more secular Arab parties do better. Even in Nazareth, where tensions mounted in the late 1990s over the construction of a mosque near the Church of the Basilica (see the next section), the party's performance was weak. In 1999, it secured only 23.2 percent of the Arab vote, compared to 43.8 percent for the DFPE and 21 percent for Balad.[26]

The UAL's success in 2006 raises the question whether it was linked in any way to the striking electoral gains of other Islamist parties in the region, most notably in the Palestinian Authority, where Hamas won 45 percent of the votes and 65 percent of the seats in the Palestine Legislative Council Elections of January 2006, which took place six weeks before the Israeli general elections, and in Egypt as well, where the Muslim Brotherhood sharply increased its number of seats in the parliament.

Analyzing survey data over time is one way to explore linkages. Indeed, in a poll of Arabs of voting age in November 2005, only 7.4 percent of those polled chose the UAL, a percentage that, through extrapolation, suggests that the candidate list would have won fewer than thirty thousand votes, insufficient to secure any Knesset seats, and one-third the number of votes actually cast for the party on election day.[27] By contrast, in two polls conducted at the end of February 2006, one month after the Hamas victory, the UAL was expected to take three seats, though in neither of the February polls did the UAL emerge as the party with the most support.[28]

Confessionalism, Nationalism, and Fundamentalism

Even more than the Jewish political sector, the Arab sector is haunted by the specter of political mobilization on the national level based on divisions among the three religious sects—Muslims, Druze, and Christians—that comprise the Arab sector. Most Arabs are particularly concerned about political developments that would pit the Israeli Arab Christian minority against the Islamic majority among the Israeli Arabs.

Two major developments have promoted tensions within the Israeli Arab sector: the civil war in Lebanon (particularly the internecine war between the

Druze and the Maronites, both of which are minorities within the Arab population in Israel) and the growing salience of Islamic fundamentalism (particularly the controversy that emerged in 1997 surrounding the Shihab al-Din burial site near the Church of the Basilica in Nazareth). The latter was by far the more important crisis in terms of the imprint it had on local Arab politics.

The controversy broke out when members of the Islamic Association and nonaffiliated Muslims demanded that the DFPE-dominated municipality of Nazareth acknowledge that six thousand square feet of land surrounding a small building reputedly containing the grave of Sheikh Shihab al-Din, the nephew of the legendary Salah al-Din, were Islamic communal property.[29] Nazareth, it should be noted, in addition to being one of the towns most identified with Christianity, also serves as the intellectual and political center of Arab life and is a reflection of the Arab sector's inherent heterogeneity. The DFPE-dominated municipality of Nazareth, headed by Ramiz Jeraisi, who happens to be Christian, had authorized—with the consent of the municipality's council, including representatives of the United Nazareth List, the local candidate list affiliated with the UAL—the use of land around the Church of the Basilica building to extend the square in front of the church in preparation for the millennium commemoration in the year 2000.

This authorization was challenged by Muslim citizens, some of whom were prominent activists in the Islamic Movement, on the grounds that the burial site and the building were an Islamic endowment. They argued that, instead of a church square, a mosque should be built to serve Nazareth's rapidly growing Muslim population. The mosque would change the wholly Christian character of the town center. The Islamists, using a means of protest that Palestinians commonly use against land expropriation by the state, set up a protest tent site on the property.

Just how rapid and how volatile the dispute became is shown in part by the results of the November 1998 municipal election, in which the local UAL-affiliated candidates won ten seats, whereas nine seats were secured by the competing DFPE-led list.[30] The controversy degenerated into violence between Muslim and Christian youth during the annual Christmas procession, and the violence continued for several days and once again broke out on Easter Day in April 1999. By that time, the Israeli government's adviser on Arab affairs and, increasingly, the Vatican were heavily involved in trying to settle the dispute. Even more insistent on trying to resolve the dispute were Yasser Arafat and the Palestinian Authority (PA). Arafat and the PA were busy organizing "Project 2000," which was centered on Bethlehem but included Nazareth as well. Arafat interceded personally to achieve a compromise and also sent Minister 'Imad Faluji, a former member of Hamas, to try to persuade the UAL to build a smaller mosque and earmark some of the property for enlarging the square, but to no avail.

On July 1, 2003, the Israeli authorities, operating in the darkness of the early morning, and supported by thousands of police mobilized for the occasion, demolished what had been transformed from a protest tent into a semipermanent structure. This happened soon after the district court had upheld a local court ruling, reached four months previously, authorizing the tent's destruction.[31] In the course of demolishing the structure, police arrested six municipal council members of the United Nazareth List, including Vice Mayor Salan Abu Ahmad. The authorities, and no doubt many Arabs, too, breathed a sigh of relief when Nazarenes ignored strike calls and a massive turnout for a protest prayer.[32]

The rise of political fundamentalism has also created a religious-secular divide. The success of the Islamic Movement in the 1988 municipal elections, particularly in the poorer Muslim neighborhoods of Nazareth, once a predominantly Christian city (and the unofficial capital of Israeli Arabs), awakened fears that the rise of Islamic fundamentalism would set off a reaction that would transform ideological parties into essentially religiously based organizations, as had happened in Lebanon. On the national level, such a transformation would have meant that the DFPE and Balad would increasingly reflect Christian and secular interests, while the UAL reflected Islamist leanings.

Anxious to avert these dangers, the DFPE, the PLP, and later Balad bent over backward to demonstrate their commitment to ideologies—a social universalism, on the one hand, and a nondenominational Palestinian and Arab nationalism, on the other—that transcended these divisions. The three parties not only strenuously refused to admit that ethnicity had anything to do with their choice of candidates but even refrained from accusing their opponents in the non-Zionist camp of using ethnic criteria in a campaign that respected no other ground rules.

Clearly these parties did take religious considerations into account, but they did so to weaken the link between religious affiliation and party identification rather than to enhance it. For the DFPE this stance meant increasing the number of Muslims on its candidate list; in the PLP it meant increasing the prominence of Christians. In 1992, the DFPE, having abandoned the age-old ruling of giving equal representation to Jews and Arabs, was able to place Tawfik Ziyad, the venerable mayor and incumbent member of the Knesset, in first place on its candidate list, followed by Hashim Mahamid, the former mayor of Umm al-Fahum, in second, with a Christian from 'Ablin, a Christian village in the Galilee, only in the fourth place.[33] In the PLP, a Christian was placed second. The ADP, which was courting the Islamic vote, made use of verses from the Quran in its campaign, and counted as the fifth man on its list a known Islamic Movement supporter—placed a Christian in fourth place.[34] Even the Islamic Movement was at pains to deny political sectarianism. Throughout the campaign, the movement pressed for the emergence of a unified Arab front, excluding the DFPE only on the grounds that it considered itself a Jewish-Arab party.[35]

However, ensuring "appropriate" religious representation also relates to the importance of ensuring representation for each of the religious communities comprising the Arab sector. Concealing the salience of Islam no longer became possible in the 1996 general elections, when for the first time the moderate wing of the Islamic Movement united with the ADP to form the UAL. The UAL has combined explicitly Islamist rhetoric with nationalism in its election campaigns ever since.

In retrospect, were the fears of looming religious polarization in the Arab sector justified?

A look at both exclusively Christian and exclusively Muslim, as well as mixed Christian-Muslim, localities in the 1999 elections, when the Nazareth controversy was at its height, allows one to gauge its impact on the sectarian issue. Because of the Shihab al-Din controversy, it would probably be best to focus on Nazareth, Israel's unofficial Arab capital. With 43.6 percent of the Nazarenes voting for the DFPE, over twice the average of the total Arab political sector, Nazareth remained a traditional stronghold of the DFPE. By contrast, in Nazareth Balad received less than its sectorwide share of the vote (13.3 percent compared to 16.8 percent). The UAL did just slightly better in Nazareth than in the national average (33.3 percent compared to 31.3 percent). These three parties captured 90.2 percent of the city's votes. It is generally assumed that Nazareth is currently 60 percent Muslim. Even assuming that all those who voted for the UAL were Muslims, over one-fourth of Muslim Nazarene voters would have had to vote for either the DFPE or the UAL.

Further confirmation of this reality was found in voting patterns in Umm al-Fahum, an exclusively Muslim town. Both the DFPE and Balad did better there than in the sectorwide average. Balad's strong performance may be partially due to its use of Islamic symbols during its campaign.[36] It is evident, however, that the major explanation lie in the secular nature of these parties.

Though the Arab population refrains from casting votes based exclusively on religion, religion is nevertheless important. Its importance is not so much sectarian as it is a reflection of an increasingly salient divide between the secular and the religious. An analysis of the distribution of votes for the major non-Jewish parties in the 1999 and 2003 elections, in eight villages that are populated exclusively by Christians,[37] suggests that Christians tended to favor the secular parties over the UAL (see table). In any event, the wide variation in

Voting Patterns in Exclusively Christian Localities in the 1999 and 2003 Elections (Percentages)

	1999			2003		
	UAL	**DFPE**	**Balad**	**UAL**	**DFPE**	**Balad**
Locality						
Gush Halav	11.6	43.1	12.9	12.9	50.4	6.5
Kfar Yasif	34.9	30.7	15.6	43.1	40.0	6.0
Ma'iliya	8.6	51.5	—	13.0	55.5	0.4
'Libun	41.9	20.6	10.1	37.0	35.1	4.8
Fasuta	17.3	45.2	.2	11.7	45.6	3.3
Rama	25.9	24.3	7.0	23.5	29.9	7.4
Maalot	19.4	37.4	13.2	20.5	32.3	16.5
'Iblin	26.8	35.8	13.8	33.1	29.9	6.1

Source: www.elections-yedioth.co.il.

voting patterns even in so small a subgroup cautions one against making too sweeping a generalization.

Changes in the party platforms of the secular parties provide further evidence of a growing secular-religious divide. In its 2003 election party platform, the DFPE emphasized its secular character by for the first time supporting "a democratic constitution that would defend basic human citizens' rights, social rights, and the secular nature of the state and the equality of its citizens" and, in another clause, "the separation of religion and state, the abolishment of laws of religious coercion, struggle against all forms of confessional zealotry; the institutionalization of civil marriage and divorce."[38] In taking such a brazen stand, the party was obviously hoping to secure the secular vote. Of all the states in the Middle East, only Turkey has so far placed personal law matters, such as marriage and divorce, under the exclusive jurisdiction of civil law. The change in the party platform reflected the struggle that had taken place over a Meretz-initiated Knesset law, passed in 2001, that extended the jurisdiction of the civil courts over personal law, at the expense of the religious courts. The DFPE had sided with Israel's secular parties, while the UAL representatives had sided with the Jewish religious parties in an attempt to maintain the status quo.

A similarly brazen move took place in the election campaign when the DFPE's television promotions repeatedly showed scenes of intermingling of the sexes in schools, universities, and places of work. In one commercial, young Arab men even drank beer, a clear prohibition in Islamic law. The UAL threatened to take this case to the Central Elections Committee, on the grounds that it offended the sensibilities of a large and recognized religion and therefore should be considered a form of racial incitement.[39] The DFPE, in turn, condemned the UAL for its decision to place Salam Abu Ahmad, the head of the United Nazareth List backed by the (southern) Islamic Movement, in the third slot on its candidate list.[40] The DFPE perceived Ahmad not only as the major opposition figure to Nazareth's DFPE-dominated municipal council but as a radical in the Shihab al-Din mosque controversy, which had increased tensions between Christians and Muslims in the city.[41]

We are left with an enigma. Why, in the 2003 general elections, the first elections since the violence of 2000, did neither religiosity nor secularism generate political dividends, after a presumed assault on the al-Aqsa mosque had generated riots unprecedented in the history of the state? A simple answer would be that al-Aqsa is a nationalist landmark representing a balance of power between two rival national communities and the political institutions representing them, a balance of power that the Palestinians felt must not be upset. Such an answer would not explain why other significant events did not elicit any violent response, for example, the attack on and partial reoccupation of West Bank towns (including the assault on Arafat's residence) beginning in late March and culminating in late June 2002.

Once again, it is clear that sectarian voting patterns of the type witnessed in Lebanon do not prevail among Israel's Arab citizens. It is equally clear, however, that Muslims tend to vote in a far higher proportion for the UAL than Christians, who highly favor the "secular" parties, which place Christians in secure slots on their candidate lists.

The Arab Parties and the Israeli Electorate

Arab parties form a small bloc in the Knesset and represent a minority of the electorate, as significant as that minority is. There is no doubt that the Israeli establishment has become more liberal over time. Lists of radical Arab candidates had been disqualified from elections in the distant past, but this disqualification was consistently overruled by a more activist Israeli Supreme Court in the 1980s and 1990s. However, the statements and actions of Arab party leaders in the past decade have severely tested these liberal tendencies.

Remarks and actions taken by Arab leaders after Israel's withdrawal from Lebanon in 2000 were bound to antagonize the majority of Jewish Knesset members and their constituencies. For example, Knesset member Azmi Bishara, in "the victory celebration and the celebration of the resistance" (*ma-*

harajan al-nasr wa-mahrajan al-muqawanna) that his party held on June 5, linked the withdrawal with Israel's victory on the same day in 1967: "This is the first fifth of June that has transcended the low morale that 1967 left in its wake. For the first time we can feel a ray of hope concerning the Arab situation. We now have a small sample. After all Lebanon is the weakest Arab state. We can draw a lesson from it, but the most important lesson is the desire for victory."[42]

Darawsha, the head of the ADP, which had been established in 1987, soon after the outbreak of the First Intifada, threatened that the ADP would dissolve its coalition with the Islamic Movement if the latter's representatives, 'Abd al-Malik Dahamsha and Tawfiq al-Khatib, agreed to attend the special session of the Knesset in Kiryat Shmona near the Lebanese border, which had come under repeated rocket attacks by Hizbollah. The Knesset had decided to hold the special session in the city of Kiryat Shmona near the Lebanese border to express solidarity and calm the apprehensions of upper Galilee residents concerning future Hizbollah moves along the northern border with Lebanon after the withdrawal.[43] Darawsha's threat worked. Several days later the UAL announced that its representatives would not attend the special session.[44] Meanwhile, al-Sana, the Knesset member from the UAL, proposed that Hassan Nasrallah, the secretary-general of Hizbollah, be nominated for the Nobel Peace Prize.[45]

These remarks and positions were soon placed in the context of the Palestinian insurgency, as Israeli analysts debated whether the Palestinians in the territories were following a Lebanese strategy.[46] And rather than trying to calm the situation after the outbreak of the intifada, at least one Knesset member, Azmi Bishara, stoked the fires. In July 2001 he praised Hizbollah in a rally in Umm al-Fahum, and then, on a trip to the burial site of Syrian leader Hafiz al-Asad in Kardaha in Syria in the summer of 2001, urged Arab political forces to engage in resistance against Israel. By that time, Hamas—and Islamic Jihad—initiated homicide bombings were taking a tragic toll of Israeli civilian lives deep within Israel almost weekly.

To reign in Arab members, the Knesset, for the first time in its history, voted on November 7, 2001, to remove Azmi Bishara's immunity as a Knesset member. Voting took place over two issues. The first concerned allegations that Bishara had transgressed the Prevention of Terrorism Ordinance by advocating Arab resistance. The second concerned visits by Arab citizens of Israel to Syria. Sixty-one members of the Knesset voted to lift Bishara's immunity regarding the first charge of supporting terrorist organizations; thirty voted against, and two abstained. Regarding Bishara's organization of nineteen illegal visits to Israel's enemies, sixty-five voted in favor of lifting his immunity, twenty-four voted against, and two abstained. Minister without Portfolio Dan

Meridor was one of the abstainers. He explained that he had doubts whether praising Hizbollah incited people to violence. Shas had initiated the Knesset's move against Bishara, a fact that Bishara noted and derided: "Are these the great democrats that want to declare me beyond the law? Is this the democracy you want in the Knesset? There is no democracy here. Don't kid yourself."[47] At the start of the trial, in which he faced charges of encouraging violence and voicing support for a terrorist organization, Bishara claimed he had merely organized family reunions for elderly Israeli Arabs, separated from their families since Israel's creation in 1948. He argued he should be supported for engaging in a humanitarian act rather than be condemned. His statement was an opening salvo in a publicity campaign that created parallels between Bishara's trial and the infamous Dreyfus trial held in nineteenth-century France. A poster portraying Bishara, with the caption "J'accuse," was distributed by his party, and Adalah, a legal rights organization, mobilized to defend him. A political motif—namely an attack on the ethnonationalist basis of the state—quickly became the motto of those trying to defend Bishara.[48]

The campaign to reign in Arab politicians and movements took a second legislative turn. In May 2002, the Knesset passed an amendment to the law governing the immunity of members of the Knesset, an amendment stating that parliamentary immunity did not include "any statement of opinion or actions made that included the rejection of Israel as the state of the Jewish people, support for armed struggle by an enemy state or an act of terror against Jews or Arabs because they were Jews or Arabs."[49]

A second law against incitement to violence or terror imposed a five-year sentence not only on those calling for the commitment of an act of violence but even on those who praised acts of violence, provided, however, only that "there is a real possibility that it will bring about the commitment of an act of violence or terrorism."[50] Though the law sounded draconian, the proviso gave ample discretion to the Supreme Court, which will most probably significantly dilute the law's substance when cases are brought before it.

A third law, limiting participation in the elections, added supporting armed conflict of a terrorist organization or an enemy state as grounds to prevent a party from running in the elections.[51] Once again, any decision of the Central Elections Committee (CEC) based on this law would have to come under court scrutiny, which is likely to cancel out the law's effects entirely. However, in March 2002, a law extending the emergency regulations had stipulated that the prohibition against visiting an enemy state such as Syria extended to bearers of diplomatic passports, including, of course, members of the Knesset.[52]

Israel's parliamentary elections offered additional opportunities to constrain the behavior of Israel's Arab politicians. Whereas the procedural and legislative rules were designed to restrain the incumbents, efforts were made to prevent Arab politicians and parties from attaining office in the first place. Two months before the 2003 elections, Israel's right-wing parties moved to ban the participation of two Arab parties, Balad and the UAL, and three members of Knesset specifically, Azmi Bishara, Abd al-Malik Dahamsha, and Ahmad Tibi. Israel's right-wing parties claimed that these parties and Knesset members did not accept the democratic character of the Jewish state, a position that directly contravened Israel's electoral law.

Worse still from the viewpoint of the Arab electorate, the attorney general, Elyakim Rubinstein, had backed the right-wing position on Balad, Bishara, and Tibi, though he disagreed on Dahamsha, the leader of the UAL. The Right had its way in the Central Elections Committee vote on Balad, Bishara, and Tibi, but not on Dahamsha. In early January 2003, a mere three weeks before the elections took place, Israel's Supreme Court overturned all the decisions of the CEC and allowed the Arab parties to compete in the elections.[53] There is no doubt that the campaign to debar the UAL and Balad was a boon to Balad, the party that was attacked most. Polls conducted in November 2002, before the CEC moved to deny Balad the chance to contest in the elections, indicated that the party would lose relative to the other two non-Zionist parties. Polling survey data also suggest that, had the Supreme Court not fulfilled its watchdog role and invalidated the CEC decisions, Arab boycotting of the elections would have been far more widespread.

Questioning the loyalty of Israel's Arab elite reached new heights in April 2007, when Azmi Bishara refused to return to Israel to face charges of serious security violations (assistance to Hizbollah in time of war, the passing of information to an enemy, and contacts with a foreign agent) during the Second Lebanon War in the summer of 2006. Instead, he announced his resignation from the Knesset from the Israeli embassy in Cairo, becoming, in effect, a fugitive of justice.[54]

Conclusion

Paradoxically, political dynamics since the massive outbreak of violence in September 2000 show that although Israeli Palestinian elites may be suggesting changes in the structure and identity of the state to allow Arab cultural autonomy, the majority of Israel's Arab citizens are still working within the system. They seem to recognize both the economic and the democratic benefits of citizenship in the Jewish state, despite recent legislation to constrain the Arab political elites, and despite the drafting of documents, most notably "The Future Vision of the Palestinian Arabs in Israel," drafted under the aegis of the Higher Follow-Up Committee for Arab Affairs, which expresses a desire to work toward a binational state.

Israel's Arab citizens are well aware of their economic dependence on the Jewish majority, both in the marketplace and by virtue of government economic transfers that probably exceed the tax receipts generated within the Arab sector itself. A move toward binationalism would increase economic gaps between Jews and Arabs. This is perhaps why most Arabs continued to vote in the general elections, and why Israel's former champion football team, whose home base is Sahnin, a large town known for its participation in the Land Day protests in 1976 and in the riots at the beginning of the hostilities in October 2000, plays in European football championships under the blue-and-white Israeli flag with the Star of David at its center. Arab realism casts doubts on the visionary documents that Arab intellectuals occasionally bring out but that are divorced from reality.

The Jewish majority, however, cannot discount the possibility that over the long term an ominous process of deconstructing the Jewish state is taking place. Israeli Jews can hardly claim that Arab parties or their leaders who say they want to radically change the nature of the state do not represent their constituency. After all, Israel's Arab citizens have almost unbounded freedom in choosing between boycott and abstention, voting for Arab parties with different ideological profiles, and voting for an array of Jewish parties. Their choices reflect their affinities, tastes, and interests.

Nevertheless, it is precisely when, as today, the Jewish majority feels more threatened that it must refrain from taking refuge in iron-fist policies and must realize that judicious policies leading to a more equitable allocation of resources, respect for Arab culture and identity, and the development of institutional modes to combat discrimination will attenuate (though hardly dissipate) tensions between the Jewish majority and the Arab minority for the mutual welfare of all of Israel's citizens.

Such forbearance in the face of regional Islamic fanaticism, terrorism, and state-led wars through proxies—the cost of which was borne, during the Second Lebanon War in 2006, by Israel's Arab citizens themselves—is no small challenge. However, avoiding the alternative, a binational state (like that whose violence under the British Mandate was bloody and violent), renders the effort more than worthwhile.

Notes

1. Central Bureau of Statistics, Preliminary Findings of the 12th Knesset Elections, 1988.

2. Sara Ozacky-Lazar, *Habhirot la-Knesset ha–13 Bekerev Haaravim be-Israel, Yuni 1992* [The 13th General Elections amongst the Arabs in Israel, June 1992] (Givat-Haviva, Israel: Ha-Machon Le-Limudim Araviim, 1992), p. 14.

3. See Azmi Bishara, "Al-Arabi al-Israili: Qira'a fi al-Khitab al-Siyasi al-Mabtur," *Majal-*

lat al-Dirasat al-Falastinyya, vol. 24 (Spring 1995), pp. 26–54.

4. See an interview with Bishara, *Ha'aretz* (April 23, 1996).

5. "Barnamij Hadash (Muqtatafat)," *Majallat al-Dirasat al-Falastiniyya,* vol. 27, no. 2 (Summer 1996), p. 93.

6. Ibid., p. 94.

7. On the concept of ethnorepublicanism, see Yoav Peled, "Strangers in Utopia: Ethnorepublican Citizenship and Israel's Arab Citizens," *American Political Science Review,* vol. 86, no. 2 (June 1992), pp. 432–443.

8. Knesset Election Results, www1.knesset .gov.il/asp/election/results.asp.

9. Yosef Algazi, "Mehuhadim Neged Netanyahu," *Ha'aretz* (May 29, 1999). The Peace Studies Center in Givat Haviva publicized a poll in the Arab sector, where the average expectation of the participation rate of eligible voters amongst those polled was 87.3 percent; see *Al-Quds* (May 3, 1999).

10. *Ha'aretz* (May 19, 1999). Since one of every four new eligible voters in these elections was Arab (24.6 percent to be exact), despite the huge influx of Russian immigrants in the past decade, the Arab effective participation in Israeli elections in the future is likely to increase significantly.

11. www.knesset.gov.il/elections01/ results.htm.

12. Ibid.

13. Yair Ettinger, "New DFPE member Chenin to Push for Social Legislation," *Ha'aretz* (December 1, 2002).

14. Dr. Rashid Salim, *Al-Sinnara* (November 11, 1988).

15. *Ha'aretz* (December 16, 1988).

16. Sara Ozacky-Lazar and As'ad Ghanem, *HaHaTzba'aa Ha'Aaravit Ba'Bhirot LaKnesset Ha–14, 29 May 1996* [The Arab Vote for the 14th Knesset, May 29, 1996], *Giv'aat Haviva, Skerot 'Al Ha'Aravim Beyisrael,* no. 19 (1996), p. 11.

17. *Sawt Al-Kutla* (January 1996).

18. Khalid A'id, "Al-Taswit al-Falastiniyyi Ahl–48 fi al-Intikhabat al-Israiliyya: Nata'ij wal-Dalalat" [The 1948 Palestinian Vote in the Israel Elections: Results and Meaning], *Majal-*

lat Al-Dirasat al-Falastiniyya, No. 27 (Summer 1996), p. 27.

19. Ozacky-Lazar and Ghanem, *HaHaTzba'aa Ha'Aaravit BaBhirot LaKnesset Ha–14,* p. 11.

20. *Al-Sinnara* (April 12, 1996).

21. *Kull Al-'Arab* (January 19, 1996); also see an interview with Tibi in *Kull Al-'Arab* (February 2, 1996).

22. *Al-Sinnara* (April 16, 1996).

23. Ozacky-Lazar and Ghanem, *HaHaTzba'aa Ha'Aaravit BaBhirot LaKnesset Ha–14,* p. 11.

24. http://www.knesset.gov.il/elections17/ eng/Results/main_results_eng.asp.

25. Scott Wilson, "Arab Israelis See Lesson in Hamas Victory," *Washington Post* (March 5, 2006).

26. http://www.knesset.gov.il/elections17/ eng/Results/main_results_eng.asp.

27. *Adcan,* no. 1 (February 1, 2006), p. 5.

28. *Adcan,* no. 2 (March 1, 2006), p. 3.

29. Dani Rabinowitz, "Nazerat Zequqa Le-Shalom" [Nazareth Needs Peace], *Ha'aretz* (July 13, 1999).

30. *Al-Ayyam* (November 12, 1998).

31. Elias Karam, *Kull al-Arab* (October 10, 2003).

32. David Ratner, July 3, 2003.

33. *Sawt al-Jabha* (a special election supplement of *Rakah*) (May 15, 1992).

34. *Ha'aretz* (May 12, 1992).

35. *Arabs in Israel,* vol. 2, no. 6 (August 1992), p. 14.

36. Latif Husri, "Shas shel HaMigzar HaAravi" [The Arab Sector's Shas], *Ha'aretz* (May 27, 1999).

37. They are Gush Halav, Kfar Yasif, Miliya, Ilbun, Fasuta, Rama, Tarshiha, and Iblin.

38. Section E: The Defense of Democratic Rights, Clauses 1 and 6, The DFPE Platform in the 16th General Elections, www.knesset .gov.il/elections16/heb/lists/plat_23htm.

39. *Kull al-Arab* (January 17, 2003).

40. *Kull al-Arab* (January 10, 2003).

41. *Al-Sinnara* (January 17, 2003).

42. *Kull al-Arab* (June 8, 2000).

43. Ibid.

44. *Kull al-Arab* (June 16, 2000).

45. *Kull al-Arab* (June 8, 2000).

46. For a more detailed discussion, see Hillel Frisch, "Debating Palestinian Strategy in the al-Aqsa Intifada," *Terror and Political Violence,* vol. 15, no. 2 (Summer 2003), pp. 1–20.

47. *Ha'aretz* (November 8, 2001).

48. Nimr Sultani and Arij Sabagh Khuri, "Muqawamat al-Haimana: Muhakamat Azmi al-Bishara," *Majallat al-Dirasat al-Filastiniyya* [The Factors behind Hegemony: The Trial of Azmi Bishara], no. 54 (Spring 2003), p. 63.

49. "The Law of Immunity of Members of Knesset: Their Rights and Obligations (1951)," Amendment No 29, July 23, 2002, *Reshumot 1860* (in Hebrew).

50. "The Law against Incitement to Violence or Terror in the Penal Law (1951)," Article 1(a), Note a(1); Article 144(d), Clauses 2 and 3; Amendment Tashav (3) (in Hebrew).

51. "The Law to Prevent Participation in the Elections Owing to Support of Armed Struggle against the State," Basic Law; The Knesset, Article 7(a), (3) (22.5.02) (in Hebrew).

52. "The Law for the Prevention of Infiltration (Offenses and Judgment); The Ordinance Regarding the Prolongation of the Emergency Regulations (Departure Abroad, 1948)," Article 5, Permission to Travel to Certain Countries (Amendment 2002) (in Hebrew).

53. *Ha'aretz* (January 9, 2003).

54. Shahar Ilan, "Police Forces Search Azmi Bishara's Knesset Office," *Ha'aretz* (May 1, 2007).

7

Israel's
Supreme Court

Pnina Lahav

WHEN ISRAEL WAS BORN, the kibbutz was its most recognized and admired symbol.[1] After the Six Day War, when Yitzhak Rabin first appeared on the international scene as the glorious strategist of a stunning military victory, Israel's Defense Forces replaced the kibbutz as emblematic of Israeli values. Today, Israel's Supreme Court, or High Court of Justice (hereafter the Court), has come to take center stage, at least for those interested in politics.[2] Until the 1980s, Israel's Court was barely known outside Israel's borders, and its jurisprudence was mostly ignored. Today it is a major player in a field of increasingly influential, globalized, judicial politics. One, but by no means the only, reason for this change is the composition of the Court. Chief Justices Meir Shamgar and Aharon Barak and justices such as Dalia Dorner, Mishael Cheshin, Eliyahu Matza, and Ayala Proccacia[3] have viewed the Court as an important guarantor of the rule of law and political and civil liberties and developed a jurisprudence that reflected these values. Take the issue of torture, a means to obtain information in the fight against terrorism, so much on the minds of Americans today. Chief Justice Aharon Barak's opinion, outlawing torture, has become a focal point of American and international discourse on the subject.[4] Anyone wishing to take a stand on the subject has to address Barak's arguments in that opinion. Chief Justice Barak is the only foreign jurist ever invited by the *Harvard Law Review* to author its prestigious Foreword, an achievement that is the dream of any constitutional law professor in the United States.[5] Barak, recently retired, has shaped Israel's Court as a beacon of Israeli moral values, a major institution whose jurisprudence should be reckoned with. As this chapter goes to press, Barak is showered with recognition and honors abroad. He is also rigorously criticized at home for the changes in the court's role in Israeli society, connected with his tenure as a justice and president of the Court (1979–2006). Furthermore, something reminiscent of the 1937 Roosevelt U.S. Supreme Court packing plan has been under way in Jerusalem, and it may well be that before long the Court that Barak left in September 2006 will be considerably diminished in power and prestige.[6] This chapter primarily addresses the Court's legacy as we have known it so far. It only briefly discusses the impending changes, in its conclusion.

Four contrasting pairs will facilitate an understanding of the changing role of the Court in Israeli society: judicial activism versus judicial restraint; Israel as a democracy versus Israel as a Jewish state; unilateralism versus multilateralism in the context of the Arab-Israeli conflict; and catastrophe Zionism versus utopian Zionism.

Judicial Activism versus Restraint

By activism I mean a practice that embraces the notion of law as reflective of culture and society, as well as of law as a tool in social engineering. An activist court thrusts itself into the political arena, using its decisions as a lever to influence the direction of policy.[7] Since the 1980s the Court has shifted from a restrained demeanor and has embarked on a more activist path.[8] The litigation that challenged the legality of torture illustrates this development. May the security services use torture to obtain valuable information from detainees? It is safe to assume that a court exercising judicial restraint will decline to take a stand, leaving the question to the political branches.[9] Indeed, in the early 1990s the Court rejected a petition alleging that the security services were torturing detainees.[10] A court willing to exercise judicial activism will become involved, discuss the permissibility of using torture under the law of the land, and decide whether torture is always permitted, always prohibited, or permitted in only rare circumstances that meet certain criteria specified by law. In September 1999, Israel's Supreme Court held that in the absence of an explicit statutory authorization (an enactment of the Knesset), the executive branch could not deploy torture, euphemistically called *intensive interrogation,* as a method of interrogation.[11]

Why did the Court decline intervention in the first case and agree to adjudicate the second? One reason is the continuous criticism voiced by the international community. Another reason has been changes in Israeli society itself. Civic society in Israel has been growing. Many Israelis found it hard to accept practices that violate the core values of Israel. They joined the global movement of establishing NGOs (nongovernmental organizations) and agitated in public in favor of more ethical behavior on the part of the Israeli executive branch. Responding to (and perhaps empathizing with) these changes, the Court expanded the right of standing: Until the 1980s an individual had to show a personal stake in his or her petition. Now the requirement is much less strict. This fundamental overhaul of the right of standing allowed the Court to step into controversies that were at once legal and political. In the case of torture, it may well be that the relentless public protest of the Committee against Torture, an NGO, has paid off.[12]

Another example of activism also related to the expansion of the right of standing was fueled by the concern about legality in governance. Until the late 1980s the Court refrained from intervening in matters of governance, even in the face of severe breaches of public ethics. Since then the Court has intervened in a number of cases, thereby signaling its willingness to maintain a level of accountability and propriety in governmental processes. In 1993, an indictment had been brought against Arye Deri, leader of the Shas Party and an influential cabinet minister, alleging that he had taken bribes and used his office to benefit his self-interest. Prime Minister Rabin, navigating the Oslo Accords in very turbulent political waters, and in need of Shas Party support, decided that he would not ask Deri to leave his office as a cabinet minister unless the Knesset removed Deri's parliamentary immunity. Rabin's decision was challenged, and the Court held that an indicted person could not serve in a public office. The Court ordered the prime minister to terminate Deri as a cabinet minister until the resolution of his criminal proceedings (Deri was eventually convicted).[13] Similarly, the Court invalidated a decision by the Rabin government to appoint a former General Security Services (SGG) officer, Yossi Ginossar, as director general of the ministry of housing. Ginossar was involved in the cover-up following the Bus 300 affair (in which two terrorists who hijacked a bus were murdered in cold blood by the SGG). He was pardoned before an indictment had been issued. The Court held that, given the nature of these offenses, Ginossar could not be appointed to a position that required public trust and confidence.[14]

These are only a few examples of a very well-documented judicial involvement. Of course, they do not all necessarily raise similar questions concerning judicial review.[15] The first example (the legality of torture) focuses on the judicial protection of human rights. The last two raise the question of the independence of the executive branch in reaching its own decisions, on the one hand, and the integrity and ethics of government, on the other hand.[16] Persons who hailed the Court's torture opinion did not necessarily support its aggressive position in matters of ethics in governance. By way of summarizing a very complex field of scholarship, and at the risk of overgeneralizing, one may divide the Israeli reaction to the Court's performance into three camps.

Some supported the Court's defense of human rights and personal dignity. Members of this camp did not necessarily approve of the entire jurisprudence of the Court but, by and large, approved of the Court's agenda of enhancing the profile of Israel as a democratic and "Western" state. Others were loyalists of the principle of judicial restraint and criticized the Court for failing to adhere to Alexander Bickel's jurisprudence of judicial modesty.[17] A third camp, of assorted strange bedfellows, has been more eclectic, taking (not always self-consciously) an instrumental approach to judicial review.[18]

The rise of judicial activism may be attributed to a number of factors. Many of the judges who have served on the Court since the 1950s, including Chief Justice Meir Shamgar and later Chief Justice Aharon Barak, were responsible for its ascent because of their understanding that law does not exist in a vacuum but reflects the nation's fundamental vision.[19] The sociological and political changes experienced by Israel after the rise of the Likud Party to power and the signing of the peace treaty with Egypt contributed to the higher profile assumed by the Court.[20]

In 1992, the Knesset passed two Basic Laws known as Basic Law: Freedom of Occupation and Basic Law: Human Dignity and Freedom. These statutes were designed to join a series of previously enacted Basic Laws, which together would form a constitution for Israel.[21] Section One of Basic Law: Human Dignity and Freedom declared Israel's commitment to the principles of "human dignity and freedom," and Section Eight provided that "there shall be no violation of rights under this Basic Law except by a law befitting the values of the State of Israel, enacted for a proper purpose, and to an extent no greater than is required."[22]

It should be emphasized that Basic Law: Human Dignity and Freedom was not a constitution in the strict sense of the word. The convention in Israel law was that the Basic Laws were not different from ordinary laws. It was generally agreed that an actual constitution was a project for the future, not the present. The question of whether the Court would possess the power to invalidate statutes found to violate a Basic Law has been left open. Many believed that the Court was not authorized to exercise the power to review the constitutionality of statutes. Americans may reflect on this question in the context of the American doctrine of judicial review. The US Constitution does not explicitly provide for judicial review. *Marbury v. Madison,* the canonical case announcing the power of judicial review, based its "finding" on principles of constitutional theory and interpretation.[23]

Shortly after passage of the two Basic Laws of 1992, Chief Justice Barak declared the event a "constitutional revolution." In a famous speech, he celebrated the passage of these two statutes as heralding a new era in Israeli constitutional law. He opined that even though these Basic Laws did not explicitly provide for judicial review, they should be interpreted as endowing the Court with the power to review the conformity of statutes to their principles. Any other conclusion, Barak suggested, would render hollow the explicit normative commitment to human dignity and the normative command that any violation of the rights enshrined in the Basic Law must conform to the criteria stated in Section Eight.[24]

Soon thereafter, attorneys began to test Barak's theory.[25] Within three years the Court had endorsed Barak's position and held that these two Basic Laws indeed vested the judiciary with the power to review the validity of statutes. Mixing restraint with activism, the Court refused to declare the particular statute at hand invalid.[26]

Judicial activism should not be reduced to the power to invalidate statutes. It may take place even if the Court does not have such power. The practice of invalidation may be the jewel in the crown, but the activism of Israel's Court has taken the form of statutory interpretation and expansion of precedent.

A Democratic State, a Jewish State

The two 1992 Basic Laws, Human Dignity and Freedom and Freedom of Occupation, declared that "the purpose of this Basic Law is to protect human dignity and liberty, in order to establish in a Basic Law the values of the State of Israel as a Jewish and democratic state."[27] Why the need for the knot between democratic and Jewish? Historically, Israel's founders did not perceive a tension between the notions of *Jewish* and *democratic* and assumed the two to be inseparable. This is evident from Israel's Declaration of Independence, as well as from the fact that since its inception Israel has honored the principle of "one person, one vote" regardless of ethnic origin. Thus Israel's Palestinian Arabs were granted the right to vote even as they were placed under military rule.[28] Only after the 1967 War—with the intensification of the Jewish theme in Israeli politics as a result of the acquisition of the territories, the rise of the settlement movement intoxicated as it was by intense messianic dreams, and the concomitant rise of the Likud Party, which embraced and gave voice to the settler ideology—did discussion of the political tension between the "Jewish" and the "democratic" enter political discourse.[29] Curiously, one may trace the intensification of this dichotomy to American influence. Meir Kahana, an American rabbi who emigrated to Israel in the 1970s and established the Kach Party, agitated energetically for the idea that a Jewish state should strive to minimize the presence of other ethnic populations in its midst. Israel's raison d'être, he argued, was to enable Jews to live in the company of Jews and under Jewish law. The Jewish theme, according to this theory, should trump the democratic ideals of inclusion and egalitarianism.[30] Kahana's conception of

politics soon appeared before the Court, which found itself compelled to assess the nature of the Israeli polity.[31] Is it primarily Jewish, or primarily democratic, or should one strive to avoid conflict between the two? The question
has not been resolved, but the Knesset decided to incorporate both concepts
into the 1992 Basic Laws, refusing to indicate whether one may trump the
other.[32] The Court had to confront the question as a matter of statutory and
constitutional interpretation.

The meaning of "Israel as a Jewish state" is extremely complex. On one end
of the spectrum it refers to the Jewish right to national self-determination, a
collective right that coexists with the right of the individual Jew living in Israel
to freely pursue either a secular or a religious lifestyle and values. At the other
extreme, the national concept implies the significance of Judaism in Zionist
nationalism and anticipates the creation in Israel of a state that operates under Jewish law, perhaps not different from the Islamic republic now dominating in Iran. In between these polarities there are multiple mutations. The
complexity, I shall note in passing, is rooted in both sociological and historical
events. Sociologically, the majority of Jews in Israel have been secular and
committed to a secular state.[33] Historically, Zionist thought, from Theodore
Herzl to David Ben-Gurion and Ze'ev Jabotinsky, was predominantly secular
and, in parts, even hostile to Orthodox Jewish law and culture.[34] Some of the
original Zionist visceral reaction against Jewish Orthodoxy is still commonly
observable in Israel.

The Court has, by and large, avoided any of the radical versions of "the Jewish State," but it did appear to have sided with the principle of separation between state and church, and to prefer the secular law of the state over
conflicting halachic holdings. At the same time, the Court has also focused on
the concept of Judaism and has leaned toward the interpretation of Judaism
that embraces universal principles, rather than on the Judaism that is particularistic and preclusive. In so doing, the Court has expressed a willingness to
address and modify an agreement reached between Ben-Gurion and leading
Orthodox rabbis known as "the status quo." This agreement, dating back to
the emergence of Israel as a sovereign state, embedded a compromise between
the religious and secular leadership in such matters as the meaning of observ-
ing Saturday (Shabbat) as the official day of rest (Would public transportation be allowed? Will places of entertainment be open?), or as the law
applying to matters of personal status (Should civil marriage be allowed?
Should the Orthodox enjoy a monopoly over burials?). The Court has always
leaned toward the separation of church and state; however, it is fair to say that
its jurisprudence has become more intensified, perhaps more controversial,
since the 1990s. The reason has been the fact that the religious sector was
gaining more visibility and power in public affairs. In this area, the Court's

landmark cases have been true to the path it has taken since its inception and have been cautious and circumspect. For example, when a flat ban on the sale of pork products was challenged before the Court, it held that a balancing approach was required. The deeply rooted Jewish religious and cultural taboo on pork was to be balanced against the individual freedom of conscience and freedom of occupation. A municipality could not impose a flat ban if a minority within it (in this case, primarily Russian immigrants) was interested in buying and selling pork products; it should provide for some reasonable availability of these products to those who wished to sell them in their stores or to purchase them for consumption.[35]

One particularly divisive example of the secular-religious disagreement has been the administrative exemption from military service granted yeshiva students. Military service in Israel is a universal obligation. Among the secular public it is perceived as a symbol of one's commitment to the state and its Zionist values. However, under the "status quo" agreement, the minister of defense has granted exemptions from service to Orthodox men who spend their time studying in religious institutions (yeshivot). The religious establishment has been emphasizing the imperative of a strong connection between a Jewish state and the unhindered pursuit of Jewish learning. The Court of the 1960s and 1970s carefully avoided this explosive matter and declined to review the legality of the wholesale exemption. The Court of the 1980s, and particularly the Court of the 1990s, demanded that the Knesset address the issue and enact a more egalitarian arrangement.[36] It is important to observe that the Court trod carefully. On the one hand, it refrained from making a substantive decision, thereby exercising restraint. On the other hand, it insisted on the legislative clarification of the constitutional ramifications of the exemption, thereby putting pressure on a reluctant Knesset to address the issue. There was more than a grain of activism in such a stand. The matter has remained controversial and has not yet been resolved.

The religious public's resentment of the Court's willingness to reconsider the status quo was the glue that united the religious sector, from the ultra-Orthodox to the religious nationalists.[37] As indicated above, the 1990s saw not only the rise in judicial activism and a consciousness of rights but also the growing political power and sense of entitlement experienced by the religious sector.[38] The clash between the Court's agenda of more separation of church and state and the religious parties' agenda of exerting more religious influence in the public arena threatened to transform the verbal controversy into physical violence. Threats to the Chief Justice's life intensified, and on the heels of Rabin's assassination, Chief Justice Barak was assigned a bodyguard. The religious press was filled with hostile references to Barak as an evil tyrant and the archenemy of the Jews. In 1999, a demonstration of two hundred thousand persons was held to protest the Court's rulings.[39]

How did the Court justify its limitations on the religious sector's power to influence everyday life, and what explains the Court's willingness to reevaluate the status quo? The justifications were rooted in Israel's commitment to maintaining a democratic form of government. The Court understood democracy to require a measure of a separation between church and state, a commitment to equality, and a generous pinch of respect for individual autonomy. This understanding, particularly the growing recognition that equal protection of the laws is a crucial ingredient of a democratic order, became even more prominent after the passage of Basic Law: Human Dignity and Freedom. Ironically, equal protection was not explicitly mentioned in this Basic Law; it had to be read into the law, thereby intensifying the wrath of those alarmed by the rapid change of the legal landscape. To them Chief Justice Barak responded (and he was not alone) that Israel should strive to join the movement of the universal recognition of the significance of human rights, that it could not afford to maintain a particularism that justifies discrimination and thereby violates the grand promise of Zionism.[40]

The issue of equality takes us to the complex question of the status of the Israeli Arabs, those Palestinians who are citizens of Israel. Again, this question is a good illustration of the fundamental change in the Court's role. Israel's legal system has tolerated discriminatory practices against Israel's Arabs, practices that have not always been apparent to the undiscerning observer.[41] Until the 1990s the Court rebuffed invitations to step into the fray and address the issue. In 1995 an Arab-Israeli couple challenged the decision of a small Jewish-Israeli community in the Galilee to dismiss its application to join the community. The Court took its time, as it has been doing in most of the hard cases described here, but in the end it decided that, indeed, the practice of limiting the community only to Jews violated the fundamental values of Israel as a democratic state.[42]

This holding, while circumscribed in terms of the result (the community was asked to consider the application on its merits but was not ordered to accept the couple), was a watershed event in that it pierced the veil of official discriminatory practices and emphasized the right of Israeli Arabs to equal treatment under the law.[43] It should also be emphasized that the willingness to recognize official discrimination against Israeli Arabs followed on the heels of substantial gains made by women and by gays and lesbians.[44] To conclude, under the banner of Israel as a democratic state the Court advanced the rights of minorities in Israeli society and encouraged inclusion and equal treatment under the law in a way unprecedented in previous decades.

Unilateralism versus Multilateralism

The Court felt less inclined or able to protect the rights of Palestinians under occupation in the West Bank and the Gaza Strip. Let me explain why this matter should be understood within the context of the tension between unilateralism and multilateralism, terms familiar to any student of foreign affairs. By *unilateral* I mean Israeli policy that expects to resolve the Arab-Israeli conflict more-or-less on Israel's own terms; by *multilateralism* I mean a conflict resolution process that takes into account conventional principles of international law: negotiations with the enemy and the enlistment of major players in the international community as brokers and assistants in resolving disputes. Within Israel itself, unilateralism calls for centralizing the management of the conflict in the hands of the executive (particularly top military officers), whereas multilateralism would mean opening the channels to include more actors by reaching out to the Knesset (including the opposition) as well as to other important actors in the body politic, such as the judiciary, the scholarly community, and a panoply of NGOs.[45] The Court has served as an important agent in encouraging multilateralism and discouraging unilateralism. Here are three of the many available examples. The first is the question of the validity of torture as an interrogatory technique, a case already mentioned above. It may well be that torture became a practice in the Israeli security services after the Six Day War, when Israel suddenly found itself in control of a very large and unfriendly population. For almost a quarter of a century the Court refused to look into the practices of the General Security Services (GSS), insisting that these practices belonged exclusively within the jurisdiction of the political branches. In the 1990s, the Court agreed to consider the matter, probably emboldened by its own judicial activism, by Basic Law: Human Dignity and Freedom, and by the Oslo Accords, and quite possibly embarrassed by the repeated criticism of Israel by international human rights groups. Again, the Court took its time but finally held that torture, as well as aggressive methods of interrogation, was illegal.[46] The decision illustrates how Israel's Court, under the leadership of Chief Justice Aharon Barak, became a major player in the international community of human rights. The so-called torture decision was released in English, on the Court's Web site, simultaneously with its publication in Hebrew, a signal of the conscious awareness of all involved of its international significance and media value. Thus it became an important element in Israel's diplomacy and public relations.[47]

The second example of the role of the Court in curbing unilateralism and encouraging multilateralism was the decision concerning the legality of the fence separating Israel from the West Bank. One result of the intensifying

terrorist attacks on Israeli civilians inside the Green Line (Israel's borders before the 1967 War) was a decision to build a wall that would help prevent suicide bombers from entering Israeli cities and towns. A petition challenging
the barrier (note the multiple names describing the same phenomenon)[48] as
violating international law came before the Court in 2004. The Court held
that security considerations should be balanced against the rights of the inhabitants under humanitarian international law, and that the Court would
evaluate the military commander's decision to ascertain that the rights of the
Palestinian residents were indeed not being violated beyond what proportionality required.[49] In other words, and without entering into the technical
details, the Court held that it would subject the government's action in
building the barrier to the requirement that the fence may infringe on the
Palestinian inhabitants' rights only in proportion to the needs of enforcing
security, not more.[50]

It is important to understand the context of this decision. The Court was
considering the matter while the International Court of Justice was preparing
its Advisory Opinion on the Legal Consequences of the Construction of a
Wall in the Occupied Territory.[51] Some opine that the Court intended to as-
sure the international community that Israel could and would address the
issue of legality internally, thereby deflecting the need for international intervention in its actions.

The third example is one of Chief Justice Barak's last opinions, delivered in
December 2006, in the matter of the legality of targeted assassinations. The
opinion is studded with references to international law (thereby acknowledging its authority) and imposes strict limitations on the power of the government to resort to targeted killings. It has been argued that in imposing these
limitations the Court was attempting to reconfirm Israel's commitment to the
community of nations. Under the principle of complementarity, developed in
the 1990s, foreign and international tribunals will not try citizens of another
state for violations of international criminal law if that state applies these very
norms in its own courts. By acknowledging the authority of these international norms, both the torture opinion and the one related to targeted assassination (among others) also shelter Israeli officials from prosecution abroad.
Foreign jurisdiction may be avoided because Israel's courts themselves consider whether international norms have been violated.[52]

At the same time, it is worth emphasizing that at no time has the Court
agreed to consider the legality of the settlements themselves or the larger
question of the legality of the occupation. This matter has consistently been
left to the political process. However, in a good number of dicta the Court
opined that international humanitarian and customary laws apply to the territories because they are occupied. Thus, while the status of the settlements

themselves has never been directly addressed, the Court has indirectly conceded that to the extent the settlements do not fulfill a security purpose, they are illegal.[53] In doing so the Court has encouraged multilateralism by emphasizing that Israel abides by the consensus of the international community. It is important to appreciate the contingent nature of this discussion. The point of emphasizing multilateralism over unilateralism is not that the Court prefers norms of international law over domestic norms passed by the Knesset. Nor is the point that the Court coerces Israel to choose multilaterism when it prefers a unilateral approach. Rather, the Court situates Israel within the community of nations and under the umbrella of international law. In doing so, the Court subtly encourages Israelis to develop a worldview that accepts that umbrella as a part of the natural landscape. In other words, it is the integration of international norms into the deliberation that tilts the decision-making process in the direction of multilateralism and away from unilateralism.

Catastrophe versus Utopian Zionism

This pair sheds light on the previous three pairs of tensions. Utopian Zionism stands for the proposition that Israel aspires to behave as a model state, a light unto the nations. Its ideology holds that universal values, doing the right and just, should guide Israeli society and its government. Catastrophe Zionism sees Israel primarily as a safe haven from the various calamities Jews have experienced throughout history, and as a state under siege that cannot afford the luxury of lofty universal values. The pair does bear a resemblance to idealism and realism in the theory of foreign affairs. In Israel itself, persons influenced by utopian Zionism hold the worldview that peaceful Arab-Israeli coexistence and cooperation in the Middle East are possible and depend partially on the policies adopted by Israel's government. Those influenced by catastrophe Zionism hold the worldview that negotiations with the enemy are impossible as "there is no one to talk to," and that "the Arabs are the same Arabs and the sea is the same sea," meaning Arabs do and always will aim to annihilate the Jewish inhabitants of Israel. Both Utopian Zionism and catastrophe Zionism struggle for influence on the Court's jurisprudence. Judicial activism, in the context of Israel today, pulls toward a limited and restrained executive branch, thereby reining in the instinct to subordinate all means to the ultimate goal of survival. The emphasis on Israel as a democratic state likewise echoes utopian Zionism and operates to curb particularistic tendencies of "a nation unto itself."[54] A stark example of this deeply rooted tension is the opinion in the family-unifications case of 2006. As the number of terrorist attacks within Israel increased, some thought that a useful prophylactic measure would be to limit the right of Palestinians residing in the occupied territories to marry Israeli citizens and thereby obtain a permit to reside in Israel. An amendment to the citizenship law was passed and then was duly challenged before the Court. By a vote of six to five the Court sustained the amendment.[55]

Justice M. Cheshin spoke for the majority, whereas Chief Justice Barak dissented. In justifying his refusal to invalidate the law (as violating the right to experience family life embedded in the concept of human dignity), Justice Cheshin reported a fantasy. He wrote that he had dreamed he was visiting Sir Thomas More's Utopia, where he met the legendary jurist and asked him whether the laws of Utopia were similar to those of the state of Israel. Cheshin attributed to More the following answer: "At this time you are fighting for your lives, for the survival of the state, for the ability of the Jewish people to live as a community in its own state, like all nations. The laws of Utopia—in your current circumstances—are not for you." By implication, Cheshin was assuring his audience that he had gotten approval from More to refrain from implementing in the state of Israel the great universal values that were pronounced by the ancient prophets of Israel, and that have been seen as a Jewish legacy. Wars, pogroms, and the imperative of survival have made them irrelevant. Barak and his fellow dissenters held that the amendment was overbroad and that ad hoc proceedings would suffice to eliminate those who might use a fictitious marriage to earn a residency permit and engage in acts of terrorism. This disagreement reflected the age-old arguments among the founders of Zionism, between those who sought a safe haven and fortress for persecuted Jews and those who wanted a Jewish state based on justice and human rights.

The Court in Comparative and Historical Perspective

Before a brief discussion of some of the reasons for the shift in the Court's role since the 1980s, let me address the interesting form of dispute resolution developed by the Court under Chief Justice Barak's leadership. In general, the raison d'être of courts is said to be dispute resolution (in US constitutional parlance, the resolution of "cases or controversies")[56] with a remedy offered as a conclusion of the dispute. In the adjudication before Israel's Court a different function may be discerned. The Court tries to influence the parties (the individual and the government) to deliberate, to back down from extreme positions, and often to reach a compromise. Many petitions are dismissed because the parties have reached an agreement. The Court has also been known to drag out the petitions for a very long time, thereby creating an incentive for compromise, or thereby delivering an opinion in a political climate more sympathetic to the result desired by the Court. From this perspective the

Court has served as a skilled mediator rather than a conventional tribunal.[57] Some would say that by acting in this fashion the Court has overstepped its boundaries and entered the political arena. However, one should also recognize the benefits of an approach that helps the parties to understand each other better and accept the values and passions underlying the claims of the other side.

I should also add that it is important to embrace a comparative perspective when evaluating the changes on Israel's Court. Chief Justice Barak's technique was quite similar to techniques practiced by constitutional courts in Europe. Professor Alec Stone Sweet, who studied European constitutional courts, observed that "judicialization is the process by which legislators [and administrators] absorb the behavior norms of constitutional adjudication, and the grammar and vocabulary of constitutional law, into those repertoires of reasoning and action that constitute political agency. In judicialized politics, legal discourse mediates partisan debate and structures the exercise of legislative [and administrative] power."[58] Furthermore, in the last decade many national courts have used arguments from international law in curbing excessive violations of human rights, and the thesis has been advanced that national courts "coordinate outcomes across national jurisdiction," thereby putting pressure on their governments to adhere to international norms. From these perspectives, the developments by Israel's court are not exceptional or unique but in keeping with a general trend in the world today.[59]

Another important factor that has contributed to the changes delineated above has been the legal theory in which the Court has grounded its general approach. Until the 1980s, Israel's Court had been rather formalistic in its understanding of the meaning of law and judicial decision making. It observed the distinction between law and politics and the distinction between law and justice rather rigidly and, in general, refrained from challenging the political branches.[60] The arguments generally provided by the Court in its opinions were of the lean type, restricted to the traditional reliance on stare decisis or textual interpretation. Thus, for example, the Court was not keen to rely on the values of Israel's Declaration of Independence as a guiding tool in resolving disputes. It should be emphasized that this was the general approach dominating the Court, and there has always been a competing tradition, which would come to prevail from time to time. This tradition, known in the United States as sociological jurisprudence, came to eclipse legal formalism in the Israel of the 1980s.[61] From then on, the opinions of the Court became longer, the rhetoric grew richer, and a reliance on arguments from history, political theory, and Zionist theory became commonplace.[62] Formalistic opinions became rare and unfashionable. This development came with a price. The rise of sociological jurisprudence exposed the political component of law. Law, particularly constitutional law, could no longer hide behind the veil of neutrality and objectivity as a science unto itself that is divorced from moral values. The Court thereby has come to be perceived as political, just another actor in the political arena. Its pristine reputation as an impartial institution that stands above the fray of everyday politics has been cracked. An intense interest has developed in the worldviews of the justices, in their personal lives, and in the method of appointing judges. The public scrutiny of this method nurtured intense doubts about the alleged impartiality and professionalism of the method of appointing judges.[63] Curiously, these processes resulted in skepticism about law and judicial decision making. On the one hand, there emerged an understanding that the strict distinction between law and politics is mythical; one may call it a loss of innocence and a hardheaded acquisition of a more sophisticated (if less enchanting) understanding of the role of law in society. On the other hand, nostalgia for the "golden age" was accompanied by a naive belief that this distinction may be restored so that judges (other judges, who will replace the ones currently serving) may once again "apply the law and not their political preferences." Israel has not yet come to accept a sober worldview in which the political element of law is recognized. The simplistic dichotomy of "law" and "personal values" still informs the public discourse.

The intensification of the struggle in the theater of law reflects a number of factors that have been thrown into sharp relief since the 1990s. Some attribute the high profile of the Court to an increasing process of ungovernability.[64] The collapse of the two big parties (Labor and Likud), the proliferation of small parties, the rise of the politics of special interests, and the deep divisions in Israeli society created by the conflict over the fate of the territories, and also by internal and external pressures that have changed Israeli society—all of these have led to a loss of public trust in the competence of the government to govern and have placed pressure on the Court to enter the vacuum and draw lines between the acceptable and the unacceptable. In addition, the shift from a highly regulated, socialist economy to a market economy, as well as the impact of globalization, have contributed to the sense of crisis and disorientation. Ordinary people tend to accept the capitalist model as a better strategy for an economically stronger, more prosperous Israel; at the same time, they resent and fear the loss of the social safety net of yesteryear. Another factor is the huge wave of immigration from the former Soviet Union, exacerbated by immigration from Ethiopia, and the increasing dependence on guest workers from the Philippines, Romania, Poland, and China (this is a partial list), designed to replace Palestinian labor in Israel. All of these factors have contributed to an atmosphere of social upheaval.[65] Yet another factor is the consolidation of the settlement movement, often perceived as having created irreversible "facts of the ground," and simultaneously the violent eruption of the two intifadas and the rise of Hamas, which thus far has denied Israel's right to exist. The increasing incidents of corruption at the highest levels of government are yet an additional factor. All of these have created a severe collective identity crisis. Simultaneously, the democratization of Israel and the Court's commitment to political and civil liberties have encouraged the proliferation of NGOs, private groups that take various sides in the disputes born out of the tensions just described, and that place more pressure on the Court to enter the fray and set the crooked straight.[66] Needless to say, each side before the Court expects to win and is unhappy with anything but a full victory. The failure of the Court to deliver resolutions that satisfy all parties has turned the Court into a popular punching bag. Finally, there has been a growing discontent among members of the legal profession, a sizable portion of whom began to experience the Court as too interested in matters of public concern and not sufficiently attuned to run-of-the-mill cases and controversies in the area of private law. The willingness of the Court to entertain petitions related to the entire spectrum of Israeli politics, from ethics in government to church and state, security matters, and political and civil liberties, has led to the creation of a strange coalition of the willing, factions that do not necessarily agree with one another, but that unite in their hostility to the Court. It may well be that the government, as well as some members of the Knesset, were pleased, even secretly encouraging this focus on the Court because it deflected attention from their own performance and misdeeds.

A simplistic theory of majoritarianism enables this coalition to hide behind the banner of democracy. They all claim to defend the "will of the people" against what they call "the tyrannical rule of the appointed few." Democratic theory is much more complicated than pure majoritarianism or the implementation of majority rule, and yet, as a slogan for doing battle, this tactic has worked quite well.

One reason for the success of this offensive is the increasing role of the media in reflecting and sometimes aggravating public controversies. Again, I can sketch only in very general terms the developments in this area. The Court's contribution to free speech jurisprudence in Israel is well documented. Ever since Justice Meir Shamgar joined the Supreme Court, first as an associate justice and then as Chief Justice, the expansion of the protection of freedom of expression has been accelerated. The protection of expression has extended not only to aggressive ideology (including racism) and to criticism of public officials, but also to criticism of the judicial process.[67] At the same time, deep structural changes have transformed Israel's media. The printed press, television, the Internet—all have come to adopt the capitalist-business model and have accepted profit and the naked preferences of the owners as the overwhelming factors in decisions about whether "to print or not to print." The result has been an unprecedented exposure of the justices and increasingly gloves-off criticism of the Court.[68] Very few journalists have paused to reflect on the significance of the Court's agenda of rights, and many reporters have preferred to focus on the sensational or have presented the coalition of special interests as reflecting the majority will.

Events in 2007 confirmed this sad state of affairs. Israel's cabinet, which now enjoys very little public support, targeted the Court as at least one part of its problems. Attacks representing the Court as "the gang of the rule of law" (note the marriage between *gang* and *the rule of law*) are on the rise. In the spring of 2007, when Israel's minister of justice Haim Ramon was convicted of a sexual offense, his vocal defender, Tel Aviv University law professor Daniel Friedman, was appointed by Prime Minister Ehud Olmert as Ramon's replacement. Professor Friedman's disenchantment with the Court was well known prior to his appointment, and he wasted no time in making his agenda clear: to clip the wings of the Supreme Court, to restore judicial modesty, to narrow down substantially the Court's power to declare statutes unconstitutional, and to give the politicians more power to change the composition of the Court.[69] His agenda of reform also includes a more substantial power to the government in appointing Israel's attorney general and solicitor general.[70] Friedman's feud with the new president of the Court, Chief Justice Dorit Beinish, is well documented in the many articles he has published criticizing her performance and leadership. Friedman is a highly regarded law professor; likewise Beinish is a jurist of excellent credentials, long judicial experience, and a mild judicial temperament that leans toward a minimalist constitutional jurisprudence.

There may be a number of reasons behind the choice of Friedman for minister of justice and the support he evidently received from the prime minister for his unprecedented attack on the Chief Justice. The prime minister is himself the subject of several criminal investigations and may be indicted. In this event, he will lose his job. It may well be that the attack on the attorney general is designed to lower the chances of an indictment. It is not unthinkable that the attack on the judicial system, at the same time that the attorney general is attacked, is meant to create the appearance that comprehensive and genuine reform measures are at stake, not an effort to discourage a criminal investigation. If this idea is correct, then Friedman is merely a pawn in the hands of the savvy and experienced prime minister. It may also be that Friedman's personal resentment of the Chief Justice makes him a particularly enthusiastic candidate for his task.[71] At the same time, even the Chief Justice herself concedes that some reforms are useful and should be seriously and cautiously contemplated. If Friedman is successful, the Court will no longer serve as a check and balance on the political process, and the freedom of the political branches to violate minority rights will be enhanced. In the current Israeli climate, judicial passivity may lead to the strengthening of a particularistic view of the Jewish state over the democratic character of Israel, to increased authoritarianism and intolerance, and to the preference of unilateralism over multilateralism. The worldview of Catastrophe Zionism may come to trump the worldview of Utopian Zionism.

It is not yet clear how successful Minister Friedman will be. Chief Justice Beinish is fighting back, and the Knesset, while resentful of the Court's power, is not yet of one mind about how it should proceed. Public opinion, as well as the academy, is split. Some support Friedman's plans as necessary reforms. Others fear that Israel is facing a baby-and-bathwater problem, and they anticipate with trepidation the morning after, when the baby has been thrown out and the power of the Court to protect the rule of law is handicapped.

In this crisis, one thing is clear: The significant presence of the Court in Israeli civic and political life shows that, as Israel celebrates its sixtieth birthday, it is experiencing a welcome level of maturity. Israelis and their government have begun to deliberate the importance of political and civil liberties, of due process, and of checks and balances. Even if the Court modifies its activism, it will still be true that Israeli society has come to accept the idea that a government of laws, not of men, is a good ideal to uphold. The current struggle in Israel shows that there is always a wide gap between theory and practice, and that lessons learned are not always lessons applied. It is not unreasonable, however, to expect that a consciousness of law and justice, nurtured by the Court, will affect Israeli politics in the years to come.

Notes

1. I wish to thank Aeyal Gross, David Kretzmer, and Michal Shaked for comments and suggestions that significantly improved this work. All errors are my responsibility.

2. Israel's judiciary has three tiers: courts of the peace, district courts, and one Supreme Court. The Supreme Court serves in two capacities: as an appellate tribunal and as the high court of justice. In the latter capacity it accepts petitions challenging the legality of governmental actions.

3. This is by no means an exhaustive list of the justices who partook in the shift from judicial restraint to judicial activism. It is also important to note that there have been justices who opposed the trend and whose opinions advocated judicial modesty and deference to other branches of the government.

4. H.C. 5100/94, *Havaad Ha-tziburi Neged Inu-yim B'Yisrael v. Memshelet Yisrael* [The Public Committee against Torture in Israel v. Government of Israel), 43(4) PD 817 (1994). Trans. On June 20, 2007, a Westlaw search of law review articles that discuss this case yielded eighty-two articles.

5. "Foreword, A Judge on Judging: The Role of a Supreme Court in a Democracy," *Harvard Law Review,* vol. 116 (2002), p. 16.

6. For the court-packing plan, see P. Irons, *A People's History of the Supreme Court* (New York: Viking, 1999), chap. 24.

7. These conceptions of law are also related to sociological jurisprudence (see below). It is important to realize that while an activist Court does thrust itself into the political arena, it does not choose its agenda and depends on litigants to bring the suits before it. At the same time, its performance may encourage or discourage litigants from coming forth.

8. Surely the Court has had important breakthrough opinions since Israel's establishment, most notably *Kol Ha'am v. Minister of the Interior,* H.C. 73/53, 87/53 7 P.D. 871 (1953) (in Hebrew); I Selected Judgments of the Supreme Court of Israel, 90 (1948–1953) (in English). For discussion see P. Lahav, *Judgement in Jerusalem* (Berkeley: University of California Press, 1995), chap. 5. But in general a restrained orientation was emphasized. See Ronen Shamir, "'Landmark Cases' and the Reproduction of Legitimacy: The Case of Israel's High Court of Justice," 24 *Law and Society Review* (1990), p. 781.

9. Various techniques of deploying minimalist jurisprudence may help the Court avoid the question of the legality of torture, among them the doctrines of ripeness, standing, and justiciability. For the dilemmas facing a court addressing the permissibility of torture—the case of Israel in particular—see Eyal Benvenisti, "The Role of National Courts in Preventing Torture of Suspected Terrorists," 8 *EJIL* 596 (1997), p. 596. For a discussion of minimalism, see Cass Sunstein, *One Step at a Time: Judicial Minimalism on the Supreme Court* (Boston: Harvard University Press, 1999).

10. *Salachat v. Government of Israel,* H.C. 2581/91, 47(4) 837 (1994).

11. It is worthwhile noting that the opinion of the Court not only prohibited torture but also explicitly listed the illegal methods of interrogation. Thereby, the Court preempted an executive interpretation that would distinguish between harsh interrogatory methods (e.g., extensive deprivation of sleep, humiliation) and torture.

12. The Israeli Association for Civil Rights (ACRI), an equivalent of the US American Civil Liberties Union, was also a petitioner, as well as several Palestinian individuals who were SGG detainees. For a description of these detainees' activities prior to detention, see the Court's opinion, at *The Public Committee against Torture in Israel v. Government of Israel,* 43(4) PD 817, 825–826 (1999). Also detainees-petitioners who alleged torture always had a right of standing under Israeli law. See generally Z. Segal, *Locus Standi in the High Court of Justice* (Tel Aviv: Papirus, 1993) (in Hebrew). For the NGO opposing torture see http://www.stoptorture.org.il/eng/publications.asp?menu=5&submenu=1.

13. *Hatenuaa L'e-chut Ha-shilton* [The Movement for Quality Government in Israel] *v. The Government of Israel.* See http://www .mqg.org.il/.

14. *Eisenberg v. Minister of Housing,* 47(2) P.D. 229 (1992). For a discussion, see Pnina Lahav, "A Barrel without Hoops: The Effect of Counterterrorism on Israel's Legal Culture," 10 *Cardozo Law Review* (1988), p. 529.

15. An encyclopedic and detailed review of the Court's opinions is found in Amnon Rubinstein and Barak Medina, *The Constitutional Law of the State of Israel,* 6th ed. (Tel Aviv: Schocken, 2005) (in Hebrew).

16. For a review and critique of the Court's intervention in Knesset decisions challenged as unethical or violative of substantive notions of the rule of law, see D. Kretzmer, "Judicial Review of Knesset Decisions," 8 *Tel-Aviv University Studies in Law* (1988), p. 95. In recent years the Court has modified its position in this area. See, for example, *HaT'nua L'Maan Eichut Ha-Shilton B'Yisrael v. The Prime Minister,* 59[3], P.D. 145 (2004).

17. R. Gavison, M. Kremnitzer, and Y. Dotan, *Judicial Activism: Pro and Con* (Jerusalem: Magnes, 2000) (in Hebrew). See Alexander M. Bickel, *The Least Dangerous Branch* (Indianapolis, IN: Bobbs Merrill,

1962). For a fierce critique of judicial review in Israel, in a comparative context, see R. Hirschl, *Towards Juristocracy* (Boston: Harvard University Press, 2004).

18. For example, Dean Amnon Rubinstein, a leading constitutional law scholar and father of Israel's Basic Law: Human Dignity and Freedom (see below, Note 21), strongly advocated judicial restraint in avoiding the question of whether the statutory prohibition on family unification of mixed couples who wish to reside in Israel violated the fundamental right to marriage. In Rubinstein's view, the limits placed by the law had full security justification; see A. Rubinstein and L. Orgad, "Security of the State Jewish Majority and Human Rights: The case of Marriage Migration," 48 *Ha-Praklit* (2006), p. 315 (in Hebrew). Still others would welcome judicial support of the right to demonstrate in matters related to religious freedom (for example, the right of religious persons to protest limitations on their free exercise of religion) but would oppose the right of gays and lesbians to demonstrate in support of gay pride. It should also be noted that Israeli scholars reflecting on judicial review tend to recognize a distinction between the judicial protection of rights and judicial intervention in matters of the integrity of governance. They support the former and discourage the latter. However, it is not clear that where the integrity of governance is compromised, political and civil liberties may flourish. The torture case is again relevant. Torture may be seen as a pure matter of civil rights, but it may also be perceived as a matter of governance, that is, the power of the executive to use the necessary means to obtain intelligence. Similarly, when the Court held that persons with the background of Mr. Ginossar (who was allegedly involved in the murder of the captured terrorists and subsequently participated in a cover-up) cannot serve in public office, it was precisely facing this dilemma. See Note 14 above.

19. The vision they promoted was, by and large, a vision anchored in Israel's Declaration of Independence, a vision that embraces liberal values, human rights, and equality. One should not confuse this collective vision with "judges promoting their personal values."

20. See generally, Uri Ram, *The Globalization of Israel* (Tel Aviv: Resling, 2005) (in Hebrew).

21. For the text of the Basic Laws, see http://www.knesset.gov.il/description/eng/eng.mimshal yesodl.htm.

22. http://www.knesset.gov.il/laws/specihe.al/eng/basic3 eng.htm.

23. The decision in *Marbury v. Madison* triggered significant criticism. President Thomas Jefferson considered Chief Justice John Marshall's exercise of judicial review a usurpation of constitutional powers. See James F. Simon, *What Kind of Nation? Thomas Jefferson, John Marshall, and the Epic Struggle to Create a United States* (New York: Simon & Schuster, 2002).

24. Aharon Barak, "The Constitutional Revolution: Protected Basic Rights," 1 *Mishpat U-Mimshal* (1992), p. 9.

25. Sensing that Barak meant to import the US rather than the continental model of judicial review, attorneys challenged the statutes in all courts of the judicial system, including the fact that lower court judges assumed power to invalidate laws passed by the Knesset provided additional ammunition to critics of the Court.

26. *Bank Hamizrahi, v. Migdal*, 49 P.D. 221 (1995). The Court later declared that other Basic Laws, Basic Law: The Knesset and Basic Law: The Government, also enjoy constitutional status. See Rubinstein and Medina, *The Constitutional Law*. In later opinions the Court grew bolder and did invalidate several statutes.

27. See http//nnwknesset.gov.il/laws/special/eng/basic-eng.

28. The reader should distinguish between the Palestinian Arabs who live within the Green Line and Palestinians in the occupied territories of the West Bank and the Gaza Strip. The latter group has neither rights of Israeli citizenship nor the right to vote. For a discussion see D. Kretzmer, *The Legal Status of Arabs in Israel* (Boulder, CO: Westview Press, 1987), and David Kretzmer, *The Occupation of*

Justice (Albany: State University of New York Press, 2002). See also Ilan Peleg, *Human Rights in the West Bank and Gaza* (Syracuse, NY: Syracuse University Press, 1995).

29. Ehud Sprinzak, *The Ascendance of Israel's Radical Right* (London: Oxford University Press, 1991).

30. This is not the place to discuss Kahana's American roots, but it may well be that his experience with the rise of the black power movement in the United States in the late 1960s propelled him to reject the principle of egalitarianism in favor of an ethnicity-based political ideology.

31. The issue came up primarily, but not exclusively, in the litigation addressing the question of whether Kahana's Kach Party should be banned from running in the elections. See generally, Rubinstein and Medina, *The Constitutional Law,* p. 589.

32. Ironically, Kahana had to rely on a democratic principle—his right to participate in the political process—as he sought protection of his nationalist agenda. The concept of Israel as a "Jewish and democratic state" first appeared in the 1985 amendment to Basic Law: The Knesset, Section 7A, enacted in response to the phenomenon of Kahana's political agenda: "A candidates' list shall not participate in elections to the Knesset if its objects or actions, expressly or by implication, include one of the following: (1) negation of the existence of the State of Israel as the state of the Jewish people, (2) negation of the democratic character of the State, (3) incitement to racism." See http://www.knesset.gov.il/laws/special/eng/basic2.eng.htm. Discussion of the term *Jewish and democratic* first appeared in *Yeredor v. Chairman of the Central Elections Commission,* E.A. 1/65, 19(3) P.D. 365 (1965) (in Hebrew); for discussions see Lahav, *Judgment in Jerusalem,* chap. 11.

33. Thus the majority of Israelis do not observe the halachic (Jewish law) principle of the sanctity of the Shabbat and prefer to spend the day shopping, getting a tan on the beach, or watching a soccer game.

34. See generally, Shlomo Avinery, *The Making of Modern Zionism* (New York: Basic Books, 1981); see also Gad Barzilai, *Communities and Law* (Ann Arbor: University of Michigan, 2003), particularly chap. 5.

35. *Solodkin v. Iriyat Beit Shemesh,* 58 PD 595 (2004).

36. *Rubinstein v. Minister of Defense,* 52 PD 481 (1998).

37. Another area that fed the religious sector's resentment was the increasing limitations placed on the power of the rabbinical courts. One such example is *Bavli v. Supreme Rabbinical Court,* 48(2) PD 221 (1994), where the Court held that the halachic law in matters of the division of marital property because of divorce discriminates against women and that therefore the rabbinical courts must apply the egalitarian secular law of the state.

38. See M. Mautner, "Years of Anxiety," *Tel Aviv University Law Review* (2002), p. 645, and M. Mautner, "Years of Reconciliation?" 26 *Tel Aviv University Law Review* (2002), p. 887.

39. See Nomi Levitzky, *Your Honor (A Biography of Aharon Barak)* (Tel-Aviv: Keter, 2001), particularly chaps. 1 and 2.

40. A. Barak, *The Judge in a Democracy* (Princeton, NJ: Princeton University Press, 2006), p. 285: "We, the judges in modern democracies, are responsible for protecting democracy both from terrorism and from the means the state wants to use to fight terrorism. . . . Since its founding Israel has faced a security threat. As a justice of the Israeli Supreme Court . . . I must take human rights seriously during times of both peace and conflict. I must not make do with the mistaken belief that, at the end of the conflict, I can turn back the clock."

41. See generally, Kretzmer, *The Legal Status of Arabs.*

42. *Qa'adan v. Israel Land Authority,* 54(1) PD 258 (2000); for analysis see Alexandre S. Kedar, "A First Step in a Difficult and Sensitive Road," *Israel Studies Forum,* vol. 16, no. 3 (2000), p. 3.

43. A good source of information on the legal status of Israeli Arabs is the NGO

Adalah. Adalah's litigation has spurred the Court to address the inequality of allocation of state resources to the Arab sector and has caused considerable pressure on the government to allocate resources more evenly. See Note 66 below. On July 18, 2007, a bill proposed to the Knesset passed the preliminary reading. If enacted, the bill will restrict the sale of land in the possession of the Jewish National Fund to Jews only, thereby circumventing the ruling in *Qa'adan*. For a critique see http://www.adalah.org/eng/kkl.php.

44. A few of the many examples are *Shakdiel v. Minister of Religion*, 42 (2) PD 221 (1998), holding that a government-appointed religious council cannot bar women from membership; *Shdulat Hanashim B'Yisrael v. Government of Israel*, 48(5) PD 501 (1998), ordering the implementation of affirmative action appointments of directors to government-owned companies; *Alice Miller v. Minister of Defense*, 49(4) PD 94 (1995), holding that the air force cannot deny women applicants access in its pilots' school; and *El Al v. Danilovitz*, 48(5) PD 749 (1994), holding that employers should offer same-sex partners the same benefits it offers heterosexual couples. As this chapter goes to press, the Supreme Court has ordered the municipality of Jerusalem and the police to facilitate a "pride march" by gays and lesbians: HC 5277/07, *Marzel v. Chief of Jerusalem Police*, decided on June 20 2007, http://elyoni .court.gov.il/Files/07/770/052/n03/07052770 .n03.HTM. It should be emphasized that the principle of gender equality has taken root. Currently five of the thirteen justices, including the Chief Justice, are women.

45. See Zeev Maoz, *Defending the Holy Land, A Critical Analysis of Israel's Security and Foreign Policy* (Ann Arbor: University of Michigan Press, 2006). See also Yoram Peri, *Generals in the Cabinet Room: How the Military Shapes Israeli Policy* (Washington, DC: US Institute of Peace, 2006).

46. There is a disagreement among scholars about the question of whether the Court simply bounced the ball to the Knesset's court, challenging it to specifically permit tor-

ture, or whether the Court hinted that such legislation could not withstand the language of Basic Law: Human Dignity and Freedom. On the question of whether the SGG continues to use aggressive methods that were outlawed by the Court's opinion, see http:// www.stoptorture.org.il/eng/background.asp? menu=3&submenu=3.

47. Another illustration that the Israeli government finds the Court's jurisprudence useful in its international relations is the fact that the Court's opinions related to alleged violations of international law in the occupied territories have been quickly translated into English, bound in glossy paper, and distributed free of charge by Israeli institutions abroad. See, for example, *Judgments of the Israel Supreme Court* and *Fighting Terrorism within the Law* (two volumes). The publisher of these volumes is not specified, but the back of each volume invites interested readers to go to "the diplomatic missions of Israel"; to the "internet: www.mfa.gov.il," the Web site of the ministry of foreign affairs; or to the Court's Web site, www.court.gov.il. It is important to remember, however, that most of the Court's opinions are not translated into English. The Court's acquiescence with violations of rights in the occupied territories, through its excessively deferential stand toward claims of "national security," is well documented, but only in Hebrew.

48. On the ground, the structure called *fence, wall,* or *barrier* is "a network of barbed wire, electrified fencing, concrete walls, ditches, guard posts, and military roads." The Palestinians prefer to call it *wall*, thereby evoking the Berlin Wall or a prison. The Israelis prefer *fence*, invoking Robert Frost's line "Good fences make good neighbors." The *New York Times* adopted a policy calling it "the barrier," often with the phrase "along and inside parts of the West Bank." E-mail message from Ethan Bronner, Deputy Director of the *New York Times* Foreign Affairs desk.

49. HCJ 2056/04 *Beit Sourik Village Council v. Government of Israel*, 58(5) PD 807 (2004), translated in 38 *Israel Law Review*

(2005), p. 83. The 2006 issue of the *Israel Law Review* contains useful analyses of the problem of the wall from the Israeli domestic as well as the international perspective.

50. For a critique and review of subsequent opinions, see Aeyal M. Gross, "The Construction of a Wall between the Hague and Jerusalem: The Enforcement and Limits of Humanitarian Law and the Structure of Occupation," 19 *Leiden Journal of International Law* (2006), p. 393.

51. Judgment of July 9, 2004, reprinted in 38 *Israel Law Review* (2006), p. 17.

52. Clearly shelter will follow only a serious official investigation of the misdeeds ending with a decision not to prosecute, or a proper prosecution. See Orna Ben-Naftali, "A Judgment in the Shadow of International Criminal Law," 5 *Journal of International Criminal Justice* (2007), p. 322; E. Benvenisti, "Case Review: *Ajuri et al. v. IDF Commander in the West Bank et al.*, 9 Eur.Pub.L.481, 491 (2003), suggesting the expectation of Israeli officials that the Court's rulings might clear them of international criminal liability; and Amichai Cohen, "Domestic Courts and Sovereignty," http://papers.ssrn.com/s013/papers.cfm?abstract_id=917048. For a discussion of the influence of norms of international law on the jurisprudence of the Court, see Daphne Barak-Erez, "The International Law of Human Rights and Constitutional Law: A Case Study of an Expanding Dialogue," 2 *International Journal of Constitutional Law* (2004), p. 611.

53. The Court has held on numerous occasions that the military commander in the occupied territories must be guided by either security considerations or the benefits to the local population or both. Thus, if the settlements fail to meet either of these considerations, they lose their legal justification. See Kretzmer, The *Occupation of Justice*, p. 77, and Orna Ben-Naftali, Aeyal M. Gross, and Keren Michaeli, "Illegal Occupation: Framing the Occupied Palestinian Territories," *Berkeley Journal of International Law*, vol. 23 (2005), pp. 551–614.

54. See Pnina Lahav, *Judgment in Jerusalem* (Berkeley: University of California Press, 1995).

55. HCJ 7052/03, *Adala v. The Minister of Interior and others*, http://elyonl.court.gov.il/Files/03/520/070/a4703070520.a47.HTM (in Hebrew). For an English summary of the ruling, translated by Adala, see http://www.adala.org/newsletter/eng/may/06/fet.pdf. For a discussion, see N. Carmi, "The Nationality and Entry into Israel: Case before the Supreme Court of Israel," *Israel Studies Forum*, No. 22 (2007), p. 26. For defense of the government's position, see Rubinstein and Orgad, "Security of the State."

56. US Constitution, Article 3, Section 2, "The judicial power shall extend to all cases [and] controversies."

57. Mediation has been particularly pronounced during ongoing hostilities, where the Court's presence prevailed upon the military to rein in considerations of expediency because of the requirements of international humanitarian law.

58. Alec Stone Sweet, *Governing with Judges: Constitutional Politics in Europe* (Oxford: Oxford University Press, 2000).

59. Eyal Benvenisti, "United We Stand: National Courts Reviewing Counterterrorism Measures" (forthcoming). See also A. Barak, *The Judge*, p. 98, echoing this sentiment: "Did all the democracies established after World War II and after the fall of the Soviet bloc err in explicitly writing into their constitutions provisions for judicial review of the constitutionality of statutes? Why should we not be allowed to continue this multinational experiment?"

60. See, for example, Pnina Lahav, "The Intellectual Foundations of Civil Liberties in Israel," *Israel Law Review*, vol. 24 (1991), p. 1.

61. Theorists of legal formalism hold that law is a set of rules and principles independent of society and politics. Theorists of sociological jurisprudence think of law as a reflection of social and historical processes.

62. See Lahav, *Judgment in Jerusalem*, pp. 251–253.

63. See, for example, journalist Nomi Levitzki's book *Ha-elyonim* (Tel Aviv: Hakibutz Hameuchad, 2006) (in Hebrew), which reveals personal details about the various justices and reviews the Court's judicial decision making behind the scenes.

64. See Shlomo Mizrahi and Assad Meidani, *Public Policy between Society and Law: The Supreme Court, Public Participation and Policy Making* (Tel Aviv: Carmel, 2006) (in Hebrew).

65. See, for example, Attorney General Mazuz's speech to the graduating class at Bar-Ilan Law School: "The symbols of government are collapsing one after another; the feeling is that the state is knocking out its values one by one. . . . Studies show the growing erosion of trust that the public has toward the different government institutions, including the judicial system." *Jerusalem Post* Online, June 20, 2007.

66. The number of NGOs in Israel is too many to list here. I shall only mention three that are very involved in adjudication. The Association for Civil Rights and Civil Liberties (ACRI) is the oldest and most versatile and has litigated a good number of the landmark cases before the Supreme Court (http://www.acri.org.il/english-acri/engine/index.asp); Adalah, the Legal Center for Arab Minority Rights in Israel (http://www.adalah.org.eng/index.php), promotes, as its title suggests, the rights of Israeli Arabs; and the Religious Action Center (IRAC) is dedicated to promoting religious pluralism and free exercise of religion in Israel (http://rac.org/advocacy/irac/).

67. For example, the offense of contempt of court, which has previously kept the courts insulated when judging in matters of pending cases has been weakened. See M. Negby, *Freedom of the Press in Israel* (Jerusalem: Jerusalem Institute, 1995) (in Hebrew).

68. One example is the recent publication of Levitzki, *Ha-elyonim*. Another example is Justice Cheshin's rhetorical barb at Chief Justice Barak in the context of the family unifications opinion (see Note 55 above). Justice Cheshin told a journalist that "Chief Justice Barak is willing to tolerate that 30–50 people die in a terrorist attack provided that human rights [of the alleged terrorists] are respected. I am not willing. . . . Fortunately I was in the majority"; quoted in Yuval Yoaz, Cheshin about Barak, May 24, 2006, http://news/walla.co.il/?w=//911848.

69. Since the early 1950s Israel's judges have been selected by a committee composed of three justices of the Supreme Court, including the Chief Justice; two cabinet ministers; two members of the Knesset; and two members of the bar. The committee is chaired by the minister of justice. Under Friedman's proposal, two of the three Supreme Court justices will be replaced by lower-court judges, who will thus partake in choosing judges superior to themselves in the judicial hierarchy; see Yuval Yoaz, "Friedman Initiates a Change in the Composition of the Committee to Select Judges," *Ha'aretz* (March 5, 2007). He also proposed limiting the term of the Chief Justice's tenure to seven years; see Yuval Yoaz, "Friedman Initiates a Statute: Court Presidents Will Serve Only Seven Years," *Ha'aretz* (March 8, 2007). At the same time Friedman announced he would work on a bill to limit the power of the Supreme Court to invalidate statutes and allow the Knesset to overrule the Court with a majority of sixty-one members (a regular majority reflecting the coalition government); see Yuval Yoaz, "The Minister of Justice Will Not Promote His Suggestion to Impair the Powers of the High Court of Justice in the Coming Few Months," *Ha'aretz* (March 7, 2007). On July 9, 2007, the Knesset approved an amendment to the Court's law that would limit the tenure of presidents of the courts (including the Supreme Court) to one term of seven years. See http://www.knesset.gov.il/privatelaw/data/17/3/298 3 2.rtf.

70. For examples see Yuval Yoaz, "Eight Reforms in Five Months of Service," *Ha'aretz* (June 8, 2007), and Zeev Segal, "Politicization of Selecting the Attorney General," *Ha'aretz* (June 8, 2007).

71. Friedman has been intensely involved in lobbying for the appointment of his

colleague, Professor Nili Cohen, to the Supreme Court. Chief Justice Beinish (prior to her elevation to position of Chief Justice) opposed the appointment. It is widely thought that Cohen was a well-qualified candidate. Many believe that Friedman's frustration with Beinish's failure to appoint Cohen triggered his bitter and aggressive assault on the Chief Justice and his determination to undermine the Court; see, for example, "Ha-Mefarek" (He who pulls the system apart), *Ha'aretz* (May 25, 2007), pp. 18, 22.

8

The Israeli Economy

Ofira Seliktar

ISRAEL'S UNIQUENESS among immigrant nations is well known. Its east European Zionist founders were influenced by a hybrid socialist-nationalist ideology of Marxist dogma mixed with utopian agrarianism. This ideology called for "social redemption" and "normalization" of the Jewish people. To this end, the Yishuv, the Jewish community in Palestine, glorified agricultural endeavor and labored to create an egalitarian society supervised by the Histadrut, the labor trade union that also owned much of the economy. Many activities were undertaken to further political and social causes as interpreted by the dominant Mapai (Labor) Party. Market rationality embedded in the laws of economic profitability and efficiency was either ignored or sacrificed on the altar of larger communal goals. As one observer put it, the socialist-Zionist dreams "were assumed to be achievable by the sheer will power of the pioneer."[1]

The creation of a sovereign state in 1948 and the twin burdens of security and absorption of a mass immigration tested cherished tenets of socialist Zionism. Reluctant to give up the founding ideology, the Labor leadership struggled to adjust it to the new domestic and international economic realities. At the normative level, Labor was concerned that the new immigrants, as well as many of the veteran settlers, would reject the communal and egalitarian ethos of the Yishuv. To ensure an equitable distribution of resources the state-supervised economy was designed to limit the individual's pursuit of "selfish interests." The network of government interventions—including price and wage controls, capital market controls, and foreign exchange controls, complemented by extensive state and public ownership of production—created the most socialist economy outside the Soviet bloc.

The cost of preserving such ideological purity was daunting. The inefficient and bloated public sector—some 80 percent of the total economy—could neither create enough jobs nor provide the standard of living that the West-looking Israelis expected. Fearful that real or perceived economic hardship would impede further immigration or, worse, trigger a large-scale emigration, the government resorted to deficit spending to support an array of subsidies and other transfer payments. By the mid-1970s the systemic consequences of such policies were clear. The inflation rate, partially related to the increase in oil prices following the 1973 War, exceeded 30 percent. At the same time economic growth had virtually stopped; the high rate of unemployment and a more generalized sense of malaise triggered a large-scale emigration, under-mining the Zionist mission of "ingathering of exiles."

The Likud Party, which came to power in 1977, promised to reverse these trends through market-oriented reforms. The new government asked the liberal Milton Friedman, the free-market economist from the University of Chicago, to develop a blueprint for turning Israel into a competitive player in the global economy. Friedman's suggestions included liberalizing foreign exchange transactions, lowering import duties, privatizing the public sector, and other market measures. While Likud implemented some of these reforms, the party's core constituency of lower-class Sephardi immigrants made the removal of subsidies and transfer payments politically imprudent. By replacing socialism with populism, the government abandoned all controls over government spending. By 1985, the huge budget deficit triggered an inflation of more than 400 percent annually, and the trade imbalance left Israel with a perilously low foreign currency reserve.

The Likud-Labor national unity government formed in June 1984 launched the Stabilization Program, an emergency plan to introduce market reforms. As if to underscore the structural problem of socialism, the government was forced into expensive bailouts of the Histadrut-owned Koor Company, the banks, and even the kibbutz movement. Still, instead of privatizing the bankrupt companies, the state became their biggest owner.

Sensing an opportunity, a small circle of market advocates mobilized to push Israel toward a "Thatcherite revolution," a reference to the successful free-market transformation of Great Britain under Margaret Thatcher. Among its leaders was Daniel Doron, a disciple of Friedman and the head of the Israel Center for Social and Economic Progress. Doron was a member of Chicago Committee on Social Thought, a group inspired by the conservative philosopher Leo Strauss and the economist Frederick von Hayek. Strauss and von Hayek argued that economic freedom is a basic component of human freedom, and they predicted that rational self-interest, exercised without undue economic constraints, would create prosperity for all. Doron, who called socialism and Zionism a "deadly mix," devoted much of his time to educating the Israeli public about the working of markets. Alvin Rabushka, the head of economic policy at the Institute for Advanced Strategic and Political Studies, was another early market proponent. In the Institute's *1991 Scorecard on the Israeli Economy*, Rabushka wrote that the country was rife "with money-losing enterprises, Histadrut's debt ridden industrial conglomerates, a huge government bureaucracy, massive public spending consuming three quarters of national income . . . and [infested] with dozens of official monopolies and cartels."[2]

Yitzhak Rabin, who led Labor to victory in 1992, vowed to continue market reforms, but distracted by the Oslo peace process and hampered by labor unrest organized by the left wing of his own party, he had little scope for maneuver. Following his assassination in November 1995, Shimon Peres, one of the architects of the Stabilization Plan, took over, only to be replaced in May 1996 by Likud's Benjamin Netanyahu.

Adjusting Zionism to the Age of Globalization

Well before reaching the prime minister's office, Netanyahu had lent his voice to the growing group of neoliberals. In his programmatic book *A Place among the Nations*, Netanyahu declared that socialism was not only ill prepared to cope with the emerging global economy but uniquely incompatible with Zionism's core mission of the "ingathering of exiles." Netanyahu suggested that the failure to absorb the large wave of Soviet Jews properly was a clear indication of the bankruptcy of socialist Zionism and warned that without reforms Israel would not be able to attract immigrants or even hold onto the more enterprising segments of the native-born population.[3]

Neoliberal critics added that the Zionist ethos should be adjusted to account for the information technology (IT) revolution, which made the movement of workers across national boundaries commonplace. Global IT was especially attractive to the so-called knowledge workers, who could move easily to pursue more rewarding professional and economic opportunities. According to statistics published in the late 1990s, IT workers formed the bulk of emigrants among both native Israelis and new Russian arrivals. Such a brain drain was especially painful in view of Israel's historical failure to attract large-scale immigration from the United States and other Western countries.[4]

Abandoning the normative vocabulary of *aliya* and *yerida* (ascent to Israel and descent from Israel) to place immigration within the general push-pull theory of migration was only part of the neoliberal critique of socialist Zionism.

The other part was a sharp rebuke of the ethos of a "new Jew," socialist-Zionist shorthand for its ambitious social engineering program to turn Diaspora Jews into proud and resourceful individuals imbued with a communal spirit. Neo-liberal observers noted that the highly paternalistic Israeli state had produced an antithesis of this ideal: people beholden to politicians and state bureaucracy, whose spirits were stunted by economic dependency and bondage. Doron asserted that the socialist leadership of the Yishuv had betrayed and corrupted Theodore Herzl's vision of building a Jewish national home "with a prosperous market economy"; they had replaced it with socialist fantasies "that impoverished the Zionist enterprise demographically, economically and socially." Doron and others urged the adoption of a "new Zionist manifesto" that would put the ethos of economic freedom at the center of the society. The Shinui Party, co-founded by Doron in 1973, carried this message to the Israeli public.[5]

That communal interests could be best served through individual endeavor was anathema to the entire Israeli left-wing camp, which mounted a vigorous intellectual counteroffensive. The radical Left was represented by the post-Zionist New Sociologists, a group inspired by two neo-Marxist academics, Shlomo Swirski and Uri Ram. New Sociologists contended that the hegemonic Zionism created by white European men marginalized the minorities: Sephardim, Arabs, and women. They decried the impact of globalization led by the United States and blamed it for replacing the "Zionist consensus" with a "Washington consensus."[6]

The mainstream Left took the more conventional view that a large public sector, bolstered by generous subsidies and other transfer payments, was crucial to maintaining the egalitarian ethos of Zionism. These critics pointed out that the individualistic spirit of the market economy was utterly alien to the Jewish concern for social justice, equality, and mutual responsibility.

While conceding that Jewish values mandated social compassion, market advocates retorted that the public sector had undermined such concerns because of its built-in inefficiencies. At best, a state-run economy misallocated resources; at worst, it suffered from featherbedding, inflated salaries for the managerial class, and chronic labor unrest. Such practices were said to cost the Israeli society in lost productivity, a key element in the creation of wealth. They noted that during the 1990s, the productivity rate in Israel had increased by a meager 0.6 percent compared to the average of 3 percent customary in market economies.[7]

The neoliberals explained that the public sector was rife with corruption fueled by politicians who used public appointments to reward supporters or otherwise manipulated and defrauded the public coffers. Indeed, the Movement for Quality Government in Israel, dubbed the "corruption busters," had documented hundreds of cases of fraud in the public sector since the early

1990s. In comparative terms, the annual Transparency International (TI) Global Corruption Barometer ranked Israel with some highly corrupt Third World states where the public sector dominated the economy. Not incidentally, statistics published by TI and other international corruption watchers showed a strong correlation between a statist economy and corruption and poverty.

With the philosophical groundwork laid, the Netanyahu government vowed to turn Israel into a global economic player along the lines first suggested by Milton Friedman. However, plagued by widespread labor unrest and facing harsh criticism for his handling of the peace process, Netanyahu made little headway. Labor's Ehud Barak, who replaced Netanyahu in 1999, made even less progress. Overwhelmed by the unprecedented violence of the al-Aqsa Intifada, the public climate was hardly auspicious for a fundamental debate on the virtues of a market economy. But in a surprising twist of events, the slowdown that started in 2000—a combination of a global recession, the fallout from the intifada, and deepening structural problems in the economy— brought a new urgency to the issue.

Helping the renewed discourse was a significant shift in the Israeli electorate. In the 2003 election, Shinui, under the leadership of the maverick politician Tommy Lapid, garnered fifteen Knesset seats, becoming the third largest party in the Knesset after Likud and Labor. Ariel Sharon, Likud's leader, opted to include Shinui rather than the ultra-Orthodox religious parties in his coalition. Although Lapid was best known for his harsh critique of the ultra-Orthodox, the free-market crusaders in his party seized on the opportunity to finally bring the Thacherite revolution to Israel. They found an enthusiastic ally in Benjamin Netanyahu, the finance minister in the Sharon cabinet.

Resuscitating the Israeli Economy

Netanyahu, whose appointment was met with widespread skepticism, wasted little time in promoting a radical restructuring of the economic system. To generate public support, Netanyahu took to describing the economy as "sick," "bleeding to death," and in urgent need of a radical cure. He vehemently criticized analysts who tried to link the recession to cyclical or random factors like the global slowdown and the intifada, which had wiped out the tourist industry. In Netanyahu's opinion the "sickness" was structural, a product of the failure to implement market reforms going back to 1985. The prestigious Israel Democracy Institute (IDI), a liberal think tank, backed Netanyahu's position. The head of its Project on Structural Reform in the Israeli Economy, Avi Ben Bassat, a former director general of the ministry of finance and the chair of the Public Commission for Tax Reform launched on May 4, 2000, lent credibility to the neoliberal cause.[8]

In diagnosing structural failure, the finance minister, his Shinui backers, and other market advocates had plenty of statistical evidence. By any measure, by 2003 Israel had entered its longest recession since the 1960s. Unemployment exceeded 10 percent; in February 2003 the budget deficit stood at $579 million, the largest such monthly deficit on record. In March Netanyahu unveiled his "four-pillar" reform plan, aptly titled Program for the Resuscitation of Israel's Economy.

Shrinking the public sector, the first pillar, was the number one priority of the government. Netanyahu's favorite metaphor was of a fifty-five-kilogram "fat man" riding on the back of a forty-five-kilogram "thin man," meant to illustrate the economic imbalance. The nonproductive public sector, some 55 percent of the GDP (gross domestic product), was supported by the 45 percent generated by the productive private sector, especially the IT enterprises. Netanyahu argued that to compete more effectively, Israel needed to bring down the public-sector–GDP ratio to some 30 percent, a level that had helped Ireland to stake out a strong position in the European Union.

To achieve fiscal reasonability, the government proposed cuts in public sector salaries, which had steadily risen over the past decade without a corresponding increase in productivity. In addition, Netanyahu pledged to cut by a yet-to-be-determined percentage the number of public sector jobs.

The government also vowed to trim subsidies, welfare, and other transfer payments. Child allowances, paid by the National Insurance Institute (NII; the equivalent of the American Social Security Administration), were an item of major concern. Over the years, Israel has experimented with variations of the universal formula (benefits were paid to families according to size) and the selective formula (means-tested allowances). In 1993, under pressure from the left-wingers in his cabinet, Rabin returned to the universal model. The formula changed yet again when Barak's government lost its majority in the Knesset in 2000. The opposition parties supported the Halpert Bill, a private initiative by an ultra-Orthodox Knesset member, which dramatically increased child allowances for the fifth child onward. Under the Halpert Bill, a family with five children received a 12 percent increase, bringing its allowance to $440 a month; a family with ten children saw its stipend go up by 30 percent, to $1,303.

The steep increase in child payments added to the already substantial cost of other forms of welfare, including unemployment benefits, old-age pensions, and income support payments, the so-called last resort safety net. Critics noted that transfer payments had grown from 6.09 percent of the GDP in 1985 to 8.8 percent in 2003. By that time transfers consumed almost half the annual state budget of $70 billion without alleviating poverty.[9]

To stimulate the private sector, the government moved to implement Netanyahu's second pillar: vigorous privatization and tax reform. Even though privatization had been on the table since the Stabilization Plan of 1985, the results up to 2003 had been meager. By the end of the Rabin-Peres tenure, only $3.6 billion's worth of companies had been sold, a fraction of the state's holdings. During his short-lived tenure as prime minister, Netanyahu had tried, with modest success, to sell off public companies; however, by 2000 only $8.6 billion had been raised. This time around the ministry of finance announced an ambitious schedule to privatize within five years the largest public holdings: Haifa Chemicals, the shipping company Zim, the national airline El Al, the ports, and the banks.

In yet another boost to the private sector, the government promised to lower the high rate of corporate taxes, as well as to reduce taxes on the higher income brackets. In early 2000 the government of Israel took, as part of its income, almost 60 percent of individual tax receipts, compared to 40 percent in the European Union and 29 percent in the United States. Last revised in 1975, the tax code was viewed by critics as inimical to creating wealth. In the opinion of liberal economists, the tax was "irrational" and "confiscatory" because it penalized the wealthier and more productive members of the population. Ben Bassat stated that the Israeli tax system should be adjusted to "the nature and composition of economic activity today," and he promised that the new tax would stimulate employment, improve productivity, and accelerate growth. Once implemented, the marginal tax rate was expected to gradually go down to EU (European Union) levels.[10]

Netanyahu's third pillar included the plethora of monopolies and cartels. He and Bank of Israel economists argued that despite a growing number of highly competitive Israeli ventures, many of the locally oriented firms were either monopolies or cartels. Inevitably, such enterprises lacked market motivation and discipline, maintaining high profit margins through price collusion. Since many of these concerns were publicly owned, price manipulation by their bureaucrat managers was easy. Monopolistic practices extended to imports as well, where "exclusive" state-licensed importers blocked cheaper foreign goods. Market reformers held that monopolistic practices, combined with a large public sector, inflated costs, increased unemployment, and were responsible for anemic productivity and very low real wage growth. In addition, they argued, low productivity and monopolies/cartels had cost Israel $100 billion in cumulative GDP; the "monopoly tax" increased the price of every consumer item by 30–50 percent, depressing the purchasing power of the lower sectors and forcing them to rely on welfare to survive. According to such logic, dismantling of the monopolies would have reduced the number of people below the poverty line and thus reduce the amount of transfer payments.[11]

Dismantling the monopoly/cartel structure was also part of Netanyahu's fourth pillar, the restructuring of the highly abnormal Israeli capital market. It is a truism that transfer of capital from savers to investors is most efficient when multiple financial intermediaries—banks, pension funds, and insurance companies—participate and compete in the process. However, Israel's banking industry had been dominated historically by two large institutions: Bank Leumi, which originated in the Jewish Agency, and Bank Hapoalim, a Histadrut creation. The much smaller Discount Bank was privately owned but followed the monopolistic practices of the larger institutions. In 1983, the so-called shares scandal forced a government bailout and a subsequent takeover of the banks, but state management changed little in the financial system.

Market advocates argued that the twin problems of excessive concentration and conflict of interest had starved Israel of credits and retarded economic growth. Dominated by a duopoly (the Leumi and Hapoalim groups), which controlled some 80 percent of savings, banks were able to pay below-market interest rates on savings but charged high interest on household and small- and medium-business loans. Worse, a tiny group of big-business borrowers— about 1 percent of the population, often in highly speculative ventures—were beneficiaries of some 70 percent of bank loans. By some accounts, in 2003 the banks carried $13 billion in questionable loans on a capital base of $10 billion.[12] Such practices were said to deprive the market of capital for productive investment, making it especially hard on small and medium businesses. Conflicts of interest occurred because banks were allowed to own provident and mutual funds as well as to engage in underwriting stock issues. Quite naturally, the publicly owned banks invested much of their funds in the badly managed public-sector conglomerates, where returns were paltry and defaults frequent.

The Bachar Commission, appointed by Netanyahu in September 2004, noted that such a dysfunctional system made capital expensive and difficult to obtain. It recommended that banks sell their provident and mutual funds and urged the removal of their underwriting role. In spite of considerable pressure from the banking lobby, which had defeated all previous attempts at reform, the Knesset voted the recommendations into law in 2005.[13]

While not under the commission's purview, the finance ministry was also keen to tackle the pension funds of the Histadrut, which, with some seven hundred thousand workers registered, had a commanding lead over the thirty-thousand-strong non-Histadrut sector. Spanning more than a decade, reports by the comptroller general highlighted corruption and mismanagement of the funds; fund managers were said to place too many of their assets in poorly performing Histadrut concerns and to charge exorbitant management fees to cover bloated administrative expenses. Conflicts of interest drove the funds into further decline; union members who sat on the boards often pressured management to act against rational investment policy. In fact, by 2000, the Histadrut pension funds were in actuarial deficit, the value of their future claims far exceeding their assets. As with the bank investments, the finance ministry wanted to channel this capital to the better-performing private sector.

In attempting an extreme makeover of the economy, Netanyahu could count on the United States and the International Monetary Fund (IMF). Indeed, the Republican administration of George W. Bush signaled that it would demand market reforms in return for $9 billion in loan guarantees to Israel. The IMF, a powerful market advocate in its own right, was equally stringent; in their annual presentation before the IMF, Israeli officials were compelled to report on the progress of privatization, fiscal solvency, and other market measures.

Domestically, Netanyahu benefited from the support of the Bank of Israel, headed since 1991 by strong market advocates. Jacob Frankel, a former professor at the University of Chicago and an adviser to the World Bank, was replaced in 2000 by David Klein, whose previous assignments included a stint at the International Monetary Fund. Klein, a strict monetarist and advocate of fiscal discipline, developed an econometric model to assess the impact of budgetary imbalances on the Israeli economy. Upon Klein's retirement in early 2005, the Sharon government picked the American Stanley Fischer, a one-time chief IMF economist who had helped to privatize the economies of the former Soviet bloc.

Even with such a powerful array of allies, Netanyahu's reforms faced an uphill battle against a powerful coalition led by the Histadrut, the Labor Party, and the social lobby. Amir Peretz, the militant Histadrut chief, who had made his name by launching frequent general strikes, understood well that the Netanyahu plan would not only shrink the public sector, the mainstay of his support, but also rob the trade union of its pension fund empire. To make matters worse, the Histadrut was forced to curb excessive salaries of senior officials, a curb that greatly angered the Histadrut elite.

In his frequent public appearances Peretz denounced the neoliberal policy as "the extreme right-wing tendency to create a new class of working poor" and promised to challenge the government with strikes and industrial actions. At its peak in 2004, the wave of stoppages and a general strike had brought the country to a standstill. However, such aggressive tactics backfired; there was a public backlash, and the courts ordered the strikers back to work. Bereft of public support and facing legal hurdles, Peretz was compelled to negotiate with Netanyahu, but he redoubled his efforts to defend the "suffering of pensioners, workers, the unemployed," and other fragile groups.[14] With Histadrut support, the large social lobby mounted a public relations campaign against neoliberalism that centered on the emotional issues of poverty and inequality in the Jewish state.

Deconstructing Poverty and Inequality

Leading the intellectual charge was the influential Adva Center for Equality and Social Justice, which billed itself as an independent, nonpartisan research and advocacy group. Still, Adva's academic director, Shlomo Swirski, and Uri Ram, a board member, held the neo-Marxist view that globalization and the antecedent market reforms had created a great class divide in Israel, a thesis argued in great detail in Ram's coedited book, *The Power of Property: Israeli Society in the Global Age*. Swirski, who had previously complained that Israel's transformation into a regional "military-industrial power" was hurting the poor, noted that global economic change legitimized an ethnonational "class differentiation." The Marxist scholar Yoav Peled explained that market reforms had shifted resources from the state to capital markets, creating a new "capitalist class" and spearheading an "economic onslaught" against Israeli society, not unlike Israel's aggression against the Palestinians.[15]

Using the Gini coefficient, a measure of societal equality, Adva demonstrated that in the early 2000s, Israel's inequality had reached some 39 points on a scale of 1 to a 100. Comparative United Nations statistics placed Israel at the level of Ireland but below the equality standard of the Scandinavian countries and Japan. The New Sociologists found this trend truly alarming; they pointed out that in the 1950s socialist Israel had had a very low Gini coefficient, with the top "20 percent of the population earning only 3.3 times the income of the bottom 20 percent." In their view, this trend was yet another example of the "regressive government income policies to subsidize the few by the many" and part of the ongoing Zionist practice of marginalizing Sephardi Jews, Arabs, and women.[16]

While acknowledging that gaps had been on the rise since the 1950s, Neoliberals faulted the neo-Marxist analysis of poverty and inequality. Some of the critiques pertained to the statistical pitfalls of using the Gini Index, but others were more substantive. Neoliberals claimed that the inequality had been brought on by the IT economy, which disproportionally rewards education, most notably by favoring college graduates with advanced degrees in science, engineering, and management.

Asher Meir, the head of the Business Ethics Center of Jerusalem, suggested that two related factors enhance the earning potential of this population: IT workers work longer hours than their blue-collar counterparts and tend to form two-paycheck families. As in other advanced economies, married female college graduates holding a full-time job have been a key factor in upward mobility in Israel. Indeed, in the decade after 1995 the number of college-educated women in the Israeli workforce increased by 37 percent; the comparable number for low-skilled women was 11 percent.[17]

These inequality-engendering "universals" were compounded by a uniquely local phenomenon of low participation in the labor market, especially among males between the ages of twenty-five and fifty-five. Compared to the their average of 92 percent participation in advanced economies, the Israeli rate stood at 83 percent, a result of the low market engagement of ultra-Orthodox men and Arabs. The large number of children in these populations has pushed families below the poverty line. The ultra-Orthodox and the Arabs have constituted 67 percent of families below the poverty line; ultra-Orthodox children formed the largest category of below-poverty children, followed by the Bedouins of the Negev. Three smaller categories have rounded out the demography of poverty: (1) the Israeli underclass, mostly from Sephardi multigenerational welfare families with children at risk; (2) poorly educated older immigrants; and (3) the chronically unemployed and immigrant retirees dependent on NII payments.

Neoliberals have suggested that generous welfare payments have contributed to high fertility rates in the ultra-Orthodox sector, where male employment by 2006 stood at only 46 percent. In other words, far from being victimized by Zionism-gone-global, the ultra-Orthodox have used the state to support their ideal of "blessed families" (large families) and full time, lifelong religious study by men. For all their concern for the poor, leftist Laborites voted with Netanyahu to repeal the Halpert Bill, and prominent members of the social lobby denounced the ultra-Orthodox for freeloading. One Tel Aviv University sociologist went so far as to suggest that "blessed families" should actually be called "cursed families" because they are a "prescription for a national catastrophe." An Adva report explained that, together with allocations for ultra-Orthodox education, government support amounts to a "selective welfare system which assures a minimal standard of living for some of the ultra-Orthodox families."[18]

If the lifestyle of the ultra-Orthodox poses a huge challenge to fighting poverty, the traditional nature of the Arab society is not far behind. High school graduation rates of Arabs have been well below those of Jews; in the older cohorts (fifty-five to sixty-five) only some 40 percent of men and 20 percent of women have finished high school. Moreover, in traditional Arab families women have been expected to stay home and bear children, an expectation that perpetuates the cycle of poverty.[19] The ministry of finance suggested a number of programs to enrich the human capital and marketability of these groups, including vocational training and newly created college programs designed for ultra-Orthodox sensibilities.

As for the underclass, neoliberals used the American experience to argue that lifelong welfare dependency has helped to create and perpetuate a culture of poverty. Netanyahu's finance ministry adopted the Wisconsin welfare-to-work plan, known in Hebrew as *Mehalev*, to move individuals into the workplace. *Mehalev* was also expected to tackle the chronically unemployed and older immigrants with limited Hebrew and few marketable skills.

While social engineering designed to enrich human capital in underperforming populations is slow, the speed of economic recovery has caught even the most optimistic market-economy boosters by surprise. Two years after Netanyahu left office in 2005, Israel was widely being described as an "economic miracle."

Israel as a Market Economy

All leading economic indicators in 2006 and the first quarter of 2007 were on the upturn. GDP per capita rose above twenty thousand dollars, surpassing the average for the European Union. In terms of purchasing power parity (PPP), the sum was actually thirty thousand dollars. The inflation rate stood at below 1 percent, better than the projected Consumer Price Index increase of 1–3 percent and a first in the country's history. Crucial in this context was the strengthening of the shekel against the US dollar, a development that was influenced by a hefty surplus in the balance of trade. In another historic first, Israel's exports exceeded imports by some $66 billion in 2006, and the current surplus is expected to grow in the next few years.

Direct foreign investment has also gone up; in addition to the IT sector, where "country risk" matters little, investors have poured billion of dollars into traditional industries and the real estate market. Warren Buffett's decision to purchase an 80 percent share of Iskar, a precision toolmaker, was emblematic of such a vote of confidence. Israel's status as a new economic powerhouse was acknowledged by the international financial community. Standard and Poor upgraded the country's international credit rating from A- to A, and the Organization for Economic Cooperation and Development (OECD) invited Israel to join. The Global Competitiveness Index based on a list of indices, including economic freedoms, upgraded Israel to the respectable rank of 15.

As expected, the structural reforms have had a positive impact on the economic well-being of Israelis. The unemployment rate went down to 7.7 percent in the last quarter of 2006, the lowest in a decade, and the percentage of families below the poverty line dropped from 20.6 percent in 2005 to 20 percent in 2006. According to the Index of Social Confidence, the sense of economic confidence went up from 57 in 2006 to 62 in the first quarter of 2007.[20] What is more, Israel's impressive integration into the global economy has come without the Oslo-related "peace dividend" and in spite of continued violence in the Palestinian Authority and the Second Lebanon War in 2006.

Zvi Ecstein, deputy governor of the Bank of Israel, expressed confidence that such a "conflict-proof" economy could attain true excellence if a number of issues were addressed. Israel's low labor participation is still the most pressing problem. The government-funded ultra-Orthodox educational system is not mandated to offer a market-related curriculum, a circumstance mirrored in the growing number of Islamic schools in the Arab sector. Foreign workers employed in agriculture, construction, and caregiving have pushed down the wages for low-skilled Israelis. Because of coalition considerations, the Mehalev program has come under threat and may be replaced with more generous welfare benefits to those deemed to be unemployable, a prescription for more poverty.[21]

The still strongly unionized labor force, coupled with a failure to introduce cutting-edge technology, has thwarted productivity in the traditional economy, especially as compared to that in other developed nations and to that in the IT sector. Residual monopolistic practices in manufacturing and banking have hurt competitiveness and kept the prices of goods and services high.

While the pace and degree of success in addressing these issues are difficult to determine, it is quite clear that Israel, as part of a global revolution, has made an irreversible transition to a market economy. In the process, the historical debate about the nature and mission of the Jewish state has been settled.

Conclusion

To the founding fathers of the Yishuv, the classical liberal view of the economy in which individuals, pursuing enlightened self-interest, create collective well-being was anathema. Yet after decades of struggle to adjust, the model of socialist collectivism clashed with economic realities and collapsed amid high inflation, high unemployment, a huge balance-of-trade deficit, corruption scandals, and a general sense of malaise.

Starting with the 1985 Stabilization Plan, the country began a slow and painful transition to capitalism. Arrayed against a market economy was a formidable coalition of statist interests, buttressed by much of the intellectual elite. However, difficulties in absorbing the Russian immigration, a core Zionist mission, coupled with emigration of native-born cohorts, cast doubts on the socialist ideology. Widespread corruption and the glaring inefficiency of the system helped to delegitimize it altogether. As Israel moved to adopt a market economy, Zionism was redefined to embrace Herzl's original vision for the Jewish state.

Notes

1. Yair Aharoni, *The Israeli Economy: Dream and Realities,* (New York: Routledge, 1993), p. 320.

2. Ofira Seliktar, "The Changing Political Economy of Israel: From Agricultural Pioneers to the 'Silicon Valley' of the Middle East," in Robert O. Freedman, ed., *Israel's First Fifty Years* (Gainesville: University of Florida Press, 2000), pp. 197–218.

3. Benjamin Netanyahu, *Place among the Nations* (Tel Aviv: Yedioth Ahronot Books, 1995), p. 301.

4. Reuben Gronau, *Globalization: The Israeli Economy in the Shadow of Global Economy* (Jerusalem: Israel Democracy Institute, 2002), p. 42.

5. Daniel Doron, "Theodore Herzl's Vision Betrayed," *Jerusalem Post* (May 21, 2007); Yitzhak Klein and Daniel Polisar, *Choosing Freedom: Economic Policy for Israel, 1997–2000* (Jerusalem: Shalem Center, 1997), p. 147.

6. Shlomo Swirski, *Not Naturally Inept but Socialized to Be Inept: A Sociological Analysis and Discussion with Socialist Activists* (Haifa: Haifa University Press, 1981); Uri Ram, *The Changing Agenda of Israeli Sociology: Theory, Ideology and Identity* (Albany: State University of New York Press, 1995); Jonathan Nitzan and Shimshon Bichler, *The Global Political Economy of Israel* (London: Pluto Press, 2002), p. 29.

7. "One on One: Market Values," *Jerusalem Post* (March 29, 2007).

8. Mat Plen, "Privatization vs. Welfare State: Israel's Economic Crisis," *Hagshama* (November 22, 2004); Avi Ben Bassat, *The Israeli Economy 1985–1998: From Government Intervention to Market Economics* (Jerusalem: Israel Democracy Institute, 2002).

9. Joseph Zeira, *Reducing Unemployment and Closing Income Gaps on the Road to Economic Growth* (Jerusalem: Israel Democratic Institute, 2004), pp. 29–30.

10. Klein and Polisar, *Choosing Freedom,* p. 61; Bassat, *The Israeli Economy.*

11. Kimberley A. Strassel, "Israel Gets a Taste of Friedman," *Wall Street Journal* (March 1, 2004).

12. Israel Center for Social and Economic Progress Conference, New York City, cited in *New York Sun* (June 27, 2005).

13. Guy Rolnik, "Banking Fees on the Front Page," *Ha'aretz* (November 21, 2006).

14. Interview with Amir Peretz (June 2005).

15. Uri Ram and Dani Filk, eds., *The Power of Property: Israeli Society in a Global Age* (Jerusalem: Van Leer Institute, 2004); Shlomo Swirski, "Israel in the Global Space," in Ram and Filk (eds.), *The Power of Property;* Yaov Peled, "Profits or Glory?" *New Left Review,* vol. 29 (September–October 2004); Shlomo Swirski, *Politics and Education in Israel* (New York: Falmer Press, 1999), pp. 215–216.

16. Jonathan Nitzan and Shimshon Bichler, *The Global Political Economy of Israel* (London: Pluto Press, 2002), p. 351.

17. Asher Meir, "The Shrinking Middle Class," *Jerusalem Post* (December 12, 2005).

18. Abraham Doron, "Social Security in Israel at the Beginning of the 21st Century: Adaptation or Dismantlement," paper delivered at the Fourth International Research Conference on Social Security, Antwerp, May 2004; Shlomo Swirski et al., *Government Allocation to the Ultra-Orthodox Sector in Israel* (Tel-Aviv: Adva Center, August 1998).

19. Ronni Frish, *The Causal Effect of Education on Earnings in Israel* (Jerusalem: Bank of Israel Research Department, February 2007).

20. Nehemia Strasler, "National Insurance Institute Report: Growth Reduces Poverty," *Ha'aretz* (January 26, 2007); Ruth Eglash, "Israelis Feel Highest Economic Security in Six Years," *Jerusalem Post* (June 3, 2007).

21. Zvi Eckstein, "Maintaining a Thriving Economy in the Shadow of Terror," *Jerusalem Issue Brief,* vol. 7 (June 18, 2007); Asher Meir, "The Shrinking Middle Class," *Jerusalem Post* (December 12, 2005).

PART TWO

Israel's Foreign Policy

9

Israel and the Palestinians

Barry Rubin

DURING THE 1980S AND THROUGH THE 1990S, the Israeli-Palestinian conflict seemed to be approaching peace, yet, instead, went into sharp reverse.
The process's failure in 2000, followed by a Palestinian war on Israel and
Hamas's electoral triumph over Fatah, has now pushed back for decades any
hope of a negotiated solution.

Of all the factors involved in shaping this history the key was the Palestinian movement's inability to define the conflict in nonexistential terms, and to
accept a two-state solution as a permanent outcome. The critical year was
2000, when the two sides came closest to peace and this chance was rejected
by Arafat himself.

In the late 1980s, and even more by the start of the 1990s, key world, regional, and local developments reduced conflict in the Middle East on a
state-to-state level. These developments included lagging Arab economic
development and growing domestic opposition; the threat from Iran and the
danger of radical Islamism; and inter-Arab quarrels. Oil producers had less
money to finance military spending. The Arab states were passive during the
Lebanon war and First Palestinian Intifada. Next came the cold war's end
and the USSR's collapse, making the United States the world's sole superpower, weakening radical Arab regimes, giving moderate ones an incentive to
improve relations with Washington, and reducing US constraints on using its
own power.

Through all these tests, the Palestine Liberation Organization (PLO) suffered as a result of its own mistakes and these wider developments. In 1991,

the defeat of Iraq in the war over Kuwait led to the Madrid conference, which began a series of negotiations. Secret talks in Oslo produced a 1993 Israel-PLO agreement that gave rise to a seven-year-long peace process, culminating in the July 2000 Camp David meeting and President Bill Clinton's framework plan for negotiations. PLO leader Yasser Arafat rejected these offers, even as a basis for talks, and instead launched a new war.

In 2005, some months after Arafat's death, this war ended with a Palestinian defeat. Israel's withdrawal from the Gaza Strip and January 2006 Palestinian elections brought victory for the Islamist Palestinian group Hamas. In June 2007, Hamas seized control of the Gaza Strip. The era of PLO and Fatah hegemony over the Palestinian movement was finished. And the hopes for a negotiated peace, which began in the late 1980s and flourished in the 1990s, had been pushed back, probably for decades.

The 1993–2000 peace process was complex but did not fail due to small issues, technical matters, or US or Israeli errors. The ultimate problem was that the Palestinians failed to come to terms with making peace because of their goals, their ideology, their internal politics, and their leaders' need for the advantages of continuing conflict.

The result was not necessarily that Arafat went into the peace process knowing he would not reach an agreement in the end; his failure to make a deal in 2000 may have been a logical consequence of his basic worldview rather than a conscious design on his part. If he expected to get an agreement with Israel without reining in terrorism, or thought that the peace treaty would grant Palestinian refugees a full "right of return," or considered it possible to arrange things so that the door would remain open to destroying Israel in a later stage of conflict, or expected the United States and Europe to force Israel to make unilateral concessions to him without responding in kind, then he was taking into the peace process notions that doomed it to failure.

Equally, Arafat did nothing to prepare Palestinians for compromise during the seven-year-long process and instead led them to believe they would get everything they wanted through negotiation or violence. Simultaneously, Arafat had ensured support for his ultimate decision and was also able to use this same public opinion as an excuse for his refusal to make an agreement. In private, he told colleagues in 1993, "We entered Lebanon through a crack in the wall and we ended up controlling Beirut. We're entering Palestine through a crack in the wall and we'll see where it gets us."[1]

On January 20, 1996, Arafat won election as head of the Palestinian Authority (PA). This mandate could have been his launching pad for reaching a peace agreement that would make him ruler of a Palestinian state. Within days, however, the peace process faced its greatest crisis. A wave of Palestinian terrorist attacks profoundly shook Israeli trust in Arafat's intentions and abilities. In response, four months after Arafat's triumph at the polls, the Israelis elected a conservative government far more hostile to Arafat than the previous government.

Yet, despite this and numerous other problems, Arafat could still have made peace if he had provided decisive leadership to close a deal with Israel at the process's end. It was understandable to expect Arafat to act as dozens of other Third World leaders had all over the world. Scores of nationalist leaders had transformed themselves into presidents of peaceful, if hardly utopian, states. Moreover, the Oslo agreement existed only because Arafat had acted boldly on that occasion. Why, then, shouldn't he have repeated this feat to make a peace treaty with Israel?

Arafat's political pattern was unique: a strange mixture of dictatorship and pluralism, repression and conciliation, weakness and tight control. In his pluralistic-conciliatory stance, he sought to avoid confrontation and build a united front. As he had once mollified PLO member groups, he now worked to coopt the Islamist opposition, reconcile former Palestinian exiles with local residents of the West Bank and Gaza Strip, and bridge gaps between wealthy notables and young activists. As a "weak" leader, he let other groups do as they pleased—as long as they did not challenge his power and generally followed the political line and strategy he advocated.

As long as Israel could be presented as a danger and there was no peace treaty, Arafat's position as total ruler was sacrosanct. All criticism could be swept away, national unity preserved, and demands for a wider distribution of power rejected. His real domestic risks would begin only once peace arrived and a state was created. This fact gave him less incentive to cross that finish line, especially since many PLC (Palestine Legislative Council) members—like others in the PLO and Fatah elites—made it clear that any concession to Israel would be one too many for them.

On April 22, 1996, the PNC (Palestine National Council) convened in Gaza, and Arafat proved himself the master of persuasion, showing he could be an effective advocate of peace when he chose to be. He insisted that talks with Israel would produce a Palestinian state and demanded the delegates revise the PLO Charter. "All revolutions end in agreements. Do you think you can get everything you want?" he said in an angry exchange with Abd al-Shafi. During a closed session, he warned that those who demanded Israeli concessions before changing the PLO Charter were delaying the creation of a Palestinian state. "Where do you want to be buried, nowhere or in Palestine?" Arafat shouted.[2]

It was the moment when Arafat seemed closest to piloting the movement to a genuine transition. The final vote was 504 to 54 to remove the charter's passages that were contrary to the Palestinians' new commitments and to have the PNC Legal Committee look into composing a new charter.[3] The Israeli and US governments hailed this action as an important step toward peace. On three different occasions thereafter, Arafat wrote formal letters to President Bill Clinton certifying the abrogation of the charter's clauses demanding Israel's destruction through violence.

And yet even here, despite such an apparently iron-clad decision, Arafat managed to maintain ambiguity. He carried on no public discussion or educational effort among Palestinians about this huge apparent change in their historical goals. Meanwhile, when the PNC's own leader, Salim al-Za'nun, one of Arafat's closest allies, and those in the Fatah hierarchy responsible for ideology denied that the charter had been changed at all, Arafat did nothing to contradict or discipline them. The media he controlled broadcast material and interviews hinting that the goal was still Israel's elimination. As a result, Israelis critical of the Oslo agreements insisted that Arafat had shown his true nature.

The same principles applied to Arafat's unwillingness to force radical groups to accept or at least not violate the agreements he had made as the Palestinians' leader. Despite Arafat's overwhelming power, he did not want to foreclose either his own military option or the possibility of an alliance with Hamas. As a result, in 1995 alone, there had been thirty-three successful Palestinian armed attacks on Israelis that caused casualties. Hundreds more such operations had been foiled by Israeli security forces.[4]

Prime Minister Yitzhak Rabin's assassination by a right-wing Israeli extremist actually increased Israeli support for a compromise agreement. Every poll showed increased backing for a compromise peace with the Palestinians, and a confident Shimon Peres decided to call for new elections. Everyone expected Peres to defeat the Likud Party candidate, Benjamin Netanyahu, and to carry forward the peace process vigorously.

Precisely because he was considered much softer on Arafat and security issues than Rabin, Peres authorized the killing of the most effective Hamas terrorist, Yahya Ayyash, nicknamed the Engineer by the Israeli press. Peres had to act against Ayyash because Arafat had refused to do so. Ayyash had made the bombs for a series of deadly attacks on buses in Israel—including those in July, August, and October 1994—and his campaign was continuing. The Israelis knew Ayyash was in Gaza, but Arafat insisted he was in Sudan. Israel finally took matters into its own hands. In January 1996, Ayyash was killed in Gaza when he answered his cellular telephone, which was packed with fifty grams of explosives.

Now Hamas launched a wave of terrorist attacks in late February and early March 1996, making that the bloodiest period of terrorism in Israel's history.

While maintaining publicly that these acts were to revenge Ayyash's death, Hamas had many other motives as well. At Arafat's earlier urging, Hamas had suspended terrorism, although only temporarily, so as not to interfere with Israel's withdrawal from West Bank towns and then with the PA elections. These goals having been accomplished, Arafat had less incentive to stop terrorism, and Hamas, eager to return to action, had less reason to believe he would crack down on it.

Arafat had many tools he could have used to push Palestinians toward a moderate course and to reduce violence, and occasionally he used them, most notably when he needed to quiet down the upsurge of fighting following the Hamas terrorist attacks in February-March 1996. But he rarely deployed his key assets: his popularity; his legitimacy as the national leader; his command of the PLO, Fatah, and the PA; his ability to reward friends with money or jobs; and his threat of punishment. His sizable security forces, which ate up a very large portion of the PA's budget, could also have been used to ensure that the radicals would not block a compromise peace with Israel. Instead, he held them back.[5] For him, the security forces' real purpose was to ensure his rule at home, to provide jobs for followers, and to be an army to fight in a future confrontation with Israel. He thus supported efforts to smuggle in arms and expand his forces to a size forbidden by the agreements he had made.[6]

In February, March, and August 1997, Arafat organized meetings with Hamas, the PFLP (Popular Front for the Liberation of Palestine), and the DFLP (Democratic Front for the Liberation of Palestine) to bring them into his coalition. But these exchanges made no progress. The opposition told Arafat he must end talks with Israel, release its activists from PA jails, and launch a serious anticorruption effort.[7] Rather than make the substantive changes they demanded, Arafat found it easier to let these groups continue their activities, including preparing and sometimes launching attacks on Israel.

But after May 1996 Arafat would face a new challenge in dealing with a truly hostile Israeli prime minister. Netanyahu had opposed the Oslo agreement and viewed Arafat as a terrorist who had not changed his stripes. True, as Arafat had predicted, Netanyahu had to accept the agreements negotiated by his predecessors. But while Rabin and Peres had unwillingly slowed or suspended talks due to terrorist attacks and the difficulties of negotiating with Arafat, Netanyahu was happy to do so.

While Rabin and Peres accepted the notion that many problems—such as Arafat's oversized security agencies and continued anti-Israel incitement in the Palestinian media—could be deferred to after a full peace agreement had been reached, Netanyahu intended to hold Arafat to full compliance with all his commitments. Finally, while Rabin and Peres had looked on the Jewish settlements in the West Bank and Gaza as a problem, Netanyahu and his government backed them.

Whether from fear of Netanyahu's toughness or for other reasons, Arafat tried more energetically to prevent violence after 1996 than he had done before.[8] Shaken by Netanyahu's threat to send the Israeli army into PA territory, Arafat reacted decisively, arresting hundreds of Hamas and Islamic Jihad activists, warning Hamas to stop its offensive or face serious retribution, and thus drastically reducing terrorism.[9] Arafat had shown he could certainly stop attacks when he wanted to. But he did not always want to.

In September, Netanyahu ordered the opening of a tourist tunnel in East Jerusalem that let people see the buried Western Wall of the Jewish Temple, now also the al-Aqsa mosque's retaining wall. The Muslims had been given permission to open a new prayer room at this site—that is, on Temple Mount—as part of a deal. But Palestinians, encouraged by the PA-controlled media, spread rumors that the tunnel was a plot to destroy the al-Aqsa mosque itself. In the ensuing riots and gun battles between PA and Israeli troops, eighty-six Palestinians and fifteen Israelis were killed and many more wounded. The PA media controlled by Arafat incited violence daily.[10]

While Netanyahu spent months renegotiating the deal Peres had made for the security arrangements and for the redeployment of Israeli forces in Hebron—the only West Bank Palestinian city where Jewish settlers lived—in the end he had to sign virtually the same agreement that had previously been made. Abu Mazin, Arafat's deputy and later his successor, took the lead in getting Arafat to agree, though it was clear that Arafat did not understand the complicated arrangements dividing the town into different zones.

In January 1997, the PA took over 80 percent of Hebron, and Arafat visited to be welcomed by sixty thousand cheering Palestinians. The speech he made on that occasion was one of the peak moments in Arafat's conciliatory tone. "We have made a peace agreement with all the Israeli people" and all their political parties, he said. "There were 87 votes in the Knesset for peace . . . and that is something new in the Middle East. . . . Therefore I say, that all forces of peace in Israel have voted for this decision and together with the Palestinian side will make a just and comprehensive peace in the Middle East."[11]

Perhaps Arafat was forthcoming precisely because he thought that Netanyahu would not be. Indeed, shortly thereafter the Israeli prime minister announced a provocative decision to build sixty-five hundred housing units on Jerusalem's southeastern edge in an area called Har Homa. It was part of a strategy to ring East Jerusalem with Jewish neighborhoods so that it could never come under Palestinian rule. This action angered Arafat and raised the level of bilateral friction with Israel, but it also opened an opportunity for Arafat to move closer than ever to the United States.

Arafat appeared to hold fast to his belief that violence would increase his leverage in negotiations and strengthen him regarding internal Palestinian politics. On March 21, 1997, a Hamas suicide bombing in a Tel Aviv café killed three Israelis and injured forty. The PA condemned the bombing in statements aimed at the West. Netanyahu accused Arafat of giving a green light for terrorism and demanded the PA crack down on the groups carrying out these attacks, as it had pledged to do in all previous agreements. A wave of Palestinian attacks against Israel culminated in a major bombing in Jerusalem on July 30, 1997. In messages directed toward the West, Arafat condemned the bombing and said he would do all he could to prevent such incidents in the future. But a statement issued by the PA information ministry, for internal consumption, charged that the suicide bombings were a result of Israel's policies of "expanding settlements, confiscating Palestinian land, building new settlements, Judaizing Arab Jerusalem, isolating the Palestinian territories, and closing the labor market to Palestinian laborers."[12]

Netanyahu talked frequently about how he would force Arafat to engage in "reciprocity." Israel would make more concessions only if Arafat honored his own commitments. Yet Netanyahu's attempt to pressure Arafat into stricter compliance had no effect. The PA made no serious, consistent effort to collect weapons, break up terror networks, or dismantle bomb factories.

Through a strange twist of events, Netanyahu did give Arafat one interesting opportunity to test his claims. In October 1997, Israel released Hamas leader Ahmed Yasin. Yasin urged Palestinian unity and praised Arafat. But soon Yasin was attacking Arafat and urging Hamas to continue armed attacks. Instead of calming the situation, Yasin's release was followed by more attacks, including a November 4 bombing at a Jerusalem mall killing 4 Israeli civilians and wounding 170. This attack took place just as Israel was starting to lift the restrictions imposed after earlier attacks. The restrictions were immediately reinstated.[13] Criticized by the United States and threatened by Israel, Arafat again, as he had in March 1996, temporarily arrested Hamas and Islamic Jihad members and closed a Hamas-run newspaper, television station, and charities.

With an end nearing for the five-year transitional period designated by the Oslo Accords, Arafat faced the possibility that deadlock might turn the transitional arrangements into a permanent situation. To avoid this outcome, Arafat pledged in April 1998 that he would unilaterally proclaim statehood in 1999 and implied that Palestinians could turn to violence if their demands were not met.[14] Netanyahu immediately warned that such a proclamation would nullify the previous agreements and lead to Israel's annexing parts of the West Bank and Gaza still controlled by Israel.[15]

In October 1998, Arafat, Netanyahu, and Clinton held a summit meeting at the Wye Plantation conference center on Maryland's eastern shore. The negotiations centered on Arafat's goal of getting another Israeli withdrawal to give him more land and Netanyahu's objective of getting in exchange some way of ensuring Arafat that would comply more with his earlier unmet commitments.

On October 23, after nine days of work, Arafat and Netanyahu signed an agreement with a complex timetable of interlocking steps. A US-Israel-Palestinian security plan was to be drawn up to limit violence. The PA would imprison thirty murderers on Israel's wanted list—Netanyahu had dropped his demand for extradition—and collect the radical groups' weapons. The PLO's highest bodies would confirm the revision of the PLO Charter to eliminate clauses calling for Israel's destruction and an Israel-PA anti-incitement committee would seek to reduce media encouragement of violence and terrorism. The Palestinians would receive their own Gaza–West Bank safe passage route, airport, and seaport. The agreement accepted the PA's violation of earlier commitments to build a thirty-thousand-strong security force and set that number as the new limit. Israel would make three redeployments of its troops to turn more West Bank territory over to the PA and release 750 Palestinian prisoners involved in past violence.[16]

Israel's Knesset approved the Wye agreement, but the right wing of Netanyahu's coalition rebelled against his concessions, and he was forced to call new elections for May 1999. Israel released 250 Palestinian prisoners and made its first redeployment on the northern West Bank. Later, the PA would get its airport and seaport. But there was no change in the Palestinian media's tone, no collection of weapons, and no long-term imprisonment of terrorists. The security plan never materialized either.

Instead of cracking down on incitement against Israel in PA institutions, Arafat used the Wye agreement's anti-incitement clauses to block Palestinian criticism of his own policies or officials, then blamed these measures on alleged Israeli demands.[17]

On May 17, 1999, Israelis elected as prime minister Ehud Barak, a man who had promised to make a deal with Arafat even if it required big Israeli concessions. Barak's colleagues included the Oslo agreement's creators.

Arafat had been complaining that Israel's leader, Netanyahu, did not want to implement the agreements. Now he had a counterpart who was staking his whole political career on doing so. Arafat had been the one insisting on arriving at an agreement that would bring the creation of a Palestinian state. Now he had an Israeli leader ready to accept that outcome.

In 2000, Arafat would get his way on many of these points, as well as his best chance ever to fulfill his expressed goals and program. Barak worried that continuing the step-by-step approach, in which a series of partial agreements would be made over a long period of time, meant Israel would keep turning over more West Bank land without the Palestinian side making any compromises for a final settlement or even implementing its earlier pledges.[18] So Barak preferred, as Arafat said he also did and the Oslo plan mandated, to move quickly and steadily toward a comprehensive peace treaty.

Clinton presented the proposal to Arafat during the July, 2000, Camp David II Summit. On borders, the Palestinians would receive an independent state whose territory would include all the Gaza Strip, the equivalent of 92 percent of the West Bank (including a 1 percent trade of land with Israel), and most of east Jerusalem. The state would be demilitarized, though it is worth noting that Arafat's PA was already defined as demilitarized, since it had huge security agencies but no formal armed forces.

According to this plan, settlements on the 9 percent of West Bank land to be annexed by Israel would remain, while Jewish settlers would leave those areas becoming part of the Palestinian state. During the refugee committee meetings, Israeli delegates had even raised the idea that the buildings and other assets of Jewish settlements would be turned over as part of the compensation for Palestinian refugees, who could either live in those buildings or sell them.

On East Jerusalem, Barak took a step hitherto unthinkable for any Israeli prime minister by proposing that the Palestinian state include seven or eight of the nine Arab neighborhoods in the city, plus the Muslim and Christian quarters of Jerusalem's Old City. Israel would annex the Jewish quarter and also the tiny Armenian quarter, which consisted mainly of Christian religious buildings with virtually no residents. This area was needed to provide access to the Jewish quarter from Israeli territory, which even then would comprise a corridor only a few yards wide. There would be some shared security control in several other neighborhoods under Palestinian control.

As for the most controversial place, Temple Mount, containing the remains of the Jewish Temple, the only true Jewish holy site in the world, and the al-Aqsa mosque, as well as the Dome of the Rock, of great importance to Muslims, US officials came up with several creative solutions. They proposed having the UN Security Council make the Palestinians custodians of the mosque area, giving them control and barring Israeli forces from entering, while Israel retained overall symbolic sovereignty. Since the Temple's ruins lay within the Mount, Israel did not want to give total authority over it to the Palestinians, but for all practical purposes, they were ceding full control. The analogy used was that of a country's embassy, which is considered legally part of that country's territory, though the land formally belongs to the host country.[19]

More than any other issue, the Palestinian position demanding a total "return" of all Palestinian refugees to live in Israel persuaded the Israelis that Arafat was not really interested in a deal and had not given up his hope of destroying Israel. Some Palestinian leaders were aware that their stance on this point would make peace impossible.

The Palestinians rejected the Camp David II Summit proposal but made no counteroffer. On every point, Arafat was sticking to his traditional position: all the West Bank and Gaza, all East Jerusalem, and all refugees offered a right to live in Israel. Arafat rejected this proposal even as a framework for further negotiations. By turning down this deal, Arafat not only denied his people a state and ensured prolonging the occupation and their refugee status but also threw away an opportunity to gain huge material benefits for every Palestinian. US delegates estimated that the Palestinians could receive more than $20 billion in refugee compensation to be raised internationally.[20] The United States proposed to lead a global fund-raising campaign for money to be administered by a special international committee.[21]

Two months after Arafat's decision at Camp David, Palestinians began a new uprising under his leadership. More than four thousand Palestinians and one thousand Israelis were killed during the al-Aqsa Intifada.

Any agreement on the terms offered would have created a tremendous incentive for Israel and Palestine to get along peacefully but, by the same token, would inevitably have left both sides vulnerable to violations of the accord. In this respect, Israel would have been no better off than the Palestinians. What if, as happened a few months later, Palestinian terrorists attacked Israel and an Arafat-led government denied responsibility and did nothing to stop them? What if, after independence, the Palestinian government rejected the demilitarization clause or even invited in help from the army of some other Arab state? Israel's only recourse would have been to go to war under very unfavorable security and international conditions.

What would Arafat do next? At Camp David, he had predicted on many occasions that if he did not get everything he wanted, the Palestinians would erupt in violence.[22] This was no mere political analysis on his part but a threat to gain leverage over the other parties and an alternative if and when the talks broke down. Immediately after the summit ended, his Fatah movement announced a general call-up of young men for weapons training.[23]

As had happened before, Arafat saw violence as an alternative to negotiations, as a way to get what he wanted either by intimidating or defeating his foe. In this effort, he used his old tactic of seeking international sympathy and an even older one of trying to wear down Israel through terrorism. In addition, Arafat's popularity had been at a low point for some time, with growing complaints about corruption, repression, and the failure of a state to materialize. Once the fighting began, however, all the Palestinians' anger was turned away from Arafat and toward Israel.

Some informal contacts did continue after the Camp David meeting, since both sides wanted to show they were not responsible for any diplomatic breakdown.[24] On September 25, 2000, Barak even invited Arafat to his home. The atmosphere was friendly, but no progress was made.

There were more meetings at New York's Waldorf Astoria Hotel and at the Ritz-Carlton Hotel near the Pentagon in Virginia during the last few days of September. But nothing new was said.[25] Meanwhile, the US side was pulling together Clinton's follow-up peace proposal, which they planned to present on October 1.

But then, on September 28, the explosion that Clinton had prophesied and Arafat had threatened at the summit's end began. Ariel Sharon, Israel's opposition leader, made a one-hour visit to the Temple Mount/Haram al-Sharif area in Jerusalem's Old City.[26]

Marwan Barghouti, Fatah's leader on the West Bank, saw Sharon's visit as an opportunity: "I knew that the end of September was the last period [of time] before the explosion, but when Sharon reached the al-Aqsa Mosque, this was the most appropriate moment for the outbreak of the Intifada."[27]

After Sharon left, Palestinian activists held a two-hour meeting on how to spread the battle to all PA-controlled areas.[28] At al-Aqsa the next day, a large number of Palestinians demonstrated. Some threw stones, and Israeli police replied with rubber-coated metal bullets and live ammunition to disperse the demonstrators, killing four and injuring about two hundred of them. Fourteen Israeli policemen were also hurt. Violence spread quickly. By the end of the first week, over sixty Palestinians and five Israelis had been killed. Madeleine Albright, the US secretary of state, called Arafat and asked him to stop the violence. But he did nothing.[29]

The Palestinians called the new uprising the al-Aqsa Intifada, a name inflaming religious passions. But few of those demonstrating in what they thought to be the defense of an endangered holy site knew that Arafat had already been offered sovereignty over al-Aqsa at the Camp David Summit. For Arafat, the conflict was actually a Palestinian war to gain independence without compromise or negotiations.

On October 4, after Arafat rejected the first American call for a cease-fire, Barak and Arafat met with Albright at the US embassy in Paris with plans to continue talking in Egypt the following day. During the meeting, Arafat expressed reluctance to issue a public statement calling for an end to the uprising, and Barak refused to accept Arafat's demand for an international investigation of the origins of the violence without even getting a cease-fire in exchange.

With his popularity plummeting and his coalition splintered, Barak resigned on December 10 and called for early elections, a desperate move apparently aimed at giving himself some slim chance of victory, since his opponent would be Ariel Sharon rather than the more popular Netanyahu.

On December 23, Israeli and Palestinian negotiators met at Bolling Air Force Base near Washington for Clinton's last effort to make peace. He offered new concessions to the Palestinians going beyond even what had been offered at the end of Camp David.[30] According to the new offer, the Palestinian state would include between 94 and 96 percent of the West Bank, plus a 1–3 percent land swap between Israel and Palestine. Thus the Palestinians would get roughly the equivalent of the entire pre–1967 land area of the West Bank. The goal would be to incorporate 80 percent of the Israeli settlers into areas that would become part of Israel, while also maximizing the territorial contiguity of the Palestinian state. In addition, there would be three Israeli early-warning stations in the West Bank to ensure that foreign armies were not moving to cross into that area, with Palestinian officials present to inspect the use of these places.

On Jerusalem, too, the offer was improved for the Palestinians. Now they would have total sovereignty over the Temple Mount/Haram al-Sharif and Israel would have sovereignty only over the Western Wall; Israel's only influence over the Temple's site would be that its permission would be required to excavate, while the Palestinians would also be able to veto any Israeli digging behind the Western Wall.

Finally, regarding refugees, the US offer tried to meet Palestinian demands. An international commission would be established to handle this issue. Two alternative ideas were offered that might meet both parties' wishes. One idea was for both sides to recognize a right of Palestinian refugees to return to "historic Palestine" and "their homeland," which could be fulfilled by migration to the Palestinian state. Alternatively, the agreement would list a number of acceptable destinations for the refugees: the state of Palestine, areas of Israel transferred to Palestine in the land swap, Arab states where they now lived, another country, or Israel. Both Israel and Palestine would decide their own policy on admitting refugees.

The Clinton plan came close to giving the Palestinians 99 percent of their demands, aside from the "return" issue, while transcending any of Israel's previous interpretation of its goals and security needs. Clearly, the package was tailored to winning Arafat's acceptance.

The Israelis approved the plan despite reservations, which Israeli foreign minister Shlomo Ben Ami called "minor and dealing mainly with security arrangements." The Palestinian press declared that the US proposal was unacceptable because it would allegedly divide a Palestinian state into three sections, undermining its ability to survive; split Palestinian Jerusalem into disconnected islands; and constitute an unacceptable surrender of the so-called right of return. Rather than accept the plan as a framework for negotiations, Arafat said it would first have to be totally changed. In fact, his responses amounted to merely a repetition of all his earlier claims, without even the one or two small compromises he had offered at Camp David.

The Palestinians later maintained that Arafat had accepted the agreement with reservations. But Palestinian accounts make clear that this was not so. At most, Arafat said he viewed the agreement as containing interesting elements that the negotiators might study without being bound to them.

Arafat never told his own people what he had been offered. But his Fatah group's most comprehensive official analysis of the plan shows what he wanted them to believe about the proposal and the reasons they should reject it completely.[31] Fatah's argument begins by insisting that the peace process "was launched on the basis of international legitimacy." In its second point, the Fatah document denounces "the monopoly of the Zionist Clinton administration" as mediator, even though Arafat had constantly sought to increase the American role in the negotiations. Equally telling was the Fatah paper's broader conclusion. Unless all Palestinian demands were met, stated Point 9, the conflict would not end.

What was most telling of all, however, was Arafat's perception of the "right of return," ultimately the issue that really blocked any chance of an agreement. He always spoke as if UN Resolution 194 was a virtually sacred document guaranteeing a "right of return," a total misstatement of that document's purpose and contents. The resolution was, in fact, a nonbinding set of instructions given for a short-lived, abortive mediation effort that the Arab side had rejected shortly after the 1948 war.

What was most shocking about Arafat's approach, however, was how irrational it was from the standpoint of a genuine Palestinian nationalist. Nationalists want their people to live in their own country in order to maintain an identity, and to increase its population, power, and prosperity. If the goal was to build a strong, stable Palestinian state living in peace alongside Israel, everything would have been done to discourage any notion of a return. Why should a Palestinian state apparently make a gift of these people, their money, and their talents to Israel? Aside from any other consideration, Palestine would lose hundreds of thousands of them merely because they would seek jobs and better living standards in Israel. These bizarre contradictions seem to show Arafat's belief that a "return" would subvert Israel and put it under Palestinian rule. In that case, the returnees would not be lost to Palestine but would soon be making a real "return" to that state while bringing all of Israel with them.

After the Clinton plan, for all practical purposes the peace process was over. There was one last attempt at Taba, Egypt, on January 21–27, 2001, but neither Arafat nor Barak were there, and it was more an exchange of opinions than a negotiation.[32] While initially Abu Alaa, the Palestinian team's head, stated, "There has never before been a clearer gap in the positions of the two sides,"[33] Palestinian leaders later proclaimed that the meeting had come close to success. Their motive was to consolidate Israel's new concessions as the starting point for future negotiation. On Jerusalem, Israel proposed a special regime for the whole city, but the Palestinians again demanded control over all East Jerusalem.[34] On borders, however, the Palestinians offered to swap 2 percent of the West Bank for an equal amount of land from Israel, an echo of Abu Alaa's idea at Camp David, and agreed to three Israeli settlement blocs.[35] But this exchange would include only the actual land on which buildings stood. All land adjacent to the settlement and the roads would remain in Palestinian hands, making them unviable and undefendable.[36]

While this was clearly not the case, Arafat told his own people that there had never been a reasonable offer by the United States or Israel. "Was a real opportunity for peace lost? I think not," he told a major rally in March 2001. He claimed that since Israel had withdrawn the proposal, this proved that it had never intended to implement a deal. This argument ignored the fact that the offers had been clearly made only on the basis of his acceptance. Moreover, Arafat's own rejection of peace plans, war against Israel, and refusal to stop attacks were the cause of Israel's rethinking its offer to make concessions. But Arafat simply insisted to Palestinians, "There was no opportunity that was wasted."[37]

On January 3, 2002, Israeli commandos captured the freighter *Karine A* in a lightning-fast raid. Bound for Gaza, the vessel had aboard fifty tons of weapons ordered by Yasser Arafat's forces, including Katyusha rockets, Sagger and LAW antitank missiles, mortars, mines, sophisticated explosives, sniper rifles, and bullets. If all this equipment had arrived as planned, Arafat's troops could have greatly escalated their war on Israel.

Discovery of this ship's mission implicated Arafat as the one behind the violence that had been raging since September 2000 and the difficulty in ending it. But there was even more to the story that might discredit Arafat internationally. The weapons had been purchased through Hizbollah and supplied by Iran. Just four months after the devastating September 11, 2001, terrorist attack on America, Arafat was aligning himself with a movement and country the United States saw as principal elements in an "axis of evil," foes in its war against terrorism, and even allies, to a degree, with the forces of Osama bin Ladin.

Arafat felt secure that his survival skills made up for his penchant for making bad decisions. He and his lieutenants disclaimed any link to the shipment.

He argued, rather unpersuasively, that he did not need to buy weapons because he had his own arms depots all over the world and that Arab countries would give him whatever he wanted.[38] Instead, he insisted the raid on the freighter was all a plot by Israel to frame him.[39]

Indeed, the renewed battle against Israel reinforced Arafat's popularity. Palestinians overwhelmingly backed his policy and the violent tactics being used. Instead of talking about mismanagement, corruption, and economic woes, Palestinians, convinced they had no choice, again rallied behind Arafat's leadership against an enemy portrayed as diabolical and intransigent. They believed that neither Israel nor the United States had ever made a reasonable or attractive offer for a peaceful resolution of the conflict. Since their leadership made it clear to them that negotiations had failed and the enemy was uninterested in ever ending the occupation and letting them have a state, violence was the only alternative.

As the war continued in 2002 and Israeli forces periodically advanced deep into the West Bank, Palestinian grumbling increased. It became clear that the war could not defeat Israel and was causing far larger losses on their own side. Palestinians increasingly expressed their sense of insecurity, complaints about the lack of PA relief efforts, declining living standards, the loss of educational opportunities, and such maladies as stress, depression, and sleep deprivation.[40] The intifada's first fifteen months cost the Palestinian economy an estimated $2.4 billion. Real income fell by 30 percent, to a level lower than in the late 1980s; unemployment tripled. The PA could barely, and not always, pay its employees.[41]

The landslide electoral victory of Ariel Sharon, Arafat's old nemesis, in early 2001 should have bothered Arafat. Sharon had been responsible for Arafat's great defeat of 1982 in Lebanon, had refused to shake his hand at the 1998 Wye meeting, and had opposed Barak's peace plan as far too generous. Yet there was every sign that Sharon's victory pleased Arafat, who preferred facing his military reprisals rather than Barak's diplomatic offensives. Arafat thought Sharon would be unpopular with Western and Arab governments, media, and public opinion. He could easily portray Sharon as a war-loving reactionary opposed to peace or compromise.

The most detailed evidence of Arafat's direct involvement in terrorist attacks came from documents taken by Israel during its March 2002 siege of his Ramallah office compound. The al-Aqsa Martyrs Brigade, nominally an independent group ignoring Arafat's authority, was shown to be led by local Fatah leaders who were on Arafat's payroll and used official Fatah stationary to ask Arafat's personal approval to give money for gunmen, weapons, posters, and financial assistance to families of terrorists who had been captured or killed in action.[42]

On June 1, 2001, a Saturday-night bombing by Hamas outside a Tel Aviv disco killed twenty Israeli teenagers. After a direct appeal from German foreign minister Joschka Fischer, who was visiting him at the time, Arafat agreed to speak on Palestinian television promising to "exert the utmost efforts to stop the bloodshed of our people and of the Israeli people."[43] But aside from this broadcast he did nothing. A few days later, the suicide bomber's family received a letter from the PLO embassy in Jordan, over Arafat's signature, calling the bomber's act a "heroic martyrdom operation . . . the model of manhood and sacrifice for the sake of Allah and the homeland."[44] When Israel identified the two men who had run the operation and, with US support, asked the PA to arrest them, a PA security agency spoke to the terrorists. They admitted their involvement. The security officers then told them to sign an agreement not to do it again and let them go home.[45]

Yossi Sarid, leader of the left-wing Israeli party Meretz, and one of the peace process's main champions, advised Arafat in March 2001, "Maybe it's time you stopped flitting from one country to another. Settle down in Gaza and Ramallah and start bringing order, because this anarchy is going to bring a terrible disaster upon our people as well as on yours. . . . Do not make us suspect that you . . . care more for an armed and violent struggle for a Palestinian state than for the Palestinian state itself."[46]

But this is exactly what Israelis did suspect. Yossi Beilin, an architect of the Oslo agreement and the most important Israeli politician still friendly toward him in April 2001 stated that even the leftists now believed that "the Oslo agreement was a plot and not a historic program of conciliation. At the critical moments of test—at Camp David, at Sharm al-Shaykh and at Taba—Arafat's true face was revealed. What he wanted was not a peace treaty, but the implementation of the Palestinian plan of stages for annihilating Israel."[47]

In April 2001, an international commission—which had originated with Arafat's own demand to look into the causes of the new intifada—issued what is usually called the Mitchell Report. Although the commission did not accept Arafat's request to send an international force to the West Bank, many points in the report were favorable to Arafat's position, for example, the demand for a freeze on settlements, a plan for returning to negotiations, and an analysis of the violence that avoided blaming Arafat.[48] Arafat could have ended the fighting and demanded that Israel implement the commission's provisions.[49] Instead, he merely complained about the sections he didn't like and continued the fighting.

Despite the opportunities offered by the Mitchell Report and the September 11 crisis, as well as the pleas of European leaders who wanted to help him, Arafat made no serious attempt to end the fighting as it dragged on through 2001. In August, Israeli forces killed PFLP leader Abu Ali Mustafa, whom it accused of planning terrorist attacks. Two months later, the PFLP slew Israeli tourism minister Rehavam Ze'evi at a Jerusalem hotel. Despite PFLP claims of responsibility for the latter shooting, Arafat denied that Palestinians were involved and suggested that Ze'evi's death was an Israeli conspiracy. When Israel accused four Palestinians of culpability, Arafat protected them.[50]

Sensitive to international pressure and to his own reputation as an extremist, Sharon acted with relative restraint at first. He knew that Israeli ground forces could seize control of the West Bank, destroy the PA, and force Arafat into exile, but he refrained from such a strategy. Arafat had to be aware that Sharon always retained that option. As the terror attacks escalated, there was no sign of a cease-fire, and as Arafat lost Arab and Western support, Sharon had less incentive to hold back his full retaliation. On December 1, 11 Israelis were killed and about 180 injured when explosive devices were detonated by two Hamas suicide bombers at a pedestrian mall in the center of Jerusalem. The next day 15 Israelis were killed and 40 injured in a Hamas suicide bombing on a bus in Haifa; on December 4, as a warning to Arafat, Israeli missiles destroyed his three helicopters and tore up the landing strip at Gaza International Airport.

Still, the terrorist assaults on civilians within Israel continued and even accelerated at times when Sharon was not meeting with US president George W. Bush. On March 27, 29 people were killed by a suicide bomber at a Passover celebration in Netanya. This was the final straw for Sharon. Israel's army was now ordered to advance into PA territory to damage facilities, kill or arrest terrorist leaders and planners, and destroy bomb or munitions factories. Arafat's compound in Ramallah was surrounded and he was under siege. The specific quarry in the encirclement of Arafat was Ze'evi's assassins, whom Arafat had moved into his headquarters for protection.

Battles broke out, especially in Jenin, which attracted international attention. PA leaders, including Arafat, claimed that Israel had massacred many Palestinians. While at first the Western media reported or accepted such assertions, it was soon shown that they were untrue. Despite inflicting casualties on Israeli forces, the Palestinians suffered far higher losses and a humiliating military defeat.[51]

Meanwhile, Arafat promised political reforms, but once again none of the measures were made. Even in the face of national disaster, the only step the PLC took was to reject Arafat's proposed new cabinet in September 2002, which it had come close to doing on at least three previous occasions.[52] Even then, Arafat merely had to make some small alterations in the cabinet in order to win the PLC's overwhelming approval six weeks later.[53] When the real showdown might have come at the October 2002 Fatah Central Committee meeting, the opposition collapsed. Abu Mazin and Abu Alaa did not even show up, and no one there would fight for the demand that Arafat name a powerful prime minister. Arafat was still in control and, as so many times before, had easily defeated attempts to reform his behavior without significant domestic costs.[54]

At about the same time, though, his traditional failure to manage external forces was once more on view. Israel's army staged its second siege of Arafat in Ramallah for ten days beginning on September 19. Like the previous siege, the operation came after suicide bombings within Israel and was aimed at capturing men wanted for their involvement in planning attacks on Israelis. This time, few prisoners were taken, but the army brought in bulldozers and tore down most of the compound's buildings. Arafat's office was left surrounded by empty shells of structures and piles of rubble.[55] Once again, saved by the Americans, Arafat emerged flashing his hand in a V-for-victory sign and blowing kisses to a crowd of chanting supporters.[56]

Nevertheless, this was to be Arafat's last political hurrah, as he had lost all credibility with both the United States and Israel. In mid-June 2003, under heavy international pressure, he had agreed to partially change the Palestinian system of governance to allow for an "empowered" prime minister, as Bush had demanded. However, the prime minister, Mahmoud Abbas, was to resign only three months later, claiming that Arafat had undercut him. From then until his death in November 2004, Arafat was a "nonperson" as far as the United States and Israel were concerned. Indeed, arguing that there was no Palestinian partner for peace, Sharon embarked on his unilateral withdrawal policy.

Arafat's successor as president of the Palestinian Authority was Mahmoud Abbas, and Abbas initially raised hopes that he would help revive the peace process. However, his March 2005 agreement with Hamas to settle their disagreements only through "dialogue," instead of cracking down on the terrorist organizations as Israel and the United States demanded, undermined his position in Israeli eyes. Abbas also proved ineffectual in reforming the corrupt Palestinian Authority and proved unable to solve the conflict between Fatah's old guard and young guard, factors that, in part, helped explain Fatah's loss to Hamas in the January 2006 Palestinian Legislative Council elections.

The victory of Hamas, the Palestinian Islamist group, in the January 2006 parliamentary elections seemed like an earthquake transforming the Arab-Israeli conflict, Palestinian politics, prospects for democratization, and even the region as a whole. Yet this development should not have been a surprise. More than just heralding the rise of Hamas and Islamists, it was both based on and ensured the Palestinian nationalist movement's overdue collapse.

In the long run, Fatah and the nationalists had outlived their usefulness. On one hand, they were responsible for almost forty years of failure. True, the PLO did get back into the West Bank and the Gaza Strip in 1994, but only by making an agreement with Israel. Yet, while Israel let two hundred thousand Palestinians return, a government was formed (the Palestinian Authority), and international aid reached the highest per capita levels for any people in history, the Palestinians' situation improved only marginally.

Compared to Hamas's toughness and proud extremism, the Fatah nationalists were paralyzed by overweening smugness. Believing their own slogan that they were the Palestinians' sole legitimate representatives, they could not conceive that they could be replaced. Rather than improve their performance, they ignored all the problems that were bringing them down.

In facing the Hamas challenge, the PA and Fatah could certainly have done well enough to survive even within their own traditional approach. Yet the real solution would have been to develop a truly new program based on self-criticism of past errors and a sense of reality about the present. They could have made a deal with Israel to end the conflict and obtain a state. The nationalists might have focused on raising living standards; convincing refugees to return to a Palestinian state (rather than demand they move to Israel); gaining credibility with Israel as a peace partner; creating a strong economy, schools, and health system; and other such steps. There is no evidence that the leadership of Fatah or the PA—except for a handful of people—ever seriously considered such a program.

Only Arafat's death in 2004 forced the Palestinians to seek a new leader, but his legacy—constantly reaffirmed by most of his colleagues and successors—continues to shape the Palestinian experience. By three critical factors Arafat posthumously ensured the collapse of the nationalist movement and of his own Fatah group.

First, Palestinian institutions and governmental structures were a mess. Second, in strategic terms, the movement is in an extremely weak position. Third, in ideological terms, Arafat ensured that militancy would be the dominant ideological force. All of these factors played into the hands of Hamas, which promised to provide a strong, honest, caring institution in comparison to Fatah's anarchy. As for strategy and ideology, Hamas implicitly offered to continue Fatah's line but to do it better and more systematically. By extolling extremism and militancy, Fatah sowed the seeds and Hamas reaped the crop.

While the Fatah and PA establishment rejected any reforms or moderation, it still had good reasons for having Abbas as nominal leader. He is one of them, a man who could be trusted to support their interests against the younger generation and Islamists. At the same time, they knew he was too weak to challenge their own power. Yet he was extremely valuable, since he could still present a more moderate face to the world, thus retaining Western support and money better than the openly hard-line leaders.[57]

Challenging the establishment was a group of younger Fatah militants, including the terrorist al-Aqsa Martyrs Brigade and Fatah's grassroots Tanzim group. Its best-known leader was Marwan Barghouti, now serving a life sentence in an Israeli jail as the main organizer of the 2000–2005 terrorist campaign. The young insurgents view Fatah's establishment leaders with contempt, as having failed to win victory and instead becoming corrupt bureaucrats. The insurgents wanted a concerted war on Israel, which they believe would force its withdrawal to the pre–1967 boundaries without any political concessions on the Palestinians' part.

All three of the most powerful Palestinian political groups—the Fatah establishment, the Fatah young guard, and Hamas—have the same basic worldview, goals, and strategy. Against this combination, Abbas's shaky belief that a moderate course was needed and his timidity in implementing anything had no chance of even partial success.[58] Ironically, after helping make Abbas's administration a failure, the Fatah young guard and Hamas posed as the alternatives to this unsatisfactory leadership. Yet by running so many competing candidates in the January 2006 parliamentary election, the Fatah young guard ensured a landslide victory for Hamas and a defeat for its own organization.

Consequently, in the January 2006 elections, Hamas won a big victory: seventy-four parliamentary seats to only forty-four for Fatah.

Why did Palestinians vote for Hamas? In the past, 20–25 percent of Palestinians had identified with Hamas. In the 2006 elections, in very rough terms, about half those voting for Hamas supported its entire program, and the other half backed it due to disillusionment with Fatah's rule.

Following the election, the West announced plans to cut links to the regime, but in practice, aid actually increased, though most went to Palestinian institutions rather than the government itself. Hamas and Fatah fought sporadically, and anarchy also allowed a proliferation of armed and criminal groups, adding to the chaos. A Saudi-mediated agreement for a coalition soon fell apart. Hamas seized full power in the Gaza Strip against disorganized Fatah opposition. Fatah retained the West Bank, and Abbas declared that his government there was the legitimate Palestinian government. While failing to build one state, the Palestinian movement had in fact created two warring entities. Although Israel was ready to deal with the Fatah–West Bank entity, the prospects for successful negotiations for a comprehensive peace were close to zero.

Notes

1. Author's interview with Palestinian official.

2. *Jerusalem Post* (April 25–26, 1996).

3. Author's observations; 111 other delegates either abstained or didn't participate. Among those opposing the change were Ashrawi and Abd al-Shafi, an important reminder that those who were seen as moderates when it came to democracy were often extremists when it came to the peace process.

4. Many examples are given at the Internet site of the International Policy Institute for Counterterrorism Chronology, http://www.ict .org.il.

5. *Ha'aretz* (April 1, 1998).

6. *Ma'ariv* (March 1, 1998); *Yediot Aharonot* (March 25, 1998).

7. *Al-Dustur* (May 24 and 31, 1997).

8. Author's interview with Netanyahu.

9. Author's interviews.

10. *Palestine Report* (October 4, 1996).

11. Author's observations at the rally.

12. *Jerusalem Post* (August 3, 1997).

13. *Financial Times* (September 5, 1997).

14. *Jerusalem Post* (April 19, 1998).

15. *Al-Quds* (September 28, 1998), in *Foreign Broadcast Information Service Daily Report: The Middle East.*

16. For the text of the agreement, see Walter Laqueur and Barry Rubin, *Israel-Arab Reader* (New York: Penguin, 2001), pp. 529–534.

17. *Middle East Monitor* (January 4, 1999).

18. Author's interview with Sher, May 3, 2001.

19. This was also referred to as giving "functional sovereignty" to the Palestinians and "residual sovereignty" to Israel.

20. *Palestine Report* (July 15, 2000); Rashid was said to be preparing a $40-billion claim, including refugee compensation, infrastructure projects, development assistance, and even a pension fund.

21. Author's interviews with Dennis Ross and Toni Verstandig.

22. Author's interview with US official.

23. *Al-Hayat al-Jedida* (July 20, 2000).

24. *New York Times* (July 26, 2001).

25. Author's interview with US official.

26. *60 Minutes,* CBS Television, November 17, 2000; *The Guardian* (April 30, 2001).

27. *Al-Hayat* (September 29, 2001).

28. Ibid.

29. Dennis Ross, Margaret Warner, and Jim Hoagland, "From Oslo to Camp David to Taba: Setting the Record Straight," *Peacewatch,* no. 340 (August 14, 2001).

30. For the text of the Clinton plan, see Laqueur and Rubin, *Israel-Arab Reader,* pp. 562–564.

31. "44 Reasons Why Fateh Movement Rejects the Proposals Made by U.S. President Clinton," *Our Opinion* (Fatah Movement Central Publication) (January 1–7, 2001), originally obtained at the PA's official Web site, http://www.pna.gov.ps/peace/44.resons.htm.

32. Author's interview with Ehud Barak.

33. *l-Ayyam* (January 28, 2001), translated in *Middle East Media Research Institute,* no. 184 (February 1, 2001).

34. *Al-Ayyam* (January 29, 2001); *al-Hayat* (January 28, 2001).

35. Author's interview with Ehud Barak.

36. *Al-Ayyam* (January 26, 2001), translated in *Middle East Media Research Institute,* no. 184 (February 1, 2001); *al-Quds* (January 26, 2001).

37. *New York Times* (March 11, 2001).

38. *Al-Sharq al-Awsat* (August 1, 2002), translated in *Foreign Broadcast Information Service Daily Report: The Middle East.*

39. Itim news agency release, January 25, 2002.

40. See poll series by the Birzeit University Development Studies Program and the Jerusalem Media Communications Center.

41. World Bank, "Fifteen Months—Intifada, Closures and Palestinian Economic Crisis: An Assessment," http://Inweb18.world bank.org/mna/mena.nsf/61abe956d36c23df38 525690b00775b5e/81299af1b1220c528525680 e0071d721?OpenDocument. See also *al-Sharq*

a-Awsat (August 1, 2002), translated in *Foreign Broadcast Information Service Daily Report: The Middle East.*

42. See, for example, al-Aqsa Martyrs Brigades, Southern Area, to Yasser Arafat, text printed in Israel Defense Forces (IDF), "The al-Aqsa Martyrs Brigades and the Fatah Organization," May 3, 2002, TRI 319–02, Document 2, pp. 9, 11.

43. *New York Times* (June 2, 2001).

44. The letter's text was shown on the German television station Westdeutscher Rundfunk on June 24, 2001, in the scrapbook of a suicide bomber's family. It was sent by the Palestinian embassy in Jordan over Arafat's signature; *Al-Ayyam* (June 24, 2001), translation in *Middle East Media Research Institute*, no. 237 (July 8, 2001).

45. *Ha'aretz* (June 22, 2001).

46. *Ha'aretz* (March 29, 2001).

47. *Ha'aretz* (April 12, 2001).

48. For the full text of the report, see http://usinfo.state.gov/regional/nea/mitchell.htm.

49. Yezid Sayigh, "Arafat and the Anatomy of a Revolt," *Survival,* vol. 43, no. 3 (Autumn 2001), pp. 47–60.

50. *Al-Sharq al-Awsat* (August 1, 2002).

51. On these events, see the beginning of this chapter.

52. *New York Times* (September 12, 2002).

53. *New York Times* (October 29, 2002).

54. *Jerusalem Post* (October 2, 2002).

55. *New York Times* (September 22 and 23, 2002). For Arafat's version, see his interview in *al-Hayat* (September 29, 2002).

56. *New York Times* (September 30, 2002).

57. The Western policy of "supporting the moderates" could be sustained only in regard to Abbas as the PA's leader, since his Fatah counterparts—with the exceptions of Abu Alla, Dahlan, and Fayyad—barely manifested any moderation at all.

58. Abbas was very strongly attached to the "right of return" idea, so such an agreement was impossible. See, for example, his statement in *al-Ayyam* (January 26, 2001).

10

Israel and
the Arab World

David W. Lesch

IT IS INTERESTING TO SPEAK WITH Arab officials today regarding the state of Arab-Israeli relations or, more particularly, how things have stagnated, if not deteriorated, in recent years. Almost invariably they wax nostalgic about former Israeli prime minister Yitzhak Rabin. Many truly believe that had he not been assassinated and had completed his time in office, a comprehensive Arab-Israeli peace would have been secured by now—in fact, by the late 1990s. With the assassination and subsequent events, a hard-line Likud prime minister, Benjamin Netanyahu, was able to come to power and mute, if not set back, the peace process, stifling the momentum that had been achieved on multiple tracks to date. Although an acolyte of Rabin came to power in Israel in 1999 in the person of Ehud Barak, he was politically naive, and he did not carry the same domestic weight that Rabin had enjoyed to push through the process amid internal political dissent. Barak was also hampered by the Rabin assassination itself and the Israeli domestic environment that had produced it, which compelled him to be more secretive in his diplomacy, yet also much more sensitive to public opinion. Many a leader in the Arab world suffered the same hesitation following the assassination of an Arab leader who had broken ranks and gone out on a limb for peace, Anwar Sadat.

This nostalgic retrospective of Rabin may be seen a bit too much through rose-colored glasses, but it is also a reflection of how far the Middle East has traveled away from a legitimate peace process since the assassination—and possibly away from leaders who stick their necks out for peaceful rather than violent causes. There were plenty of Arab leaders and Palestinian officials who

castigated Rabin while he was in office, and some of the castigation he probably deserved, but at least there was a legitimate peace process. One finds the
same sort of nostalgia in the Arab world toward the administration of US
president Bill Clinton; indeed, many will say they cannot believe that they are
even entertaining such positive thoughts about Clinton's negotiating team,
but when compared with George W. Bush, that team appears in retrospect to
be very agreeable.

Since the assassination of Rabin, the Arab-Israeli peace process has proceeded in fits and starts—or not at all. Most of the time what has deleteriously
affected an announced or existing peace plan or prevented the resumption of
negotiations has been a lack of consensus about peace among the relevant parties, as well as a serious lack of preparation in laying the necessary groundwork
prior to the enunciation of a plan (see, for example, the Camp David II Summit, the Saudi-inspired 2002 Beirut Arab League summit peace plan, and the
Road Map). The events in the Arab-Israeli arena since 2000 have threatened to
divide—or have already divided—the Arab world or even transformed the
Arab-Israeli dynamic into a completely different paradigm entailing a different
set of potentialities and possibilities. As a result, we may now be witnessing our
last, best chance to initiate a process that may finally bring about that elusive
comprehensive Arab-Israeli peace.

The Setting for Rabin's Assassination

Two events realigned the Arab-Israeli conflict prior to Rabin's assuming the
office of prime minister in 1992: the 1979 Egyptian-Israeli peace treaty and
the 1991 Gulf war. The Egyptian-Israeli peace treaty eliminated the possibility, for the foreseeable future, of an all-out Arab-Israeli war of the kind that
had occurred in 1967 or, especially, 1973. Although directly and indirectly
leading to an enhanced environment for subregional conflict, such as the Iraqi
invasion of Iran in 1980 and the Israeli invasion of Lebanon in 1982, the peace
treaty increasingly transformed the Arab-Israeli paradigm into an Israeli-
Palestinian one. After Egypt, the most powerful, populous, and influential
country in the Arab world, signed on the dotted line, it instantly became more
acceptable for other Arab countries (and entities such as the Palestine Liberation Organization) to pursue subregional and national interests separate from
the Arab-Israeli and/or Arab nationalist arenas. This became even more of an
imperative with the end of the superpower cold war and, by the late 1980s, the
concurrent weakening of the Soviet Union, the traditional superpower patron
of the Arab states.

These shifting currents in the Middle East became manifest in the
1990–1991 Gulf crisis and Gulf War. With the Soviet Union no longer willing

to play the game, a number of Arab states—first and foremost Syria, the traditional leader of the Arab states confronting Israel—immediately realized that they, too, needed to realign their relations with the West in order to obtain much-needed economic support and foreign investment. This is when Syrian president Hafiz al-Asad decided to make his "strategic choice for peace" with Israel. Conflict with Israel, as seen at the time, was no longer a viable option. The 1990 Iraqi invasion of Kuwait, which precipitated the Gulf War waged by the US-led UN coalition that evicted Iraqi forces from Kuwait, presented an opportune moment to effect such a realignment.

The 1991 Gulf War had a salutary effect on the Arab-Israeli arena. When the US administration of George H.W. Bush began to recruit countries into the UN coalition arrayed against Iraq, it was to be expected that the Gulf Arab states as well as Washington's traditional allies in the Arab world, such as Egypt and Morocco, would join up. With the end of the cold war and a Soviet Union on its last legs, desperately needing economic assistance from the West, it was also not surprising that Moscow supported the formation of the coalition by not using its veto in the UN Security Council. The participation of Syria, however, was the most important of all the Arab states' participation in the coalition. Syria's inclusion looked as if almost the entire Arab world was against Iraq, rather than just the usual pro-West countries, especially since Damascus had been in the vanguard of the anti-Israeli front for decades.

In 1989, Syria's position had seemed to take a turn for the worse. Iraq had emerged victorious in the Iran-Iraq war, an Iraq that wanted to reexert its influence in the Middle East. Saddam Hussein remembered Syrian support for his enemy in the war and would make life as difficult as possible for Syria in Lebanon by supporting anti-Syrian groups such as the Christian militia, led by Michel Aoun. Iraq also drew Jordan deeper and deeper into its orbit through economic integration and dependence, as it did the Palestine Liberation Organization (PLO) through financial and political assistance. The latter case led to Yasser Arafat's monumental mistake of tacitly supporting Saddam Hussein at the outbreak of the 1990 Gulf crisis. Almost overnight the Palestinians lost what international goodwill they had garnered during the first years of the First Intifada. More important, the PLO lost crucial financial and political support from the Arab Gulf states, which were angered by Arafat's stance. What emerged was, again, a weakened PLO and an intifada that seemed to be going nowhere.

Furthermore, for Syria (and the PLO), the pillar of Soviet support that had braced the Syrian regime for most of the decade virtually crumbled with the ascension to power of Mikhail Gorbachev in 1985 and the Red Army exit from Afghanistan by early 1989. Both of these events led to a dramatic reassessment of Soviet foreign policy that emphasized a drawing down of

Soviet commitments abroad, more concentration on domestic restructuring, and improved ties with the United States. This change did not bode well for Syria, as Moscow first urged and then backed the PLO's decision to pursue a negotiated solution to the Israeli-Palestinian conflict. In the process of all this, the Kremlin improved its relations with Israel. Gorbachev made it clear to Hafiz al-Asad, when the Syrian president visited Moscow in April 1987, that Syria's "reliance on military force in settling the Arab-Israeli conflict has completely lost its credibility," and he went on to suggest that Damascus abandon its doctrine of trying to attain strategic parity with Israel and seek to establish a "balance of interests" toward a political settlement in the Middle East.[1] In addition to these problems in the foreign policy arena, Syria's economy continued to deteriorate, owing in large measure to the concentration of economic resources in the military, as well as to the inherent frailties of its public-sector-dominated state capitalist economy. Therefore, Syria joined the coalition. Not only was it participating in an alliance whose objective was to weaken, if not destroy, the war-making capacity of its archenemy in the Arab arena, but Syria was also clearly situating itself in the Arab world's moderate camp and opening up its economic doors to investment and aid from the West and grateful Arab Gulf states.

Israel was not a member of the US-led UN coalition, despite Saddam Hussein's attempts to draw it into the fray by lobbing Scud missiles into Israel proper, hoping to turn a Persian Gulf conflict into an Arab-Israeli one, and thus prying away at least the Arab members of the UN coalition; the Arab states and Israel were de facto on the same side in the war, with similar objectives, which at the very least eliminated an important psychological barrier. For Israel, the destruction of Saddam's war machine diminished any serious threat emanating from the Arab east, which had been a strategic concern for some time; indeed, this concern was behind the strategic relationship that Israel had established with the shah of Iran before the Iranian revolution of 1979, both parties being interested in containing and/or weakening Iraq.

The end of the superpower cold war and the First Gulf war compelled Hafiz al-Asad, by force of circumstance and opportunity, to engage in what became known as the Madrid peace process, launched by a plenary session held in the Spanish capital on October 30, 1991. Asad had already begun to reposition Syria toward the end of the 1980s, seeing the writing on the wall concerning continued support from the Soviet Union. He was, indeed, taking Gorbachev's advice. In December 1988, Asad "acknowledged the importance of Egypt in the Arab arena," the first time he had publicly praised Egypt since the 1979 Egyptian-Israeli peace treaty.[2] By the end of 1989 Damascus had reestablished full diplomatic relations with Cairo, as Egypt became fully rehabilitated in the Arab fold. And with an eye toward isolating Iraq as well as building bridges with the United States, Syria also began to improve its relationship with Saudi Arabia. Asad and other Arab leaders in the Gulf War coalition had stressed to the Bush administration that the United States must address the Arab-Israeli situation after evicting Saddam Hussein from Kuwait. It was an unspoken quid pro quo on which the Bush team made good by organizing the conference in Madrid.[3] As the US Middle East envoy Dennis Ross noted, "Asad's choice [to attend the conference] put him in the center of post-Gulf war diplomacy," while Yasser Arafat's tacit support of Iraq sidelined the PLO leader.[4] For Syria, the road to regaining the Golan Heights, to economic growth, and to protection from an Israel that was getting stronger as Syria grew weaker all went through Washington. Paradoxically, the road to Washington went through Israel. Ultimately, this is why Syria made some important concessions to launch the Madrid process, and without Syria's participation, the conference would not have happened.

The Bush administration worked diligently to organize the initial conference and establish parameters acceptable to the pertinent parties—a tall task indeed. Secretary of State James Baker made numerous visits to the region during the summer and early fall of 1991 to push the respective leaders of the countries involved to the negotiating table. It was important to the Arab states, especially Syria, for at least the opening session to appear to be international. The Arab states much preferred an international setting in which the United States, the Soviet Union, the United Nations, and multiple Arab parties would participate in order to maximize Arab leverage. Israel, on the other hand, traditionally preferred one-on-one negotiations with individual Arab states, in which Tel Aviv believed it had a clear bargaining advantage. This obstacle had to be overcome to get the proceedings under way. It was successfully bridged by holding an opening plenary session with all of the participants seated at the table, the two superpowers as cosponsors of the meeting presiding. This was to be the "international conference" the Arab states had demanded; yet, following this opening session, the parties would break onto separate bilateral negotiating tracks, an Israeli-Jordanian track (including a non-PLO Palestinian delegation) and an Israeli-Syrian/Lebanese one. The Arab participants were the remaining countries bordering Israel that were still officially at war with the Jewish state. Egyptian and Saudi Arabian representatives were also present in the background and working the corridors, so to speak, when necessary. Egypt used its political muscle in the inter-Arab arena as the only Arab country at the time that had signed a peace treaty with Israel, and the Saudis used the power of the purse, for any agreements would most certainly require enormous amounts of financial aid to multiple parties as an added inducement and incentive to remain at the negotiating table and consummate agreements.

What Yitzhak Rabin inherited when he came to power in 1992 was a Madrid peace process that was continuing in fits and starts. Rabin sensed an opportunity to deal in advantageous terms with a weakened PLO. He also recognized the opportunity to negotiate with Syria, which was the track he always preferred because it involved, relatively speaking, a much more straightforward land-for-peace deal than the Palestinian situation. Because of complications regarding a mutually acceptable delineation of where exactly the June 4, 1967, line was along the Golan Heights, in addition to Asad's typically plodding negotiating style, Rabin gave the green light for Israeli officials to pursue secret ongoing negotiations with the PLO. The Oslo process, which was in many ways tangential to the Madrid process, culminating in the signing of the Oslo Accords and then the Declaration of Principles signed on the White House lawn in September 1993, is covered elsewhere in this book. But the PLO's signing on the dotted line now cleared the road even further for countries such as Jordan and Syria to more actively pursue their own national interests vis-à-vis Israel. No longer would they be seen as abandoning the Arab or Palestinian cause, because Yasser Arafat himself had agreed to enter peace negotiations with Israel. Therefore it is no surprise that in an almost anticlimactic fashion an Israeli-Jordanian peace treaty was signed in October 1994. And Syrian representatives negotiated seriously with Israeli representatives in 1994 and 1995 as part of the continuing process launched at Madrid. Concurrently a series of regional economic talks began in 1994 in Casablanca that included Arab and Israeli officials and representatives as well as businessmen from all over the world. There was also a series of multilateral talks in various locales about more specific items, such as water sharing, arms control, and economic development. Although Syria did not participate in these ancillary conferences, there seemed to be a real momentum toward a comprehensive Arab-Israeli peace.

Fallout from the Assassination of Rabin

On November 4, 1995, Yitzhak Rabin was assassinated by a Jewish zealot.

Foreign Minister Shimon Peres was asked to form a new government, and with the outpouring of sympathy in Israel following the assassination, he had little trouble in doing so; he became the next Israeli prime minister. Even though the vast majority of Israelis expressed support for the peace process in the wake of Rabin's assassination, many of these same people had certain qualms about Peres, who did not have the perceived security credentials and often appeared too eager to trade land for peace. Peres committed himself and his government to taking up the mantle of Rabin and continuing the peace process; in fact, he even accelerated it, hoping to use the favorable post-Rabin political environment as a base of support.

On the Syrian track, Peres redoubled Israel's efforts to come to an agreement with Damascus, and two rounds of talks between Syrian and Israeli negotiators were held at the Wye Plantation in Maryland, one in December 1995 and the other in January 1996.

But just as a Jewish extremist had potentially blunted the peace process with the assassination of Rabin, in early 1996 it was the turn of Palestinian Islamic extremists. In February and March, Hamas carried out a series of suicide bombings in Israel that killed fifty-nine Israelis and wounded hundreds more. The attacks were ostensibly a response to Israel's assassination of Fathi Shqaqi, an Islamic Jihad leader, in Malta in October 1995, and of Yahya Ayyash, otherwise known as the Engineer for his ability to organize suicide bombings, in January 1996, when his cell phone, rigged by Israeli intelligence agents, exploded in his ear.

Despite Arafat's condemnation of the terrorist acts, peace negotiations on all fronts were suspended by Peres. Since Hamas locates its political offices in Damascus, Israel expected Hafiz al-Asad to publicly condemn the attacks, which he chose not to do, on top of his noticeable silence following the assassination of Rabin. Indeed, quite the opposite, exhortations over Syrian radio tacitly supported the suicide bombings. This was a major diplomatic faux pas on the part of Asad. Scheduled meetings between Syria and Israel at the Wye Plantation were subsequently called off. This episode certainly paints in stark relief the totally different wavelengths of Syria and Israel with regard to public diplomacy. Asad was always someone who played his cards close to the vest, never giving up any of them until he absolutely had to. The pace of Peres's march toward a Syrian-Israeli agreement was already uncomfortably fast for the methodical Syrian president. The Israelis, who had in mind the overtly dramatic public gestures of Anwar al-Sadat, which had jump-started the Egyptian-Israeli peace process, expected Asad also to do something in the public arena that might reassure the Israelis about his sincere desire for peace.

Asad was a notoriously private man. He was consciously devoid of the dramatic flare of Sadat, who he felt had relinquished his most expensive bargaining chips by de facto recognizing Israel before an agreement. The Israelis may have expected too much from Asad in this regard and never really appreciated the fact that even though he was at the apex of an authoritarian structure, he also had a constituency to play to among the Syrian elite, the Syrian population, and the wider Arab world. In addition, various elements in the Syrian regime were not shy about firing some warning shots through state-controlled media outlets to send subtle and not-so-subtle signals to Asad that he needed to slow down a bit in his march toward a peace agreement with Israel, for many of these elements might be deleteriously affected by an Israeli-Syrian peace treaty. He could not go too far out in front of them, just as Rabin, Peres, and later Ehud Barak could not be seen to be too far out in front of their own domestic constituencies. But Asad's hesitancy fed into the claims of those Israelis who from the beginning had doubted the sincerity of Syria's interest in peace. In this situation, Syria's traditional position in the vanguard of Arab nationalism, and the rejectionist anti-Israeli front, and in its oft-stated commitment to the Palestinian cause possibly hampered its ability to break out of this self-professed paradigm and embrace ameliorating opportunities such as that presented following the suicide attacks. Unfortunately, Hafiz al-Asad probably did not even know what the term *public diplomacy* really meant—and he was never much interested in finding out.

With the Israeli-Syrian negotiations offtrack for the moment, Hizbollah began to launch Katyusha rocket attacks against towns and villages in northern Israel, coupled with intensified operations against Israeli forces in the south Lebanon security zone. Although Hizbollah acts with more independence from Syria than most perceive, Damascus has used it indirectly as necessary leverage against Israel. Asad considered Hizbollah the other side of the peace negotiation coin, to be cashed when necessary to pressure Israel in the few remaining ways it could. The use of Hizbollah showed—at least it was supposed to show—Israel that there was something to be gained (i.e., quelling the Hizbollah threat) by returning the Golan Heights and something to be lost by not doing so. Hizbollah, as well as its other state sponsor, Iran, provide Damascus with some strategic depth in case of war with Israel, a military consideration that was a central feature of Hafiz al-Asad's overall strategic conception vis-à-vis Tel Aviv.

Israel, however, tends to see Syrian influence over Hizbollah as a threat that must be met with force, to convince Damascus to delink itself from or contain the Shiite Islamist group. Unfortunately for Peres, in February, before the Hamas suicide bombings, he had called for early elections to take place in May 1996, which originally had been scheduled for the following October. At the time it seemed to be a politically astute move, taking advantage of the post-Rabin sentiments that favored the Peres government. But with the Hamas bombings followed so closely by the Hizbollah attacks, the Israelis began to see the peace process as unraveling before their very eyes and adopted a more belligerent attitude. This type of political atmosphere was very uncomfortable for Peres, perceived as more of a peacenik, whereas it indelibly improved Likud's position as the party that placed security before anything else. Peres could not just sit back and do nothing in response to these attacks in the midst of what was, in effect, an election campaign against Likud Party leader Benjamin Netanyahu.

The Hizbollah attacks on Israeli proper had violated an unwritten agreement brokered by Warren Christopher in 1993 following another round of Hizbollah and Israeli military exchanges. After Israel's Operation Accountability in 1993, consisting mostly of Israeli air attacks and artillery barrages in Lebanon, a cease-fire agreement had been reached in which Hizbollah committed itself to launching attacks against Israeli positions only in the security zone and not in Israel itself. Peres's response this time, on April 11, was to launch Operation Grapes of Wrath in Lebanon as punishment for the Hizbollah attacks.[5] The military campaign was directed not only against Hizbollah positions but also against various manifestations of the Lebanese government, such as power grids, to convince Beirut that it would suffer, too, by turning a blind eye on what Hizbollah was doing in the south. There was also the hope that the general Lebanese population would turn against Hizbollah for bringing the wrath of Israel down upon them. This operation turned out to be a public relations nightmare, as it led to the displacement of over four hundred thousand Lebanese civilians and the deaths of over a hundred noncombatants due to an Israeli artillery barrage that mistakenly hit a refugee camp in the village of Qana on April 19; of course, all of this destruction and suffering was instantly shown to the world through the global media. By April 27, Christopher had again intervened to broker an agreement that temporarily led to a cessation of hostilities—and this time the agreement to confine attacks to the security zone was written down, accompanied by a monitoring committee composed of the pertinent parties (Israel, Lebanon, Syria, France, and the United States).

While Peres may have sanctioned Operation Grapes of Wrath in part to toughen up his image for the Israeli electorate prior to the election, because of the international uproar associated with the civilian casualties and displacement in Lebanon in a military campaign that seemed disproportionate to the act that had precipitated it, the Israeli prime minister's gamble actually had quite the opposite effect. If anything, it raised doubt among Israeli voters about the ability of Shimon Peres to navigate Israel through an increasingly more hostile regional and domestic environment. This doubt was just enough to allow Benjamin Netanyahu to eke out a victory in the May election, and to become the next Israeli prime minister. Significantly, Israeli actions in Lebanon angered a great many Israeli Arabs, who make up almost one-fifth of the population in Israel and 12 percent of the electorate. Many of them had relatives in Lebanon. They certainly did not vote for Netanyahu, but they stayed at home in droves, depriving Peres of much-needed votes. Netanyahu

was a hard-line Likudnik and a proponent of Vladimir Jabotinsky's Revisionist program, who preached "peace with security" instead of "land for peace,"
and he had vociferously opposed the Oslo process.

Netanyahu's victory was less than overwhelming; he won by a very narrow
margin over Peres. Therefore the new prime minister had a difficult time
patching together a coalition of parties that would provide him with at least
61 votes in the 120-member Knesset. As was to be expected, Netanyahu relied
heavily on nationalist and religious parties to form a governing coalition, the
result being their enhanced influence despite their small numbers in the
Knesset. In return for joining a coalition, these smaller parties would gain a
desired portfolio in the cabinet or other concessions, usually involving financial assistance for various pet projects. Because he had to rely on elements opposed to the peace process to form the coalition, Netanyahu adopted a more
critical view of Oslo and Madrid than expected. He did not want just to "slow
down" the process, but to effectively terminate it.

In these circumstances, Netanyahu naturally gravitated toward his support
base in Likud and cozied up further to Orthodox Jewish parties such as Shas
with financial subsidies. He seemed to many in the Israeli electorate to be beholden to Israeli special interests at the expense of pursuing peace; as with
Shamir, his frosty relationship with Clinton did not enhance his electability.
The result was the decisive victory (50 percent to 44 percent of the votes) of
the new Labor Party leader, Ehud Barak, in the election on May 17, 1999.

New Opportunities with Barak?

In the person of Ehud Barak, Israel elected a prime minister in the mold of
Yitzhak Rabin; indeed, Barak had been something of a protégé of Rabin. The
new prime minister was a military man as a former chief of staff of the Israel
Defense Forces (IDF) and the most decorated soldier in Israeli history. Israelis
could be more trustful, then, of Barak's efforts to reignite peace talks without
sacrificing Israeli security, as was the case with Rabin. Barak was a "dovish
hawk."[6] Again similar to Rabin, although he reengaged with the Palestinians,
Barak tended to prefer the Syrian track, if anything, to help facilitate one of
his primary foreign policy objectives: the withdrawal of Israeli troops from
Lebanon. Barak also had some Anwar al-Sadat in him: He was prone to the
dramatic, bold move to secure a peace agreement—and his place in history.
But as discussed earlier, this approach was the antithesis of Hafiz al-Asad's negotiating style, to which a succession of US negotiators can attest. Dennis Ross
notes that "Asad did not like to rush under any circumstances; it was not his
style. He was never in a hurry lest it appear that he needed an agreement more
than the other side. And that, of course, was the very message Barak would be

sending—he was anxious, and if so, why would Asad concede anything?"[7] By early 2000, the differences in negotiating style would prove to be fatal under the bright lights of international attention and expectations.

Lebanon had long been a quagmire for Israeli troops due to the effective guerrilla campaign carried out by Hizbollah. With Israeli deaths mounting in south Lebanon, the Israeli public had grown quite tired of the whole ordeal. Barak wanted a withdrawal from Lebanon to be part of an overall settlement with Syria. In this way, Israel would not be seen as cutting and running, and Hizbollah would not be perceived as having won. In addition, Syria could be brought on board as a guarantor of security along the Israeli-Lebanese border. If there was an Israeli-Syrian peace agreement, what need then would Damascus have for Hizbollah vis-à-vis Israel? Also, Barak seemed to prefer dealing with Asad rather than Arafat, whom no Israeli leader ever trusted. Asad was, from the Israeli perspective, difficult to deal with as well. The Syrian president once commented, "Our stance in the battle for peace will not be less courageous than our stances on the battlefield."[8] Or as Shimon Peres once observed, Asad was "conducting the peace process just as one conducts a military campaign—slowly, patiently, directed by strategic and tactical considerations."[9] As a result, however, Asad could be trusted to comply with any agreement reached, and he was more straightforward with regard to the issues that needed to be discussed. As Ross states, Barak "knew that what mattered to the Syrians was the land, and that what most mattered to Israelis was security and water."[10] In addition, Hafiz al-Asad's son, Bashar, the putative heir to his father, had praised Barak following the election, this praise, many Israelis believed, being a signal sent by Damascus, and thus encouraging even more attention to the Syrian track.

Syrian-Israeli negotiations heated up with behind-the-scenes contacts during the summer and fall of 1999, especially as the second-term Clinton administration was eager to broker a comprehensive Arab-Israeli peace before it left office in January 2001. Such a peace would be a capstone to Clinton's presidency, creating a legacy apart from the scandals and impeachment that had rocked his administration in the second term. In addition, Hafiz al-Asad may well have wanted to make a deal with a willing Israeli prime minister while he could, so that Bashar could inherit a more congenial regional environment when the time came. Asad's deteriorating health, which outside observers had been commenting on for years, also appeared to become an issue of increasing concern. American negotiators could see for themselves that Asad was becoming more gaunt and frail in late 1999 and early 2000. They had also heard reports from other Arab state officials that his ability to engage in everyday affairs was limited and that even his lucidity had been questionable at times. One sensed that the momentum building toward direct Syrian-Israeli negotiations in late 1999 was a race against time, a last-ditch attempt to orchestrate an agreement before a crisis, namely, the death of Hafiz al-Asad.

The climax came in January 2000, when Barak and his support staff met with Syrian foreign minister Farouk al-Shar'a and his staff at a retreat in Shepherdstown, West Virginia, about an hour and fifteen minutes from Washington by car. Camp David was especially not chosen because the Syrians in no way, shape, or form wanted to be associated with Sadat and the Egyptians at Camp David in 1978, and the Wye Plantation was no longer a viable option since it had been the locale used by Arafat and Barak to produce the Wye accords in October 1998. Yet Shepherdstown was still close enough to Washington for Clinton to fly back and forth by helicopter to help mediate the talks when necessary. A good deal of progress was made at Shepherdstown, building on the Syrian-Israeli talks of 1994–1996. Ross, who was present at the meetings, was very impressed by the flexibility of the Syrians, which to him showed the seriousness with which they were pursuing a peace agreement; indeed, while acknowledging that there was enough blame to go around for the failure of a definitive agreement emerging out of the talks at Shepherdstown, Ross explicitly states that "Barak was more at fault than the Syrians."[11] Even so, the process was not dead after Shepherdstown, especially with a US president who was willing to take some risks in the pursuit of an agreement. Syrian officials commented at the time that an agreement was 80 percent accomplished.

It did not happen, however. An ill-timed leak of a draft agreement between Syria and Israel, crafted by the Americans at Shepherdstown soon after the parties had adjourned, inestimably complicated the progress that had taken place. It is highly likely that the draft was intentionally leaked by someone in the Barak government as a trial balloon, for Barak was very concerned about public support for his position. It could also have been designed to drum up domestic support for Barak in the negotiations, as well as for an Israeli public referendum promised by Barak on any Syrian-Israeli accord. The leak, which confirmed some significant concessions by Damascus, embarrassed, if not infuriated, Asad, who received indirect criticism in Syria for having gone too far without the requisite guaranteed returns. The leak certainly compelled him to lurch backward from the negotiating table.

Nevertheless, contacts continued at the insistence of the United States, and President Clinton threw the full weight of his office into the fray by meeting personally with Hafiz al-Asad in Geneva, Switzerland, in March 2000, in what appeared to be a last-gasp attempt to salvage an accord. The fact that Asad met him in Geneva created a great deal of anticipation that an agreement was at hand. Everyone would be disappointed.

Stories differ on all sides on what happened at Geneva that resulted in a failed summit. The Syrians believe they had been promised an agreement that confirmed Israel's withdrawal from the Golan Heights to the June 4, 1967, line, and when something less was offered by Clinton, they backed away. Jeremy Pressmen argues it appears that the offer the United States presented Syria in Geneva was a withdrawal to the June 4 line in name only, since the map Dennis Ross was showing the Syrians moved the June 4 line even farther back to the east of the 1923 line, and thus farther away from the Sea of Galilee. According to this view, perhaps the United States and Israel were trying to get Syria to agree to the demarcation, calling it the June 4 line while knowing that it probably was not. If this is true, then it follows that Barak probably, in the end, did not agree to withdraw to a June 4 border more consistent with Syria's idea of where it was. Thus it is little wonder that Asad cried foul, and the summit became a stark failure.[12] In an interview I conducted with Syrian president Bashar al-Asad in May 2004, who at the time of the Geneva summit was thoroughly integrated into the regime and, by most accounts, was being systematically groomed to succeed his father, he described the Geneva meeting:

The last time my father met with Clinton in April 2000 [*sic*], Clinton called my father, and [Saudi Crown] Prince Abdullah was involved. There were good relations between my father and Clinton. My father asked Clinton what he wanted to discuss, why a summit, as my father did not think it was appropriate. But then Clinton called him to meet with him because he was on his way back from Asia, Pakistan I think, and he stopped in Oman, then he went on to Geneva. He called my father and told him he was on his way to Geneva and that he would like to meet there because he had good news, that Barak accepted the June 4th line. However, at Geneva my father was told that Barak accepted to withdraw from 95 percent of the land, so my father was angry and he wanted to leave. He was surprised and Clinton was surprised; Clinton was surprised he [Hafiz al-Asad] refused, so somebody told him that we would accept this offer. When he stopped in Oman, Clinton met with some Omani officials along with [US national security adviser] Sandy Berger and [US ambassador to Syria] Chris Ross—they told Clinton at the time that since my father was sick he wants to have a peace before he dies so that he can help his son be president . . . so he [Hafiz al-Asad] will accept anything. And they hinted to Clinton that they had asked my father and that he had said o.k. So Clinton presumed that my father had agreed to the proposal. What happened was that Barak was a little bit weak in Israel, and he wanted to play two cards, one for peace and one not for peace. For those who wanted peace he would tell the world he is a peacemaker, for the extremists in Israel he would say he would take peace but not give all the land back, so this is how it failed. It was not Clinton's fault or the Syrians, but then the Israelis said my father was not interested in peace. In

this way Barak could say my father only wanted peace on his conditions, and therefore the Arabs are responsible [for the breakdown].[13]

Others believe that Asad, his health having deteriorated even more, was not
really interested at all in peace negotiations at that moment because he was
concentrating more specifically on preparing the way for Bashar to come to
office with cabinet and military personnel reshuffling. Domestic politics was
the immediate priority, and Asad could not be locked into another protracted
round of negotiations with the Israelis. He attended the summit meeting with
Clinton, according to this view, as a show of strength to those who had been
criticizing him at home. As Dennis Ross stated, he would "stand up to the
President of the United States and not compromise vital Syrian interests,"
thus shoring up the support of powerful elements within Syria that would
help ensure Bashar's succession.[14] Regardless of which view is more accurate,
the Syrian-Israeli track was effectively moribund. This became even more apparent when Hafiz al-Asad died in June, ending his thirty-year reign. His son,
Bashar, did indeed succeed to the presidency in a relatively smooth transition.
The way had been well prepared, but for the foreseeable future the new Syrian
president, while recommitted to Syria's "strategic choice for peace" with Israel
in his inaugural speech in July, would concentrate on consolidating his power
base and dealing more with domestic issues, particularly the deteriorating
Syrian economic situation.[15] After witnessing what had happened on the
Syrian-Israeli front over the previous six months, Bashar was reluctant to enter into the diplomatic fray so soon.

With the Syrian track dead, Barak moved forward with what had been one
of his primary objectives as prime minister: getting out of south Lebanon.
Even before the failed Asad-Clinton summit meeting in Geneva, the Israeli
cabinet had agreed in early March 2000 to withdraw from Lebanon by July.
Since it was apparent that a withdrawal would not be linked to a Syrian-Israeli
peace agreement, Barak decided to withdraw unilaterally in May. That this decision was unilateral attests to the breakdown by that time of the Madrid
peace process on the Syrian-Lebanese front. By May 24, Israel had completely
withdrawn its forces from Lebanon, and a very divisive and dark chapter in
Israeli history had apparently been put to rest. Syria stood on the sidelines, in
part satisfied that a threat to its position in Lebanon had been reduced, but
also concerned that it would have less leverage to use against Israel (by supporting Hizbollah attacks against Israel) vis-à-vis a return of the Golan
Heights.

Hizbollah, on the other hand, was jubilant. The Shiite Islamist group became widely perceived in the Arab and Muslim worlds as the only combat-
ant ever to have defeated Israel. It would parlay this added popularity in

Lebanon into enhancing its role in the country as a legitimate political party and increasing its representation in the Lebanese parliament. It would slowly but surely position itself as a Lebanese national entity rather than a supranational Islamist party. This new position became evident when Hizbollah's leader, Sheikh Hassan Nasrallah, spoke of the "victory" with the Lebanese flag—in addition to Hizbollah's traditional yellow flags—in the background. Just as important, however, the Israeli withdrawal from Lebanon outside the auspices of an agreement gave rise in the Arab world to belief in the effectiveness of the Hizbollah "model"; that is, steady, consistent, low-level resistance and guerrilla warfare were the only way to inflict enough pain on Israel, without confronting it directly, to compel the small Jewish state, which was so sensitive to the loss of each and every Israeli soldier, to give up territory. Palestinians took note.

The inability of the Syrians and the Israelis to consummate a peace treaty may well be one of the great missed opportunities in the Middle East in the modern era. A peace treaty *should* have materialized, given the solubility of the issues dividing the two states and the tangible progress made on most of these issues in the discussions throughout the 1990s. History could have been quite different in the event of a Syrian-Israeli peace treaty. Lebanon would certainly have signed on the dotted line soon thereafter, and the Arab Gulf states would not have been very far behind (and North African members of the Arab League, with the exception of Libya, most likely would have joined the chorus). And with Lebanon at peace with Israel, Hizbollah would most certainly have been emasculated by now, the Israeli-Hizbollah conflict of the summer of 2006 would not have occurred, and Iranian influence in the heartland of the Middle East would have decreased. Although many believe the "Syrian option" and its regional repercussions would have weakened the Palestinian negotiating position due to the lack of collective Arab support, it is also possible that Israel, feeling more safe than ever before following peace treaties with its Arab neighbors, would have felt more comfortable making certain concessions than in an environment characterized by an official state of war with most of the Arab countries. In this scenario, then, the Palestinians might still have received a viable independent state. The holdouts to peace with Israel, such as Iraq, would have become more isolated. Saddam Hussein's resuscitation in the Arab world, due in part to the breakdown of the Arab-Israeli peace process by the end of the decade, would not have occurred, his ability to maintain power may have lessened, and the US-led invasion of Iraq in 2003 may therefore have been precluded. In addition, there is no telling how a comprehensive Arab-Israeli peace might have deleteriously affected al-Qaeda and other Islamic extremist groups, especially in terms of recruitment. Even though their existence was not predicated on Arab-Israeli hostility or the plight of the Palestinians, these issues have played a prominent role in al-Qaeda propaganda. What would history be without these tantalizing what-ifs?

Camp David II and the Second Intifada

With the Israelis out of Lebanon and the Syrian-Israeli peace negotiations dead, diplomatic attention shifted back to the Palestinian-Israeli track in the summer of 2000. The result was the fateful Camp David negotiations between Barak, Arafat, and Clinton in July, in what turned out to be a last-ditch attempt to salvage a peace agreement—and maybe more important, individual legacies.

In the view of some observers, the Camp David II Summit probably should never have happened. It was premature, with very little preparation on any of the hard issues that needed to be discussed. The Arab heads of state had not been consulted or brought on board ahead of time to give Arafat some political cover, the fault being largely the Clinton administration's. It may have no longer been the *Arab*-Israeli conflict, but the Arab world, if brought on board appropriately, could have played a useful role. Essentially, the summit involved two political leaders desperate for a political milestone that would redefine their political careers and a third (Arafat) who believed that not attending the summit would be worse than attending because he would then be portrayed as not really being interested in peace (it was almost a no-win scenario for Arafat, who did not expect summit success to begin with, and who therefore insisted on not being blamed if Camp David failed). Barak's negotiating inexperience, and even brusqueness, was also on display at the site of the summit in Maryland. He avoided directly discussing matters with Arafat, and he often made proposals without consulting the rest of the Israeli delegation. For his part, Arafat's denial that Jewish temples had ever existed in Jerusalem poisoned the negotiating atmosphere. In addition, like Carter in 1978, the American president in July 2000 placed more pressure on the Arab party than on Israel to make concessions, usually in terms of trying to explain the vulnerable domestic situation of the Israeli prime minister without taking into adequate account the very real and equally vulnerable political arena of the Arab participant.

Most important, though, the failure of Camp David II seemed to embolden radical elements in both the Israeli and the Palestinian populations who had been opposed to the Oslo process from the very beginning. The years of seemingly fruitless negotiations, which appeared merely to exacerbate violence and despair, legitimized the more confrontational view that the ultimate answer lay only in militancy, repression, and separation. A decade of hope had been replaced by frustration on both sides. The Oslo process was effectively over.

An air of rising tension was filling a balloon that was ready to burst—and burst it did with the so-called al-Aqsa Intifada in September 2000.

The Arab world was outraged by Israel's strong response to the intifada, this time the images being sent via the Arab satellite news agency, al-Jazeera, into the homes of anyone with a satellite dish. The lasting image for Arabs in the early part of the intifada was the death from an Israeli-Palestinian crossfire of twelve-year-old Muhammad al-Dureh in the arms of his father at Netzarim Junction, although who actually killed the boy remains in dispute. An emergency Arab League summit meeting was convened in Cairo on October 21–22. The anti-Israeli rhetoric spewed by one Arab leader after another harked back to the heyday of the Arab-Israeli conflict. Some Arab leaders bombastically—and unrealistically—called for an Arab military response, while also demanding the reimposition of a full Arab boycott of Israel. As Arab moderates, Egypt and Jordan did everything they could to maintain the hope of a diplomatic resolution in the meeting's communiqué, which, in the end, called on the international community to actively intervene to bring the crisis to an end. The Egyptian-Israeli peace treaty had weathered many storms over the years, and Hosni Mubarak had long since decided that its maintenance was a sine qua non for stability in the region, which served Egyptian (and Jordanian) interests. Even so, Egypt did recall its ambassador as a sign of displeasure with Israeli tactics; Jordan, as well, kept its new ambassador to Israel at home instead of replacing the outgoing one as scheduled. Other moderate Arab states, such as Morocco, Oman, Tunisia, and Qatar, downgraded or severed the unofficial (mostly economic) ties they had established with Tel Aviv in the 1990s. As the Arab public had been integrated into the information age by this time, the daily repetition over the airwaves of Israeli "brutality" and Palestinian "suffering" began to be reflected across the sociocultural spectrum in the Arab world, not unlike in the aftermath of the 1967 Arab-Israeli war. As Yoram Meital comments:

> The Intifada, as an expression of the legitimate struggle of the Palestinian people, was upheld by the broader Arab public and lauded by writers, poets, artists, and intellectuals. Television and radio, the Internet, newspapers, and magazines all revolved around it. Literature, poetry, theater, documentaries, and feature films served as rich, unique sources, conveying how different Arab polities perceived, embedded, and accepted the Intifada from September 2000 on.[16]

All of this, of course, tended to restrict the flexibility of moderate Arab leaders, compelling them to at least be seen as doing as much as possible to assist the Palestinians. On the other hand, the vitriolic anti-Israeli rhetoric just resuscitated the latent fears among Israelis of their country's isolated location in a hostile environment, fears that again fed into a growing sentiment in Israel that security rather than any sort of peace process was the priority in such a climate—a sentiment reinforced by the lynching of two Israeli reserve officers in the West Bank in the early months of the intifada.

In any event, the constituencies of both Arafat and Barak had been radicalized over the preceding six months, so that public support for a new peace initiative was lukewarm at best. The most immediate manifestation was the landslide victory of Ariel Sharon in the February 2001 Israeli election, bringing Likud back to power and electing as prime minister, for the first time, a man who was considered one of the prime architects of the settlement movement, a vociferous opponent of the Oslo process, and someone who had tremendous personal animus for Arafat.

The Regional Effects of 9/11 and US Foreign Policy

US president George W. Bush assumed office on January 20, 2001. In the early months of his term in office, his administration was not much inclined to turn its attention to the Middle East, particularly the Israeli-Palestinian situation. This stance was certainly understandable at first. Bush had just witnessed his predecessor engaging directly in the Israeli-Palestinian process and committing the prestige of the office of the US president to an attempt to seek a final agreement, with little to nothing to show for it. Indeed, the Clinton administration's efforts unintentionally contributed to the outbreak of the al-Aqsa Intifada, which was now in full force. There seemed to be nothing to gain from involving the administration in intensive diplomacy, especially since President Bush's domestic situation was less than ideal: He had won the presidency by only a razor-thin (and controversial) margin; he was presiding over an economic downturn; and the Republican edge in the US Senate had been whittled down to a mere one in the November 2000 election (a margin it would lose several months later when a liberal Republican became an Independent who voted primarily with the Democrats).[17] In addition, with Ariel Sharon as prime minister, there was no longer a willing Israeli partner for peace in Israel, and the Palestinians were carrying on an increasingly bloody intifada. For all intents and purposes, the Oslo process was dead. Finally, the partisan bitterness that had come to characterize Washington politics found its way into foreign policy as well, with the new administration embracing what was amusingly called the "ABC" (i.e., "Anything but Clinton") approach.

Representative of this relative lack of interest in Middle East affairs at the time was the fact that a new Assistant Secretary of State for Near Eastern Affairs was not appointed until late May 2001.[18] The US special envoy to the Middle East, Dennis Ross, who had served the two previous administrations, retired in January 2001, yet no replacement was named. Colin Powell stated succinctly the bent of the administration in December 2000 before taking office as secretary of state: "We will facilitate, but at the end of the day, it will have to be the parties in the region who will have to find the solution."[19] In addition, the Bush administration supported Sharon's position regarding the Camp David and Taba talks; that is, they were off the table once his new government was formed. In March, Powell would comment in more specific terms that "the US stands ready to assist, not insist. Peace arrived at voluntarily by the partners themselves is likely to prove more robust . . . than peace widely viewed as developed by others, worse yet, imposed."[20] This stand was very close to the Israeli view of dealing with Arab parties directly and not in an international setting, where there was a greater likelihood that a peace agreement would be imposed on the Jewish state. And in what would become a mantra of the administration throughout the intifada, Bush, clearly placing more of the blame for the violence on the Palestinians, stated, "The Palestinian Authority should speak out publicly and forcibly in a language that the Palestinian people [understand] to condemn violence and terrorism. . . . The signal I am sending to the Palestinians is stop the violence and I can't make it any more clear."[21] All of this countered the high optimism in the Arab world (and in the Arab-American community in the United States) that George W. Bush would be as impartial an arbiter on the Arab-Israeli conflict as his father, President George H.W. Bush, had been. They would be bitterly disappointed. Instead, the United States remained an aloof observer, casting a virtual blind eye on Sharon's settlement expansion activities, the use of targeted assassinations of suspected Palestinian militants, and the employment of verbal prestidigitation, as when Sharon claimed that the West Bank and the Gaza Strip were not "occupied" but "disputed" territories, and thus that their disposition was subject to negotiation (although the US State Department did issue a forceful rebuke of Sharon's use of these words; however, nothing was heard from the White House).[22]

This was the general predisposition of the Bush administration toward the Middle East on the eve of the most lethal terrorist attack in history on September 11, 2001, which has simply become known as 9/11.

As is well known, soon after the workday had begun on the morning of September 11, passenger planes hijacked by terrorists slammed into the World Trade Center Twin Towers in New York City and the Pentagon in Washington, DC, killing almost three thousand people (including those who crashed in Pennsylvania in the fourth plane). The attacks had been organized and carried out by the transnational terrorist network called al-Qaeda ("The Base"), led by Osama bin Laden. Bin Laden and many al-Qaeda leaders had taken refuge in and were operating from Afghanistan under the protection of the puritanical Sunni Islamist Taliban regime. The global repercussions of 9/11 would be enormous, with distinct reverberations in the Arab-Israeli arena.

The initial US riposte to 9/11 was an invasion of Afghanistan in October 2001, to rid the country of the Taliban and the al-Qaeda presence. With the considerable assistance of local Afghani factions that had opposed the Taliban regime for years, the United States did just that by early December. Article V of the NATO (North Atlantic Treaty Organization) Charter was invoked, legitimizing the US-led military response as an act of collective self-defense. The 9/11 attacks were roundly condemned by governments throughout the Middle East, even by traditional foes of the United States such as Iran and Libya, even though there were Arabs who celebrated the event. While the cynic may doubt the sincerity of these government condemnations, seeing them more as a convulsive gesture to let Washington know these countries had had nothing to do with the terrorist acts (and therefore should not be subjected to the expected US military response), there was an outpouring of grief at the grassroots level. Religious figures across the Islamic world condemned the attacks, stating that they were totally inconsistent with the teachings of Islam. Sheikh Yusuf al-Qaradawi, who is a very influential figure in the Islamic community and hosts a popular religious program on the Arab satellite news network, al-Jazeera, condemned all suicide attacks. President Bush went out of his way to make sure that the Islamic world understood that Washington was not castigating an entire religion or culture, just the extremists who perverted the true meaning of Islam. Saudi Arabia, from which fifteen of the nineteen hijackers originated (not to speak of Osama bin Laden himself), quietly increased its supply of oil to the United States to soften the anticipated economic blow following the attacks.

For a short while in the aftermath of 9/11, the Bush administration actively courted the Arab world as an ally against the new terrorist threat and in its Afghani campaign, attempting to construct a broad coalition not unlike that his father had formed for the 1991 Gulf War.[23] Indeed, Ariel Sharon was getting a bit nervous about the repercussions that this new American bent might have on Israel's policies vis-à-vis the Palestinians. In fact, Bush began to pressure Sharon to agree to a cease-fire in the intifada in order to facilitate the US attempt to attract allies against the Taliban in the Arab and Muslim world. In a terse statement that he would later soften, Sharon shot back that "Israel would not be sacrificed as part of the West's appeasement of the Arab world."[24] Of course, ever since the end of the cold war and the breakup of the Soviet Union, both Labor and Likud governments had feared that Israel's reduced strategic utility, combined with soaring government deficits and calls by the US Congress to cut back on foreign aid, would degrade the US-Israeli relationship and lead to a significant reduction in the annual $3 billion the United States provided Israel.[25] By the mid-1990s, Israeli leaders were warning the United States of the brewing threat of Islamic extremism, hoping to position Israel once again as a key US ally in the fight against a global menace arising in the wake of the fall of communism. As we shall see, Sharon's fears, while understandable at that specific moment, would turn out to be very much unfounded.

The goodwill the United States garnered following 9/11, however, began to dissipate toward the end of the year. European states began to question whether Article V of the NATO charter had been too hastily invoked. Media coverage, especially by al-Jazeera, of civilian casualties in Afghanistan, as well as questions about the legality and morality of the treatment of Afghani and al-Qaeda prisoners taken to the American naval base at Guantánamo Bay in Cuba, began to erode the international support for US policies. To many in the Muslim world, the US actions were indeed becoming a war against Islam, and this perception was reinforced as the US prepared to invade Iraq.

The shifting sands in Washington by the end of 2001 served to align the Bush administration with Ariel Sharon's view of the Palestinians, that is, that what Israel was doing was indeed not different from what the United States was attempting to do in Afghanistan: root out terror. Yasser Arafat and the PLO, therefore, were nothing more than another version of Osama bin Laden and al-Qaeda, and slowly but surely the Bush administration began to come around to this same point of view. As National Security Adviser Condoleezza Rice stated in reference to Arafat in November 2001, "You cannot help us with al-Qaeda and hug Hizbollah or Hamas. And so the President makes that clear to Mr. Arafat."[26] Thus the Israeli-Palestinian conflict became a function of the US global war on terror, despite attempts by a number of Arab and European states to convince the Bush administration to delink the two and treat the Arab-Israeli arena on its own terms.

It was in this moribund diplomatic environment that the Arab world took the lead in offering a plan to reinvigorate the peace process. Saudi Arabia, with Crown Prince Abdullah as its de facto ruler (with King Fahd increasingly incapacitated by the stroke he had suffered in the mid-1990s), laid out for the first time in Arab quarters a set of principles for a permanent Arab-Israeli peace.[27] He introduced the plan at an Arab League summit meeting in Beirut in late March 2002.[28] The Saudis were concerned about the dangerous drift of events in the al-Aqsa Intifada, which could undermine regional stability. In addition, it was not a bad propaganda move to play the part of peace brokers following the bad press Saudi Arabia had received in the United States following 9/11 because fifteen of the nineteen hijackers had been Saudis.[29] The peace plan called for Israel's withdrawal from all Arab territories it had acquired in the 1967 War; the establishment of an independent Palestinian state with East Jerusalem (al-Quds) as its capital; an end to the Arab-Israeli conflict with peace treaties signed between Israel and the Arab states; and a just resolution of the Palestinian refugee problem, based on UN Resolution 194. In the summit's closing statement, however, the Arab League reiterated the "suspension of establishing any relations with Israel in view of the setback to the peace process and the reactivation of the Bureau of the Arab Boycott of Israel until Israel responds by implementing the resolutions of international legitimacy."

It was not a detailed peace plan "but a common Arab statement of principles for a political settlement of the Israeli-Arab conflict," which would entail complex negotiations based on this "Arab vision for achieving peace in the Middle East."[30] The Sharon government was not very responsive, revealing its own consciously adopted lack of vision at the time regarding any sort of peace process. As Henry Siegman comments, the Saudi peace plan "seems to have been greeted with a yawn by the Israeli government."[31] In any event, even if Israel had been more forthcoming, the plan most certainly would have been derailed by another round of lethal Palestinian suicide attacks, which once again reversed any momentum toward peace. Since an end of the violence was a precondition for resuming negotiations, extremists were automatically given virtual veto power over the peace process. This time, on March 27, the first day of the Jewish Passover holiday, twenty-nine Jews were killed in a suicide bombing in the Israeli coastal resort town of Netanya. Over the next three days, seventeen Israelis were killed in a series of suicide bombings in Tel Aviv, Haifa, and Jerusalem, events that led to Israel's reoccupation of the large cities of the West Bank that had been given over to Palestinian control following the 1995 Oslo II agreement.

Awash in victory immediately following the US-led invasion of Iraq in March 2003, and probably hoping (with considerable encouragement from British prime minister Tony Blair) to utilize the postwar environment and regional balance of power to orchestrate a peace process much in the way his father had, Bush attended a conference at Sharm al-Shaykh in early June, meeting with Egyptian president Hosni Mubarak, King Abdullah of Jordan, Crown Prince Abdullah of Saudi Arabia, Prime Minister Mahmoud Abbas of the Palestinian Authority, and the emir of Bahrain, Sheikh Hamad bin Isa Al Khalifa. The next day (June 4) Bush traveled to Aqaba, Jordan, to meet again with Mahmoud Abbas and Ariel Sharon. He again met with Abbas and Sharon in July in Washington. Bush was certainly investing his considerable prestige in trying to get Phase I of the so-called Road Map off and running. (The Road Map was a three-stage peace process under which a Palestinian state was to emerge by 2005 as part of a two-state solution to the Israeli-Palestinian conflict.) Unfortunately, the Road Map, for all intents and purposes, collapsed in August 2003, just a few months after it was launched, as a result of a Hamas terrorist attack in Jerusalem, and Abbas was soon to resign as prime minister, blaming both Arafat and Israel. Seeing no Palestinian partner, and wishing to preserve Israel as both a Jewish and a democratic state, Sharon outlined a policy calling for a unilateral withdrawal of Israeli settlements and military bases from Gaza. After consultation with the United States, the plan was expanded to include the uprooting of four Israeli settlements in the northern part of the West Bank. In return Sharon received US support to return to the vacated territories if they became bases of terrorism, as well as an acknowledgment by Bush that any final borders would have to reflect "new realities on the ground."[32]

Even the death of Yasser Arafat in November 2004 did not change Sharon's plan for a unilateral withdrawal, although there were talks with the newly elected president of the Palestinian Authority, Mahmoud Abbas, about coordinating the withdrawal from Gaza. The United States tried, with limited success, to facilitate the coordination. At the same time, given his concentration on the unilateral withdrawal—which caused a major political storm in Israel leading to Sharon's breaking away from the Likud Party to form a new Israeli political party, Kadima—Sharon had little interest (or political capital) to respond to hints from Syrian leader Bashar Asad that he was interested in resuming peace talks with Israel.

After completing the unilateral withdrawal, Sharon was hit by a series of strokes, the second of which totally incapacitated him. He was succeeded, as acting prime minister, by Ehud Olmert, who had left the Likud Party with Sharon to form Kadima. Olmert was almost immediately confronted by the Hamas victory in the Palestinian legislative election in January 2006, which led to the formation of a Hamas government. Given the Hamas position calling for the destruction of Israel, it is not surprising that Israeli-Palestinian relations sharply deteriorated, and two months after Olmert's Kadima Party had won the Israeli elections in April 2006, a Hamas-directed military operation from Gaza resulted in the kidnapping of an Israeli soldier, Gilad Shalit, which caused an escalation in Israeli military operations against Gaza, from which Qassem rockets continued to be fired into Israel, despite the Israeli unilateral withdrawal from Gaza in 2005.

Summer 2006

Three weeks into the Gaza military operation without obtaining the release of Corporal Shalit, and amid rising internal criticism of Olmert and his inexperienced defense minister, Labor Party head Amir Peretz, Israel was unexpectedly hit again, this time in the north. On July 12 Hizbollah carried out a daring daylight raid into Israel just across the border, killing eight Israeli soldiers and capturing two. In an almost cathartic response, Israel launched punitive air strikes into Lebanon against Hizbollah positions as well as transit routes, including Beirut International Airport, to prevent the transfer of the two soldiers out of the country. Hizbollah responded by firing scores of Katyusha rockets into northern Israel, launching a thirty-four-day conflict. Several thousand more Katyushas were fired indiscriminately into Israel as far south as Haifa, and the Israelis launched an intensive air campaign over most of Lebanon, especially in south Beirut and south Lebanon against Hizbollah strongholds, and eventually a ground campaign to root out Hizbollah positions in southern Lebanon. During the conflict 159 Israelis (118 soldiers and 41 civilians) and some 1,070 Lebanese were killed; hundreds of thousands of Lebanese and Israelis fled the warfare to safer environs.[33] The level of destruction in Lebanon itself reminded many of 1982, and the destruction in northern Israel—and perhaps even more important, the fears generated—showed Israelis that they were not yet safe in the Middle East despite their overwhelming conventional military strength.

As in the case of the Hamas raid, the reason for the Hizbollah attack was unclear. Perhaps the reason was simply, as Hizbollah leader Sheikh Hassan Nasrallah said, to help the Palestinians under attack in Gaza by diverting Israel's attention; Nasrallah is widely known to say what he means and to do what he says. This action allowed Hizbollah to transcend its Lebanese Shiite roots to the broader Arab-Islamic arena, amply displaying that it alone in the region had the temerity to take on Israel and fight on behalf of the Palestinians. Others claim the action was either ordered by Hizbollah's patron, Iran, or carried out independently by Hizbollah on behalf of Tehran in order to show the West that Iran has lethal means to employ if the international pressure on its nuclear enrichment program escalates into military action. Hizbollah's launching the attack on the day of an important UN deadline for receiving a response from Tehran regarding its nuclear enrichment activities lends some credence to this view. In addition, ever since the passage of UN Security Council Resolution 1559 and the subsequent Syrian withdrawal from Lebanon, Hizbollah had seen its position in the country being undermined. It was resisting attempts by the Lebanese government to disarm it, as ordained in Resolution 1559. Stirring up trouble with Israel, this line of thought proceeds, would confirm Hizbollah's role as a legitimate resistance organization; thus it would be able to retain its arms as well as position itself more favorably in the constellation of political forces that make up the Lebanese polity.[34]

Syria, which also supports Hizbollah—namely, with logistical assistance in transferring Iranian arms and funds—might also, by default, enhance its influence in Lebanon and gain a seat at the diplomatic table in any sort of resolution of the conflict and in postconflict attempts to restart Arab-Israeli peace negotiations. Hizbollah's rationale may have been one or all of the above.

There was widespread support in Israel for Olmert's military response in Lebanon, although many outside Israel saw it as disproportionate to the provocation. It was a response that definitely caught Hizbollah by surprise, although Hizbollah was effectively prepared to resist it. Despite the desperate pleas for help from the pro-US government of Lebanese prime minister Fuad Siniora, the Bush administration appeared to delay inserting itself actively into the mix to arrange a cease-fire, as previous administrations had when Israeli-Hizbollah violence had flared up and threatened to escalate beyond Lebanon. The United States clearly was allowing Israel the opportunity to deal Hizbollah a decisive blow, which would not only allow the Lebanese government to extend its control but also damage Syrian and Iranian interests. Indeed, it seemed that in Washington the Arab-Israeli conflict was being folded neatly into a US versus Iran dynamic, even though Arab-Israeli conflict in general, and in Lebanon specifically, long predated the 1979 Iranian revolution and had unique dynamics of its own that needed to be addressed directly. But the Bush administration believed that the events of the summer of 2006 could weaken both Hamas and Hizbollah, and that the Israelis were poised to inflict irreversible damage.

But Israel was unable to "defeat" Hizbollah. As Robert Malley stated, Olmert, "who claimed that Hizbollah would be destroyed, defined victory in terms that ensured a loss." Hizbollah's leader, Hassan Nasrallah, whose stated goal was to withstand the onslaught, had characterized success in a way that ruled out defeat. A war waged to reassert Israel's power of deterrence and to spoil Hizbollah's image achieved the opposite of both goals.[35] Hizbollah military preparations (including underground tunnels and bunkers) and stockpiles of weapons were much more extensive than Israeli intelligence had anticipated. In addition, Olmert and Peretz came under heavy internal criticism for not carrying out the war effectively, that is, depending too much on air power and not enough on a ground campaign, which in any event was too little, too late.

With both Israel and Hizbollah appearing to seek a way out as civilian casualties mounted and a military solution appeared fleeting, US and UN diplomacy engaged in arranging a cease-fire. By August 14, UN Security Council Resolution 1701 (passed by the Security Council on August 11) had been accepted and implemented by the governments of Lebanon (which included Hizbollah representation) and Israel.[36]

Both sides, of course, claimed victory. But it was also clear that the Olmert government had been rattled and weakened. The right-wing parties were empowered, as they had consistently opposed unilateral withdrawal, fearing what had actually come to pass: Withdrawal had opened the door for groups such as Hamas and Hizbollah to operate freely and build up their military ability to launch attacks against Israel. The survival of the Olmert coalition was certainly in doubt. As a result, any talk of further withdrawal (or realignment) from the West Bank was put on hold indefinitely. Equally clear was the failure to carry out withdrawal within the framework of a negotiated settlement that would hold a legitimate party such as the PA in Gaza or Syria in Lebanon (in 2000) responsible for maintaining the terms of the agreement. Although unilateral withdrawal is off the table for the time being, perhaps a negotiated withdrawal along the lines of the Egyptian-Israeli peace treaty will eventually gain some traction.

For Hizbollah the conflict was a mixed bag. In the span of a month, Hizbollah and Nasrallah became the most popular group and leader in the Arab and Muslim worlds. Its reconstruction efforts in Lebanon through its already existing and pervasive social welfare networks and institutions—along with copious amounts of Iranian money—seemed to have improved Hizbollah's political position in Lebanon and solidified its demand, as a resistance group, to keep its weapons. On the other hand, the damage to Lebanon, especially in the Shiite-dominated south, was extensive. In fact, Nasrallah pointed out, with refreshing honesty, that had he known beforehand the extent of the damage that Israel would inflict, he absolutely would not have ordered the July 12 raid. In the early stages of the conflict some Arab leaders (notably Sunni countries such as Saudi Arabia and Egypt) and a number of Lebanese openly pinned the blame for initiating the war on Hizbollah. While these sentiments disappeared under the weight of Arab solidarity as the death and destruction in Lebanon grew, some level of opprobrium is likely to return, especially inside the country, once the postconflict political dust settles.

A Final Opportunity?

Bashar Asad of Syria wasted no time in trying to put his newfound leverage to use. There was no shortage of signals emanating from Damascus and from Syrian diplomats in a variety of locales that Syria was prepared to resume negotiations with Israel. To Bashar, Israel is not an existential enemy, as it is to some other entities in the Middle East, such as Iran, elements of Hamas, and Islamic extremist organizations. Rather, Syria sees Israel as a strategic threat, and it has certainly presented a manifest and serious strategic challenge from time to time. But it is also a country with which Syrian officials have held negotiations, and it is the only country that can return the Golan Heights, a prime foreign policy objective ingrained into Bashar's being—and just about every other Syrian's as well. Bashar commented to me last summer that he would be a "hero" if he was able to effect a return of the land that Israel seized in 1967, with the clear implication that it might be worth cashing in some chips to reacquire the Golan Heights, such as Syrian influence regarding Hamas and Hizbollah, both of which became much more a concern to Israel in 2006.

A debate ensued in and outside the Israeli government on whether to explore Syrian intentions. But Prime Minister Ehud Olmert remained steadfast in rejecting Bashar's peace overtures, in part because he did not want to negotiate from a position of perceived weakness following the debacle in Lebanon. It was also widely believed that in order to maintain the US-led isolation of Damascus, the Bush administration was pressuring Israel not to reengage with Syria. Since Israel's primary strategic threat is an Iran with nuclear weapons capability, and since the United States was taking the lead in trying to contain if not eliminate this possibility, Olmert did not want to cut off his nose to spite his face by upsetting the Bush administration over Syria. So nothing happened.

Nonetheless, this may be the last chance to create the foundation for an Arab-Israeli peace process during the Bush administration. The timing may be perfect in this regard in terms of the US position. In recent US history, dramatic peace overtures have been attempted during the final two years of second-term administrations, for example, the Reagan and the Clinton administrations. Second-term presidents no longer have to be concerned about a presidential election, and the second-term midterm congressional elections are over. In other words, presidents begin to think more about their legacy than about their domestic political constituencies. The constraints of domestic politics are less, and presidents can be bolder in their foreign policy initiatives. The chastening of the Bush administration because of its foreign policy in the Middle East may augur a change in Washington's foreign policy approach. Unfortunately, the Bush administration is working from such a deficit, especially in terms of the level of mistrust, that there may not be enough time to create a process, much less bring it to fruition. A number of Arab states have invested in US-led peace processes over the years, only to be let down more often than not; therefore they may be less willing to invest themselves in such a process in the near future. It is a sign of the times that in lieu of positive US leadership—from the Arab point of view—Saudi Arabia is assuming the regional mantle in an attempt to fill the void before Iran does. The Saudis have attempted to do this in the past, with limited success at best, but maybe they can help rehabilitate Syria while pushing the Bush administration to take more concerted action.

Historians like to ponder the counterfactual in history, wondering what would have happened had some event not taken place. The answer is difficult, to say the least, because it must be totally hypothetical. In some important ways, though, today, we are seeing the counterfactual to peace in the Arab-Israeli arena. An Israeli-Syrian peace treaty—and a close to overall Arab-Israeli settlement—should have occurred in 2000; in its absence, we have had the al-Aqsa Intifada, the war in Iraq, and the 2006 Israeli-Hizbollah conflict. The United States must take advantage of the current opportunity. Let it not make this opportunity another what-if that historians a generation from now regretfully speculate about. As recent history has shown, we perpetuate the absence of peace at our peril.

Notes

1. Quoted in Moshe Maoz, "Changes in Syria's Regional Strategic Position vis-à-vis Israel," in Moshe Maoz, Joseph Ginat, and Onn Winckler, eds., *Modern Syria: From Ottoman Rule to Pivotal Role in the Middle East* (Brighton, England: Sussex Academic Press, 1999), p. 266. See also David W. Lesch, *The New Lion of Damascus: Bashar al-Asad and Modern Syria* (New Haven, CT: Yale University Press, 2005), pp. 52–56. For an illuminating treatment of the transformation of Soviet policy toward the Middle East under Gorbachev, see Georgiy Mirsky, "The Soviet Perception of the U.S. Threat," in David W. Lesch, ed., *The Middle East and the United States: A Historical and Political Reassessment* (Boulder, CO: Westview Press, 2007), pp. 437–445.

2. Quoted in Maoz, "Changes in Syria's Regional Position," p. 267.

3. For Syria, another quid pro quo was the Bush administration's looking the other way in late 1990 when Syrian troops helped to force out Christian militia leader General Michel Aoun, thus securing for Damascus the dominant position in Lebanon. Aoun had actually been receiving support, mostly financial, from Saddam Hussein as something of a payback for Syria's backing of Iraq during the Iran-Iraq war.

4. Dennis Ross, *The Missing Peace: The Inside Story of the Fight for Middle East Peace*

(New York: Farrar, Straus, & Giroux, 2004), pp. 48–49.

5. And just days after former US president George H.W. Bush visited with Hafiz al-Asad in Damascus during a Middle East trip to several countries.

6. William L. Cleveland, *A History of the Modern Middle East* (Boulder, CO: Westview Press, 2004), p. 514.

7. Ross, *The Missing Peace*, p. 523.

8. Quoted in Patrick Seale and Linda Butler, "Assad's Regional Strategy and the Challenge from Netanyahu," *Journal of Palestine Studies*, vol. 26, no. 1 (Fall 1996), pp. 36–37.

9. Quoted in Raymond Hinnebusch, "Does Syria Want Peace? Syrian Policy in the Syrian-Israeli Negotiations," *Journal of Palestine Studies*, vol. 26, no. 1 (Fall 1996), pp. 44–45.

10. Ross, *The Missing Peace*, p. 517.

11. Ibid., p. 569. The Syrians, for instance, agreed for the first time to an American presence at an early-warning station in Mount Hermon for five years after the Israeli withdrawal from the Golan Heights, which had been a major hurdle to that point. Along these lines, Ross also states the following: "Amnon Shahak [former deputy chief of staff of the IDF, minister of tourism under Barak, who was involved in the Syrian negotiations] was to tell me in the summer of 2002 that the Middle East changed the day in Shepherdstown when, unbeknownst to us, Barak re-

ceived the results of a poll that made doing the deal with Syria more problematic than he had thought. It was at that time that Barak decided to hold fast in Shepherdstown regardless of the Syrian moves. It was then that a deal was probably lost," p. 589.

12. Jeremy Pressman, "Lost Opportunities," *Boston Review,* (December 2004/January 2005), pp. 44–45.

13. Lesch, *The New Lion,* p. 259.

14. Ross, *The Missing Peace,* p. 589.

15. For a small portion of Bashar's inaugural speech devoted to Israel, see Lesch, *The New Lion,* pp. 156–157.

16. Yoram Meital, *Peace in Tatters: Israel, Palestine, and the Middle East* (Boulder, CO: Lynne Reinner, 2006), p. 103.

17. Robert O. Freedman, "The Bush Administration and the Arab-Israeli Conflict: The First Term and Beyond," in David W. Lesch, ed., *The Middle East and the United States: A Historical and Political Reassessment,* 4th ed. (Boulder, CO: Westview Press, 2007), p. 280.

18. Ibid.

19. *Washington Post* (December 17, 2000).

20. *Financial Times* (March 20, 2001).

21. *Washington Post* (March 30, 2001), as quoted in Freedman, "The Bush Administration," p. 282.

22. Again, while the US State Department condemned the use of targeted assassinations, Vice President Cheney stated in a Fox TV interview on August 4, 2001, that "if you've got an organization that had plotted or is plotting some kind of suicide bomber attack, for example, and they have hard evidence of who it is and where they're located, I think there's some justification in their trying to protect themselves by preempting," as quoted in Freedman, "The Bush Administration," p. 285. And it was very clear to the Israelis that Cheney spoke with much more authority than the State Department at the time. Cheney's statement also foreshadowed what would become known as the Bush doctrine, which sanctioned preemptive US military action to protect the country from terrorism. It also hints at the ideological framework, pushed by Cheney's office, behind the more liberal rules regarding the US interrogation of terrorist suspects, which many have claimed went beyond the pale of internationally sanctioned behavior.

23. In fact, on October 8, 2001, the UN General Assembly elected Syria to a nonpermanent, rotating two-year seat on the UN Security Council. The fact that the United States did not lobby against the choice of Syria was a clear indication that Washington was courting the Arab world at the time in the new war against terror and the war in Afghanistan. Syria would actually cooperate with US intelligence organizations and provide valuable information regarding al-Qaeda in the months ahead.

24. *Financial Times* (September 5, 2002).

25. For an interesting essay on this dynamic, see Scott Lasensky, "Paying for Peace: The Oslo Process and the Limits of American Foreign Aid," *Middle East Journal,* vol. 58, no. 2 (Spring 2004), pp. 210–234.

26. Quoted in Freedman, "The Bush Administration," p. 287.

27. Interestingly, according to a *Washington Post* report, Crown Prince Abdullah was absolutely furious upon hearing President Bush's televised comments on August 24, 2001, when he stated that "the Israelis will not negotiate under terrorist threat, simple as that . . . and if the Palestinians are interested in a dialogue, then I strongly urge Mr. Arafat to put 100 percent effort into . . . stopping the terrorist activity." Believing Bush to be totally partial in favor of Israel, Abdullah apparently immediately fired off a very strongly worded message to the American president through Prince Bandar bin Sultan, the Saudi ambassador to the United States. In the note to Bush, Abdullah basically threatened that Saudi Arabia would be compelled to go its own way from now on, essentially ending its unique relationship with the United States. This letter reportedly "shocked" the Bush administration, which scrambled to patch things up with the Saudi crown prince. Bush sent an ameliorating letter back to Abdullah professing his impartiality as well as endorsing the

idea of a viable Palestinian state in the West Bank and Gaza Strip, along with an invitation to Abdullah to visit with Bush at his ranch in Crawford, Texas. Abdullah was mollified and began to work assiduously as an intermediary between Bush and Arafat, hoping to set up a meeting between the two at the upcoming UN General Assembly meeting in late September. On September 8 and 9, US and Saudi officials were reportedly discussing the possibility of a major speech by Bush or Colin Powell that would jump-start the peace process and end the intifada, and it appeared that the Bush administration was eager to do this. Of course, then came the events of September 11, 2001, and all bets were off; Robert G. Kasier and David B. Ottaway, "Saudi Leader's Anger Revealed Shaky Ties," *Washington Post* (February 10, 2002).

28. Apparently, *New York Times* columnist Thomas Friedman helped Abdullah come forward with his plan in a meeting he had with the Saudi crown prince in February 2002. See Friedman, "An Intriguing Signal from the Saudi Crown Prince," *New York Times* (February 17, 2002).

29. Elie Podeh, *From Fahd to Abdullah: The Origins of the Saudi Peace Initiatives and Their Impact on the Arab System and Israel* (Jerusalem: Harry S. Truman Research Insti-

tute for the Advancement of Peace, 2003), p. 19. Podeh asserts that the Saudi initiative was also an attempt to strengthen the moderate faction within the Saudi elite against Islamic radicals in the country as well as to assert Saudi primacy over Egypt regarding the Palestinian issue; indeed, Mubarak did not attend the Arab League summit in Beirut, although he quietly supported the summit communiqué.

30. Meital, *Peace in Tatters,* p. 150.

31. *New York Times* (February 21, 2002).

32. Quoted in Freedman, "The Bush Administration," p. 298.

33. Over four thousand Lebanese and over one thousand Israelis were wounded.

34. Especially, as Hizbollah has done in the past (even when Sharon was in power), if it could arrange for a prisoner exchange.

35. Robert Malley, "A New Middle East," *New York Review of Books,* vol. 53, no. 14 (September 21, 2006), pp. 10–15. See also the chapter by Elli Lieberman in this book.

36. The resolution actually called for a "cessation of hostilities" and not a formal cease-fire, with a combination of the Lebanese army and a beefed up UNIFIL moving into the south to act as a buffer to take up positions that were vacated by Israeli forces as the international troops took up their positions.

11

Israel's Strategic Relations with Turkey and India

Efraim Inbar

AFTER THE COLD WAR, Israel's strategic environment improved considerably. It succeeded in maintaining good relations with the United States, the hegemonic power. Moreover, the ascendance of the United States in world politics and the decline in power of the Arab states at the regional and global level fueled the Arab-Israeli peace process—a reluctant recognition of Israel as a fait accompli in the Middle East.[1] The systemic change and the regional dynamics of the balance of power improved Israel's international status. The changes in Israel's international fortunes were reflected also in its improved relations with many states. For example, major international players, such as Russia, China, India, and Turkey, established full diplomatic relations with Israel. Similarly, other Asian states, such as Laos, Cambodia, and Vietnam, as well as countries once in the Soviet orbit (Eastern Europe and Central Asia), renewed or established full diplomatic relations with Jerusalem during that period.

The decision of these international actors to upgrade relations with Israel was also the result of the disappearance of several inhibiting factors. First, a change in the trends in the political economy of energy sources lessened the political leverage of the Arab states' bloc, and in particular of the oil-producing states. By the end of the 1980s, the fears of an energy crisis had already subsided substantially, and the oil market had become a "buyers" market, so that the weight of Arab objections to the enhancement of relations with Israel was diminished.

Second, in the aftermath of the 1991 Gulf War, the Arab-Israeli peace process, reactivated by the Americans with great fanfare, further marginalized the objections of Israel's regional enemies to third-party ties with Jerusalem. The October 1991 peace conference in Madrid, a formal gathering with Israel to which almost all Arab countries sent senior diplomatic delegations, served as a convenient pretext for hitherto reluctant states to develop a closer relationship with Israel. The upgrading of relations with Israel was therefore part of a larger post–cold war international phenomenon, characterized by the desire to normalize relations with an increasingly important international actor, to tap Israel's advanced technologies, and possibly to profit from Jerusalem's good relations with Washington.

This chapter reviews Israel's significantly improved relations with two important states, Turkey and India. In the 1990s Jerusalem was able to forge close relations with Ankara and New Delhi. To a great extent these strategic partnerships were in accordance with Israel's Periphery Doctrine, which guided Israel's foreign policy in the 1950s and the 1960s. This doctrine envisioned good relations with important states beyond Israel's hostile Arab neighbors.[2] The improvement in relations with the Arab world in the 1990s, however, was not a one-way process; it lent continuous validity to the premises of the Periphery Doctrine. Therefore, as this chapter demonstrates, the new links with Ankara and New Delhi are very beneficial for Jerusalem and strengthen further Israel's position in the region.

Special Relations with Turkey

Turkey was the first—and for decades the only—Islamic country that recognized the Jewish state, opening diplomatic relations in 1949. While Turkey became a member of the North Atlantic Treaty Organization (NATO) in 1952, and Israel served during the cold war as a Western ally to counter Soviet alliances in the Arab world, relations between the two states were low-key throughout the decade of wars fought between Israel and the Arabs. Yet Turkey never severed the relationship despite Arab pressure to do so. With the end of the cold war, Israel and Turkey emerged as the most democratic and economically dynamic states in the region. Their pro-Western orientation, their self-perception as bastions of democracy, and their free-market values in an unruly neighborhood put them again, as during the cold war years, in the same strategic boat.

In the early 1990s, with the end of the cold war, and when the Arab-Israeli peace process gained momentum, Israeli-Turkish relations also moved into high gear. Diplomatic ties were upgraded to embassy-level status, joint military exercises began, and intelligence cooperation was expanded. In addition, economic relations boomed. The annual economic trade between the two nations grew to $2.4 billion in 2006, up from $200 million in 1993, and since the mid-1990s, Turkey has ranked as the number one tourist destination for Israelis. Moreover, a series of military agreements were signed expanding intelligence cooperation, beginning joint military exercises, and enhancing military cooperation in many areas.

The remarkable upgrading of relations with Israel was the result of the emergence of a new international constellation following the breakdown of the Soviet Union and the subsequent adoption of a different Turkish approach to a newly defined Greater Middle East. Turkey only partially benefited from the "peace dividend" at the end of the cold war because it still found itself in a volatile environment. It perceived itself as encircled by many areas of instability and as threatened by dangerous neighbors, while the country was free to adopt a more assertive foreign policy than during the cold war.[3] Thus the main context for Turkey's rapprochement with Israel was Turkey's reorientation of its foreign policy and its greater emphasis on the Middle East.

Indeed, the many similarities in the strategic outlook of Israel and Turkey in the post–cold war regional environment strengthened the bilateral relationship. The countries shared similar regional concerns regarding Syria, the proliferation of weapons of mass destruction, the challenge of Islamic radicalism, and the geopolitical destiny of Central Asia. These mutual concerns intensified in the 1990s as a result of the end of the cold war, which allowed for greater freedom of action, particularly for the revisionist states in the region: Iran and Syria. At the global level, Israel and Turkey have displayed a strong pro-American orientation in their foreign policy, have had problematic relations with Europe, and have been suspicious of Russian aspirations.[4] The parallels outlined here were also clear to the other players in the region, which generally view the entente in strategic terms.[5]

This perception is reinforced by the close relationship reached between the defense establishments of the two states in the 1990s. Turkey benefited from the ability to purchase advanced weaponry from Israel that the United States and/or other Western states were reluctant to sell to it directly. Transfer of military technology has become increasingly important to the Turkish industrial-military establishment.[6] These interactions included a huge deal for Israel Aircraft Industries (IAI) to upgrade Turkey's F-4 Phantom jets. Local Israeli defense industries have also sold Turkey other electronic systems, including unmanned aerial vehicles (UAVs), radars, Delilah antiradar drones, Ehud debriefing systems, and Popeye advanced guided weapons. In 2002, Israel Military Industries (IMI) secured a contract to upgrade Turkish M-60 main battle tanks. Turkey has also provided the Israeli Air Force with a huge airspace where combat pilots can train in unfamiliar surroundings and practice long-distance attacks. In turn, Israel has provided Turkish pilots with advanced training at its Air Combat Maneuvering Instrument Range in the Negev. The Israeli, Turkish, and US fleets have undertaken annual "Reliant Mermaid" joint naval exercises in the eastern Mediterranean.

Throughout the years, Turkey has capitalized on its strategic partnership with Israel and has actively thwarted organizations working against Turkey. In 1998, it coerced Syria to expel the Kurdish Workers Party (PKK) leader, Abdullah Ocalan, and (with US help) it prevented the deployment of Russian-made S-300 surface-to-air missiles in Cyprus. In 2000, Turkey reportedly prevented Iran from supplying arms to Hizbollah through Turkish airspace. Again, in 2001, Turkey probably moved with tacit Israeli and American support against Iran when Iran threatened Azerbaijani oil in the Caspian Sea.[7]

All these ties and sales, of course, have taken place with the quiet encouragement of the United States. Moreover, Ankara believes that Jerusalem can be useful in neutralizing the hostile Greek and Armenian lobbies in Washington. For Israel, reaching out to Turkey was also a way to show its acceptance by a Muslim state in a hostile Arab and Islamic neighborhood despite the unresolved conflict with the Palestinians. The evolving Israeli-Turkish relationship in the 1990s became an important feature of the post–cold war Middle East.

The broad common strategic agenda of the 1990s served as a foundation for the Israeli-Turkish entente. However, changes in the international and regional environment could erode mutual interests and exacerbate differences.[8] Domestic links could also affect the bilateral relationship. Generally, Turkey needs Israel less than Israel needs Turkey, so Ankara is more likely to adopt a cooler disposition toward Jerusalem if international circumstances require such a realignment. Yet common perceptions about the regional and the global environment of the 1990s still bind the two states strategically and seem to be prima facie evidence of continuous relevance. The Middle East does not change rapidly and will continue to be a zone of turmoil for the foreseeable future. While the intensity of the current conflicts in the region may vary over time, and new alliances among past rivals may emerge, old enmities and suspicions will not easily fade away. Moreover, Turkey is gradually becoming more involved in Middle Eastern affairs, and the Arab states have been more receptive to its return to regional affairs.[9]

So far, the Israeli-Turkish entente has weathered problematic domestic preferences and disagreements over a variety of regional issues. The growing power of Islamic parties in Turkish politics did not bring about a reversal in the bilateral relationship, an indication of the primacy of strategic considerations in foreign-policy making. During 1996–1997, when Ecmettin Erbakan of the Islamist Refah Party served as prime minister, the course of the government's foreign policy vis-à-vis Israel remained basically unchanged, despite Erbakan's announced intention to minimize contacts. A more significant test came with the October 2002 electoral victory of the Justice and Development Party (AKP), a conservative party with Islamist roots.[10] It held out the prospect of a new rapprochement between Turkey and its Muslim neighbors and a cooling of ties with Israel.

Such an inclination could have been augmented by the September 2000 outbreak of the Palestinians' war against Israel (the al-Aqsa Intifada), which had clear Muslim overtones. For many Turks the war launched by the Palestinians reflected the religious dimension of the conflict. They also saw the war as an aspect of a national conflict in which most Turks sided with the Palestinians. Since its outbreak, pro-Palestinian demonstrations and vigils on campuses have increased considerably, and the press has contributed a steady stream of anti-Israeli articles. On such occasions, protestors typically burned Israeli and American flags and chanted slogans against the two states.[11] Israel's war against the Hizbollah in the summer of 2006 provided the anti-Israeli elements in Turkish society another opportunity for Israel-bashing. As in many other places in the world, traditional anti-Semitism and radical leftist ideologies converged vigorously with expressions of Islamic animosity toward the Jewish state.[12]

Except for occasional protests (sometimes quite harsh) over the treatment of the Palestinians or over the perceived disproportionate use of force by Israel during the Second Lebanon War in 2006, the good relationship between Israel and Turkey continued. Prime Minister Recept Tayyip Erdogan made it clear to Jewish organizations in America, which he met with immediately following his electoral victory, that he was in favor of continuing and expanding the bond with Israel.[13] His government allowed high-level contacts and visits to continue at all military and government levels. Turkey even hosted a high-profile visit of the Israeli president Moshe Katsav in July 2003, which generated much rhetoric about the virtues of the relationship and hopes for further cooperation. The most recent high-level visit was that of Prime Minister Ehud Olmert in February 2007. And Erdogan paid an official visit to Israel in May 2005, signaling business as usual.

Generally, the international criticism of the slowdown in the peace process, particularly the Israeli-Palestinian track and the great amounts of force used by Israel, have not affected the relationship. Ties between the two countries have also overcome persistent Arab criticism of Turkey's behavior. Turkey has withstood continuous pressure from Arab states and the Organization of Islamic Countries (OIC) to limit its links to Israel. Moreover, Ankara has helped Israeli diplomacy at Islamic summits to tone down some of the anti-Israeli resolutions.[14] Abdullah Gul, the foreign minister of the AKP government, even demanded in October 2003 that the OIC members be more realistic about the Israeli-Palestinian conflict.[15] Under the AKP, Turkey also hosted and mediated the breakthrough meeting between Pakistani foreign minister Khursheed Mehmood Kasuri and his Israeli counterpart, Silvan Shalom, in September 2005.

The Turkish arms market has remained open to Israeli firms, although the volume of sales has diminished considerably, primarily due to a general reduction in arms imports by the Turkish army and a growing preference for domestic products. Under the AKP, Turkey has not canceled the contract to upgrade tanks despite promises to do so in its election campaign. Significantly, Ankara decided in April 2005 to grant Israeli firms a $200-million contract for fifty Harop mini-UAVS. Additional potential deals include the purchase of long-range standoff weapons, various systems for F-4s and F-16s, the LORA type of surface-to-surface missiles and components for submarines.[16] An Israeli security fence was procured for construction in southeast Turkey. Cooperation between the two states in the security sphere has continued uninterrupted.

International developments in the twenty-first century have had mixed effects on the relationship. The events since September 11, 2001, seem to have strengthened the Israeli-Turkish strategic partnership, as the two countries face similar terrorism threats. Muslim Turkey has also been subject to attacks by Muslim terrorists. Prime Minister Erdogan urged strengthened intelligence cooperation between the two states in their counterterror activities.[17] In addition, both states strongly support the US global war on terrorism, which targets Islamic radicals. The Turkish and Israeli leaderships are afraid of the growth of radical influences in pro-Western countries (such as Jordan and Egypt) that could destabilize these regimes.

The American plans to invade Iraq created uncertainties in bilateral relations. Jerusalem followed with concern Turkey's rejection of the American request to open a northern front from Turkey's territory, a rejection that created tensions between Ankara and Washington.[18] The tensions continued due to fears that the American policy in Iraq would encourage Kurdish aspirations for independence and allow a renewal of PKK terrorism. The US-Turkish disagreements were also fed by stronger anti-American sentiments in public opinion. Israel and its lobby in Washington have done their best to mend the relations between Ankara and Washington.[19] The most recent examples (spring 2007) were the attempts to prevent the US Congress from adopting an Armenian genocide resolution. These attempts were appreciated in Ankara. Moreover, the basic interests of Israel and Turkey clearly converge in Iraq. Both states want the United States to remain there and hope it will be successful in generating a process of political change for the better. While neither country anticipates the development of an Iraqi democracy in the near future, both favor the emergence of a stable Iraq that is not a threat to its neighbors.

However, the potential for Iraq's disintegration into three states, including one for the Kurds, has clouded relations between Israel and Turkey. In the spring of 2004, Turkish officials issued harsh statements against Israel and re-called the Turkish envoy after reports that Israelis were heavily involved in Iraqi Kurdish affairs. The media inaccurately perceived these moves as a crisis in bilateral relations.[20] Official Israeli statements in favor of the territorial in-tegrity of the Iraqi state were not always taken at face value due to past Israeli support of the Kurdish nationalist movement in Iraq as part of a strategy of seeking alliances with non-Arab minorities.[21] Occasional articles in the Israeli press in favor of an independent Kurdish entity were viewed as an indication of Israel's desire to bring about the division of the Iraqi state into three smaller states, including an (Iraqi) Kurdistan, and to further its quest to weaken the Arab world. Foreign Minister Abdullah Gul was reported to complain about Israeli banks funding land purchases by Kurds from Arabs and Turkomans in an attempt to change the demographic profile of the oil-rich city of Kirkuk.[22] Turkey expressed its fears and anger over Israeli economic activity, and partic-ularly Israeli military assistance to the Kurds in northern Iraq.[23]

However, the idea that Kurdish independence serves Israel's current inter-ests is wrong. Israel supported the Kurds in the 1950s and 1960s in order to weaken Iraq. This support took place *before* the emergence in 1979 of the Is-lamic republic in Iran, Israel's major regional foe. Strategically, the breakdown of Iraq does not serve Israel's interests; a relatively strong Iraq that would counterbalance Iran's strategic preponderance in the Gulf area does. Only a unified Iraq can play such a role. Moreover, Israel must also contend with the possibility that a landlocked Kurdish political entity threatened by Turkey would fall under Iranian influence and allow Tehran to establish a contiguous corridor from north Iraq, through Syria, and extending to its protégé, Hizbol-lah, in Lebanon. Even if such a prospect does not materialize, Israel would not risk jeopardizing an important strategic relationship with a regional power, such as Turkey, in order to ally with a new, small, and weak state. Ankara and Jerusalem have a common goal in Iraq, namely, to see the emergence of a sta-ble state, strong enough to be a counterweight to Iran, but not a revisionist power that would threaten its neighbors. Finally, both have displayed appre-hensions about a premature exit of American forces from Iraq.

The future of northern Iraq seems to have elicited greater cooperation on the part of Turkey with Syria and Iran, Israel's regional rivals, which do not favor a Kurdish state. The interests of Turkey, Syria, and Iran are not identical, however. Damascus and Tehran are clearly pursuing policies intended to create American misfortune and instability in Iraq, and neither minds the Kurds continuing to be a constant thorn in the side of their powerful Turkish neighbor, although Iranian troops occasionally clash with Kurdish rebels. Syria's and Iran's past behavior clearly indicates that they have actively or tacitly supported Kurdish insurgent activities against Turkey. Therefore an explicit Turkish-Syrian-Iranian regional alliance is likely to be tactical rather than strategic.

It is true, however, that the AKP government believes that Turkey has been successful in improving relations with its neighbors, thus creating a more benign strategic environment. Syria gave in to Turkish military superiority in 1998. The subsequent overtures of Damascus to improve relations with Ankara were a reflection of Syria's realpolitik assessment that the circumstances dictated limiting hostilities with Turkey.[24] Ankara, like Jerusalem, presumably would welcome the emergence of a moderate pro-Western orientation in Damascus. Yet it would take a lot to convince a skeptical Turkey of Syrian moderation.[25] Similarly, the removal of Saddam Hussein has eliminated a source of immediate threat to Turkey (as well as to Israel) and may lead Ankara to conclude that there is less need to rely on Jerusalem to balance threats in the Middle East.

An increase in threat perception, as a result of more aggressive policies in the rogue states in the region or an increase in their ability to harm Turkey and Israel, would probably bring about greater cooperation between the two. This is a likely scenario, as Syria and Iran are both engaged in programs to extend the range and accuracy of their surface-to-surface missiles. One binding issue could be missile defense. Faced with a growing Iranian missile threat, Turkey has shown interest in the Israeli Arrow–2 ballistic missile defense system—the only operational antimissile system in existence. The fact that it will be coproduced by an American company added somewhat to its attraction.[26] The prospects of a nuclear Iran would make ballistic missile defense an urgent security need.

Indeed, Iran's nuclear ambitions bring the two states closer together. Both fear a nuclear Iran and prefer that the international community, primarily the United States, prevent its emergence, which Israeli decision makers consider an existential threat.[27] Turkey has upgraded its evaluation of the threat coming from Iran. Turkish defense minister Vecdi Gonul stressed that Iran has become a major threat to Turkish security, primarily because Tehran is actively seeking to acquire weapons of mass destruction and remains a major sponsor of international terrorism.[28] Reflecting the views of his government, Turkey's ambassador to the United States, Faruk Logoglu, said, "Iran's nuclear weapons would be a serious threat to the security of the Middle East."[29] Similarly, Turkey's key National Security Policy Document, formulated in November 2005, singled out Iran as a potential source of instability in the region due to its nuclear program.[30] Threatening postures could lead to increased collaboration between Israel and Turkey.

Energy is an emerging area of strategic cooperation between Turkey and Israel. Following the completion of the Baku-Ceyhan pipeline, supported by Israel, and the growing Turkish aspirations to become a global energy hub, Turkey and Israel began negotiating the construction of a network of pipelines to transport Caspian and Russian oil and natural gas to Lebanon, Jordan, Israel, and the Palestinian Authority. Moreover, a link to the Ashkelon-Eilat (Israel's Red Sea port) pipeline is necessary to ship oil via the Mediterranean Sea to Far East markets. This project envisions the inclusion of a pipeline to carry Turkish water to relieve Israel, the Palestinian territories, and Jordan of water shortages. The European Union (EU) decided to fund a feasibility study concerning this ambitious project.[31] Israel's national infrastructure minister, Binyamin Ben-Eliezer, who oversees the country's energy and water matters, said in April 2007 that the project could be finished in three years if ongoing feasibility studies supported it.[32]

Turkey and Israel do not see eye to eye on all issues, but they have learned to ignore their differences on secondary issues and concentrate on the main matters. For example, Turkey's sympathy for the Palestinians and the AKP's soft spot for Hamas (a Hamas delegation visited Turkey soon after the Hamas election victory in January 2006) were ignored in Jerusalem, while Israel's delays in buying water from Turkey and its ambiguous position a Turkish role in peacemaking left only a few scars in Ankara, and Israel did invite a Turkish delegation to observe its reconstruction of a ramp to the Temple Mount. Thus the different perspectives on marginal issues and various irritants in the bilateral relationship have not yet changed the calculus of expediency in the strategic partnership.

The future direction of Turkish foreign policy is uncertain. Much depends on the outcome of the Turkish "identity crisis." The political fortunes of political Islam in Turkey, or of the ultranationalist forces, could play an important role in distancing Turkey from the West. Turkey's problematic EU accession process has had a corrosive effect on Turkish-European ties.[33] Nowadays, public opinion in Turkey is less supportive of efforts to join the EU. Rising Turkish nationalism, which includes a great deal of anti-Western, and particularly anti-American, feeling, has infiltrated many aspects of society and could lead Turkey into a more isolationist posture.[34] The American and European efforts to incorporate Turkey into their political and military architecture are an important factor in determining Ankara's foreign orientation, including its relations with Jerusalem.[35] Wise policies are needed to maintain Turkey's pro-Western stance. Yet even a Turkey less enamored of the West might see Israel as an important regional ally. Indeed, to some extent, it was attracted to Israel because of its disappointment in the West.

The Blooming Relations with India

India recognized Israel in September 1950 but refused to establish full diplomatic relations, only allowing the opening of a consulate in Bombay in 1953. Within the ruling Congress Party, most of the Indian leadership linked the Zionist enterprise to Western colonialism. Furthermore, Israel was born as a result of the partition of Palestine, an unacceptable idea in the Indian context, which further undermined the legitimacy of the nascent Jewish state. Moreover, under the premise that Muslims tended to support the Arab cause, the Indian government was loath to estrange its Muslim minority.[36] Israel was very interested in improving relations with New Delhi, one of the Nonaligned Movement (NAM) leaders, but had little success.[37] India was dissuaded from accepting the Israeli overtures due to pressure by the Arab bloc and the adoption of an anti-Israeli policy by the NAM.[38] Gradually, Israel became identified as an American ally in the 1960s, and this alliance further hindered good relations with India, which was suspicious of American foreign policy. The limited Israeli military assistance rendered to India during its 1962 confrontation with China and during the Indo-Pakistani wars (1965, 1971), as well as the low-key cooperation between the intelligence services over the years, did not elicit a change in New Delhi's approach to Jerusalem. Even the 1979 peace treaty between Egypt and Israel did not change the formal hostility displayed by the Indian political elite against Israel.[39]

As in the case of Turkey, the change in India's attitude toward Israel occurred in the post–cold war era.[40] India felt strategically vulnerable as its quasi ally, the Soviet Union, collapsed, thus reducing a main source of diplomatic support and military technology. India reassessed its foreign policy, including its relations with Israel. Additionally, India did not want to lag behind China, which had been gradually improving its relations with Israel since the 1980s.[41] Changing domestic politics also contributed to the upgrading of Indo-Israeli relations. The ascendance of the Bharatiya Janata Party (BJP) in Indian politics helped remove hesitations about Israel. The BJP's nationalist and Hindu outlook viewed the Jewish state not as a diplomatic burden, but as a potential ally against Pakistan and radical Islam. Normalization was also the result of the economic liberalization initiated by Prime Minister Narasima Rao of the Congress Party. Under his policy, India depended heavily on economic and technological interactions with the West. Israel was seen as part of the new globalized economy that India wished to enter.[42] India announced full diplomatic relations with Israel on January 29, 1992, linking the announcement to the upcoming visit of Prime Minister Rao to the United States. New Delhi believed that a detente with Israel would be conducive to a better atmosphere in the United States due to the closeness between Washington and Jerusalem. Thus domestic and external perceptions converged.

Following the upgrading of Indian-Israeli diplomatic relations, a stream of visits by senior officials of both countries provided the architecture for concrete cooperation in many areas. The high-profile visit to India in December 1996 of Israel's president, Ezer Weizman, signaled new bilateral warmth. The closeness between the two states was further reflected in the historic September 2003 visit of Ariel Sharon to India, the first ever by an Israeli prime minister. This visit was an opportunity to enhance each other's understanding at the highest levels and to further promote bilateral defense and trade relations.[43]

In the economic arena, the two states signed various trade agreements, including double taxation protocols. Direct airline connections were established, facilitating economic interactions and tourism. In the early part of the trade relations, the accent was on diamonds, followed by cooperation in agriculture. Today there is a flourishing trade in high-tech, software, telecommunications, biotechnology, medical equipment, machinery, chemicals, and pharmaceuticals, among other areas. By 2006 the civilian bilateral trade had reached $2.7 billion—a volume thirteen times larger than in 1992 ($202 million)—and India became Israel's ninth largest global trading partner and second largest in Asia. India turned into the world's fourth largest economy in terms of purchasing-power parity after the United States, China, and Japan and is among the fastest-growing economies. It offers a plethora of opportunities, which Israeli entrepreneurs are taking advantage of.

The Israeli foreign ministry's Center for International Cooperation, MASHAV, has conducted activities in diverse fields with India. Since 1992, over sixty courses in India have been attended by twenty-three hundred trainees, including courses in health, agriculture, education, and management. Israel has also invited over nine hundred Indians for training at its institutions/facilities in areas like agriculture, community development, medicine and public health, management, science and technology, and education. India also receives Israeli diplomats for the Professional Course for Foreign Diplomats conducted by the ministry of external affairs.[44] Similarly, cultural contacts have been intensified by the exchange visits of art exhibitions, dance and music groups, and academics. Both states have sponsored cultural delegations.

In the late 1990s, the long-feared backlash from India's Muslim community failed to materialize, and the two countries discovered significant similarities in their outlooks on their respective regional disputes, as well as a common strategic agenda. The American decision of January 1999 to lift some of the sanctions against India, imposed after India's May 1998 nuclear tests, removed a serious snag in Jerusalem's relations with New Delhi, paving the way for even closer ties. The September 11, 2001, attacks and the ensuing war against international terror appeared to have created a political climate even more conducive to Indo-Israeli strategic collaboration. Finally, the growing realization that the Palestinian Authority had degenerated into a failed state unable to proceed in the peace process moved the differences of opinion between Israel and India on the Palestinian question to a back burner.

As in the Turkish case, India's relations with Israel have overcome problematic domestic changes. The United Progressive Alliance (UPA), led by India's Congress Party, came to power after the May 2004 elections. The new government, whose components had been quite critical of the closer ties with Israel, and which continued to criticize Israeli policies toward the Palestinians and Lebanon, nevertheless kept the relationship with the Jewish state on course. UPA ministers continued to conduct business with Israel. Additional bilateral agreements were signed, including one in July 2005 (Industrial Initiative for Research and Development), one in November 2005 (Economic Cooperation), and one in May 2006 (Agriculture). Relations between Jerusalem and New Delhi expanded and defense ties continued as before.

The additional improvements in US-Indian relations in the twenty-first century, which the UPA government endorsed, as well as the growing cooperation between the pro-Israeli and pro-Indian lobbies in Washington, have greatly reduced the differences in global orientation. Israel was satisfied to see India vote with the United States at the International Atomic Energy Agency on holding Iran in breach of its international commitments. Moreover, the tentative nuclear deal between Washington and New Delhi, which would allow Indian access to American nuclear technology despite the Indian nonsignatory status in the Nuclear Nonproliferation Treaty, was seen in Jerusalem as a welcome precedent. If the deal goes through, Israel, which was in the same boat as India on the nonproliferation issue, might enjoy similar access to the American nuclear market.

Similarity in Outlook on Regional Disputes

India and Israel display extremely high levels of threat perception, as both have been engaged in protracted conflict and have waged several major conventional wars against their neighbors. Moreover, they experience low-intensity conflict and terror, and they fear weapons of mass destruction (WMD) reaching the hands of regional rivals.

Indians, like Israelis, feel beleaguered in their own region. Indians believe that Pakistan wants India's disintegration. The prevalent perception is that Pakistan engages India in a proxy war by supporting Muslim separatists who employ terrorist tactics. Furthermore, despite adroit diplomacy to reduce Sino-Indian tensions, most of the Indian strategic community shares the view of many other countries along China's periphery that the massive economic progress of China has threatening national security implications.[45] Generally, there is much potential for strategic turbulence in Asia around India.[46]

As noted, Israel's strategic situation has improved considerably in the post–cold war era. Nevertheless, existential threats still exist, particularly from the Iranian nuclear program. Israel still meets profound hostility in the Arab world, as parts of it still want Israel's demise. The unrealistic expectation that the peace process would bring about the end of the Arab-Israeli conflict was proven wrong.

Indeed, the two states display similar attitudes toward the international community, which seems incapable of understanding their protracted and complex ethnic and religious conflicts with their neighbors. In Indian eyes, international attention is shifting from pressuring Islamabad to act against terror to pressuring New Delhi to make it worth Pakistan's while to end terrorism.[47] Similarly, Israelis feel pressured to make concessions to the Palestinian leadership under the problematic assumption that the latter must be able to show achievements to their people in order to muster support for ending the violence. The similar postures of India and Israel to forgo negotiations as long as their rivals use violence is often viewed as an unnecessary hard line. Another example of perceived bias is the human rights organizations' perspectives, which are often critical of the methods used by Israelis and Indians in their counterterrorist activities.

The current source of threat to the two nations is similar: the radical offshoots of Islam in the greater Middle East. It has been over the issue of radical Islam that the threat perceptions of India and Israel have clearly converged. India regards parts of the Arab world—Saudi Arabia, in particular—as hubs of Islamic extremism. The threat is felt closer to home regarding Saudi-Pakistani relations, which India views with suspicion. The Pakistani nuclear arsenal is viewed with trepidation in New Delhi, particularly the danger of nuclear warheads falling into the hands of Islamic radicals. For Israel, the Islamic radicals in the Arab world and in the Islamic republic of Iran constitute a constant security challenge. The links between Iran and Hizbollah and Hamas, radical Islamist organizations that have acquired great influence in their political systems, pose great security challenges. The combination of Iran's fanatic hatred and nuclear potential especially constitutes a clear existential threat.[48] Generally, the two states espouse affinities in their strategic cultures, entertaining similar notions about behavior during conflict.

The Common Strategic Agenda

The common strategic agenda, whose content is described below, has not turned the evolving relationship between India and Israel into a military alliance. Neither side wants to be drawn into the regional conflicts of the other. Both emphasize that their defense ties are meant only to enhance national self-defense capabilities and stability and are not directed against any third party. Israel does not want to be seen as Pakistan's enemy and displays considerable caution in its relations with China. Similarly, India has many political and economic interests in the Arab world, a growing Indian diaspora in the Gulf, and residual emotional support for the Palestinians. India's views on Iran differ from Israeli perceptions of Tehran. Nevertheless, the significant overlapping strategic concerns lend the relationship a quality quite different from regular bilateral relations.

Burgeoning Defense Cooperation

The institutional framework for defense cooperation is already in place. Mutual high-level visits of military and defense bureaucrats frequently occur. A bilateral joint Working Group on Counterterrorism, established in 2002, enables the two sides to share experience, information, and training techniques to deal more effectively with this global threat. The last meeting took place in New Delhi in March 2007. Discussions include terrorist financing, the transfer of weapons to terrorists, the menace of narcotics trafficking, and cooperation at multilateral forums. The intelligence services of the two states have similar concerns and focus on radical Islamist groups. India and Israel have been actively involved in the global campaign against terrorism and are committed to coordination with each other and with other democracies against this menace. There are also mechanisms for exchange between the national security councils of the two countries. In addition, most of Israel's military industries have already established offices in India to facilitate contact.

India is one of the fastest-growing defense markets in the world and is the third largest importer of arms, spending about $4 billion annually. New Delhi has even considered doubling its defense outlays in the coming years.[49] Israel's advanced military firms have succeeded in penetrating the Indian market. By the end of 2006 Israel had become the second largest arms supplier to India, after Russia, while in that year India was the leading customer of Israel's defense companies, with purchases valued at $1.5 billion.[50] According to India's defense minister A. K. Anthony, in 2002–2006, Israel's military industries secured deals in India for approximately $1 billion each year.[51]

Initially, India was interested in retrofitting some of its aging Soviet weapons, and it turned to Israeli companies. Over the years, Israel has developed a good reputation for retrofitting old military equipment of all kinds, from all sources. Israel had an advantage in upgrading Russian equipment because some immigrants to Israel had worked as technicians and engineers in the Soviet military industry. Israeli firms signed several large contracts with the Indian Air Force to supply avionics for the upgraded Russian-made MIG-21 and also to upgrade the ground attack aircraft with laser-guided bombs. Upgrades of avionics for Su-30 fighters were also acquired from Israel. Soltam Systems, the Israeli artillery company, won the contract to upgrade Soviet 133-mm artillery pieces.[52] Israel provided state-of-the-art fire control systems and thermal imagers for the Indian army's Russian-made T-72 tank fleet.[53] It also upgraded the Russian-made ZSU-23 air defense systems. Currently these types of deals are on the decline because India is gradually moving away from Russian equipment, particularly as Moscow makes greater royalty demands on foreign companies retrofitting its systems and also has difficulty providing parts for previously delivered systems. Moreover, Russian technology often lags behind that of the West. For example, after negotiations with Russia and Israel, the plans to retrofit TU-142 aircraft were called off in April 2006.

India, whose own military industry has had difficulty developing advanced systems, realized quickly the potential of the Israeli military industries and became an important customer. The largest arms deal (over $1 billion, which required US approval in 2003) has been two Green Pine Radar systems and three Phalcon airborne warning and control systems (AWACS) to be mounted on Russian IL-76 aircraft. Indian military forces rely primarily, if not exclusively, on Israeli-made UAVs. India turned to Israel Aircraft Industries, recognized as one of the leaders in developing military and commercial aerospace technology, for its UAV requirements. The need for UAVs was highlighted after the Kargil border conflict with Pakistan in 1999, when the Indian military realized that intrusions could have been spotted earlier if India had had the pilotless spy planes. In the absence of AWACS aircraft, the Indian navy relies on UAVs. In 2001, India's defense ministry signed a deal with IAI for $7.2 million per UAV. During 2003, India awarded a $130-million contract to IAI for eighteen medium-altitude, long-endurance Heron UAVs to be delivered within a year.[54] Following the great success with the Heron, Israel sold an additional fifty UAVs in a deal worth $220 million, clinched by the new UPA government in 2005.[55]

Since 2003, the Indian navy has operated the ship-based surface-to-air Barak system, which is intended to protect ships against aircraft and stealthy, supersonic sea-skimming missiles. The navy put in service Israeli Super-Devorah fast patrol boats and purchased beyond-vision-range Derby air-to-air missiles (AAMs) for its Harriers and avionics for upgrading these airplanes. The Indian army relied on Israeli firms for the massive upgrade of three hundred T-72M1 tanks and mounted the Israeli TISAS (thermal-imaging stand alone system) on five hundred BMP-2 infantry combat vehicles. The list of arms deals mentioned here is, of course, not exhaustive; it presents only an overview of the breadth of the cooperation.

Israeli military industries are also attractive because of their interest in technology transfer and coproduction, playing to the strength of Israeli firms in the area of research and design and to the strength of Indian firms in the area of manufacturing. Cooperation also involves technology transfer to Indian industries and the expanded sale of Israeli components. In September 2002, India's state-owned Hindustani Aeronautics Limited (HAL) and Israel's Israeli Aircraft Industry reached an agreement to jointly produce an advanced light helicopter, the Dhruv. HAL produced the ALH, which was equipped with Israeli avionics to be marketed by IAI.[56] To support India's UAV requirements, IAI and HAL set up a division in Hyderabad for maintenance and other services. IAI has provided testing equipment and the Bangalore-based HAL produces spare parts for the UAVs. In turn, IAI buys spares made by HAL for its own use.[57] HAL also announced in July 2006 that it had signed an agreement with Elbit, an Israeli defense electronics company, to make aircraft and helicopter simulators.[58] Israel's Armament Development Authority provides the technology to produce in India the Spike antiarmor and the Python-4 air-to-air missiles.[59] Ongoing production projects based on Israeli technology include hand-held thermal imagers and a LORROS (long-range reconnaissance and observation system).[60]

Similar Israeli technological input has been secured for the Indian Nishant UAV project.[61] Agreements on technology transfer have also been reached for the production of artillery.[62] The deal for purchasing six Super Devorah fast-attack naval craft allowed for the building of four vessels of this type by the Goa Shipyard. In January 2006, India's state-owned Defense and Research Development Laboratory (DRDL) in Hyderabad and IAI signed a deal for the joint development and production of the long-range Barak air defense system for the Indian and Israeli militaries. A conservative estimate of the cost is $350 million.[63] This deal will allow Israel to share with an important partner the research-and-development costs for a system it needs in the future.

A new development is offset arrangements with foreign arms makers. They are required to give Indian firms subcontract work worth 30 percent of their defense contracts.[64] For example, Rafael (Israel's Weapon Research Authority) won a $325-million contract from the Indian air force to supply Spyder mobile air defense systems (armed with Python and Derby missiles) and plans to return offsets worth more than $90 million to Indian industry.[65] This kind of contract enhances technological transfer and Israeli-Indian cooperation.

Closer American-Indian relations and the eagerness of the American military industries to sell their products could compete with Israel's weaponry sales to India. Yet Indian officials have expressed apprehensions about becoming dependent on American arms. They question the political reliability of Washington and its willingness to transfer technology.[66] Israel is not concerned that US entry into the Indian market will detract from Israeli defense sales. According to Major General (Reserves) Yossi Ben-Chanan, head of Sibat, the Foreign Defense Assistance and Defense Export Department in Israel's ministry of defense, Israeli military industries rarely compete with the United States because it sells primarily large weapons platforms, that is, airplanes and tanks. This could work to Israel's advantage, as Israel could sell the accompanying systems needed for the larger US platforms.[67] For example, Lockheed-Martin is offering the Israeli version of the F-16 to the Indian air force as a low-cost, high-performance alternative to competing French, Russian, and EU models. The Israeli version would also allow technology transfer to Indian military industries.[68]

The future of the cooperation over military equipment looks bright. India invited Israel's Elbit Systems to bid for a $500-million tactical-communications-systems procurement project, part of the Indian military's quest to build a network-centric warfare system.[69] Elbit is a front-runner in an international competition in the production of high-technology gear intended to boost soldiers' firepower, communications, and surveillance capabilities.[70] India also invited Israeli firms to bid on a multi-million-dollar army purchase of a number of integrated electronic warfare systems.[71] Future potential sales include that of the Arrow missile, since India already has the Green Pine radar, the core sensor of the Arrow-2 BMD (ballistic missile defense).[72] According to Indian defense officials, cooperation is sought in the area of UAVs, missiles, and electronic warfare.[73] The space industry is also an area of potential cooperation. India, which has good launching facilities, is negotiating with Israel for the lease of its Ofeq-5 satellite.

Cooperation has extended to the area of low-intensity conflict (LIC), as both countries are actively engaged in fighting terrorism and insurgencies. This fighting intensified after September 11, 2001, when dealing with terrorism gained a higher priority on the strategic agenda of many countries, and the need for international cooperation became more urgent.[74] While comparing national doctrines and operational experience, India and Israel exchanged information on terrorist groups' finances, recruitment patterns, training, and operations.[75] India started using Israeli counterterror-tailored equipment and border-monitoring tactics, such as fences and radars. Portions of India's special forces are already receiving Israeli arms and training.

Central Asia

India has long-standing strategic and cultural links to energy-rich and newly accessible Central Asia.[76] Nowadays it describes this region as its "extended strategic neighborhood," where it fights its regional rivals, China and Pakistan, for influence.[77] Israel similarly takes an interest in this area. Like India, Israel sells military equipment to Central Asian states and has a modest diplomatic and business presence there. Israel, as well as India, aims at limiting the influence of the Iranians and Saudis, which contributes to the spread of radical Islam. They prefer the system of Turkey, which has a Muslim population, but whose political character is secular. They hope that the Central Asian states will emulate the Kemalist Turkish model rather than the Iranian model.

Both states also want stability in Central Asia, to allow an uninterrupted flow of oil and gas. While there may be differences over the direction of the planned pipelines, India and Israel prefer low energy prices. India's economy needs it, while Israel's perspective is more political. As noted, Israel is interested in a project for bringing oil and natural gas from Central Asia to Israel via Turkey. The project calls for the construction of pipelines beneath the Mediterranean Sea between the ports of Ceyhan (the final destination of the Baku-Ceyhan pipeline) in Turkey and Ashkelon in Israel. The oil can then be pumped to Israel's Red Sea port of Eilat through an existing pipeline system and afterward can be exported to countries like India, Japan, and China. With India's growing appetite for energy, its petroleum minister, Shankar Aiyar, welcomed this idea in June 2005.[78]

Indian Ocean

India has become a significant maritime player in the Indian Ocean because of its location and its increased naval investments. Israel has shown increasing interest since the 1990s in the Indian Ocean because of its growing apprehensions about Iran and Pakistan and its burgeoning strategic relationship with India. Recently, there has been greater cooperation between the two navies, and Israel has hosted several visits by Indian ships. India's interests are not averse to a greater Israeli presence in the Indian Ocean. Historically, Israel has seen the Indian Ocean as the transit area for its links to countries in the East, particularly because it could not use land routes, which were blocked by its hostile Arab neighbors. Jerusalem is particularly interested in one of the Indian Ocean choke points, the Bab el-Mandeb Straits, through which all its exports to South and East Asia pass. Israel's overtures to Ethiopia and then Eritrea had these straits in mind. Kenya, Oman, and South Africa, also states on the Indian Ocean littoral, have similarly attracted the attention of Israeli strategy.

In response to the existential threat posed by Iran, Israel has increased its strategic reach by air and sea. Since the beginning of the 1990s, Israel has developed the ability to project air and naval power to distances exceeding fifteen hundred kilometers. Israel has built an oceangoing navy that compares with its new airpower reach. Israeli Saar-5 corvettes are able to remain at sea for long periods of time and have been seen in the Indian Ocean. The three new Israeli submarines are equipped with long-range cruise-missile-launching capability. One such missile tested in the Indian Ocean generated reports of Indian-Israeli naval cooperation.[79] Israel has plans to triple its submarine force and to build additional Saar-5 corvettes.

China

The great economic success of China and its military spending are causing a great deal of strategic concern to India, Israel, and the United States. The Bush administration termed Beijing a "strategic competitor." While India moves closer to the United States, China is perceived as a growing threat.[80] China's January 2007 ASAT (antisatellite) test shocked the Indian defense establishment.[81] Israel is also apprehensive of Chinese diplomacy in the Middle East[82] because any rising competitor of Washington is likely to favor the Arab perspective. Recently, Israel has been worried that the proliferation of ASAT technologies will endanger its own space capabilities, which are crucial for battle superiority.[83]

The American Aspect

With American hegemony in world affairs well established, Jerusalem and New Delhi can hardly ignore the wishes of Washington. Israel is interested in a smooth American-Indian relationship, just as it is interested in good relations between Ankara and Washington. Its strategic partnerships cannot diverge from its main pro-American foreign policy orientation.

As noted, New Delhi believes that upgrading relations with Israel has had a positive effect on the American disposition toward India, just as India has benefited from the political leverage of the Jewish lobby. American Jewish organizations are politically astute enough to understand the importance of India to the United States and to Israel, as well as the potential advantages of nurturing good relations with the burgeoning Indian diaspora in America, whose congressional power is on the rise. These organizations have nourished ties with India and with the Indian lobby in Washington, which was formed only in September 2002. The relations between the two diaspora communities are excellent, and they are working closely together on a number of domestic and foreign affairs issues, such as hate crimes, immigration, antiterrorism legislation, and the backing of pro-Israel and pro-India political candidates. The Jews and the Indians worked together to gain the Bush administration's approval for Israel to sell four Phalcon early-warning radar planes to India. Moreover, in July 2003, they were successful in adding an amendment to a congressional bill giving aid to Pakistan that called on Islamabad to stop Islamic militants from crossing into India and to prevent the spread of weapons of mass destruction.[84]

Cooperation between India and Israel is useful in overcoming American hesitation in approving the sales of sophisticated equipment to India, not only Israeli-made systems, such as the Green Pine, the Phalcon, and the Arrow-2, but also US-made equipment, such as advanced Patriot missiles. In addition, India is interested in preventing Pakistan from procuring the latest American military equipment, especially aircraft. Israel is not averse to such limitations, as Israeli-Pakistani relations remain frozen.[85] India, as well as Israel, is also interested in military technology transfer from the United States, and Israel and India want the American-Indian nuclear deal to go through.

Conclusion

In the 1990s, Turkey and India recognized Israel as a geopolitical partner with a common strategic agenda. The relations that Jerusalem fostered with Ankara and New Delhi seemed to take on a stable appearance beyond an ephemeral meeting of interests between sellers and buyers in the arms bazaar. Israel's relations with Turkey and India have weathered important domestic tests, demonstrating the robustness of the realist paradigm in international relations. Moreover, Ankara and New Delhi have decided to relegate the Palestinian issue to a low priority and not to hold their relations with Jerusalem hostage to the oscillations in the Arab-Israeli conflict.

There is also a Muslim aspect in the rapprochement with Turkey and India. Israel is interested in normalizing its relations with important Muslim states such as Turkey, particularly as there is no foreseeable end to its conflict with the Palestinians. Similarly, cordial relations with India allow access to a very large Muslim community (over 100 million). Engaging large Muslim populations could contribute to the diluting of the Islamic dimension in the Arab-Israeli conflict—a clear Israeli foreign policy goal.

Forecasts for the strategic landscape of the twenty-first century appear turbulent, and this turbulence will probably consolidate Israel's relations with

Turkey and India. Yet each relationship has widespread geostrategic implications beyond the strength it gives each participant. The rapprochement between Israel and its two new partners is an important component of a new strategic landscape in the Greater Middle East that includes Central Asia and parts of the Indian Ocean littoral. It clearly solidifies the Arab nations' reluctant acceptance of Israel as a fait accompli and enhances the deterrence capabilities of India and Turkey, each one an important regional power. The cooperation of Israel with India and Turkey is also valuable to the US-led campaign against terrorism. In addition, Washington can capitalize on Jerusalem's good relations with Ankara and New Delhi to promote closer cooperation among Asian democracies, which face comparable security challenges— terrorism, ballistic missiles, and weapons of mass destruction—from US rivals. Australia, Japan, South Korea, and Taiwan are prime potential additions to India, Israel, and Turkey in such a comprehensive security alignment.

Notes

1. Efraim Inbar, "Arab-Israeli Coexistence: Causes, Achievements and Limitations," *Israel Affairs,* vol. 6, nos. 3–4 (Summer 2000), pp. 25–270.

2. For the Periphery Doctrine, see *Michael* Brecher, *The Foreign Policy System of Israel* (London: Oxford University Press, 1972), p. 278.

3. Kemal Kirisci, "The End of the Cold War and Changes in Turkish Foreign Policy Behavior," *Dis Politika,* vol. 18, nos. 3–4 (1993), pp. 1–43; Malik Mufti, "Daring and Caution in Turkish Foreign Policy," *Middle East Journal,* vol. 52, no. 1 (Winter 1998), pp. 32–50; Alan Makovsky, "The New Activism in Turkish Foreign Policy," *School of Advanced International Studies Review,* vol. 19, no. 1 (Winter–Spring 1999), pp. 92–113; Heinz Kramer, *A Changing Turkey: The Challenges to Europe and the United States* (Washington, DC: Brookings Institution Press, 2000), pp. 93–96.

4. For a comprehensive analysis of the bilateral relationship in the 1990s and its regional ramifications, see Efraim Inbar, *The Turkish-Israeli Entente* (London: King's College Mediterranean Studies, 2001); see also Ofra Benjio, *The Turkish-Israeli Relationship* (New York: Palgrave, 2004).

5. See Ofra Bengio and Gencer Ozcan, "Old Grievances, New Fears: Arab Perceptions of Turkey and Its Alignment with Israel," *Middle Eastern Studies,* vol. 37, no. 2 (April 2001), pp. 50–92.

6. Namik Kemal Pak, "Changing Concepts of National Security in the Post–Cold War Era and Turkish Defence Industry," *Perceptions,* vol. 7, no. 2 (June–August 2002), pp. 115–117.

7. Robert Olson, "Turkey-Iran Relations, 2000–2001: The Caspian, Azerbaijan and the Kurds," *Middle East Policy,* vol. 9, no. 2 (June 2002), pp. 118–119.

8. Stephen M. Walt, "Why Alliances Endure or Collapse," *Survival,* vol. 39, no. 1 (Spring 1997), pp. 156–179.

9. For a review of recent Turkish foreign policy, see Kemal Kirisci, *Turkey's Foreign Policy in Turbulent Times,* Chaillot Papers No. 92 (Paris: Institute for Security Studies, September 2006).

10. The most comprehensive treatment of the Islamic factor in Turkish politics is M. Yavuz Hakan, *Islamic Political Identity in Turkey* (New York: Oxford University Press, 2003); see also Gamze Cavdar, "Islamist New Thinking in Turkey," *Political Science Quarterly,* vol. 121, no. 3 (Fall 2006), pp. 477–497.

11. For reports of such demonstrations, see "Intifada Ripples in Turkey," *Mideast Mirror,* vol. 14, no. 200 (October 17, 2000); Agence France Presse release, "Thousands Demonstrate in Turkey against Israel" (April 5, 2002); Associated Press release (April 27, 2002); Financial Times Information, Global News Wire release, "Students Protest U.S., Israel at Istanbul University" (October 21, 2002); Financial Times Information, Global News Wire release, "Demonstrators Protest Israeli Attacks on Hamas in Istanbul" (September 8, 2003); Associated Press (Turkey) release, "Thousands Protest Gaza offensive" (July 9, 2006).

12. For growing anti-Semitism and spreading conspiracy theories about Jews, see "An Unfamiliar Spectre Rises—Turkish Anti-Semitism," *The Economist* (August 5, 2006), p. 27.

13. Jewish Telegraphic Agency release (December 11, 2002).

14. Author's interview with David Sultan, Israel's Ambassador to Turkey, Ankara, November 25, 2001.

15. Sami Kohen, "Advice from Gul," *Milliyet* (October 30, 2003).

16. *Defense News* (June 14, 2004), p. 20; *Jane's Weekly* (June 9, 2005); Middle East News Line release, (December 31, 2006).

17. *Aksam* (January 2, 2004).

18. For an analysis of this event, see James E. Kapsis, "The Failure of U.S.-Turkish Prewar Negotiations: An Overconfident United States, Political Mismanagement, and a Conflicted Military," *Middle East Review of International Affairs (MERIA),* vol. 10, no. 3 (September 2006).

19. See, among other sources, the April 2, 2003, declaration of the American Jewish Committee supporting financial aid to Turkey.

20. See, among other sources, "A Strategic Friendship Cools," *The Economist,* (June 24, 2004); Bulent Aras, "A Big Chill: A Duo Divided by Democratic Legitimacy," *Daily Star* (Beirut) (August 10,, 2004). For a more balanced analysis, see Mustafa Kibaroglu, "Clash of Interests over North Iraq Drives Turkish-Israeli Alliance to a Crossroads," *Middle East Journal,* vol. 59, no. 2 (Spring 2005).

21. For a recent denial, see *Turkish Daily News* (April 20, 2007). For past Israeli-Kurdish ties, see Shlomo Nakdimon, *A Hopeless Hope: The Rise and Fall of the Israeli-Kurdish Alliance, 1963–1975* (Tel Aviv: Miskal, 1996) (in Hebrew).

22. See "Israel Said Financing Northern Iraqi Kurds to Purchase Turkoman Property," *Milliyet* (December 11, 2003); Ferai Tinc, "Land Sales to Kurds with Israeli Credit," *Hurriyet* (October 27, 2003).

23. Middle East News Line (MENL) release (December 21, 2003); Reuters (Ankara) release, (June 22, 2004); Seymour Hersch, "Plan B: As June 30th Approaches Israel Looks to the Kurds," *New Yorker* (June 2004).

24. Syria, which has been labeled in Washington as a state sponsor of terrorism, has been afraid of American or Israeli attacks since the beginning of the American war on international terrorism following September 11, 2001, as well as the 2003 American invasion of Iraq, and because of Syrian behavior in Lebanon.

25. Omer Taspinar and Emile el-Hokayem, "Syria Loves Ankara but Will the Relationship Last?" *Daily Star* (Beirut) (April 19, 2005).

26. MENL, June 19, 2001; *Jerusalem Post,* July 10, 2001; *Jerusalem Post,* January 6, 2002.

27. See Efraim Inbar, "The Need to Block a Nuclear Iran," *MERIA,* vol. 10, no. 1 (Spring 2006). See also the chapter by Steven David in this volume.

28. Worldtribune.com (November 5, 2003); MENL release (November 12, 2003).

29. Metehan Demir, "Turkish Ambassador to U.S.: Iran Dead Set on Obtaining Nukes," *Jerusalem Post* (December 22, 2005).

30. Ibid.

31. Jay Bushinsky, "Turkey, Israel Make Undersea Connections," *Washington Post* (April 30, 2006), and Etgar Lefkovits, "Israel and Turkey Plan Energy Pipeline," *Jerusalem Post* (May 11, 2006).

32. *Turkish Daily News* (April 20, 2007).

33. Turkish-EU membership talks had been partially suspended for eight of the thirty-five chapters in December 2006, due to disagreements on the Cyprus issue. The talks

on the second chapter of Turkish accession negotiations were reopened in March 2007.

34. See reports by Umit Egensoy and Burak Ege Bekdil in *Defense News:* "Turks' Anti-U.S. Sentiment Threaten Ties" (February 28, 2005), p. 10; "Rising Turkish Nationalism Concerns West" (April 18, 2005), p. 21; "Is Turkey Drifting into Political Isolation?" (May 2, 2005), p. 23; "Faltering EU Process Erodes Turk-European Ties" (November 20, 2006), p. 22.

35. For an Israeli perspective on the advantages and disadvantages of Turkey's European membership, see Efraim Inbar, "Israeli Concerns over Turkish Membership," *Dis Politika* [Foreign Policy], vol. 29, nos. 3–4 (2004), pp. 28–31.

36. Yaakov Shimoni, "India—The Years of Estrangement," in Moshe Yager, Yoseph Govrin, and Ariyeh Oded, eds., *Ministry of Foreign Affairs: The First Fifty Years* (Jerusalem: Keter, 2002), p. 539 (in Hebrew).

37. Ibid., p. 540.

38. For Israel's growing isolation as a result of Third World activism, see Efraim Inbar, *Outcast Countries in the World Community,* Monograph Series in World Affairs (Denver, CO: University of Denver Press, 1985), pp. 26–31.

39. Moshe Yager, "Fundamental Factors in Asia-Israel Relations: Introductory Remarks," in Moshe Yager, Yoseph Govrin, and Aryeh Oded, eds., *Ministry of Foreign Affairs: The First Fifty Years* (Jerusalem: Keter, 2002), p. 534.

40. For any early analysis of the bilateral relations in the post–cold war era, see P. R. Kumaraswami, *Israel and India: Evolving Strategic Partnership,* Mideast Security and Policy Studies No. 40 (Ramat Gan, Israel: Begin-Sadat Center for Strategic Studies, September 1998). See also Efraim Inbar, "The Indian-Israeli Entente," *Orbis,* vol. 48, no. 1 (Winter 2004), pp. 89–104.

41. For the upgrading of Indo-Israeli relations, see Moshe Yager, "How Was Normalization Achieved in Indo-Israeli Relations?" *Nativ,* no. 90 (January 2003), pp. 1–11 (in Hebrew); Giora Bachar, "The Normalization in

Indian-Israel Relations," in Moshe Yager, Yoseph Govrin, and Ariyeh Oded, eds., *Ministry of Foreign Affairs: The First Fifty Years* (Jerusalem: Keter, 2002), pp. 543–549. Both authors were involved as Israeli diplomats in the upgrading of relations.

42. P. R. Kumaraswami, "India-Israel: Emerging Partnership," *Journal of Strategic Studies,* vol. 25, no. 4 (December 2002), p. 198.

43. Amy Waldman, "The Bond between India and Israel [Has] Grown," *New York Times* (September 9, 2003).

44. Speech by Indian ambassador in Tel Aviv, 2006, http://www.indembassy.co.il/amb_speech_telavivuniv_march8-final.htm.

45. Stephen P. Cohen and Sumit Ganguly, "India," in Robert Chase, Emily Hull, and Paul Kennedy, eds., *The Pivotal States. A New Framework for U.S. Policy in the Developing World* (New York: Norton, 1999), pp. 50–51. For a recent view, see "China: Through Indian Eyes," http://www.c3sindia.org/ind/87/china-through-indian-eyes/.

46. Paul Dibb, David D. Hale, and Peter Prince, "Asia's Insecurity," *Survival,* vol. 41, no. 3 (Autumn 1999), pp. 5–20; Wendell Minnick, "Surrounded by Turmoil," *Defense News* (February 5, 2007), pp. 11–12.

47. K. Shankar Bajpai, "Untangling India and Pakistan," *Foreign Affairs,* vol. 82, no. 3 (May–June 2003), p. 114.

48. For this dominant threat perception, which has been shared by all Israeli governments since Yitzhak Rabin (1992–1995), see Efraim Inbar, *Rabin and Israel's National Security* (Washington and Baltimore: Wilson Center Press and Johns Hopkins University Press, 1999), p. 138. See also Efraim Inbar, "The Need to Block Iran," *MERIA,* vol. 10, no. 1 (2006).

49. See Vivek Raghuvanshi, "Indian Army Chief Promotes $10B Wish List," *Defense News* (January 22, 2007), p. 14, and his "India Plans 7% Increase in Defense Budget," *Defense News* (March 5, 2007), p. 14.

50. Rajat Pandit, "Israel Sneaks to No. 2 Spot as Arms Supplier," *Times of India* Online (February 9, 2007), timesofindia.indiatimes.com/articleshow/1581346.cms; Yaakov Katz,

"Israeli Defense Companies Sell $4.4 Billion of Goods in 2006," *Jerusalem Post* (February 21, 2007). For several years, the United States was the leading defense market, spending around $1 billion a year.

51. Rajya Sabha, "Arms Purchases from Israel Touch $5 Billion," *Times of India* (May 16, 2007).

52. *Ha'aretz* (June 2, 2002).

53. Amrith K. Mago, "India-Israel Military Ties Continue to Grow," Jewish Institute for National Security Affairs Online (April 8, 2003), www.Jinsa.org/articles.html/function/view/categoryid/1948/doc.

54. *Defense News* (February 24, 2003). South Africa's Denel, too, had offered a variety of UAVs to India, but India has been content to stick with IAI due to the fixed price it offered. This has happened despite a delay of over a year in IAI's supply of six Searcher-II UAVs for the Indian army.

55. *Defense Industry Daily* (November 11, 2005).

56. *Globes* (September 26, 2002).

57. *Defense News* (February 24, 2003).

58. *Defense Industry Daily* (July 31, 2006).

59. *Defense News* (February 24, 2003).

60. Rajat Pandit, "Quietly, India Israel Ties Growing," *Times of India* Online (March 9, 2007), timesofindia.indiatimes.com/article show/1581346.cms.

61. Vivek Raghuvanshi, "India Orders a Dozen Domestic UAVs," *Defense News* (December 6, 2004), p. 22.

62. Ibid.

63. Vivek Raghuvanshi, "India Makes Progress on Big Artillery Plans," *Defense News* (April 30, 2007).

64. Vivek Raghuvanshi, "Indian Firms Expect Offset Boon as Spending Rises," *Defense News* (February 5, 2007).

65. "India Buys Israeli Missiles," *Defense News* (May 29, 2006).

66. Karen Walker, "U.S. Firms Seek Larger Slice of India's $100B in Projects," *Defense News* (January 1, 2007).

67. Katz, "Israeli Defense Companies."

68. Barbara Opall-Rome, "Israeli F-161 May Join Indian Fighter Fray," *Defense News* (June 12, 2006).

69. Vivek Raghuvanshi, "India to Invite Bids for Tactical Communications Systems," *Defense News* (March 12, 2007).

70. Vivek Raghuvanshi, "India Plans New Gear for Solders," *Defense News* (December 4, 2006).

71. Vivek Raghuvanshi, "India Invites Digital Command Center Bids," *Defense News* (April 16, 2007).

72. For Indian thinking on missile defense, see Ashley J. Tellis, "The Evolution of U.S.-Indian Ties: Missile Defense in an Emerging Strategic Relationship," *International Security*, vol. 30, no. 4 (Spring 2006), pp. 113–151.

73. Vivek Raghuvanshi, "Indian Firms Expect Offset Boon as Spending Rises, *Defense News* (February 5, 2007), p. 14.

74. In February 1992, the Indian defense minister Sharad Pawar had already admitted cooperation with Israel on counterterrorism; *Statesman* (New Delhi) (February 28, 1992), quoted in Kumaraswami, *Israel and India* , p. 11.

75. See the remarks of Major General Uzi Dayan, National Security Adviser, in Amit Navon, "The Indian Knot," *Maariv* Weekend Magazine (September 20, 2002), p. 22.

76. Cohen and Ganguly, "India," p. 40.

77. Olga Oliker, "Conflict in Central Asia and South Caucasus," in Olga Oliker and Thomas S. Szayna, eds., *Faultlines of Conflict in Central Asia and the South Caucaus: Implications for the U.S. Army* (Santa Monica, CA: RAND, 2003), pp. 225–226.

78. "India to Use Israeli Pipeline for Crude Imports," Press Trust of India, Baku, June 9, 2005, www.hindustantimes.com/news/181_1393414,0002.htm.

79. See "Israel sneaks to No. 2 spot as arms supplier," *Times of India* Online (June 17, 2002), timesofindia.indiatimes.com/articles how/1581346.cms.

80. See Jing-don Yuan, "The Dragon and the Elephant: Chinese-Indian Relations in the 21st Century," *Washington Quarterly,* vol. 30, no. 3 (Summer 2007), pp. 131–144.

81. Vivek Raghuvanshi, "China's ASAT Galvanizes Indian Efforts," *Defense News* (April 9, 2007).

82. See Yitzhak Shichor, "China's Upsurge: Implications for the Middle East," in Efraim Inbar, ed., *Israel's Strategic Agenda* (New York: Routledge, 2007), pp. 52–70. As a result of American pressure, Israel reduced its defense trade with China to nearly zero.

83. Barbara Opall-Rome, "Israel Wary of China's ASAT Test," *Defense News* (February 5, 2007).

84. See Larry Ramer, "Pro-Israel Activists Seeking Allies among Immigrants from India," *Forward* (October 11, 2002), and Alan Cooperman, "India, Israel Interests Team Up," *Washington Post* (July 19, 2003); "Canny Friends, Indian and Jewish Lobbies at Capitol Hill Are Discovering the Benefits of Working Together," *India Today* (April 19, 2004), http://Indiatoday.com/itoday/20040419/index.html.

85. The public meeting between the Pakistani foreign minister, Khurshid Kasuri, and his Israeli counterpart, Sylvan Shalom, on September 1, 2005, in Istanbul did not lead to any change in bilateral relations.

12

Israel and
the United States

Robert O. Freedman

IN THE MORE THAN SIXTY YEARS since the establishment of the State of Israel, the relationship between the United States and Israel has changed dramatically. From a country that was seen as a security liability by most of the Washington establishment in 1948, by 2007 Israel had developed into a major security ally of the United States. In addition, while in 1948 there was limited American public support for the creation of the state of Israel, by 2008 support for Israel had become widespread in the American public. Finally, despite some ups and downs over the years, the personal relationships between American presidents and Israeli prime ministers have grown very close, as epitomized by US President Bill Clinton's declaration "Shalom, Haver" ("Good-bye, good friend") at the burial of assassinated Israeli prime minister Yitzhak Rabin in November 1995. This chapter, after briefly reviewing the course of US-Israeli relations from 1948 to 1995, takes a close look at US-Israeli relations from 1995 to 2007 and, in the process, compares the policies of the Clinton and George W. Bush administrations, which, during their tenures in office, dealt with six Israeli prime ministers (Rabin, Shimon Peres, Benjamin Netanyahu, Ehud Barak, Ariel Sharon, and Ehud Olmert).

From 1948 to 1995: The Security Factor

Security issues have become an increasingly important element of the Israeli-American relationship since 1948, although they did not become significant until 1970. At the time of Israel's birth in 1948, the Jewish state was seen as a security liability. In 1948, President Harry Truman (1945–1953), while recognizing Israel de facto against the advice of his secretaries of state and defense, nonetheless imposed an arms embargo on Israel—and the Arab world—during Israel's 1948–1949 War of Independence, even though Britain was arming Jordan, Egypt, and Iraq, which were among Israel's adversaries in the war, thus making the US embargo against Israel very much a one-sided policy. US secretary of state George Marshall and secretary of defense James Forrestal, with the cold war in full swing, saw Israel as a major political and security liability for the United States. Marshall feared driving the Arabs into the arms of the Soviet Union, while Forrestal feared that US troops—which he had too few of—would be needed to rescue the Jews of Palestine, whom he felt would most likely be defeated by the invading Arab armies if a Jewish state were proclaimed. In addition, heavily influenced by the anti-Israeli position of the British, both Marshall and Forrestal saw Israel, if it were to survive the Arab invasion, as a likely Soviet client state in the Middle East.[1] There was also resistance in both the US State and Defense Departments to de jure recognition of Israel, and to a loan from the Export-Import Bank, although, following the Israeli elections of January 1949, both were granted by Truman. Nonetheless, Truman also pressured Israel to allow the return of hundreds of thousands of Palestinian refugees from Israel's 1948–1949 War of Independence, which Israel won thanks in part to arms from Czechoslovakia (agreed to by Moscow, which also gave Israel diplomatic support during the war), central lines of communication, divisions among the invading Arab armies, and better soldiers and officers. The Truman administration also called on Israel to cede some of the land it had captured during the war. Israel refused both US demands.

Israeli security ties with the United States were to remain cool during most of the 1950s under the Eisenhower administration (1953–1961), and personal ties between the American president and Israeli prime minister David Ben-Gurion were very chilly as well. Thus, in the so-called Alpha Plan, the US secretary of state, John Foster Dulles, sought, albeit unsuccessfully, to pressure Israel to give up some of the territory in its south (in the Negev region) to create a land bridge between Egypt and Jordan and strongly criticized Israel for its retaliatory strikes against Egypt and Jordan, which harbored terrorists who were attacking Israel. In addition, the main security structure for the Middle East (the Baghdad Pact), which the United States and Britain constructed in the mid-1950s, had no place for Israel. Perhaps most serious of all, the Eisenhower administration refused to sell arms to Israel even after the major Soviet-Egyptian arms deal of 1955, which provided Israel's primary Arab enemy with heavy bombers and tanks that were a strategic threat to Israel. This refusal, in part, prompted Israel to join with Britain and France in the tripartite attack on Egypt in 1956 (the Suez War), for which the United States severely condemned all three countries. Eisenhower, who as the US military hero of World War II was relatively immune to domestic pressure on foreign policy issues, also compelled Israeli prime minister David Ben-Gurion to return to Egypt both the Sinai Desert and the Gaza Strip, which had been captured during the 1956 war, although the US president did support the emplacement of UN soldiers along the Egyptian-Israeli border to serve as a buffer between the two countries, and at the Straits of Tiran to protect Israeli shipping going through the straits. Following the Iraqi revolution of 1958, however, relations between the United States and Israel began to improve, as Israel's value as a stable and democratic state in an increasingly volatile Middle East began to be more greatly appreciated in Washington.[2]

It was not until the presidency of John F. Kennedy (1961–1963), however, that the United States began to sell arms to Israel, in the form of Hawk antiaircraft missiles to counter the long-range bombers that the Soviet Union had supplied to Egypt. Nonetheless, there were frictions between the United States and Israel during the Kennedy presidency, primarily over Israel's nuclear program.[3] The presidency of Lyndon Johnson (1963–1969) had a mixed record on meeting Israel's security needs. Because the United States was badly bogged down in Vietnam, it did not respond favorably to Israeli requests for help in the period immediately before 1967's Six Day War, when Egypt moved troops to Israel's border, joined in an anti-Israeli alliance with Syria and Jordan, and closed the Straits of Tiran to Israeli shipping. The most the United States would do was to suggest a Straits of Tiran Users Association, an idea that generated little diplomatic support. Similarly, when the war broke out, the US proclaimed its neutrality as a nonbelligerent, although it did serve as a buffer to protect Israel against possible Soviet action. Nonetheless, there was some US-Israeli friction during the war when Israeli jets mistakenly attacked the USS *Liberty,* an American intelligence ship that was sailing near the coast of the Sinai. Following the war, however, there was a sharp improvement in US-Israeli relations, as Israel, which had defeated Moscow's two major Arab clients, Egypt and Syria (as well as pro-US Jordan), demonstrated its security value to the United States. It was under President Lyndon Johnson that the United States began to supply Israel with sophisticated fighter-bombers. In addition, unlike the Eisenhower administration following the Suez War of 1956, the Johnson administration did not demand that Israel withdraw before a peace agreement with its Arab neighbors was signed. Indeed, it sponsored, along with Britain and the Soviet Union, UN Security Council Resolution 242, which, in the US (and British) view, did not require Israel to give back all the land it had conquered in 1967, even for a peace treaty.[4]

foundered. To make matters worse, during this period, the United States found itself confronted with increasing conflict between Israel and the Palestinians and, in the summer of 2006, a war between Israel and Hizbollah.

From the Inauguration to 9/11

When the George W. Bush administration took office in 2001, it had a number of reasons not to continue Clinton's activist policy toward the Arab-Israeli conflict. First, Bush had witnessed the major effort Clinton had made and the relatively meager results he had achieved. Bush, who sought to clearly distinguish himself from Clinton, chose not to follow Clinton's path. Second, even if he had wanted to, Bush was unwilling to risk his very limited political capital (he had won a very narrow—and questionable—victory in a hotly disputed election) and he wanted to save his political capital for more promising policy initiatives, such as his tax cuts and ABM (antiballistic missile) programs. As a result, the administration distanced itself from the Arab-Israeli conflict, a distancing shown most clearly when Dennis Ross, who had been the special US mediator for the Arab-Israeli conflict, resigned in January 2001 and was not replaced.

Distancing itself from the Arab-Israeli conflict, however, did not mean that the administration had distanced itself from Israel. On the contrary—and much to the discomfiture of Arafat and other Arab leaders—Bush quickly developed a close and warm relationship with Israeli prime minister Ariel Sharon, who was invited to visit the White House in mid-March 2001.

On the eve of the visit, the new American secretary of state, Colin Powell, gave a major speech supportive of Israel to the pro-Israel AIPAC lobbying organization. In the speech he echoed Israel's position that the starting point for peace talks had to be the end of violence. In a clear slap at Arafat, Powell publicly stated that "leaders have the responsibility to denounce violence, strip it of legitimacy [and] stop it." Powell also asserted the Bush administration's position that the United States would assist in but not impose a peace agreement: "The US stands ready to assist, not insist. Peace arrived at voluntarily by the partners themselves is likely to prove more robust . . . than a peace widely viewed as developed by others, or worse yet, imposed."[32]

In a meeting several days later, Bush again reassured Sharon that the United States would facilitate, not force, the peace process. Bush also sought to enlist Sharon in his campaign to develop a national missile defense system, something the Israeli leader, whose country was a prime target of such "rogue" states as Iran and Iraq, was only too happy to agree to. Sharon, for his part, pressed Bush not to invite Arafat to the White House unless Arafat publicly called for an end to the violence, a request endorsed by nearly 300 members of

It was during the presidency of Richard Nixon (1969–1974) that security cooperation between the United States and Israel reached a new high, although initially there were strains in the US-Israeli relationship, as Nixon administration officials talked about a more "evenhanded" role for the United States in the Arab-Israeli conflict, and the new US secretary of state, William Rogers, put forth a plan, which ultimately proved a nonstarter, that would have minimized Israeli territorial gains from the 1967 War. Rogers was more successful in the summer of 1970, when he secured a cease-fire between Israel and Soviet-backed Egypt in their fighting along the Suez Canal, which had threatened to escalate after Israeli pilots shot down five Egyptian planes that were piloted by Soviet airmen. Rogers was, however, severely criticized by Israel for not preventing Egypt from exploiting the cease-fire to complete its deployment of surface-to-air missiles along the Suez Canal, which had the potential of providing antiaircraft cover for an Egyptian attack into the Sinai Desert, as indeed was to happen in 1973.

As the cold war between the United States and the Soviet Union in the Middle East intensified in 1970, Israel's assistance to the United States in protecting Washington's client, Jordan, against Moscow's client, Syria, during the Palestinian uprising against Jordan's King Hussein in September 1970 set the stage for significant security cooperation between the United States and Israel, including the provision of major arms systems to Israel. During the 1973 Yom Kippur War, large shipments of US arms helped Israel repulse the attacks of Syria and Egypt and then take the offensive against both Arab countries.

Following the war, Henry Kissinger, who had become secretary of state just before the conflict (the first American Jew to hold that position), embarked on a program of "shuttle diplomacy" between Israel and Egypt, which moved the two countries from conflict toward peace (a similar effort with Syria was less successful). While there was some friction between the United States and Israel over Kissinger's diplomacy, especially following the resignation of Nixon and the onset of the Ford administration (1974–1977)—at one point Ford and Kissinger threatened an "agonizing reappraisal" of US policy toward Israel as a means of pressuring Israeli prime minister Yitzhak Rabin to make more concessions—the Egyptian-Israeli peace process continued. Indeed, the signing of the Sinai II agreement between Israel and Egypt in August 1975 demonstrated a stronger US commitment to the peace process, as, under the agreement, American troops were to occupy the Gidi and Mitla passes in the Sinai Desert between the Egyptian and Israeli armies. The stationing of US forces, equipped with sophisticated radar systems, in the two mountain passes served as a confidence-building measure for both Egypt and Israel, as the US now had the ability to warn either side if the other was maneuvering its forces for an attack. In addition, as part of the Sinai II agreement, the United States promised Israel it would not deal with the Palestine Liberation Organization (PLO) until it renounced terrorism, recognized Israel, and accepted UN Security Council Resolution 242.

The presidency of Jimmy Carter (1977–1981) marked a new watershed in US-Israeli relations. The somewhat naive American president initially sought to settle the Arab-Israeli conflict through a major international conference at Geneva, with the help of the Soviet Union (whose Middle East position had been severely weakened by Kissinger), and with the presence of "representatives of the Palestinian people." Vehement opposition by Egyptian president Anwar Sadat, who had become strongly anti-Soviet, and by Israel, which feared that PLO members would be included among the Palestinian representatives, doomed the conference before it could be convened. Indeed, Sadat, following this episode, chose to travel to Israel, where he began to negotiate a peace treaty with Israeli prime minister Menahem Begin. While this development caught US diplomats by surprise, and Carter was somewhat discomfited, US help was needed when Israeli-Egyptian negotiations bogged down. In September 1978 Carter convened a three-way summit with Sadat and Begin at the residential retreat: Camp David, Maryland. After thirteen days of often difficult negotiations and considerable friction between Carter and Begin, the principles of a peace agreement were worked out, setting the stage for the Egyptian-Israeli peace treaty of March 1979. As part of the peace agreement, the United States pledged to give Israel $3 billion and Egypt $2.2 billion, which became an annual allocation, and the United States pledged to maintain its position in the Sinai passes as part of what was to become a multinational force. Nonetheless, Carter remained highly critical of Begin's settlement-building policy in the Israeli-occupied Gaza Strip and West Bank, although the Iranian revolution in 1978 and the subsequent hostage crisis diverted his attention from the Arab-Israeli conflict in the last two years of his administration.

Security relations between the United States and Israel deepened further during the presidency of Ronald Reagan (1981–1989), although not without some difficulties, as in the case of the American sale of AWACS (the airborne warning and control system) to Saudi Arabia, which Israel strongly opposed, and during the Israeli invasion and occupation of Lebanon in 1982. Soon after taking office, Reagan sought, albeit unsuccessfully, to create an alignment of Israel and Arab states such as Egypt, Jordan, and Saudi Arabia in response to the Soviet occupation of Afghanistan. Indeed, Reagan embraced Israel as a strategic partner in his struggle with the Soviet Union and supported a number of Israeli goals vis-à-vis the USSR, including the exodus of Soviet Jews to Israel and the neutralization of the USSR as the primary backer of the Arabs in the Arab-Israeli conflict. These goals were to be fulfilled in the last two years of the Reagan administration after Mikhail Gorbachev came to power in Moscow.[5]

In addition, while Washington and Jerusalem were sometimes at odds during Israel's invasion of Lebanon, it appears likely that the United States gave Israel a yellow light, if not a green light, to mount the invasion to destroy the state-within-a-state that the PLO, an ally of the Soviet Union, had established in southern Lebanon. Israel and the United States did clash, however, over "the Reagan Plan" for solving the Arab-Israeli conflict, which was issued in the aftermath of Israel's Lebanese invasion.[6] The plan included a freeze on Israeli settlement building, something Begin strongly opposed. Later in the Reagan administration, Israel and the United States cooperated in the clandestine so-called Iran-Contra affair, in which Israel served as a conduit of arms to Iran to help it in its war with Iraq, in return for the freeing of US hostages in Lebanon, the proceeds of the arms sales being used to arm the Reagan-backed Contras in Nicaragua. In addition, in November 1988, responding primarily to American pressure, PLO leader Yasser Arafat agreed to accept UN Security Council Resolution 242, to renounce terrorism, and to recognize Israel.

US-Israeli relations chilled somewhat during the presidency of George H.W. Bush (1989–1993). Bush's secretary of state, James Baker, and Israeli prime minister Yitzhak Shamir clashed over Israel's building of settlements in the West Bank, and over who should be invited to the post–Gulf War US-sponsored Madrid conference in October 1991, whose purpose was to promote the Arab-Israeli peace process. President Bush himself clashed with Shamir by withholding loan guarantees needed by Israel to resettle the hundreds of thousands of Soviet Jews, many with higher education and scientific and technological expertise, who were pouring into Israel in the late 1980s and early 1990s. Bush withheld these guarantees until the Israeli government stopped building the West Bank settlements. Relations improved, however, when Yitzhak Rabin became Israeli prime minister in July 1992 and announced that Israel would stop building new settlements in the West Bank and would construct housing only in existing settlements. Following the Rabin announcement, Bush authorized the loan guarantees.[7]

Despite the often poor personal chemistry between Shamir and Bush, the Israeli prime minister did agree to a US request to refrain from retaliating against Iraqi missile attacks during the Gulf War, so as to enable the United States to maintain its Arab coalition fighting Iraq. As a gesture of support for Israel, the United States placed Patriot missiles in Israel, manned by US troops, to engage the Iraqi Scud missiles fired against Israel during the war. While the Patriot missiles proved to be ineffective, the symbolism of the US action—deploying its troops to help protect Israel—was the key factor.

In the presidency of Bill Clinton (1992—2001), during its first term US-Israeli relations improved markedly, and Clinton developed a particularly close relationship with Israeli prime minister Yitzhak Rabin. In addition to continuing the $3 billion in annual aid to Israel, Clinton committed the United States to maintaining Israel's qualitative technological edge over the Arab world and strongly endorsed the OSLO I (1993) and OSLO II (1995) partial peace agreements between Israel and the Palestinians, as well as the Israeli-Jordanian peace treaty of 1994. Following the assassination of Rabin, however, and the election loss of his successor, Shimon Peres, to Benjamin Netanyahu in May 1996, US-Israeli relations chilled (to be discussed below).

Values and Political Dynamics
Shared by Israel and the United States

As the United States became increasingly involved in the Middle East after 1945, the differences in values between Israel, a Western-style democracy, and the monarchies, military dictatorships, and Islamist regimes in the Middle East became more and more clear to the American public. Indeed, by the end of 2007, Israel had the support of a clear majority of Americans in its conflict with its Arab neighbors. The supporters of Israel in the United States fall into five different groups, whose importance has fluctuated over time. The first group is the American Jewish community. Split over the creation of the state of Israel in 1948 into Zionists (the majority), non-Zionists (led by the American Jewish Committee), and anti-Zionists (led by the American Council for Judaism), almost all American Jews rallied behind Israel in 1967 as it faced the threat of another Holocaust (at least in the verbiage of Arab leaders) in the three weeks before the 1967 War.[8]

Following that war, the vast majority of American Jews have supported Israel, although on both the Left and the Right—especially the religious Right—of the American Jewish spectrum there have been differences with Israel over its policies toward lands captured in the 1967 War. American Jews have sought to influence US policy toward Israel through the American-Israel Public Affairs Committee (AIPAC), which is particularly influential in Congress, and the Conference of Presidents of Major Jewish Organizations.

The second important element of those supporting Israel has been American labor. In the years immediately after Israel gained its independence in 1948, American labor was a very important support group for Israel. American labor, in the form of the AFL-CIO, was very strong in the United States during the 1950s and 1960s, the same period during which the Israeli Labor Party dominated Israeli politics, and there were clear ideological ties between the two. However, since the 1970s the influence of this pro-Israeli group has declined. First, organized labor has lost a great deal of its influence in the

United States. Second, since the late 1970s, the Israeli Labor Party has no longer dominated the Israeli political scene.

A growing group that supports Israel are American Evangelical Protestants, estimated to number between forty and seventy million Americans. For the most part, they are fervent supporters of Israel—in contrast to mainline Protestant churches—and they have become a bedrock element in the Republican Party. As will be shown, Evangelical Protestants played a major role in a Capitol Hill rally for Israel on April 15, 2002, a rally organized to support Israel in its war on Palestinian terrorism, and they have been both financial supporters and political backers of Israel.

The fourth group of Israel's supporters, which was particularly important in the period from the 1967 War until the collapse of the Soviet Union in 1991, are the leaders of the US armed forces. They were pleased when US-made aircraft in Israeli hands scored massive victories against Soviet aircraft in Arab hands, and the United States also benefited when Israel shared with it captured Soviet equipment. In addition, the American military was able to improve its equipment after it was battle-tested by Israel. The recent decision by Russia to rearm Syria, as well as its ongoing armament of Iran—likely enemies of Israel in future wars—may again make this group important. In addition, despite lingering memories of the USS *Liberty* incident, the US Navy benefits from quasi-homeport status in Haifa, an Israeli Mediterranean port. The United States has also prepositioned military equipment in Israel, and the two countries regularly share intelligence.

The fifth, and largest, element in the Israel lobby comprises those Americans—liberals and conservatives, Democrats, Republicans and Independents, and Christians and Jews—who support Israel because they see it as sharing common values with the United States, most important the value of democracy. In a region that is beset by military dictatorships, Islamic theocracies, and autocratic monarchies, these Americans see the value of Israel to the United States as a genuine democracy, the basic reason Israel enjoys the popularity it does in the United States over its Arab adversaries.

US-Israeli Relations under Bill Clinton

When Bill Clinton took office as US president in January 1993, the Madrid peace process, begun by his predecessor, George H.W. Bush, had already begun to stagnate, primarily over the Palestinian issue, although there had been some progress on multilateral issues, especially economic cooperation. The peace process, however, was to receive a major boost when Israeli prime minister Rabin supported "back channel" talks with the PLO, and the talks were crowned with success in September 1993 when the OSLO I agreement, called the Declaration of Principles, was signed on the White House lawn. Here it is important to note that the 1993 Oslo agreement was directly negotiated between the Israelis and the Palestinians, with the United States serving primarily as a cheerleader once the agreement had been signed. Following the Oslo agreement, the Arab-Israeli peace process continued to make progress as Jordan and Israel signed a peace treaty in October 1994, with President Clinton again serving as a cheerleader when the treaty was signed on the Jordanian-Israeli border. There was also limited progress on the Syrian-Israeli front as the two countries negotiated in the United States under US auspices.[9]

The Israeli-Palestinian peace process made further progress, and the Oslo II agreement was signed in September 1995, despite a rising crescendo of terrorist attacks by Palestinian groups such as Hamas and Islamic Jihad, seeking to sabotage the peace process, and the murder in February 1994 of Muslims praying at the Tomb of the Patriarchs in Hebron by an Israeli terrorist. Here again, the United States served as a cheerleader in support of the agreement, rather than playing a major role in its negotiation.[10]

The peace process, however, was soon to receive a series of blows. First, Rabin was assassinated in early November 1995 by a Jewish religious fanatic opposed to his territorial concessions to the Palestinians. Rabin's successor, Shimon Peres, quickly moved to implement the Oslo II agreement, which enabled the Palestinians to gain control of all the major Palestinian-populated cities in the West Bank except Hebron, and this control, in turn, facilitated Palestinian elections for the parliament and executive of the Palestinian Authority (PA); Arafat was elected as the PA's executive. Then, however, another round of Palestinian terrorist attacks struck a nearly mortal blow to the peace process. After Peres had arranged for Israeli elections to be held in May 1996, four Hamas and Islamic Jihad terrorist attacks, killing scores of civilians in Jerusalem and Tel Aviv, undermined Israeli public support for the peace process and enabled Likud hard-liner Benjamin Netanyahu to be elected Israel's prime minister in the elections, albeit by a narrow margin—despite Clinton's efforts to support Peres by convening an international antiterrorism conference on March 13, 1996. Compounding the problem was the support given by Syria's official radio station to the terrorist attacks[11] and Syria's boycott of the antiterrorism conference—developments that effectively ended the bilateral Syrian-Israeli talks.

The Netanyahu Period

Following the 1996 Israeli elections, the personal conflict between Netanyahu and Arafat all but froze the peace process, which, according to the Oslo I agreement, was to begin discussion of the final-status issues of boundaries,

Jewish settlements, security, refugees, and Jerusalem by May 1996. Netanyahu exacerbated the problem later, in September 1996, by secretly opening the ancient Hasmonean tunnel, which was close to, but not attached to, the Temple Mount/Haram, the site of the two Jewish Temples, and the place where the Dome of the Rock and the al-Aqsa Mosque currently are located, and therefore holy to both Jews and Muslims. This act sparked severe rioting by the Palestinians, leading to seventy deaths (fifty-five Palestinians and fifteen Israelis). It took the personal intervention of Bill Clinton, with the help of Jordan's King Hussein, to bring an end to the rioting. Perhaps more important, the deep suspicion that had developed between Netanyahu and Arafat forced the United States to take, for the first time, direct control of the Israeli-Palestinian peace process; the goal was to secure an agreement over the divided city of Hebron, where the massacre of Jews by Arabs in 1929 and of Arabs by a Jew in 1994 had embittered relations. Dennis Ross, the chief American negotiator, worked intensively between October 1996 and January 1997 to secure an agreement, which split the city of Hebron between Israelis (20 percent) and Palestinians (80 percent) and called for three additional Israeli withdrawals from the West Bank, although no stipulation on the size of the withdrawals was agreed to.[12] However, following the Hebron agreement the Palestinian-Israeli peace process again stagnated. In part this stagnation was due to Netanyahu's policy of continuing to build Jewish settlements in the West Bank and also his authorization of the construction of a Jewish housing development on a hill in disputed East Jerusalem called Har Homa. A second cause of the stagnation in the peace talks was yet another outburst of Palestinian terrorism, beginning with a bomb in a Tel Aviv café in March 1997 that killed three Israelis and additional bombs in Jerusalem on July 30 and September 4 that killed twenty-one Israelis and wounded hundreds more. Netanyahu reacted to the bombings by imposing a border closure that prevented Palestinians living in the West Bank and Gaza from working in Israel (a tactic that had also periodically been used by Rabin), by withholding tax payments collected from Palestinians working in Israel and owed to the Palestinian Authority (a tactic also to be used by Ehud Barak, Netanyahu's successor, following the outbreak of the al-Aqsa Intifada in September 2000), and by threatening to send Israeli forces into Palestinian areas to root out the terrorists (a tactic to be employed by Barak's successor, Ariel Sharon).

In September 1997, after having stepped back somewhat from the peace effort because of its concentration on the expansion of NATO (the North Atlantic Treaty Organization), the United States again intervened, this time with the peace process on the verge of total collapse after the two Hamas bombings. The new US secretary of state, Madeleine Albright, who had been sworn in on January 23, 1997, but had not yet made an official visit to the Middle

East, came to Israel in an effort to jump-start the stalled peace process. She appealed to Arafat to take unilateral action to root out the terrorist infrastructure and called on Netanyahu for a time-out in settlement construction in the occupied territories, a plea Netanyahu rejected.[13] The peace process continued to stagnate until November, when the Israeli cabinet voted, in principle, in favor of another troop withdrawal but specified neither its extent nor its timing. Meanwhile, Clinton had grown exasperated by what his administration perceived as Netanyahu's stalling, and he publicly snubbed the Israeli prime minister during Netanyahu's November 1997 visit to the United States to talk to Jewish organizations. Netanyahu's ties to the Republicans in Congress and to their allies on the religious right of the American political spectrum (such as Jerry Falwell, whose Liberty University students regularly make pilgrimages to Israel)[14] helped insulate the Israeli leader from US pressure, an insulation that would continue into 1998 as a weakened Clinton got bogged down in the Monica Lewinsky scandal.

Despite his growing weakness, Clinton, acting through Secretary of State Albright, again sought in May 1998 to salvage the peace process, whose apparent demise was badly damaging the US position in the Middle East. Arab friends of the United States, as well as its Arab enemies, increased their complaints about a US double standard of pressuring Iraq while not pressuring Israel. In an effort to reverse this situation, Albright, following meetings with Netanyahu and Arafat in London, issued an ultimatum to Israel to accept withdrawal from 13 percent of its occupied territory in the West Bank. This ultimatum, however, failed due to the support Netanyahu received from Republicans in the US Congress, the pro-Israeli lobby in the United States led by AIPAC, and the Christian Religious Right.[15] Interestingly enough, American Jewry was badly split over Netanyahu's policy. Reform and Conservative Jews, already angry at Netanyahu for his favoritism to Israel's Orthodox Jews, called for Netanyahu to engage more energetically in the peace process, while Orthodox Jews (a clear minority in the American Jewish community) tended to support the Israeli prime minister.[16]

During the summer of 1998 the US effort took on a new focus: seeking to get Israeli approval by linking an Israeli withdrawal in stages to Palestinian action to combat terrorism and ensure Israeli security. Meanwhile, a new element had been added to the Israeli-Palestinian conflict: Yasser Arafat's threat to unilaterally declare a Palestinian state on the expiration of the Oslo I agreement on May 4, 1999. While Netanyahu issued the counterthreat of a unilateral Israeli response, which many interpreted as annexation of large parts of the West Bank if Arafat went ahead to declare a state, the Palestinian leader's threat may have been enough to get Netanyahu to agree to meet Arafat in late September 1998 in Washington when both leaders were in the United States to address the United Nations. At his first meeting with Arafat in a year, Netanyahu finally agreed, in the presence of Clinton, to the 13 percent withdrawal figure stipulated by the United States, but only on condition that 3 percent of the area would be a "nature reserve" on which the Palestinians would be prohibited from building, a condition to which Arafat agreed.[17]

However, besides the security questions involved in a Palestinian-Israeli agreement, there were real concerns among both Israelis and Palestinians about whether Clinton was strong enough to broker an agreement, given the Lewinsky affair. Despite the skepticism and the illness of King Hussein, Clinton was able to move the peace process several steps forward in mid-October as Netanyahu, Arafat, and King Hussein (who left the Mayo Clinic to play an important mediating role) gathered with US officials at the conference center of the Wye Plantation on Maryland's eastern shore. After eight days of intense bargaining, including the threat of a walkout by Netanyahu, a modest agreement was achieved between Netanyahu and Arafat. The agreement involved Israeli withdrawal in three stages from 13.1 percent of West Bank land (3 percent of which would become a nature preserve), the transferal of an additional 14.2 percent of land jointly controlled to sole Palestinian control, the release of 750 Palestinian prisoners, and an agreement to open a Palestinian airport in Gaza and two corridors of safe passage between the West Bank and Gaza. In return, Arafat agreed to change the PLO Charter to clearly eliminate the twenty-six articles calling for Israel's destruction, although how the change was to take place was a bit vague (reference was made to an assembly of Palestinian notables). Clinton's promise to be present during the Palestinian action, however, would serve to dramatize the event. Arafat also agreed to issue a decree prohibiting all forms of incitement to violence, to cut the number of Palestinian police to thirty thousand (from forty thousand), to arrest and confine thirty terrorism suspects wanted by Israel, and to collect illegal weapons and suppress terrorism, the US Central Intelligence Agency (CIA) being charged with attesting to the Palestinian Authority's making every effort to crack down on terrorism. The two sides also agreed to resume negotiations on final-status issues.[18]

Initially, the Wye agreement appeared to restore a modicum of confidence between Arafat and Netanyahu. Israeli troops, in the first stage of the agreement, withdrew from 2 percent of the occupied West Bank, and Israel released 250 Palestinian prisoners and allowed the opening of the Palestinian airport in Gaza. However, the momentum for peace was quickly reversed. Palestinians, complaining that the prisoners who had been released were only "car thieves," not the political detainees they wanted, carried on violent protest activities.[19] These protests led Netanyahu, under heavy pressure from right-wing elements in his governing coalition, to freeze additional troop withdrawals on December 2. The protests had been accompanied by a series of Palestinian terrorist attacks against Israelis, including an attempt to set off a bomb in the Mahane Yehudah market in Jerusalem and an attack on an Israeli soldier in Ramallah (actions that Arafat proved unwilling or unable to prevent). The Israeli prime minister conditioned the resumption of the withdrawals on Arafat's halting what Netanyahu called a campaign of incitement against Israel, forgoing his intention to declare a Palestinian state on May 4, 1999, and acceding to Israel's selection of the prisoners who were to be released.[20]

For its part, the Clinton administration, despite the ongoing impeachment process, was making major efforts to keep the peace process going. On November 29, 1998, speaking at a Palestinian donor conference he had convened in Washington, President Clinton pledged $400 million in additional aid to the Palestinians, on top of the $500 million he had pledged in 1993. All told, some $4 billion in aid was pledged to the Palestinians (the European Union had pledged 400 million euros),[21] an amount that would greatly help the beleaguered Palestinian economy, although questions were raised at the conference about corrupt Palestinian officials siphoning off previous aid for their own personal use.[22] The United States also sought to downplay the conditions Netanyahu had placed on further Israeli troop withdrawals under the Wye agreement, and State Department spokesman James P. Rubin stated on December 2, 1998, "The agreement should be implemented as signed. We do not believe it is appropriate to add new conditions to implementation of the agreement."[23]

The most important effort to restore momentum to the Israeli-Palestinian peace process was taken by Clinton himself when he journeyed to Gaza in mid-December to witness the Palestinians formally abrogating the clauses in the PLO Charter calling for Israel's destruction, an action the Netanyahu government had long demanded. Clinton's visit resulted in a warming of relations between the United States and the Palestinian Authority, which received increased international legitimacy as a result of the US president's visit—an outcome that Israeli critics of Netanyahu blamed on Netanyahu.[24]

This was the final blow to the Netanyahu government, which, suffering a series of defections and threatened defections, was soon on the verge of collapse. Under these circumstances Netanyahu moved to call for new elections before his government could fall on a no-confidence vote. With elections scheduled for May 17, 1999, the peace process was in effect frozen, this freeze leaving the United States somewhat nervously on the diplomatic sidelines, hoping that Arafat would not prematurely declare a Palestinian state and thus strengthen the chances of Netanyahu's reelection.

Fortunately for Clinton, Netanyahu was to lose the election to the new Labor Party leader, Ehud Barak, a highly decorated soldier and a disciple of Yitzhak

Rabin. Barak had run on a peace platform and won the vote 56 percent to 44 percent, a far larger margin than that by which Netanyahu had defeated Peres (50.5 percent to 49.5 percent in 1997). Following his defeat Netanyahu withdrew both from the Knesset and from the leadership of the Likud Party, to be replaced by Ariel Sharon. Yet, while Barak began his period as prime minister amid great hope, less than two years later he ended it in political disgrace, defeated in the election for prime minister by Ariel Sharon by a two-to-one margin. The peace process had been all but destroyed by the al-Aqsa Intifada, which had erupted in September 2000 while Barak was prime minister.

Clinton and Barak

When Barak took office, he switched the direction of Israel's peace policy from the Palestinian track to the Syrian track and received positive signals from Syria. Barak must also have thought that peace with Syria, which basically involved only territorial issues, could be more easily achieved than peace with the Palestinians, where negotiations had yet to deal with the highly sensitive issues of the sovereignty of Jerusalem and the plight of Palestinian refugees. Needless to say, the Palestinian leadership took a dim view of the shift in priorities, as well as of Barak's decision to allow the continued expansion of Jewish settlements in the West Bank, which Barak permitted to keep the National Religious Party, whose constituency included the West Bank settlers, in his coalition. The expansion took place primarily in areas near Jerusalem, in cities like Maaleh Adumim, which Barak hoped to annex. For his part, Clinton went along with Barak's peace process priority and invested a great deal of his personal prestige—including at a meeting with Syria's president, Hafiz al-Asad, in Geneva in March 2000—to try to obtain a breakthrough in negotiations.[25] Despite Clinton's best efforts, however, an agreement with Syria was not achieved, in part because of a dispute over Syria's claim to territory on the northeast shore of the Sea of Galilee, and in part because of Asad's rapidly deteriorating health (he died a few months after meeting Clinton in Geneva).

Barak then sought to politically outflank the Syrians by arranging a unilateral pullout from southern Lebanon in May 2000. Asad had been manipulating Hizbollah attacks against Israeli forces in southern Lebanon, as well as occasional rocket attacks into Israel proper, as a means of pressuring Israel to be more flexible in its negotiations with Syria. Indeed, just such an escalation of fighting had occurred following the collapse of the Syrian-Israeli talks in February 1996. By unilaterally withdrawing from southern Lebanon without a peace treaty, Barak may have hoped to avoid a repetition of these events, and to gain support from the international community, including the United

States, which had long pressed for such a pullback. Unfortunately for Barak, regardless of the support he received from the international community, he set a precedent for withdrawing under fire—without an agreement—from territory occupied by Israeli troops. This lesson was not lost on a number of Palestinians, who felt that if Israel could be made to withdraw from Lebanon under fire, it could also be made to pull out of at least the West Bank and Gaza under similar pressure.[26]

Following the failure of the Syrian talks, Barak turned back to the Palestinian track. After initial discussions between the two sides in May 2000, Barak pushed for a summit in July in the United States. He hoped that, at one stroke, all the remaining final-status issues, including those that had not yet been seriously discussed (such as the status of Jerusalem and the refugee problem), could be settled and a peace agreement achieved. Clinton went along with Barak's plan and devoted two weeks of scarce presidential time to the summit, which became known as the Camp David II Summit. There have been many different explanations for the failure of Camp David II, and even members of the same delegation disagree on the causes of the failure. Those sympathetic to Arafat blame Barak's negotiating style, his take-it-or-leave-it attitude, and his unwillingness to meet what they felt were even the minimal needs of the Palestinians. Those sympathetic to Barak note that he offered unheard-of Israeli concessions, including giving up all of Gaza and 92 percent of the West Bank and dividing Jerusalem. These offers threatened the viability of Barak's coalition government, especially on the issue of Jerusalem, which Israel thus far had contended was to remain united under Israeli control. Barak's sympathizers also felt that Arafat—by rejecting the Israeli concessions, by demanding the return of the more than three million Palestinian refugees to Israel proper (which would have destroyed Israel as a Jewish state), by denying the existence of Jewish temples on Temple Mount/Haram, and by making no counteroffers—had demonstrated that he was not a serious partner for peace.[27] Following the failed summit, Clinton took Barak's side in the debate over who was responsible for the failure, thereby alienating Arafat. Arafat also fared badly in the court of Western opinion, including in western Europe, where the Palestinian leader was blamed for the failure to reach an agreement. In addition to shouldering international disapproval for this failure, Arafat was criticized by Palestinians for his heavy-handed authoritarian ways and the corrupt practices within the Palestinian Authority. Arafat counterattacked, claiming he had defended the interests of the world's Muslims at Camp David by not making concessions on the Temple Mount/Haram. He also stepped up the military training given to Palestinian youth in special military camps, perhaps assuming that in the aftermath of the failure to reach a peace agreement, the only alternative was renewed conflict.

And conflict did come in late September 2000, following the visit of the new Likud leader, Ariel Sharon, accompanied by hundreds of Israeli police, to the Temple Mount/Haram, a move linked to internal Israeli politics, as Netanyahu had begun to challenge Sharon's leadership of the Likud Party. Palestinian rioting broke out, for which the Israeli police were ill prepared. As Palestinian casualties rose, the Intifada ("uprising") spread, and soon both the West Bank and Gaza had erupted. The causes of the Intifada (often referred to as the Second Intifada or the al-Aqsa Intifada, named for the mosque at the site visited by Sharon) are as much in dispute as the causes of the failure of Camp David II, as Palestinians and Israelis have very different narratives on the issue. For the Palestinians the uprising was the result of rising frustration over continued Israeli settlement expansion and the failure of the Oslo process to give them what they demanded; Sharon's visit to the Temple Mount/Haram had simply been the straw that broke the camel's back. For Israelis, the Intifada was an attempt by Arafat to get by force what he could not get by negotiation, an effort to win back international public opinion by again becoming the Palestinian David to Israel's Goliath, as Palestinian casualties rose more quickly than Israeli casualties. Many Israelis also believe that Arafat was applying the lesson learned in Lebanon, forcing Israel to withdraw by using not only stones, as in the First Intifada (1987), but also gunfire and mortar attacks: The Palestinians turned against their onetime peace partners the weapons the Israelis had given them under the Oslo agreement.[28] Many Israelis also suspected that Arafat, whether he planned the Intifada or not, was exploiting it to divert attention from Palestinian criticism of his authoritarian and corrupt practices.

Whatever the cause of the Intifada, President Clinton sought to quell it, much as he had after the eruption of violence in 1996 following Netanyahu's opening of the Hasmonean tunnel. Consequently, he convened a summit with both Arafat and Barak at Sharm al-Shaykh on October 16, 2000, and proposed an investigatory commission to analyze the causes of the conflict. The commission was headed by former US senator George Mitchell, who had been Clinton's special envoy to the conflict between Protestants and Catholics in Northern Ireland, and who was the father of the "Good Friday" agreement.

Unfortunately for Clinton, despite Arafat's pledge at Sharm al-Shaykh to stop the violence,[29] the task proved either beyond his will or beyond his ability to achieve. Not only did the Intifada continue, but the violence escalated. Clinton tried again in December, preparing, with the help of Dennis Ross and his colleagues, an American plan called the Clinton Parameters to settle all the final-status issues, including the most heavily disputed issues: Jerusalem's sovereignty and the so-called right of return of Palestinian refugees. Essentially, Clinton proposed some major trade-offs: the withdrawal of Israel from 97 percent of the West Bank; the compensation of Palestinians with Israeli territory near Gaza; the establishment of East Jerusalem as the capital of the new Palestinian state; and the partitioning of the Temple Mount/Haram area. The Temple Mount/Haram was to go to the Palestinians, the Jewish quarter of the Old City and the Western Wall would go to Israel, and a passage to both would be established through the Armenian quarter. On the issue of the Palestinian right of return, Clinton's plan called for the vast majority of refugees to go to the new Palestinian state.[30]

Barak was willing to accept the plan even though he knew that with Israeli elections looming on February 7 (which he would lose badly to Ariel Sharon), he would run into problems with the Israeli electorate. For his part, Arafat added so many conditions to his acceptance of the Clinton plan that he, in fact, rejected it, once again confirming to most Israelis that the Palestinian leader was not really interested in peace.[31]

It is possible, of course, that Arafat turned down Clinton's plan because he was expecting a better deal from Clinton's successor, George W. Bush, whose father, President George H.W. Bush, had repeatedly clashed with the Israeli leadership. If this was indeed Arafat's thinking, he was to be in for a rude awakening.

George W. Bush and Israel

The policy of the Bush administration toward Israel and the Arab-Israeli conflict moved through five distinct stages. First, from the inauguration until 9/11, Bush was generally supportive of Israel while distancing his administration from the Arab-Israeli conflict. Second, from 9/11 to June 2002, the Bush administration actively sought to solve the Israeli-Palestinian conflict in order to build Muslim support for his war against the Taliban in Afghanistan and the coming war against Iraq. The third stage, from June 2002 to Arafat's death in November 2004, witnessed periodic attempts by the United States to facilitate an Israeli-Palestinian settlement; the Road Map of April 2003 was the best example. A policy was also developed that called for democratization of the Arab world as a means of preventing terrorism. The fourth period, from the death of Arafat in November 2004 to the Hamas election victory of January 2006, witnessed an attempt to politically boost Arafat's successor, Mahmoud Abbas, while also coordinating with the Palestinians Israel's plan for a unilateral withdrawal from Gaza and the northern West Bank. The final stage, from January 2006 to June 2007, was a period marked by increasing difficulties for the United States in Iraq, which drew the administration's attention away from the Arab-Israeli conflict. At the same time the United States encountered problems with its democratization program in the Arab world, which had

Congress (87 senators and 209 House members), who also called on Bush to close the Washington office of the PLO and to cut US aid to the PA if the violence did not cease.[33]

The one bit of American activism on the peace process during this period came following the publication of the Mitchell Report in mid-May. The report contained a series of recommendations for ending the rapidly escalating Israeli-Palestinian conflict, first and foremost "a 100 percent effort to stop the violence."[34] While Israel accepted the recommendation, with Sharon ordering a cease-fire, a series of Palestinian terrorist attacks that Arafat either could not or would not stop undermined the cease-fire. Visits by the new Assistant Secretary of State for Near Eastern Affairs, Nicholas Burns, CIA chief George Tenet,[35] and Powell himself failed to resuscitate the cease-fire. Indeed, the escalating violence was now punctuated by Palestinian suicide bombings against Israeli civilian targets such as pizza parlors and discotheques, attacks that were strongly denounced by the United States. It is quite possible that the Bush administration, having witnessed the failure of its one major activist effort to resuscitate the Israeli-Palestinian peace process, concluded that its original hands-off policy toward the conflict was the correct one, and until 9/11, it distanced itself from the conflict. All of this, of course, was to change after 9/11.

From 9/11 to June 2002

Immediately after the terrorist attacks on the World Trade Center and the Pentagon, the United States changed its hands-off policy toward the Israeli-Palestinian conflict and sought to build a coalition, including Muslim states, against Osama bin Laden and his al-Qaeda terrorist organization. In an effort to gain Arab support, the United States announced its support of a Palestinian state and exercised a considerable amount of pressure on Sharon to agree to a meeting between Israeli foreign minister Shimon Peres and Arafat to establish yet another cease-fire, even though Palestinian violence had not stopped as Sharon had demanded as the price for talks. Frustrated by this US policy, Sharon called it the equivalent of British and French policy at the 1938 Munich Conference, where Czechoslovakia had been sold out to the Nazis. His comments drew a retort from the White House press secretary, Ari Fleischer, who called them "unacceptable."[36]

This point, however, was to be the low point in the US-Israeli relationship. Following its rapid military victory in Afghanistan, the United States embarked on a twofold strategy. The first part, trying to reinvigorate the Israeli-Palestinian peace process, was warmly greeted by US European allies and by pro-US governments in the Arab world. The second part of the strategy, threatening to carry the war from Afghanistan to other supporters of terror, especially Iraq, met with far less support.

The US effort to invigorate the Israeli-Palestine peace process began with a speech by President Bush at the United Nations in November 2001, where he said, "We are working for the day when two states—Israel and Palestine—live peacefully together within secure and recognized boundaries." However, in a clear warning to Arafat to crack down on terrorists, he also added, "Peace will come when all have sworn off forever incitement, violence, and terror. There is no such thing as a good terrorist."[37] Bush also pointedly did not meet Arafat at the United Nations as National Security Adviser Condoleezza Rice noted, "You cannot help us with al-Qaeda, and hug Hizbollah or Hamas. And so the President makes that clear to Mr. Arafat."[38] The United States backed up Rice's words by adding Hamas, Islamic Jihad, and Hizbollah to the post–September 11 terrorist list.

The next step in the US peace effort came on November 19 with a major speech by Secretary of State Colin Powell on the US view of a solution to the Israeli-Palestinian conflict.[39] In his speech Powell strongly condemned Palestinian terrorism, noting that the al-Aqsa Intifada was now mired in "self-defeating violence." He also stated that although the United States believed that there should be a two-state solution to the conflict—with two states, Palestine and Israel, living side by side within secure and recognized borders—the Palestinians must make a 100 percent effort to stop terrorism, and that this effort required actions, not words: Terrorists must be arrested. Powell emphasized that "no wrong can ever justify the murder of the innocent," that terror and violence must stop now, and that the Palestinians must realize their goals by negotiations, not violence. He further asserted—possibly in response to Arafat's call for the return to Israel of more than three million Palestinian refugees, a development that would have upset Israel's demographic balance—that the Palestinians must accept the legitimacy of Israel as a Jewish state.

While emphasizing that the United States and Israel were closely "bound together by democratic tradition" and that the United States had an "enduring and iron-clad commitment to Israeli security," Powell indicated that Israel, too, had to make concessions for peace to be possible. These included a stop to settlement expansion and an end to the occupation of the West Bank and Gaza, which "causes humiliation and the killing of innocents." In conclusion, Powell stated that the United States would do everything it could to facilitate the peace process, "but at the end of the day the peoples have to make peace"—a position very similar to the one Powell had held when he joined the cabinet nearly a year earlier.

In order to implement the US vision of peace outlined by Powell, in addition to promises of economic aid Assistant Secretary of State William Burns and former Marine general Anthony Zinni were dispatched to meet with Israeli and Palestinian delegations to reach a cease-fire that would lay the basis for the resumption of peace negotiations. In an effort to facilitate the Zinni mission, President Bush put his personal prestige on the line by writing to five important Arab leaders—King Abdullah II of Jordan, Egyptian president Hosni Mubarak, King Mohammed VI of Morocco, Saudi Crown Prince Abdullah (who had publicly praised Powell's speech), and President Ben-Ali of Tunisia—asking for their help in persuading "the Palestinian leadership to take action to end violence and get the peace process back on track."[40]

On November 27, soon after Zinni's arrival in the Middle East, two Palestinian terrorists, one of whom was a member of Arafat's Fatah organization (the other was from Islamic Jihad), killed three Israelis and wounded thirty others in Afulah, a town in northern Israel. Zinni responded to the violence in a balanced way, stating, "This is why we need a cease-fire. Both sides have suffered too much."[41] Zinni then met with Arafat, asking him to end the violence, but even as they were meeting, Palestinian gunmen fired at the Israeli Jerusalem neighborhood of Gilo from the neighboring Palestinian suburb of Beit Jala—despite an explicit October promise by Palestinian leaders not to do so.[42] The next day three more Israelis were killed as a suicide bomber exploded a bomb on a public bus near the Israeli city of Hadera.[43] This time Zinni's response was much stronger: "The groups that do this are clearly trying to make my mission fail. There's no justification, no rationale, no sets of conditions that will ever make terrorist acts a right way to respond."[44] Zinni's words, however, did not stem the tide of terrorism. Two days later suicide bombers killed ten Israeli teenagers who had gathered at the Ben Yehudah pedestrian mall in Jerusalem. This time Arafat condemned the attacks, stressing not the loss of life by Israel but the negative political effect the suicide bombers were having on the Palestinian world image.[45]

By now, Zinni was furious, as he saw his mission literally going up in flames: "Those responsible for planning and carrying out these attacks must be found and brought to justice. This is an urgent task and there can be no delay or excuses for not acting decisively. The deepest evil one can imagine is to attack young people and children."[46] President Bush, whose prestige had been put on the line by the Zinni mission, also responded strongly: "Now more than ever Chairman Arafat and the Palestinian Authority must demonstrate through their actions, and not merely their words, their commitment to fight terror."[47]

Arafat seemed to get the message, if rather belatedly, from US political pressure, and from Israeli military retaliation. On December 16, he called for an immediate cease-fire, condemning both suicide attacks and the launching of mortar attacks.[48] Nonetheless, the Palestinian leader did not root out the

Hamas and Islamic Jihad organizations from Gaza and the West Bank; rather, he negotiated a tenuous truce with them (a tactic later repeated by Mahmoud Abbas in March 2005), something that was clearly unsatisfactory to the Israeli government. Arafat was kept penned up in Ramallah by Israeli tanks, and in a further blow to his prestige, he was prohibited from leaving his compound to attend Christmas services in Bethlehem.

Three weeks after Arafat's call for a cease-fire, Israeli forces captured a ship in the Red Sea, the *Karine A*, which held fifty tons of concealed weapons, including C-4 explosives and Katyusha rockets—clearly weapons of terrorism. Arafat's initial denial that the Palestinian Authority had anything to do with the vessel further undermined his credibility, both in Israel and in the United States.[49] In response to heavy pressure by the United States, Arafat eventually arrested several of the Palestinian officials involved, including a major general in his own security forces and an officer in the Palestinian Authority's naval police.[50]

Meanwhile, Hamas broke the truce by attacking an Israeli military outpost in Gaza, killing four soldiers and claiming the attack was in retaliation for Israel's seizure of the *Karine A*.[51] Israel retaliated, destroying, among other things, the runway of the Palestinian airport in Gaza, and after a terrorist attack against an Israeli bar mitzvah party in Hadera, in which six Israelis were killed and thirty wounded, Israel blew up the main Palestinian radio transmitter.[52]

Thus ended the first year of the Bush administration's efforts to resolve the Israeli-Palestinian conflict. Despite two major US efforts, one in June and one in November-December 2001, Palestinian terrorism, which Arafat was either unable or, more likely, unwilling to control (he had long used terrorism as a political weapon), had sabotaged US efforts to resolve the Palestinian-Israeli conflict. Nonetheless, both Arab states and the EU (European Union) continued to urge the United States to get more engaged in the search for an Arab-Israeli peace. In response, in a remarkably frank interview with the *New York Times* on February 28, 2002, Colin Powell stated, "We have not put it [the search for an Arab-Israeli peace agreement] on the back burner. What that [US engagement] usually means is 'Go and force the Israelis to do something.' That's what many people think when they say 'Get more engaged' or 'You're standing on the sidelines. You haven't made Israel blink in the face of violence.'"[53]

Meanwhile, President Bush had sent his vice president, Dick Cheney, who often took a much harder line than Powell, to the Arab world in an effort to build Arab support for a planned US attack on Iraq. Cheney was met with strong Arab calls for the United States to work out a solution to the Israeli-Palestinian conflict before engaging in a war with Iraq. This position apparently convinced President Bush to send Zinni back for another try at achieving a cease-fire. To facilitate the Zinni visit, Sharon made a major concession by lifting his demand for the passage of seven days without violence before talks could resume. The atmosphere of the Zinni visit was further improved by the announcement of an Arab-Israeli peace plan suggested by Saudi Arabia. This plan would be introduced at the Arab summit scheduled for the end of March in Beirut and involved Arab recognition of Israel in return for Israel's return to its 1967 boundaries and a fair solution to the Palestinian refugee problem. To help reinforce the momentum for peace, the United States pushed for a new UN Security Council resolution, Resolution 1397, on March 13, 2002, which called for a two-state solution to the Israeli-Palestinian conflict; the end of violence, incitement, and terrorism; and the resumption of negotiations based on the Tenet and Mitchell plans.[54]

Unfortunately, the diplomatic momentum for peace was shattered by another series of Palestinian terrorist attacks just as Zinni was seeking to consolidate a cease-fire and the Arab summit was taking place in Beirut. On March 27, the first night of the Jewish holiday of Passover, twenty-nine Jews were murdered and more than one hundred wounded at a Passover seder in the coastal resort town of Netanya. This attack was followed by suicide bombings in Jerusalem, Tel Aviv, and Haifa over the next three days, bombings that resulted in the deaths of an additional seventeen people and the wounding of eighty-four. These events precipitated an Israeli attack on Arafat's compound in Ramallah, followed by a sweep into the major Palestinian cities of the West Bank, in what Sharon called Operation Defensive Shield.

As these events were unfolding, the United States at first strongly backed Israel, with Powell noting, "Sharon made concessions, while Arafat backed terrorism."[55] Then, when mass demonstrations broke out in the Arab world, which may have worried Bush as he stepped up his preparations for an attack on Iraq, the president decided to once again involve the United States. In a major speech on April 4, 2002, after first denouncing terrorism and pointedly noting that "the chairman of the Palestinian Authority has not consistently opposed or confronted terrorists nor has he renounced terror as he agreed to do at Oslo," Bush called for the Israelis to withdraw from the West Bank cities they were occupying.[56] Bush also announced that he was sending Powell to the Middle East to work out a cease-fire. Several days later, the president urged the Israelis to withdraw "without delay,"[57] but then he ran into a firestorm of domestic criticism for pressuring Israel. First, the neoconservatives, who were the intellectual lifeblood of the administration, attacked Bush for urging Sharon to withdraw, claiming the Israeli leader was fighting terrorism just as the United States was fighting terrorism after 9/11. Then, the Evangelical Christians, a large and energetic base of Bush's core constituency, also attacked Bush for pressuring Israel.[58] Third, on April 15, 250,000 people rallied for Israel on the Mall in Washington, a demonstration organized by the US Jewish community; the demonstration also included Evangelical Christians among its speakers. The message of the rally was that the United States should support Israel's fight against Palestinian terrorism, which was similar to the antiterrorist policy of the United States after 9/11. Finally, the administration was severely criticized by influential members of Congress, including Republican House Majority Leader Tom DeLay, a strong friend of Israel.[59]

Another factor prompting Bush to change his position was Arafat's continued sponsorship of terrorism. When Arafat's wife came out in support of suicide bombings as a legitimate form of resistance against Israeli occupation, and the Israelis gave the United States documents showing that Arafat had not only tolerated terrorism but had helped finance it, Bush further turned against the Palestinian leader. On May 26, while on a state visit to Russia, Bush noted that Arafat "hasn't delivered. He had a chance to secure the peace as a result of the hard work of President Clinton and he didn't. He had a chance to fight terrorism and he hasn't."[60]

As Palestinian terrorist attacks continued to proliferate, Sharon, who had pulled Israeli forces out of the cities of the West Bank in May 2002, sent them back in June, this time with minimal criticism from the United States. Indeed, in a major speech on June 24, Bush called for a "new and different Palestinian leadership" so that a Palestinian state could be born. In the most anti-Arafat speech in his presidency, Bush stated:

> I call on the Palestinian people to elect new leaders, leaders not compromised by terror. I call upon them to build a practicing democracy, based on tolerance and liberty. If the Palestinian people actively pursue these goals, America and the world will actively support their efforts. If the Palestinian people meet these goals, they will be able to reach agreement with Israel and Egypt and Jordan on security and other arrangements for independence. And when the Palestinian people have new leaders, new institutions, and new security arrangements with their neighbors, the United States of America will support the creation of a Palestinian state whose borders and certain aspects of its sovereignty will be provisional until resolved as part of a final settlement in the Middle East.
>
> Today, Palestinian authorities are encouraging, not opposing, terrorism. This is unacceptable and the United States will not support the establishment of a Palestinian state until its leaders engage in a sustained fight against the terrorists and dismantle their infrastructure. This will require an externally supervised effort to rebuild and reform the Palestinian security services. The security system must have clear lines of authority and accountability and a unified chain of command.[61]

President Bush then called on Israel to respond to a new Palestinian leadership when it was formed:

> As new Palestinian institutions and new leaders emerge, demonstrating real performance on reform, I expect Israel to respond and work toward a final status agreement. With intensive security and effort by all, this agreement could be reached within three years from now. And I and my country will actively lead toward that goal. . . . As we make progress toward security, Israeli forces need to withdraw fully to positions they held prior to September 28, 2000. And consistent with the recommendations of the Mitchell Committee, Israeli settlement activity in the occupied territories must stop.[62]

While Bush chided the Israelis somewhat on settlement activity, the brunt of the president's ire was clearly on Arafat, and with this speech Bush formally joined Sharon in ruling out Arafat as a partner in the peace process.

US Policy from June 2002 to Arafat's Death in November 2004

Following the June 24 speech, US foreign policy in the Middle East had two main objectives. The first was to work with the European Union, Russia, and the United Nations as part of a "Diplomatic Quartet" to fashion a road map leading to a Palestinian-Israeli peace settlement. The second was to build a large coalition to prepare for war with Iraq.

In designing the Road Map with the EU, Russia, and the UN, the Bush administration faced a major problem. Although the United States had written off Arafat as a suitable partner for peace, as had Israel, the other three members of the Diplomatic Quartet had not, and this discrepancy caused problems in subsequent diplomacy. In addition, the presentation of the Road Map, which the Quartet began planning in July 2002, was delayed on numerous occasions and was not made public until the completion of the major combat phase of the Anglo-American invasion of Iraq at the end of March 2003. As a result, many cynical, and not so cynical, Middle East observers felt that the Road Map was aimed at merely assuaging the Arabs while the Bush administration was preparing to attack Iraq.[63] Indeed, in the run-up to the war in September 2002, when the Israelis laid siege to Arafat's compound in Ramallah following another series of brutal suicide bombings, the United States chose to abstain on, rather than veto, a UN Security Council resolution condemning the Israeli action, with Condoleezza Rice reportedly telling the Israeli government that the United States expected a speedy resolution of the siege because it "doesn't help" US efforts to galvanize support for the campaign against Iraq.[64]

In any case, following delays on account of the Israeli elections of January 2003 (in which Sharon's Likud Party scored an impressive victory) and the invasion of Iraq, which began in late March, the Road Map was finally published on April 30, 2003. At the time, it appeared that Bush, spurred on by his ally British prime minister Tony Blair, wanted to prove his critics wrong by demonstrating that he was genuinely interested in an Israeli-Palestinian peace agreement. According to the Road Map, which the Bush administration announced with great fanfare,[65] the Palestinians, in phase one of the three-phase plan leading to a Palestinian state, had to "declare an unequivocal end to violence and terrorism and end incitement against Israel and undertake visible efforts on the ground to arrest, disrupt, and restrain individuals and groups conducting and planning attacks on Israelis anywhere." Second, the Palestinians had to appoint an "empowered" prime minister and establish a government based on a strong parliamentary democracy and cabinet and have only three security services, which would report to the empowered prime minister. By these measures, the United States had hoped to weaken, if not eliminate, Arafat's power base and in his place create an "empowered" prime minister who would be a proper partner for peace. For its part, Israel, under phase one of the Road Map, had to refrain from the deportation of Palestinians, attacks on Palestinian civilians, and the confiscation or demolition of Palestinian homes and property, and as the "comprehensive security performance" of the Palestinians moved forward, the Israeli military had to "withdraw progressively" from areas occupied since September 28, 2000; dismantle settlement outposts erected since March 2001; and "freeze all settlement activity (including natural growth of settlements)."

With Bush at the peak of his international influence, as a result of the apparent military victory in Iraq, Arafat was compelled to accede to the Road Map's demands to create the post of prime minister, to which senior Palestinian leader Mahmoud Abbas, also known as Abu Mazen, was appointed. Yet this appointment appeared to be a ploy; it soon became evident that Mahmoud Abbas was not the "empowered" prime minister the United States had in mind, since Arafat retained control over most of the Palestinian security forces. Apparently, the United States had overlooked this fact in the hope that Abbas, who, unlike Arafat, had never been demonized by either Sharon or the Israeli public, had sufficient power to be a credible negotiating partner for Israel. Although the Palestinian Authority accepted the Road Map, Hamas, Islamic Jihad, the al-Aqsa Martyrs Brigade, and the Tanzim (young militants tied to Arafat's Fatah organization) did not. Israel, albeit with a number of reservations, also accepted it. When the Road Map was published, it was attacked by eighty-eight US senators, who asserted that the Road Map's position against Palestinian terrorism was not as strong as that in Bush's statement of June 24, 2002.[66]

Initially, the Road Map was greeted with optimism, especially when on June 29, 2003, Abbas succeeded in eliciting a ninety-day Hudna, or truce, from the leaders of Hamas, the Tanzim, and Islamic Jihad, though not from the al-Aqsa Martyrs Brigade.

Although Israeli military leaders worried that the terrorist groups would use the ninety-day period to rebuild their forces and armaments (especially the Qassem rockets that had been fired into Israel from Gaza), Sharon proved willing to take a chance on the Hudna. He called for the withdrawal of Israeli forces from northern Gaza and Bethlehem; the closing of some checkpoints hindering traffic between Palestinian villages and cities; the shutdown of some illegal outposts on the West Bank (although other outposts were set up); the release of some Palestinian prisoners (though far fewer than the Palestinians wanted), including an elderly terrorist who had killed fourteen Israelis in 1975; and the loosening of work restrictions on Palestinians.

President Bush sought to move the peace process forward by meeting with both Abbas and Sharon in Washington in July 2003, although differences over Israel's construction of its security wall proved to be problematic during Bush's talks with the two leaders.[67] Meanwhile, during the Hudna, attacks on Israel continued, including the murder of Israeli civilians, although the number of attacks decreased significantly from the period preceding the Hudna. In addition, Abbas worked to lessen anti-Israeli incitement, painting over some of the anti-Israel slogans displayed on walls in Gaza. However, the key demand of both Bush and the Israelis—that Mahmoud Abbas crack down on the terrorists—was not met, primarily because Arafat refused to allow it. Nonetheless, Abbas tried to convince the United States that he could negotiate a permanent truce with the terrorist groups. While some in the US State Department seemed to be willing to go along with Abbas, Sharon was not, and as attacks on Israelis continued during the Hudna, Sharon decided to retaliate by attacking the Hamas and Islamic Jihad terrorists who were seen as responsible. Then, on August 19, less than two months into the Hudna, a terrorist attack in Jerusalem killed twenty-one Israelis, including a number of children. In response, Sharon stepped up his attacks on the terrorists, which led Hamas to declare an end to the Hudna. Soon afterward, blaming both Arafat and Israel for a lack of support, Abbas resigned and the peace process again came to a halt.

In the aftermath of Abbas's resignation, with the peace process stalled, the United States again distanced itself from the Israeli-Palestinian peace process, as the Bush administration increasingly concentrated on the deteriorating situation in Iraq. Bush did, however, begin to push a policy of democratization for the Middle East. Influenced by Israeli politician Natan Sharansky's book *The Case for Democracy*,[68] Bush came to argue that there were two major reasons why the US should push to democratize the Middle East. First, if young men had a chance to participate politically in their societies by joining political parties, demonstrating in the streets for their political positions, enjoying freedom of the press, and playing a role in choosing their nation's leaders through fair elections, they would be less likely to become terrorists. Second, democracies were less likely to fight each other than autocratic or totalitarian states. Thus, the administration's reasoning went, if the Middle East became more democratic it would be less likely to spawn terrorists and would be a more peaceful region of the world. Bush's democratization policy also benefited Israel. As the only genuine democracy in the region (with the partial exception of Turkey), Israel was not only an antiterrorist ally of the United States, but a democratic one as well.

While Bush was formulating his democratization policy, Sharon was developing a new strategy of his own, the unilateral withdrawal from Gaza. This was conceived in part as an initiative to prevent other diplomatic efforts' being imposed on Israel (such as the Geneva initiative of Yossi Beilin)[69] and in part to preserve Israel as both a Jewish and a democratic state by ending Israeli control over the approximately 1.4 million Palestinian Arabs living in the Gaza Strip.[70] At the same time Sharon decided to make a major effort to speed up the building of the Israeli security fence between Israel and the West Bank to prevent Palestinian terrorist attacks on Israel. The fence, however, did not run on the old 1967 border but took in a swath of land on the West Bank.

By early 2004 the United States and Israel began detailed bargaining on the unilateral withdrawal and the security fence, and under US pressure (and that of the Israeli Supreme Court), Sharon agreed to move the security fence closer to the 1949 armistice line. According to then Israeli ambassador to the United States Daniel Ayalon, Sharon also agreed to add four settlements in the northern part of the West Bank to his disengagement plan.[71]

The result of the bargaining was a meeting between Sharon and Bush in Washington in mid-April 2004 that was structured not only to reinforce the Sharon disengagement initiative but also to help each leader politically. Thus Bush went a very long way toward supporting Sharon's policies. Not only did he welcome Sharon's disengagement plan as "real progress" and assert that the United States was "strongly committed" to Israel's well-being as a Jewish state within "secure and defensible borders," but he also went on to reject any Palestinian "right of return" to Israel, stating, "It seems clear that an agreed just, fair, and realistic framework for a solution to the Palestinian refugee issue as part of any final status agreement will need to be found through the establishment of a Palestinian state, and the settling of Palestinian refugees there, rather than in Israel."[72]

Bush also reinforced Israel's position that it would not fully return to the 1949 armistice lines and that any final agreement would have to reflect the settlements Israel had built since 1967, stating, "In light of new realities on the ground, including already existing population centers, it is unrealistic to expect that the outcome of final status negotiations will be a full and complete return to the armistice lines of 1949."

Finally, Bush reaffirmed Israel's right to self-defense against terrorism, noting, "Israel will retain its right to defend itself against terrorism including to take action against terrorist organizations." This statement not only endorsed Israel's right to go back into Gaza to fight terrorism but also implicitly endorsed Israel's strategy of assassinating the leaders of Hamas, a process that continued during the spring and summer of 2004.

In his meeting with Sharon, Bush also made a number of gestures to the Palestinians. Not only did he reaffirm his commitment to a two-state solution to the Israeli-Palestinian conflict and call for Israel to freeze settlement activity and remove unauthorized outposts, but he also put limits on Israel's security wall, asserting, "As the government of Israel has stated, the barrier being erected by Israel should be a security rather than a political barrier, should be temporary, and therefore not prejudice any final status issues including final borders, and its route should take into account, consistent with security needs, its impact on Palestinians not engaged in terrorist activities." Nonetheless, returning to the theme he had emphasized since 9/11, Bush demanded that the Palestinians "act decisively against terror, including sustained, targeted, and effective operations to stop terrorism and dismantle terrorist capabilities and infrastructure."

It is clear that Sharon had scored a great diplomatic success with his visit, and he heaped lavish praise on President Bush. After noting that the disengagement plan "can be an important contribution" to the president's Road Map for peace, he went on to state, "You have proven, Mr. President, your ongoing, deep, and sincere friendship to the State of Israel and to the Jewish people. . . . In all these years, I have never met a leader as committed as you are, Mr. President, to the struggle for freedom and the need to confront terrorism wherever it exists."

Needless to say, for a president now deeply engaged in an election campaign against John Kerry, a liberal senator from Massachusetts, who normally could expect to get the vast majority of Jewish votes, Sharon's words were extremely helpful to Bush, especially in pivotal states like Florida with its large Jewish population. Indeed, not only did Bush strongly support Sharon on the disengagement plan, but the Bush administration also sent a twenty-six-page booklet, titled "President George W. Bush—A Friend of the American Jewish Community," to American Jewish organizations, stressing Bush's commitment to the state of Israel and to the world Jewish community. Prominent themes in the booklet were Bush's opposition to terrorism aimed at Israel and his opposition to PLO leader Yasser Arafat. The booklet stated, "For Yasser Arafat the message has been clear. While he was a frequent White House guest during the last administration, he has never been granted a meeting with President Bush."[73] In another effort to court Jewish support, Bush reportedly overrode State Department opposition to create an office at the State Department to monitor the rising tide of anti-Semitism around the world. Perhaps reflecting on the political nature of the proposed office, an unnamed State Department official told the *Washington Times:* "It's more of a bureaucratic nuisance than a real problem. We are not going to fight a bill that has gained such political momentum."[74] Finally, on the eve of the US presidential election, Bush sent National Security Adviser Condoleezza Rice to address the AIPAC meeting in Florida. The very fact of her presence, despite an ongoing FBI (Federal Bureau of Investigation) probe of a Pentagon analyst who had allegedly passed secrets to AIPAC, underlined the great importance the Bush administration placed on getting Jewish support in the election.[75]

Bush won the 2004 election by 3.5 million votes, and soon thereafter Arafat, seen by both the United States and Israel as the main obstacle to an Israeli-Palestinian settlement, died. Arafat's death set the stage for another US attempt to revive the Arab-Israeli peace process.

US Policy from Arafat's Death to the Hamas Victory in the Palestinian Elections

In the aftermath of the death of Arafat and the reelection victory of George W. Bush, the situation initially appeared to improve, as far as US policy in the Middle East was concerned. First, the replacement of Colin Powell by Condoleezza Rice as US secretary of state added a great deal of coherence to US policy, as the old rifts between the Department of State, on the one hand, and the White House and the Defense Department, on the other, were minimized. In addition, as Defense Secretary Donald Rumsfeld's influence declined because of the increased problems the United States was encountering in Iraq, Rice became the unquestioned administration spokesperson on foreign policy, especially on the Middle East. Second, the US democratization plan for the Middle East appeared to score some major triumphs with democratic elections being successfully held in Iraq, Lebanon, and the

Palestinian Authority. In the PA, an election was held to choose the successor to Yasser Arafat, and in what international observers considered a fair and democratic election, Mahmoud Abbas, a Fatah leader who had earlier served a brief term as Palestinian prime minister under the Road Map, was elected with 60 percent of the votes. What made Abbas such an appealing candidate for the United States was his regular denouncement of terrorism as inimical to Palestinian interests. Thus, with the Abbas election, the two main strands of US post–9/11 Middle East policy—the fight against terrorism and support for democratization—came together, and it was not long before Abbas was welcomed to the White House with full pomp and ceremony, a privilege that had been denied to Arafat, whom the Bush administration saw as closely linked to terrorism. Sharon, for his part, made a series of gestures to Abbas in February 2005, including the release of seven hundred Palestinian detainees and agreement to a cease-fire. And in order to help Abbas strengthen his position in the PA, the United States dispatched Lieutenant General William Ward to reorganize the Palestinian armed forces and James Wolfensohn, the former head of the World Bank, to help develop the Palestinian economy. Unfortunately, neither proved to be very effective. Ward was never able to transform the disparate Palestinian military groupings into an effective fighting force, and he was replaced by Major General Keith Dayton. As far as Wolfensohn was concerned, despite his heroic efforts—including the use of his personal funds to facilitate the purchase by the Palestinians of Israeli greenhouses in Gaza—the Palestinian economy remained chaotic.

While US-Palestinian relations got off to a good start after the election of Abbas, the new Palestinian leader took a risky gamble in March 2005, when, in an effort to achieve harmony among the contending Palestinian forces, he signed an agreement with Hamas and several other Palestinian organizations (but not Islamic Jihad) providing that, in return for a cease-fire with Israel, the only mode of interaction among the Palestinians would be "dialogue."[76] This agreement ran counter to Israeli and American calls for Abbas to crack down on Hamas and the other Palestinian terrorist organizations. This issue became particularly pressing as Israel prepared for its disengagement from Palestinian territories during the summer of 2005, an action involving the pull-out of Israeli settlements and military forces from Gaza and the pullout of Israeli settlements from the northern West Bank. While Hamas had signed the cease-fire agreement, Islamic Jihad had not, and there were concerns that the Iranian-supported organization might disrupt the Israeli disengagement. While this disruption never materialized, Islamic Jihad did undertake a number of terrorist attacks against Israel in 2005, and the Israeli government responded with "targeted killings" (assassinations) of Islamic Jihad operatives.

The main problem for Israel, however, was Hamas, and unless Abbas moved against the Islamic organization, it appeared unlikely that Israel would take him seriously as a peace partner. Abbas, however, appeared more interested in creating Palestinian solidarity than in satisfying Israel. Indeed, in responding to my question in late June 2005 in Ramallah about why he had chosen not to crack down on Hamas after his strong victory in the Palestinian presidential elections, Abbas replied, "What, and have a Palestinian civil war!"[77] Unfortunately for Abbas, two years later the Palestinian civil war between Fatah and Hamas did occur, at a time when Abbas was much weaker and Hamas much stronger than in June 2005.

Despite Abbas's failure to crack down on Hamas, Secretary of State Rice sought to facilitate cooperation between Israel and the Abbas-led Palestinian Authority as the disengagement took place. Thus she helped to negotiate a number of agreements between Israel and the PA, including one to haul away debris from the destroyed Jewish settlements (the PA had demanded their destruction), another on the modus operandi of the crossing points between Gaza and Egypt and between Gaza and Israel, and a third agreement on travel between Gaza and the West Bank. While the disengagement went relatively smoothly, despite the protests of Jewish settlers in Gaza, the next issue to arise was the election for the Palestinian Legislative Council (PLC). Abbas had postponed the elections from their original July 2005 date to January 2006, in part so he could get political credit for the Israeli withdrawal, and in part because he could not settle the rifts between the old and young guards of his Fatah organization. A key issue in the elections was whether Hamas would run and, if so, under what conditions. Israeli prime minister Ariel Sharon initially opposed Hamas's participation in the elections, citing the Oslo Accord requirement that no "racist" party could run in the elections; since Hamas continued to call for the destruction of Israel, it was clearly "racist." Only if Hamas renounced terrorism and recognized Israel's right to exist should it be allowed to run, Sharon asserted. The United States, however, took a contrary position. In part because forbidding Hamas to participate would hurt the US democratization plan for the Middle East, and in part because Abbas had promised to finally crack down on Hamas after the PLC elections, Rice exerted heavy pressure on Sharon to allow Hamas participation. The Israeli leader, perhaps preoccupied with Israeli domestic politics (he had broken away from his Likud Party and formed the new Kadima Party in November 2005, four months before the Israeli parliamentary elections), gave in to the US pressure. It was a decision that both the United States and Israel would come to regret.[78]

US Policy from the Hamas Electoral Victory to Its Seizure of Gaza

Capitalizing on Fatah's corruption, the PA's inability to provide law and order in the West Bank, and the continued divisions between Fatah's old and young guards, Hamas swept to a massive victory in the January 25, 2006, PLC elections. Hamas representatives were quick to claim that their victory was due to their policy of "resistance" against Israel.[79] The Hamas victory created a major dilemma for the United States, as its two main policies in the Middle East—the war against terror and support for democratization—had now come into direct conflict with each other: A terrorist organization, Hamas, utilizing democratic means, had taken control of the Palestinian legislature, and a Hamas leader, Ismail Haniyeh, had become the new Palestinian prime minister. Israel faced a different challenge. By the time of the Hamas election victory, Sharon, who had suffered a massive stroke in early January 2006, was no longer Israel's prime minister. His replacement, as acting prime minister, was his Kadima colleague Ehud Olmert, who now not only had to prepare his new party for the March 28 Israeli elections but also had to deal with the Hamas election victory. Olmert quickly decided Israel would have nothing to do with Hamas unless it changed its policies toward Israel, a position embraced by most of the Israeli political spectrum. For her part, Rice quickly convened the Diplomatic Quartet (the United States, the EU, the UN, and Russia), which agreed not to have any dealings with the Hamas-led Palestinian government until Hamas renounced terrorism, agreed to recognize Israel, and acceded to the agreements signed between Israel and the PLO, including Oslo I, Oslo II, and the Road Map. Russia, however, soon broke with the Quartet consensus by inviting a Hamas delegation for an official visit to Moscow. In April 2006, after the United States and the EU, seeing no change in Hamas policy, had decided to cut all aid to the PA (except "humanitarian" assistance), Russia again broke ranks with its Quartet colleagues by offering the PA economic assistance.

The newly elected Israeli government led by Olmert refused to have anything to do either with Abbas (who they claimed was ineffectual) or with the Hamas-led Palestinian government. For its part, the new Hamas government repeated its refusal to recognize Israel or make peace with it and supported, as "legitimate resistance," continued attacks on Israel whether in the form of Qassem rockets fired from Gaza into Israel or in the form of suicide bombings such as the one on April 17, 2006, which claimed ten Israeli lives.[80] Meanwhile, as Israel was confronting a Hamas-led government in the Palestinian territories, it also had to face a rising threat from Iran. After two years of on-and-off-again negotiations with the European Union over its secret nuclear program, in August 2005 Iran broke off negotiations and announced it was moving ahead with nuclear enrichment. Making matters worse for Israel, which along with the United States feared that Iran was on the path to developing nuclear weapons, the newly elected Iranian president, Mahmoud Ahmadinejad, called for Israel to be "wiped off the map" and declared that the Holocaust was a myth.[81] While the United States was highly supportive of Israel in the face of the Iranian leader's provocative statements (Bush, on February 1, 2006, had stated, "Israel is a solid ally of the United States; we will rise to Israel's defense if need be"[82]), the Israeli leadership had to question whether the United States, increasingly bogged down in both Iraq and Afghanistan (where the Taliban had revived), would act to eliminate the nuclear threat from Iran, or whether Israel would have to do the job itself.

Meanwhile, Israel's relations with the Hamas-led Palestinian government continued to deteriorate, with stepped-up shelling of Israeli territory from Gaza and Israeli retaliation. Then, in the summer of 2006, full-scale war broke out, first with Hamas and then with Hizbollah following the kidnapping of Israeli soldiers. In looking at US-Israeli relations during both conflicts, there are a number of similarities. The Bush administration has seen both Hamas and Hizbollah as terrorist organizations linked to Syria and to Iran and, as such, enemies of the United States. Consequently, when Israel was fighting both terrorist organizations, it was on the same side of the barricades as the United States, and the United States adopted a strongly pro-Israeli position in both conflicts. Thus it vetoed a UN Security Council resolution condemning Israel for its bombardment of the Gaza town of Beit Hanoun, from which rockets were being launched into Israel, and condemned both Iran and Syria for their aid to Hizbollah in its war against Israel. Indeed, in an "open-mike" incident at the G-8 summit in Saint Petersburg, Russia, Bush told British prime minister Tony Blair that the global powers had to "get Syria to get Hizbollah to stop doing this s___ and then it's over." Bush sought, without success, to get the G-8 to condemn both Iran and Syria for their role in the violence.[83]

In the Second Lebanon War, however, there was one additional factor that influenced US policy. The anti-Syrian Fuad Siniora government, which had come into office in Lebanon following the departure of Syrian forces in 2005, was seen as an ally of the United States, and one of the few remaining successes of its democratization program. Consequently, the United States sought to ensure that if the Israeli-Hizbollah fighting did not enhance Siniora's position, by weakening Hizbollah, at least it would not hurt it. Thus, for the first two weeks of the war, the United States gave full diplomatic backing to Israel, hoping it would destroy Hizbollah, the Siniora government's main opposition. However, in late July, after an Israeli attack in Qana aimed at a

Hizbollah bunker accidentally killed sixty Lebanese civilians,[84] it had become clear that Israeli dependence on its air force to deal with Hizbollah was not working,[85] and that Siniora's position was being threatened by the growing popularity of Hizbollah, which was successfully "standing up to Israel." This situation also negatively affected the governments of US allies Jordan, Egypt, and Saudi Arabia. Consequently, the United States began to work for a cease-fire, and the result was UN Security Council Resolution 1701, which called for the Lebanese army to move to the Israeli border and for the expansion of the UN troops in southern Lebanon to fifteen thousand. Israel was less than happy with the cease-fire because it did not lead to the disarming of Hizbollah or to a cessation of Syria's transfer of weapons to Hizbollah.

In the aftermath of the Israel-Hizbollah war, US secretary of state Rice, who had originally spoken of a "new Middle East" emerging from the conflict, sought to build on the fears of rising Iranian influence in the region following the political victory of Iran's ally, Hizbollah. She tried to construct an anti-Iranian Sunni Arab bloc of Jordan, Egypt, Saudi Arabia, and the United Arab Emirates and to align it with Israel against Iran and its allies, Hizbollah and Hamas. Helping Rice in this project was Saudi Arabia's decision to revive the 2002 Arab peace plan, which offered Arab state recognition of Israel if it withdrew to its pre–1967 War boundaries and agreed to a "fair" settlement of the Palestinian refugee problem. Unfortunately for Rice, the Democratic victory in the November 2006 US congressional elections weakened the Bush administration, which had already been damaged by the failures in its Iraq policy and in the Hurricane Katrina recovery effort. This Democratic victory gave rise to a feeling, especially in the Middle East, that Bush had become a "lame duck" president, and that any serious discussion of peace should wait until his successor took office in January 2009. Nonetheless, Rice urged Olmert to negotiate with Abbas, while the United States continued to try to strengthen him militarily while clashes between Hamas and Abbas's Fatah increased in intensity. Saudi Arabia succeeded in temporarily stopping the fighting through an agreement in Mecca in February 2007, an agreement that established a Palestinian national unity government, but neither the United States nor Israel was pleased with the platform of the new government, which was dominated by Hamas and which took positions closer to Hamas than to Fatah.[86]

Despite the new Palestinian government, Rice pressed on with her efforts to resuscitate the Israeli-Palestinian peace process, which she saw as necessary to facilitate the alignment between the Sunni Arab states and Israel. Thus she agreed to speak with non-Hamas members of the Palestinian national unity government, something that Israel feared would "sanitize" Hamas.[87] Rice also announced that at some point, the United States, in order to create a "political horizon," might suggest its own solutions to the conflict,[88] thus appearing to bring US policy back to where it had been in the Clinton administration, with the Clinton Parameters.

As part of her strategy Rice suggested the speedy implementation of the November 2005 agreement between Israel and the Palestinian Authority, under which Israel would permit bus travel between Gaza and the West Bank (Israel had suspended implementation of the agreement following the Hamas victory in the January 2006 PLC elections), as well as lift Israeli checkpoints in the West Bank, if the Palestinians stopped firing Qassem rockets from Gaza into Israel and stopped smuggling arms into Gaza from Egypt. Both Hamas and Israel rejected the plan, Israeli officials complaining that bomb makers and engineers with the knowledge to build Qassems would travel from Gaza into the West Bank, and that the checkpoints were necessary to prevent the movement of terrorists.[89]

As Rice pursued her strategy, Olmert appeared to go over her head by ingratiating himself with Bush and Vice President Cheney. Thus, speaking to an AIPAC meeting in April 2007, he publicly opposed an American withdrawal from Iraq, and in May he condemned US Speaker of the House Nancy Pelosi's "mishandling" of the Israeli conditions for peace in her discussions with Syrian leader Bashar Asad—comments that echoed Vice President Cheney's criticism of the Pelosi visit. Needless to say, leaders of the US Democratic Party took a dim view of Olmert's comments and his apparent close identification with the Bush administration.[90] Olmert also followed the US lead in refusing to negotiate with Syria despite Bashar Asad's offer to resume peace negotiations with Israel; Rice, seeking (albeit with limited success) to isolate Syria, had reportedly told Olmert, "It is best you avoid even exploring this possibility."[91]

Rice's efforts to create a "political horizon" for Israeli-Palestinian talks got an unexpected boost, however, when, in early June 2007, the escalating fighting between Hamas and Fatah led to the seizure of Gaza by Hamas forces and the crackdown on Hamas by Fatah in the West Bank. These events enabled the United States, despite the embarrassing failure of the US-trained Fatah forces in Gaza, to press ahead with negotiations with Abbas as the United States hoped to make the Fatah-controlled West Bank a showpiece, while Gaza suffered an ever-tightening Israeli blockade as Qassam rockets continued to be fired from Gaza into Israeli towns such as Sderot. Whether Abbas would be able to significantly reform Fatah and end corruption so as to make the West Bank the showpiece Rice wanted, however, remained to be seen. In any case, the Palestinian Civil War of June 2007, which led to the splitting off of Gaza from the West Bank, is a useful point of departure for analyzing US relations with Israel since the death of Yitzhak Rabin.

Conclusions

In looking at the course of US-Israeli relations since the death of Yitzhak Rabin in 1995, a number of conclusions can be drawn. First, despite occasional problems (as during the Netanyahu era and immediately after 9/11), US-Israeli relations have been very close. Thus, in addition to providing $3 billion a year in military and economic aid to Israel, the United States has strongly backed Israel at the United Nations and, especially during the George W. Bush administration, has supported the main Israeli positions on the Arab-Israeli conflict, including preserving Israel as a Jewish state, backing Israel's right to retaliate against terrorist attacks from any territory from which Israel would withdraw, asserting that Israel's borders should not be identical to the pre–1967 War borders, and maintaining that a solution to the Palestinian refugee problem has to be found in a new Palestinian state, not in Israel.

The one issue on which there was constant disagreement between Israel and the United States during both the Clinton and the George W. Bush administrations, as it had been in previous US administrations, was the building of Jewish settlements in Gaza and the West Bank. While as part of its unilateral withdrawal policy Israel withdrew from all of its settlements in Gaza, and from four settlements in the northern West Bank, the remaining Israeli settlements in the West Bank (in addition to settlement outposts that had been set up after 2001) remain the main irritant in the US-Israeli relationship, because they are a barrier to the type of peace agreement between Israel and the Palestinians that the United States has been trying to foster.

A second major conclusion to be drawn from this study is that the styles of the Clinton administration and the George W. Bush administration in promoting the Arab-Israeli peace process differed; Clinton had a special envoy to the Middle East (Dennis Ross), whereas the Bush administration's involvement was more episodic. However, both administrations were in fact deeply involved in the peace process. After being involved primarily as a cheerleader in the 1993 and 1995 Oslo I and II agreements and in the 1994 Israeli-Jordanian peace agreement during the Clinton administration, the United States, under Clinton, became heavily involved following the Israeli-Palestinian fighting precipitated by the opening of the Hasmonean tunnel in Jerusalem in September 1996. Clinton's Middle East mediator, Dennis Ross, had negotiated the 1997 Hebron agreement and Clinton himself had negotiated the Wye agreement in 1998. Unfortunately Clinton's failure to negotiate a Syrian-Israeli agreement in March 2000 and his larger failure to negotiate an Israeli-Palestinian agreement at Camp David in July 2000, together with the unwillingness of the Palestinians to accept the Clinton Parameters for an

Israeli-Palestinian peace agreement in December 2000, were factors convincing George W. Bush, who had little political capital to risk, to pull back from the Arab-Israeli peace process when he took office in January 2001. His position was to change after 9/11, when his administration threw itself into a major effort to achieve a Palestinian-Israeli settlement, sending General Anthony Zinni in both the fall of 2001 and the spring of 2002 to try to achieve a settlement—efforts that were sabotaged by Palestinian terrorism. Bush tried again with his Road Map proposal in the spring of 2003, and yet again following the death of Arafat in 2004, as the United States sought to forge a cooperative relationship between Israel and Arafat's successor, Mahmoud Abbas, to pave the way to a peace agreement. In each case, Palestinian terrorism sabotaged the peace talks, much as it had during Prime Minister Shimon Peres's premiership, in February and March 1996. Indeed, if one wishes to draw a central conclusion from this analysis of US efforts to forge a peace agreement from 1995 to 2007, it is that Palestinian terrorism by Hamas and Islamic Jihad, which neither Yasser Arafat nor Mahmoud Abbas proved willing or able to stop, destroyed whatever chance the United States had to forge an agreement between Israel and the Palestinian Arabs.

A fourth conclusion that can be drawn from this analysis is that domestic American politics has played an important role in the US-Israeli relationship. Although most Jews have traditionally voted Democratic and Bill Clinton had no trouble winning Jewish support during his election campaigns, Benjamin Netanyahu was able to mobilize both Evangelical Christian and Republican congressional support to insulate himself from pressure by Clinton to make concessions to the Palestinians in 1997–1998. During the George W. Bush administration, there was a concerted effort to increase the percentage of Jewish voters going to the Republicans and this was a factor, along with continued very strong Evangelical support for Israel and the myriad mistakes made by Yasser Arafat, who was viewed by Bush as a supporter of terrorism, that led Bush to take very strong pro-Israeli positions in both 2002, when he called for a new Palestinian government, and in 2004, when he strongly supported Sharon's unilateral withdrawal plan.

In sum, bonds of common values and strategic interests in fighting terrorism strongly tied the United States to Israel during both the Clinton and George W. Bush administrations and are likely to keep the two countries aligned for many years to come. As George W. Bush told the American Jewish Committee (AJC) in May 2006:

> My Administration shares a strong commitment with the AJC to make sure relations between Israel and America remain strong. We have so much in common. We're both young countries born of struggle and sacrifice. We're both founded by immigrants

escaping religious persecution. We have both established vibrant democracies built on the rule of law and open markets. . . . These ties have made us natural allies and these ties will never be broken. America's commitment to Israel's security is strong, enduring and unshakeable.[92]

Notes

1. The political perspectives of Marshall and Forrestal are discussed by Clark Clifford, a participant in the discussions on US policy toward the future Jewish state. See Clark Clifford, *Counsel to the President: A Memoir* (New York: Random House, 1991), pp. 3–25.

2. On these issues, see Peter L. Hahn, *Caught in the Middle East: U.S. Policy toward the Arab-Israeli Conflict 1945–1961* (Chapel Hill: University of North Carolina Press, 2004). See also Zach Levey, *Israel and the Western Powers* (Chapel Hill: University of North Carolina Press, 1997).

3. See Warren Bass, *Support Any Friend: Kennedy's Middle East Policy and the Making of the U.S.-Israel Alliance* (New York: Oxford University Press, 2003).

4. For studies of the Johnson, Nixon, Carter, and Reagan administrations' policies toward Israel, see William B. Quandt, *Peace Process: American Diplomacy and the Arab-Israeli Conflict since 1967*, 3rd ed. (Los Angeles: University of California Press, 2005), and Steven Spiegel, *The Other Arab-Israeli Conflict: Making America's Middle East Policy from Truman to Reagan* (Chicago: University of Chicago Press, 1985).

5. On the Soviet impact on US policy toward the Middle East, see Robert O. Freedman, *Moscow and the Middle East: Soviet Policy since the Invasion of Afghanistan* (Cambridge: Cambridge University Press, 1991).

6. See Quandt, *Peace Process*, pp. 250–257, and Spiegel, *The Other Arab-Israeli Conflict*, pp. 412–429.

7. On these issues, see Dennis Ross, *The Missing Peace: The Inside Story of the Fight for Middle East Peace* (New York: Farrar, Straus & Giroux, 2005).

8. On relations between American Jewry and Israel in its first decade, see Zvi Ganin, *An Uneasy Relationship: American Jewish Leadership and Israel 1948–1967* (Syracuse, NY: Syracuse University Press, 2005).

9. For an Israeli view of the negotiations by a participant-observer, see Itamar Rabinovich, *The Brink of Peace: The Israeli-Syrian Negotiations* (Princeton, NJ: Princeton University Press, 1998).

10. See Quandt, *The Peace Process*, and Ross, *The Missing Peace*.

11. See Rabinovich, *The Brink of Peace*, and Ross, *The Missing Peace*.

12. For Ross's personal account of the negotiations see Ross, *The Missing Peace*, chap. 12.

13. Albright discusses these events in her memoirs. See Madeleine Albright, *Madam Secretary: A Memoir* (New York: Miramax Books, 2003), chap. 18.

14. David Coven, "Liberty U. to Send 3,000 Students on a Study Tour of Israel," *Chronicle of Higher Education* (September 25, 1997), p. 51.

15. For an analysis critical of US strategy at this time, see Robert Satloff, "Shifting Sands: The U.S.'s Disturbing New Israel Policy," *New Republic* (June 1, 1998).

16. These divisions are discussed in Robert O. Freedman, "The Religious-Secular Divide in Israeli Politics," *Middle East Policy*, vol. 6, no. 4 (June 1999).

17. Martin Sief, "Arafat Accepts Israeli Land Deal for West Bank," *Washington Times* (September 30, 1998).

18. See Ross, *The Missing Peace*, chap. 15. Interestingly enough Ross titles this chapter, "The 13 Percent Solution."

19. Lee Hockstadter, "Attacks Kill Arab: Injure 3 Israelis," *Washington Post* (December 1998).

20. Ann LeLordo, "Israel Issues Ultimatum, Halts West Bank Pull-Out," *Baltimore Sun* (December 3, 1998).

21. See Joel Peters, "Europe and the Arab-Israeli Peace Process: The Declaration of the European Council of Berlin and Beyond," in Sven Behrendt and Christian-Peter Hanelt, eds., *Bound to Cooperate: Europe and the Middle East* (Gutersloh, Germany: Bertelsmann Foundation, 2001), p. 162.

22. Philip Shenon, "U.S. and Other Nations Plan More Aid for Palestinians," *New York Times* (December 1, 1998); Martin Sief, "Palestinians Get More U.S. Aid," *Washington Times* (December 1, 1998).

23. Cited in Hockstadter, "Attacks Kill Arab."

24. See Judy Dempsey, "Palestinians Turn the Tables on Israelis: Arafat Poses as Clinton's Friend as Netanyahu Sulks," *Financial Times* (December 16, 1998).

25. For a view of Barak's "Syria's my priority" policy, see Ross, *The Missing Peace*, chap. 20. See also Albright, *Madam Secretary*, pp. 474–482.

26. Author's interviews with Palestinians, June-July 2000. In addition Arafat's national security adviser, Jibril Ragoub, later noted that Palestinian organizations should "learn from Hizbollah"; cited in Arnon Regular, "Militants Agree to End Civilian Attacks, No Mention of Settlers," *Ha'aretz* (December 7, 2003).

27. For analyses of the failure of Camp David II see Ross, *The Missing Peace*, chap. 24; Quandt, *The Peace Process*, chap. 12; Albright, *Madam Secretary*, pp. 482–494; and Bill Clinton, *My Life* (New York: Knopf, 2004), pp. 911–916. See also the interview with former Israeli foreign minister Shlomo Ben-Ami, "End of a Journey," *Ha'aretz* (October 3, 2001) (in English); Robert Malley and Hussein Agha, "Camp David: The Tragedy of Errors," *New York Review of Books* (August 9, 2001), pp. 59–65; Ehud Barak, "It seems Israel Has to Wait for New Palestinian Leadership," *International Herald Tribune* (July 31, 2001); Alain Gresh, "The Middle East: How the Peace Was Lost," *Le Monde Diplomatique* (September 2001), pp. 1, 8–9; Barry Rubin, "The Region," (June 25, 2001), http://www1.biu.ac.il; and

Bassam Abu-Sharif, "A Call to Israel to Understand What the Palestinians Want," (September 14, 2001), http://ipcri.org.

28. For a different view of the "Lessons of Lebanon," see Roula Khalaf, "Misleading Ghosts of Lebanese Resistance," *Financial Times* (August 16, 2001).

29. Cited in Ross, *The Missing Peace*, p. 741.

30. Ibid., pp. 752–753.

31. Ibid., pp. 753–755.

32. Cited in Roula Khalaf, "Powell Sets Out Bush Line on Middle East," *Financial Times* (March 20, 2001).

33. Alan Sipress, "Lawmakers criticize Palestinians," *Washington Post* (April 6, 2001).

34. For the text of the Mitchell Report, see *Ha'aretz* (May 6, 2001), English edition online.

35. For Tenet's effort to help work out an Israeli-Palestinian peace agreement, see his memoirs, George Tenet, *At the Heart of the Storm: My Years at the CIA* (New York: HarperCollins, 2007), chaps. 4, 5, and 6.

36. Cited in Aluf Benn, "Sharon Calls Powell after White House Blasts PM Comments," *Ha'aretz* (October 5, 2001) (in English).

37. For the text of Bush's speech, see *New York Times* (November 12, 2001). See also Serge Schmemann, "Arafat Thankful for Bush Remark about 'Palestine,'" *New York Times* (November 12, 2001).

38. Cited in Bill Sammon, "Bush Will Not Meet with Arafat," *Washington Times* (November 9, 2001).

39. For the text of Powell's speech, see "United States Position on Terrorists and Peace in the Middle East" (November 19, 2001), www.state.gov/secretary/rm/2001/6219.htm.

40. Janine Zacharia, "Bush Asking Arab Nations to Pitch in for a Secure Peace," *Jerusalem Post* (November 25, 2001).

41. Cited in *New York Times* (November 28, 2001).

42. See James Bennet, "U.S. Envoy Meets Arafat and Asks for End of Violence," *New York Times* (November 29, 2001).

43. Avi Machlis, "Israeli Bus Blast Casts Shadow on Peace Process," *Financial Times* (November 30, 2001).

44. Joel Greenberg, "Envoy to Middle East Assails Palestinian Militants," *New York Times* (December 1, 2001).

45. Cited in Lee Hockstadter, "Bomber in Bus Kills 15 in Israel," *Washington Post* (December 3, 2001).

46. Ibid.

47. Cited in Peter Herman, "Terrorists Kill at Least 15 in Israel," *Baltimore Sun* (December 2, 2001).

48. Clyde Haberman, "Arafat Demands Halt in Attacks against Israelis," *New York Times* (December 7, 2001).

49. For a discussion of this point, see David Frum, *The Right Man: The Surprise Presidency of George W. Bush* (New York: Random House, 2003), p. 256. Frum was a speechwriter for Bush from January 2001 to February 2002. See also Bob Woodward, *Bush at War* (New York: Simon & Schuster, 2002), p. 297.

50. Lee Hockstadter, "Arafat Arrests Three in Arms Incident," *Washington Post* (January 12, 2002).

51. Mary Curtius, "Hamas Takes Responsibility for Attack," *Los Angeles Times* (January 10, 2002).

52. Amos Harel, "IDF Plans to Hit More PA Targets, Voice of Palestine Radio Torched in Ramallah, Police Bombed in Tulkarm," *Ha'aretz* (January 20, 2002).

53. Todd S. Purdum, "Powell Says U.S. Will Grab Chances at Middle East Peace," *New York Times* (February 28, 2002).

54. The text of UN Security Council Resolution 1397 is on the United Nations Web site.

55. For Powell's comments, see "Excerpts from Powell's News Conference of March 29, 2002," *New York Times* (March 30, 2002). See also Tracy Wilkinson, "Israel Corners a Defiant Arafat," *Los Angeles Times* (March 30, 2002).

56. Woodward, *Bush at War*, p. 34.

57. Ibid.

58. Israel has been carefully cultivating the support of Evangelical Christians. The Israeli ambassador to the United States, Daniel Ayalon, regularly visited Evangelical churches to thank them for their support, which he has called "so important in this day and age"; cited in James Morrison, "Israel Gives Thanks," *Washington Times* (Embassy Row Section) (November 27, 2003). See also James Morrison, "Praying for Israel," *Washington Times* (Embassy Row Section (October 28, 2003), citing Ayalon speaking in an evangelical church in Tampa, Florida, where he stated, "The American Christian community is a bedrock of support for the State of Israel and its people."

59. Howard Kohr, executive director of AIPAC, called DeLay, the former House Majority Leader, "one of the more important, resolute, and outspoken supporters of Israel"; cited in Juliet Eilperin, "Mideast rises on DeLay's Agenda," *Washington Post* (October 16, 2003).

60. Cited in "Bush Slams Arafat but Sees 'New Attitude' in Some PA Leaders," *Ha'aretz* (May 26, 2002).

61. For the text of the Bush speech, see *Washington Post* (June 25, 2002).

62. Ibid.

63. The skepticism was reinforced in December 2002 when neoconservative Elliot Abrams was made Condoleezza Rice's deputy for Arab-Israeli affairs on the National Security Council. For a view of the evolving thinking of Abrams and his relationship with other neoconservatives, see Connie Bruck, "Back Roads: How Serious Is the Bush Administration about Creating a Palestinian State?" *New Yorker* (December 15, 2003).

64. Cited in Aluf Benn, "U.S. Telling PM That the Muqata Siege Undermining Plans for Iraq," *Ha'aretz* (September 29, 2002).

65. The text of the Road Map is found on the U.S. Department of State Web site (April 30, 2002).

66. For the text of the letter of the eighty-eight senators, see *Journal of Palestine Studies*, vol. 32, no. 4 (Summer 2003), p. 185.

67. See Elaine Monaghan, "Bush Praises Palestinian Leader's Courage," *Times of London* (July 26, 2003); Guy Dunmore, "Bush Attacks Israelis for Building of West Bank Wall," *Financial Times* (July 26, 2003); and Brian Knowlton, "Sharon Meets with Bush but Says Security Fence Will Still Go Up," *International Herald Tribune* (July 30, 2003).

68. Natan Sharansky, *The Case for Democracy: The Power of Freedom to Overcome Tyranny and Terror* (New York: PublicAffairs Press, 2004). See also Joel Rosenberg, "Two Great Dissidents: Natan Sharansky's Vision and President Bush's," *National Review* Online (November 19, 2004). For an early critique of the democratization program, see Thomas Carothers and Marina Ottoway, eds., *Uncharted Journey: Promoting Democracy in the Middle East* (Washington, DC: Carnegie Endowment, 2005).

69. See Yossi Beilin, *The Path to Geneva: The Quest for a Permanent Agreement 1996–2004* (New York: RDV Books, 2004).

70. For an analysis of Sharon's disengagement strategy, see David Makovsky, *Engagement through Disengagement: Gaza and the Potential for Renewed Israeli-Palestinian Peacemaking* (Washington, DC: Washington Institute for Near East Policy, 2005). See also Robert O. Freedman, "Sharon: The Evolution of a Security Hawk," *Midstream,* vol. 48 , nos. 6–7 (May-June 2004).

71. Cited in Nicholas Kralev, "White House Urged West Bank Action," *Washington Times* (August 13, 2004).

72. All quotations from Bush's and Sharon's speeches are taken from *Ha'aretz* (April 15, 2004).

73. Cited in Nathan Guttman, "President Bush Woos the Jewish Vote," *Ha'aretz* (August 12, 2004).

74. Cited in Nicholas Kralev, "Anti-Semitism Office Planned at State Department," *Washington Times* (October 14, 2004). See also "State Department Opposes Anti-Semitism Bill," *Washington Post* (October 14, 2004).

75. Cited in Nathan Guttman, "Kerry and Bush Send in Top Guns to Woo AIPAC," *Ha'aretz* (October 26, 2004).

76. The agreement was published on the Associated Press Web site (March 17, 2005).

77. Author's interview with Mahmoud Abbas, Ramallah, June 26, 2005.

78. In a *Financial Times* interview on April 20, 2007, Rice clung to the democratization policy, stating, "I'll choose elections and democracy, even if it brings to power people that we don't like. . . . Without reform and democratization you're going to have a false stability in the Middle East which will continue to give rise to extremism"; interview, "What the Secretary Has Been Saying," on the US State Department Web site.

79. Hamas leader Mahmoud Zahar said Hamas would not renounce the right to armed resistance against Israel to keep the money flowing from Europe and the United States and stated, "I'm sure Israel will disappear as the Crusaders and other empires disappeared. All of Palestine will become part of the Arab and Islamic land—as the Koran promised"; cited in Paul Martin, "Leader Likely to Cut Ties with Israel," *Washington Times* (January 27, 2006).

80. Cited in Greg Meyer, "Suicide bombing in Israel Kills 9; Hamas Approves," *New York Times* (April 18, 2006).

81. Iran's policy toward Israel is discussed in Robert O. Freedman, *Russia, Iran, and the Nuclear Question: The Putin Record* (Carlisle, PA: Strategic Studies Institute of the U.S. Army War College, 2006), pp. 32–36.

82. Cited in Bernard Reich, "The United States and Israel: A Special Relationship," in David W. Lesch, ed., *The Middle East and the United States,* 4th ed. (Boulder, CO: Westview Press, 2007), p. 221.

83. Cited in Yochi Drazin., "Battle in Middle East Widens U.S.-Russia Rift," *Wall Street Journal* (July 16, 2006).

84. Cited in Marina Grishina and Yelena Suponina, "Qana Tragedy—Russia and UN Urge Immediate Cease-Fire in Lebanon," *Vremya Novostei* (July 31, 2006).

85. See the chapter by Elli Lieberman in this book.

86. See Hassan M. Fattah, "Accord Is Signed by Palestinians to Stop Feuding," *New York Times* (February 9, 2007).

87. See Harvey Morris, "Israel Pleads for Hamas to Remain in Isolation," *Financial Times* (March 19, 2007).

88. See the report by Glenn Kessler, "Secretary Rice to Try New ME Formula," *Washington Post* (March 23, 2007).

89. Cited in Avi Issacharoff, "Hamas, PRC Say Will Act to Torpedo New U.S. Benchmarks for Israel," *Ha'aretz* (May 5, 2007).

90. These statements by Olmert are analyzed in Shmuel Rosner, "Is the Democratic-Israeli Disengagement Getting Out of Hand?" *Ha'aretz* (April 20, 2007), and Nathan Guttman, "Dems Warn Olmert about Playing Politics," *Forward* (April 20, 2007).

91. Cited in Ze'ev Schiff, "U.S. Envoy Denies Pressure on Israel Not to Engage in Talks with Syria," *Ha'aretz* (May 21, 2007).

92. Cited in Reich, "The United States and Israel," p. 224.

PART THREE

Israel's Security Challenges

13

Existential Threats to Israel

Steven R. David

VIRTUALLY ALONE AMONG the countries of the world, Israel is threatened with annihilation. For some, annihilation of Israel means the physical destruction of the state in which its major cities and population are slated for destruction. For others, the threat is more subtle, not involving any immediate destruction but eliminating the Jewish nature of the state. Whatever the form of the threat may be, living under the cloud that its existence may one day end has had a profound impact on Israeli behavior, as well as on the actions of other states, both friends and foes. These threats are important for those who care about the fate of Israel, since they one day may be carried out. They also carry weight because even when the threats are not implemented, their very presence affects the dynamics of Middle East politics. It is impossible to understand the Arab-Israeli conflict, Israel's relations with the rest of the world, and American policy toward Israel without taking into account the impact of those who challenge Israel's right to exist as a Jewish state.

This chapter begins with a discussion of threats made against Israel's existence by various groups and individuals. Next, an overview of existential threats throughout history is considered, including some of the positive effects of such threats. The nature of the threats to Israel's existence is then considered, including demographic challenges to Israel's Jewish majority, the possibility of Israel's being overwhelmed in a conventional assault, and the prospect of Israel's being attacked with nuclear weapons. The chapter concludes with an assessment of the dangers presented by each of these threats.

Threatening Israel's Existence

From its very inception, Israel's existence has been called into question. When Israel agreed to the UN partition plan and declared independence on May, 15, 1948, it was immediately invaded by its Arab neighbors, which made no secret of their intention to destroy the Jewish state.[1] The Israeli victory in that conflict, though ensuring its continued survival, did not end its neighbors' efforts to eradicate Israel. The 1948 war ended with a cease-fire, not a peace treaty, as Israel's Arab neighbors vowed to continue the struggle to eradicate Israel when the balance of power proved more fortuitous. That time came in 1967, when Egypt, Jordan, and Syria formed an alliance that, with the backing of the Soviet Union, convinced Egypt's leader, Gamal Nasser, that the time was right to destroy Israel. Nasser and his allies made no secret of the fact that the annihilation of Israel was their goal, prompting Israel to launch a strike on the Arab air forces in one of the very few cases of successful military preemption in history.[2] Following Israel's success, in what became known as the Six Day War, the Arab states reinforced their refusal to accept Israel's existence when, in a conference in Khartoum, Sudan, they declared that they would not negotiate with Israel, make peace with Israel, or recognize its right to exist.

Over time, at least the stated attitudes of some of Israel's neighbors have become more moderate, no longer openly seeking its destruction. Following Egyptian president Anwar Sadat's historic visit to Jerusalem in 1977, Egypt signed a peace treaty with Israel in 1979, and Jordan followed suit in 1994. More remarkably, in 2007 the twenty-two members of the Arab League agreed to accept a 2002 Saudi initiative that offered Israel recognition and peace if it would withdraw from lands occupied in the 1967 War, accept the establishment of a Palestinian state with East Jerusalem as its capital, and agree to a just solution to the Palestinian refugee problem. Although Israel has refused to accept these terms, the Arab world's very offer to live in peace with Israel as a Jewish state is noteworthy in itself. The rhetoric of most Arab leaders has been consistent with the Saudi initiative, focusing on ending Israel's occupation of Arab lands and the creation of a Palestinian state, but not calling for the destruction of Israel.[3]

Despite the grudging acceptance of Israel, however, threats to its existence persist. Countries and nonstate actors continue to call for the end of Israel, often in an explicit and harrowing manner. Especially alarming is that many who seek the destruction of Israel represent powerful countries or have large followings, raising the possibility that their threats are not simply idle boasts but may one day be carried out. Prominent among these threats are those made by the president of Iran, Mahmoud Ahmadinejad. In a 2005 conference, appropriately titled "World without Zionism," Ahmadinejad declared, "I have no doubt that [we] will soon wipe this scourge of shame [Israel] from the Islamic world. This can be done. . . . The issue of Palestine will only be resolved when all of Palestine comes under Palestinian rule, when all the refugees return to their homes, and when a popular government chosen by this nation takes the affairs in its hands. Of course, those who have come to this land from far away to plunder this land have no right to participate in the decision-making process for this nation."[4] As if to make sure there was no room for doubt, at the same conference the Iranian president invoked statements by the Ayatollah Ruhollah Khomeini, the founder of Iran's Islamic regime, declaring, "As the Imam said, 'Israel must be wiped off the map.'"[5]

Another prominent voice calling for Israel's obliteration is the Islamic Resistance Movement (Hamas), established in 1988. Hamas surprised many by beating the secular Fatah in the 2006 parliamentary elections in the Palestinian territories, becoming the dominant party in the Palestinian legislature. The Hamas leadership continues to be bound by its charter, written in 1988, which unambiguously calls for the destruction of the state of Israel, to be replaced by a Palestinian state under the laws of Islam. The charter states, "Israel will exist and continue to exist until Islam will obliterate it, just as it obliterates others before it. . . . The Islamic Resistance Movement believes that the Land of Palestine is an Islamic Waqf [holy land] consecrated for future Moslem generations until Judgment Day. It, or any part of it, should not be squandered; it or any part of it, should not be given up. . . . There is no solution for the Palestinian question except through Jihad." As if to underscore its repugnance for Israel, the Hamas Charter blames Jews (not Israelis) for many of the world's ills, including starting World Wars I and II.[6]

Not to be outdone, al-Qaeda, on its emergence as a significant actor in international politics, added to the chorus of voices calling for Israel's demise. Bursting onto the world scene following the 9/11 attacks on the United States that it orchestrated, al-Qaeda has emerged as a major player in international politics, with thousands of fanatical followers in countries throughout the world. Though much of what it seeks remains shrouded in mystery, there is no doubting its views toward Israel. As the leader of al-Qaeda, Osama bin Laden stated in a message to the Americans in 2002, "The creation of Israel is a crime which must be erased. Each and every person whose hands have become polluted in the contribution towards this crime must pay its price, and pay for it heavily."[7] Osama bin Laden went on to argue that it is a religious obligation of Muslims to fight Jews in Israel—and wherever they live. Bin Laden said, "And whoever claims that there is a permanent peace between us [the Muslims] and the Jews has disbelieved what has been sent down through Muhammad; the battle is between us and the enemies of Islam." In a related context Bin Laden said, "It appears to us, from the writing of the Prophet, that we will have to fight the Jews under his name and on this land, in this blessed land which contains the sanctuary of our Prophet."[8]

Others have called for the end of Israel as a Jewish state without seeking the physical annihilation of its inhabitants. The linguist and leftist political analyst Noam Chomsky has repeatedly called for Israel to end its Jewish character, arguing that both Palestinians and Jews have an equal right to Palestine. In his view, it is impossible for Israel to be both democratic and Jewish while ruling over a substantial Arab minority. Chomsky's solution is to end Israel's Jewish identity by transforming the country into a binational state with equal rights for Arabs and Jews under a secular government.[9]

A similar view has been expressed by Tony Judt, a prominent historian at New York University. Judt argues that the problem with Israel is that it arrived too late on the world scene. By the time Israel was established, the notion that an ethnic or religious minority could impose itself on an indigenous population—a view that was popular in late-nineteenth-century Europe—had become unfashionable. Instead of narrowly based ethnopolitical states, the world has embraced individual rights and open frontiers, making Israel an "anachronism." Judt's solution, like Chomsky's, is to end Israel's existence as a Jewish state, and to replace it with a binational country in which Jews and Arabs would seemingly live in cooperative peace.[10]

While these arguments would, among other consequences, delegitimize most of the world's states, including all of the Arab countries, what is significant is that they have attracted a good deal of support. Therefore they represent an important strain of thought that, if fulfilled, would bring about the end of Israel as a Jewish state.

Existential Threats in History

The notion of threatening to destroy a country, and often succeeding in doing so, has a long and tragic history. In Europe, far from being unusual, the norm for centuries had been the destruction of states and other political entities. As the sociologist Charles Tilly notes, Europe in 1500 had some five hundred independent political units. By 1900, that number had been whittled down to around twenty.[11] Most of those that disappeared fell victim to wars of annihilation that proved all too successful. That such destruction occurred should come as no surprise. In a time where there was no international military force to ensure security, where countries had both the means and motivation to threaten one another, and where territorial expansion served to enhance a state's power, it was to be expected that the strong would swallow up the weak. While policies such as the balance of power served to lessen the dangers to some countries, existential threats proved effective even against major states, as the disappearance of Poland in the late 1700s and again in 1939 so vividly demonstrates.

Wars of annihilation, however, have declined markedly in the modern era, especially in the wake of the ending of the cold war. In part, the decline of wars that threaten the existence of states stemmed from the decline of international wars themselves. Wars between states used to be a very common occurrence. Between 1816 and 2002, there were 199 international wars (including colonial wars and "wars of liberation").[12] In the post–cold war era, from the 1990s through 2006, there were only three clear-cut cases of international wars: Iraq's invasion of Kuwait in 1990 and the two American interventions against Iraq (1991, 2003). The virtual absence of international wars eliminates what had been the most prominent threat to states in the modern era.[13] Moreover, since the end of World War II, norms against the destruction of states have become much stronger. Sovereignty has been enshrined as a near absolute norm, so that it is unacceptable to end states, no matter how weak and ineffectual they may be.[14] The result is that only a handful of countries have disappeared since World War II, and many more new states have been created.

It is, of course, good news that states are no longer in the habit of regularly disappearing, but it has not been an unmitigated blessing. Those countries that ultimately survived the brutal evolutionary process emerged as strong, coherent states. As Tilly famously argued, "War made the state, and the state made war."[15] Faced with impending destruction, leaders were forced to collect taxes in order to raise armies. They needed, therefore, to develop the bureaucracy and procedures to raise the revenues necessary to defend the state. The structures established for these purposes, if successful, persisted after the threat of war had passed, enabling the regimes to continue taxing their populace, a key requirement for a successful state. The threat of war also helped foster nationalism, a strong identification with the state. The natural clinging together of those under threat gives a sense of identity to otherwise disparate peoples. By creating efficient state structures and engendering a sense of nationhood to multiethnic populations, the threat and actuality of existential war played a key role in establishing today's strong European states.[16] Conversely, most of the countries in the contemporary developing world do not face existential threats and, partially as a result, have emerged as weak, ineffective countries. They are what Robert Jackson calls "quasi states, that is, countries with a flag, a seat in the United Nations and some control over their capital city—but not much more.[17] As Jeffrey Herbst argues, it is the *absence* of war threatening the existence of these countries that has enabled them to persist in such a vegetative condition.[18]

Just as the absence of existential threats has not been all good, where countries have been targeted for extinction some positive effects have resulted. The few countries in the developing world that have emerged as strong states—countries like Cuba, Vietnam, and South Korea—have all had to face continuing and pressing threats to their existence. To survive, they have had to develop a strength that translates into effectiveness across a wide range of areas, enabling the regimes to achieve what they seek far better than many of their peers. Precisely because of the threats they confront, these states have developed the revenue-raising mechanisms, the skilled bureaucrats, and the nationalist identity that set them apart from other Third World states. These benefits, of course, come at a high price: one day they may not be able to defeat the challenges to their existence and will be destroyed. Nevertheless, it is misleading and dishonest not to recognize the benefits of existential threats to those states that manage to survive.

Israel has certainly benefited from the threats arrayed against it. The invasion by five Arab armies following Israel's declaration of statehood in 1948 caused staggering casualties but also helped forge a common identity, a sense of community, and a fervent nationalism that few other newly minted countries have ever matched. Building on the foundation of the 1948 war, Israel has become a strong state, helped in its efforts by the recurring calls for its destruction. In times of relative peace, Israeli politics, always something of a blood sport, turn particularly vicious and bitter. Arguments between those who wish to give up the occupied territories and those who settle them get ugly. Disputes between the Orthodox and the secular reach a fever pitch, and relations with the Jewish communities abroad often suffer as debates over "Who is a Jew?" resurface. As soon as Israel is threatened, however, these conflicts abate, and Israel confronts existential menaces with a united front.

The tendency toward unity in the face of mortal danger is especially prominent in the Diaspora. Many have remarked on the intensity and effectiveness of Israel's supporters, particularly in the United States. Of course, other religious/ethnic communities have lobbied for their ancestral homelands, but rarely with the fervor of Israel's supporters. A major reason, undoubtedly, is that Israel's supporters recognize that the Jewish state might one day indeed be destroyed, a recognition that adds fuel to their efforts to forestall such a calamity. It would, of course, be far better for Israel and its supporters if its existence were not threatened, but it is still important to recognize that its struggle for survival has positive as well as negative implications.

Existential Threats to Israel

Despite the decline in existential threats, states have disappeared in modern times. The collapse of the Soviet Union not only brought about the end of the Soviet state but also set in motion events that led to the disappearance of

Czechoslovakia and Yugoslavia. In other countries, the national identity has been transformed, as seen in the emergence of black majority rule in South Africa. Some states have been swallowed up by their ethnic brethren in neighboring countries, as happened to South Vietnam and is threatening to happen in South Korea and Taiwan. Israel, however, is unique, in that it is the only modern country that is threatened not only by a loss of its founding identity, but by physical annihilation as well.

What, then, are the threats to Israel's existence? Of the many that are suggested, three stand out because of their plausibility. The first is the demographic threat to Israel's identity as a Jewish state. Second is the concern that Israel will be overwhelmed by its Arab neighbors (and possibly Iran) in a conventional assault. Third is the prospect of Israel's being attacked with weapons of mass destruction, particularly nuclear weapons, most likely by Iran or some extremist group.

The Demographic Threat

The demographic threat to Israel is simple and straightforward. Israel prides itself on being a democracy. Being a democracy means granting the right to vote to all citizens. If an Arab majority emerges within Israel's borders—whatever they are finally determined to be—Israel's status as a Jewish democracy will come to an end. If Israel allows the Arab population to participate in elections, presumably they will vote for an Arab leadership, thus ending Israel's claim to being a Jewish state. If Israel denies the Arab population the right to vote, it ceases to be a democracy. Whether Israel loses its democratic status or its identity as a Jewish state, an emerging Arab majority strikes at the heart of Israel's identity.

How realistic is it that the Arabs would constitute a majority in Israel in the near future? As one might expect, this is a sensitive and controversial question to which there are many responses. Israel's population in 2007 was approximately 6.4 million, including 187,000 Israeli settlers in the West Bank, about 20,000 in the Golan Heights, and around 177,000 in East Jerusalem. Approximately 76 percent of the Israeli population is Jewish and around 20 percent is Arab; the vast majority of the Arabs are Muslim.[19] The proportion of Jews to Arabs has remained remarkably constant since the founding of Israel in 1948. Given the nearly four-to-one ratio of Jews to Arabs, the notion of an Arab majority would seem to be far-fetched, except for several factors that call into question Israel's long-term Jewish majority.

The first area of demographic concern for Israel is that the Arab population is growing faster than the Jewish population. Demography, while having many complicated aspects, is relatively simple. The measurement of a population begins with a base number; then the number of births and immigrants is added, and the number of deaths and emigrants is subtracted.[20] Within Israel's Green Line (i.e., the pre–1967 borders of Israel), Jewish women average 2.7 births, and Arab women average 4.8. Within the span of a couple of generations, therefore, the emergence of an Arab majority is possible. The counter to this view has traditionally been that Jewish numbers will rise through the immigration of Diaspora Jews, what the Israelis refer to as "making *aliya*." Indeed, throughout Israel's history, successive waves of immigration have kept the Israeli majority intact. Soon after Israel's birth, some six hundred thousand Jews living in Arab countries left (or were expelled) from their homes and went to Israel, where they swelled the number of Jewish citizens.[21] The Jewish population also received a huge lift when approximately one million Russian Jews emigrated to Israel from the former Soviet Union, mostly in the wake of the communist regime's collapse.

Despite these surges, however, many argue that the days of large-scale emigration to Israel are over. The entire worldwide Jewish population is only around thirteen million. Of that number, approximately half already live in Israel, and much of the remainder (an estimated six million) live in the United States. American emigration to Israel has never been large, amounting to only a few thousand per year (many of whom later return to the United States). Barring some massive anti-Semitic outbreak in America, sources of major Jewish immigration from outside Israel no longer exist to make up for the higher Arab birthrate. The inexorable outcome is that sometime in the foreseeable future, Israel will have an Arab majority within the Green Line.

Making matters worse for Israel is the Arab population in the lands taken by Israel in the 1967 War. In terms of sheer numbers, the Palestine Central Bureau of Statistics estimated that in 2004, Gaza and the West Bank together had 3.8 million people. The bureau also assumed a growth rate (births plus immigration) of 4.94 percent, one of the highest in the world.[22] No wonder that in November 2001, the Arab Strategic Report, published by the Al-Ahram Center for Political and Strategic Studies in Cairo, wrote, "The Arabs of 1948 could become a majority in Israel in the year 2035, and they will certainly be a majority by 2048."[23] In another account, the British newspaper *The Guardian* noted that the US Population Reference Bureau estimates that Israel proper's population will double in forty-five years, the West Bank's in twenty-one years, and Gaza's in fifteen years, so that Palestinians will outnumber Jews in these three areas by 2020.[24] An Israeli demographer, Arnon Soffer, head of the geography department of the University of Haifa, agrees, arguing that if present trends continue, in 2020 there will be 6.3 million Jews in Israel (and the occupied territories), living with over 8.7 million Arabs. It would seem that in a very short time, Israel's Jewish identity will be called into question.[25]

Despite these trends, there is much to suggest that demographics do not pose an imminent threat to Israel's existence as a Jewish state. The high birthrate of Israeli Arabs today may not continue. Demographers point out that several factors, such as improving educational opportunities for women, making contraception more readily available, and bringing increasing numbers of women into the workforce, can all dramatically lower birthrates. All of these developments are taking place among Israeli Arabs and have already reduced the Arab birthrate, albeit less so among the Bedouin Arabs living in Israel's south. At the same time, the Jewish birthrate is rising, as Orthodox Jews, who typically have large families, make up a larger portion of the population. The result is a narrowing of the gap between birthrates, which delays even more the time when Israeli Jews have to worry about being a minority within Israel. Nor is it absolutely certain that waves of Jewish immigration have come to an end. Throughout Israel's history, many have claimed that large-scale Jewish immigration is over, only to be surprised by the latest surge of Jews seeking to make *aliya*. Nearly a million Jews remain in the former Soviet republics and in western Europe. A rise of anti-Semitism in Russia or France could well ignite another wave of Jews to emigrate to Israel.

It is true that the Arab population in the occupied territories brings closer the day when an Arab majority might emerge, but the nearly four million Arabs reported by the Palestine Central Bureau of Statistics as living in Gaza and the West Bank is almost certainly inflated. As an influential Israeli study noted, the Palestinian figures included over 300,000 Arabs living abroad, counted Jerusalem Arabs who had already been counted in Israel's population, assumed there would be net immigration into the territories (when more Arabs left than came in), and exaggerated the number of Arab births. As a result, instead of 3.8 million Palestinian Arabs, the true population figure is closer to 2.5 million.[26] Even more important, as Israel demonstrated by leaving Gaza in 2005, the demographic problems posed by the occupied territories can be eliminated if Israel ends its occupation. In one fell swoop, 2.5 million Arabs (the lower figure) would no longer be part of Israel's population. By returning to roughly its 1967 borders, Israel once again would push back the prospect of the emergence of an Arab population majority.

Aside from withdrawing from the occupied territories, Israel could agree to a territorial swap, in which portions of Israel within the Green Line inhabited primarily by Arabs (such as Umm el-Fahm) would become part of a Palestinian state in exchange for Israel's incorporating areas in the West Bank thick with Jewish settlements (such as Ma'ale Adunim). According to Soffer, this exchange would maintain the 80–20 percentage split in the year 2020 (with a Jewish population of 6.3 million and an Arab population of just 1.3 million) and beyond.[27] Creative solutions are also open to an Israeli government seeking to preserve its

Jewish majority. If a Palestinian state is created, Arab citizens of Israel could be given the choice of accepting citizenship in Palestine, without having to leave their homes in Israel. Instead, they could opt for permanent-resident status, which would give them the rights they enjoy now, but they would vote with their fellow Arabs in the Palestinian state.[28]

In sum, there are reasonable and humane ways to delay the challenge posed by Arab population growth in the Jewish state. At some point, an existential threat may indeed be raised by a soaring Arab population, but that day is far in the future. In the meantime, there are more pressing threats to Israel's existence that warrant close scrutiny.

Conventional Threats

It is certainly possible to imagine Israel's being destroyed by a conventional assault waged by its Arab neighbors and Iran. While Israel has a robust military, well trained and well led, its adversaries have an overwhelming advantage in sheer numbers of troops and equipment, and they are catching up qualitatively. Israel's military forces of around 170,000 troops, supplemented by some 400,000 reserve forces, is outnumbered by *each* of the militaries of Egypt, Iran, and Syria.[29] Israel's forces are also greatly outnumbered in numbers of aircraft, tanks, and artillery pieces by its Arab neighbors and Iran. Egypt alone, a country with which Israel has had four wars, has more tanks than and roughly the same number of artillery and warplanes as Israel. Moreover, the trends are not in Israel's favor. With oil selling for over one dollars a barrel, Saudi Arabia has embarked on a buying spree for new and ever more effective weapons. With Saudi F-15s based in Tabuk (despite promises not to base aircraft there), Saudi aircraft can reach targets in Israel in about six minutes. In terms of sheer military quantity, Israel's situation looks extraordinarily bleak.

The qualitative advantage of Israel is also being eroded. Since the Arab states (and Iran) pay in cash, they are able to purchase the most up-to-date technology for their arsenals. Syria, Egypt, and Saudi Arabia have been especially successful in upgrading their weaponry, especially combat aircraft and antiaircraft capabilities. This upgrading is especially worrisome to the Israelis, who rely on their air force to deter and defeat attacks. In many cases, particularly with regard to antiaircraft weaponry such as the SA-18s, the skill of the operator is not decisive. Just as Arab SAMs (surface-to-air missiles) negated Israel's air superiority in the opening days of the 1973 War and handheld antitank weapons stopped Israeli armor cold, those with rudimentary training will be able to challenge their better-educated Israeli counterparts in the twenty-first century. That the Arab military forces are improving the quality and training of their recruits only adds to the threat posed to Israel. The Summer 2006 Hizbollah-Israeli conflict clearly showed the ability of Arab forces to fight Israel to a standstill. The nightmare that Israel faces is a coalition of countries, similar to the alliance of Egypt and Syria in 1973, attacking together and overwhelming Israel's defenses, which lack any strategic depth. Such an attack would bring about the collapse of the Jewish state.

In spite of this alarming possibility, the prospect of outside invasion does not pose a serious existential threat to Israel. Part of the reason is the aforementioned overall decline in state-to-state warfare, which makes large-scale conventional conflict all but obsolete. This lessening importance of international war is mirrored in the Middle East. With the exception of Iraq, the Middle East has been a relatively peaceful region in terms of interstate conflict over the past few decades. As for Israel, which had been at the center of so much armed strife, it fought its last country-to-country war in 1973, in marked contrast to earlier times, when Israel fought wars in each decade from the 1940s to 1973.

The ending of the cold war does much to explain this time of relative peace, both globally and in the Middle East. The lessons of past wars, particularly the October war of 1973, have underscored the importance of having a superpower backer for resupply and political support before engaging in major armed conflict. With the collapse of the Soviet Union, combined with a strong American commitment to Israel's security, it is difficult to imagine the countries of the Middle East mounting an attack on Israel that would threaten its existence. Moreover, other factors that explain what historian John Lewis Gaddis has called the "long peace," such as the increasing importance of economic prosperity, the decline in the value of territory as a source of power, and changing norms regarding using force, also play a role in decreasing the likelihood of major conventional war in the Middle East.

Most important, Israel does not face a pressing existential threat from conventional attack because Israel is a nuclear power. It is estimated that Israel has around two hundred nuclear weapons as well as ballistic missiles, cruise missiles, and aircraft that are capable of delivering these weapons anywhere in the Middle East.[30] This robust nuclear force gives Israel an ironclad life insurance policy. It says to all would-be conquerors, "Even if you get lucky, even if you reach the point where you can overwhelm Israeli defenses and destroy the state, you cannot do so without incurring your own destruction as well." So long as the leaders of Israel's neighbors are rational, in the sense that they are sensitive to costs, they will not end Israel's existence knowing that they would be committing suicide in the process. Both because a conventional onslaught might not be successful and because even if successful could not be carried out without the attackers' suffering devastating retaliation, interstate war does not pose a major threat to Israel's survival.[31]

The Threat from Weapons of Mass Destruction

The greatest threat to Israel's existence comes from weapons of mass destruction. These weapons typically comprise biological, chemical, radiological, and nuclear arms. Biological weapons are living organisms that kill or maim. Some, like smallpox, are highly contagious, while others, such as anthrax, are frequently deadly. Under the right conditions, biological weapons can kill hundreds of thousands.[32] Only slightly less alarming are radiological weapons, so called dirty bombs. If radioactive material, such as cobalt or americum, is attached to a conventional explosive, large areas can be contaminated for years.[33] There are also chemical weapons, such as poison gas, that kill on contact or when breathed into the lungs.[34] Countries—and even more alarmingly, groups—throughout the Middle East either have these weapons or the ability to make them.

Although these weapons can inflict great damage, none, with the possible exception of biological arms, pose an existential threat to Israel. Rather than weapons of mass destruction, the political scientist Thomas Homer-Dixon more accurately calls them weapons of mass *disruption*.[35] Only five people were killed in the post–9/11 anthrax attacks in the United States, but offices in the Capitol Building in Washington were closed for months, mail service was drastically curtailed, and there was a heightened level of fear throughout America. Massive chemical attacks during the Iran-Iraq war caused widespread fear, but both states survived. There has never been a dirty-bomb attack, but most experts agree that if one occurs, the major cost would not be in lives but in the resulting panic. Similarly, if Israel were subject to a biological, chemical, or radiological attack, there would be much fear, and even panic, but the state would endure.

Nuclear weapons remain the only true weapon of mass destruction and the most deadly threat by far. Never before has so much destructive capability been concentrated in such a small package. A single nuclear weapon the size of a suitcase can obliterate an entire city in an instant. It is this prospect of *sudden* destruction that makes a nuclear attack so frighteningly plausible. Especially given the small size of Israel and the concentration of much of its population in the Tel Aviv–Jerusalem–Haifa triangle, a handful of nuclear bombs could devastate the country. If Israel's adversaries get nuclear weapons, Israel's survival would be called into question for the first time since the 1948 war.

Nuclear programs exist throughout the Middle East, notably in Egypt, Syria, and Saudi Arabia, but it is only in Iran that a program is on the brink of making actual nuclear weapons.

For nuclear weapons to be made, fissionable material in sufficient quantity has to be produced. The most common types of fissionable materials for bombs are plutonium and enriched uranium. Iran is well on its way to producing both types of material—no mean feat—thus creating the ability to produce nuclear weapons. In the first path, plutonium, a human-made element, is produced in nuclear reactors and then chemically separated in a special plant. Iran will soon have several nuclear reactors and the ability to separate the plutonium, which would give it a robust arsenal in a short time. The main obstacle to this path is that Iranian reactors are subject to nuclear inspection (Iran is a signatory of the international Nonproliferation Treaty (NPT), which mandates such inspection), so that it would have to violate the treaty in a manner that is likely to be made public should it seek to divert plutonium for nuclear weapons use. Iran might also choose to produce plutonium secretly, and its development of a heavy-water plant in Arak, which could supply a clandestine reactor with indigenously produced fuel, suggests that Iran is giving serious thought to this option. Whether through a public renunciation of the NPT or secret diversion, Iran has a growing capability of producing plutonium-based nuclear weapons.

An even likelier choice for Iran is to use enriched uranium to produce nuclear weapons. Uranium is a natural element that can be extracted from rocks or can simply be purchased on the open market. To make a nuclear weapon, however, natural uranium will not do. A nuclear bomb requires approximately 90 percent uranium isotope U-235, which occurs only 0.7 percent of the time in nature. The task, therefore, is to enrich or purify natural uranium (which is composed mostly of U-238) to achieve the 90 percent level of U-235 required for a functioning bomb. The most common method is to secure a large quantity of natural uranium, transform it into a gas, and then spin the gas in thousands of centrifuges linked together in a cascade. The process of spinning the gas gradually separates the heavier U-238 isotopes and allows the isolation and accumulation of enough U-235 for a bomb. Iran already has a large number of centrifuges and has announced it plans to build from thirty to fifty thousand of the machines. Since one thousand centrifuges can produce roughly enough U-235 for one bomb in a year, Iran might soon be able to produce thirty to fifty bombs each year. In addition, Iran has received assistance from the Pakistani nuclear scientist A. Q. Khan in making the necessary centrifuges to produce nuclear weapons. While Iran asserts it is building the centrifuges for "peaceful" purposes, few believe this claim. The very same technology required to enrich uranium for use in some nuclear reactors can, if the gas is spun a bit more, produce the highly enriched uranium needed for bombs. Most analysts speculate that Iran is only two to five years away from producing working nuclear weapons.[36]

Once Iran gets nuclear weapons, it will have little problem delivering them against Israel. Iran has ballistic missiles, such as the Shahab 3, whose range of fifteen hundred kilometers (about one thousand miles) threatens all of Israel. Iran could also use cruise missiles, launched from boats off Israel's coast in the Mediterranean, to strike at Israeli targets. Both ballistic and cruise missiles would be able to destroy their targets within minutes of launch. Perhaps most effective, Iran might employ militant groups such as Hizbollah or Hamas, with which it has close ties, to attack Israel. Hizbollah launched several thousand rockets into Israel proper during the Second Lebanon War in the summer of 2006, and there is little reason to believe it could not have launched a nuclear weapon if given the chance. Similarly, Hamas has sent thousands of Qassem rockets into Israel from Gaza, as well as dispatched hundreds of suicide bombers into Israel proper. By substituting a nuclear weapon for a primitive rocket or a suicide vest, Hamas could continue to strike out at Israel, only with far more catastrophic results. It is difficult to avoid the conclusion that once Iran gets nuclear weapons, its leadership will gain the ability to do what it says it wants to do, namely, end Israel's existence.

Responding to a Nuclear Iran

Israel can respond to a budding nuclear capability in several ways, all of which have serious drawbacks. First, Israel could attempt to prevent Iran from getting a nuclear weapon. Israel might rely on the international community to place economic sanctions on Iran and convince the Iranian regime that developing nuclear weapons would bankrupt its economy, which depends so much on world trade. This path, however, is not likely to succeed. Iran has many powerful friends, such as China, Russia, and France, which would complicate any international efforts to get it to change its course. Because Iran is a major supplier of oil and natural gas, most of Iran's customers do not want to see their sources of energy disappear, so they will continue to do business with Tehran and will resist any efforts at meaningful sanctions. While the United Nations has applied limited economic sanctions against Iran, there is strong resistance to any measures that would impede Iran's continuing to sell its natural resources. So long as there are willing buyers and the price of oil remains in the range of one hundred dollars per barrel, Iran's economy will remain safe even if Iran follows the nuclear path.

If economic moves are not likely to be effective, Israel could take direct military action to forestall Iranian nuclear developments. With midair refueling, Israeli F-15s are fully capable of launching bombing attacks against Iranian enrichment facilities in Natanz. Such attacks might delay Iranian efforts to manufacture nuclear weapons for several years, just as Israel's 1981 attack on Iraq's Osiraq nuclear reactor set back Saddam Hussein's plans for a nuclear capability. There are, however, serious drawbacks to an Israeli military attack.

Learning from Iraq, Iran has dispersed, placed underground, and hid much of its enrichment equipment, so it is not at all certain that an Israeli attack would destroy enough of the centrifuges to severely impair Iranian progress.[37] A large-scale Israeli raid would kill large numbers of Iranian civilians, inflame the Muslim world, and almost certainly produce a counterattack by Iran. Iran could also be expected to use its Hamas and Hizbollah proxies to launch strikes against Israel, which could easily escalate into a wider Mideast war. Finally, even if initially successful, an Israeli strike would have to be repeated time and time again to keep Iran from developing nuclear arms. At some point, such repeated attacks would become politically unsustainable, especially from a country that has nuclear arms of its own.

If preventing Iran from developing nuclear arms holds out little promise, Israel could rely on defending itself from a nuclear strike. Defense, the act of physically guarding against harm, holds much appeal, since protection does not depend on the decision of an adversary to strike or not to strike. Nevertheless, defense is a slender reed for Israel to depend on for its survival. Against Iranian ballistic missiles, Israel has the Arrow antiballistic missile system, which is designed to shoot enemy warheads out of the sky. Unlike the American antiballistic missiles, the Arrow contains an explosive charge enabling it to physically miss its target but still destroy an incoming warhead. Despite this capability, it is not at all clear that the Arrow would be successful in protecting Israel from an Iranian ballistic-missile attack. No country has ever deployed an effective antiballistic missile system, given the difficulties of "hitting a bullet with a bullet" and the various countermeasures adversaries can use, such as launching decoy warheads and jamming radar systems. More important, antiballistic missile systems are not reliable because the cost of misses is so catastrophic. What good is it to stop ten warheads if three get through to destroy Haifa, Tel Aviv, and Jerusalem? Even if the Arrow system worked perfectly, Iran could still attack Israel with nuclear weapons by nonballistic means of delivery, such as cruise missiles, aircraft, or simply the smuggling of weapons into Israel proper. Defense is necessary, but it is foolish to believe that any defensive system can protect Israel from nuclear attack by a determined adversary.

If prevention and defense won't stop an Iranian nuclear attack on Israel, the focus must be on deterrence. Deterrence is persuading an opponent not to do something it is capable of doing by threat of punishment. Nuclear deterrence worked well during the cold war. Both the United States and the Soviet Union had thousands of nuclear warheads capable of destroying one another in a matter of minutes. Neither country bothered to mount a serious defensive system, recognizing that it would not work.[38] Instead, the security of both countries was ensured through deterrence, that is, the knowledge that a nuclear attack would bring about devastating retaliation. Since no interest was worth committing suicide, no nuclear attack was ever launched, and both superpowers survived the myriad of crises that marked the cold war.

At first glance, it would appear that Israel could deter a nuclear-armed Iran the same way that the United States deterred the Soviet Union. Like the United States, Israel is believed to have a large and robust nuclear force that cannot be disarmed by a first strike. If Iran attacked Israel with nuclear weapons, the Iranian leadership would have to recognize that it was sentencing Iran to oblivion. Moreover, Iranian leaders would know that they could not escape retaliation by transferring nuclear weapons to a terrorist group such as Hamas or Hizbollah. Israel would assume that any nuclear attack came from Iran and would respond accordingly. Just to be sure, Israel could use scientific means to trace the source country of the nuclear weapon.[39] If the Iranian leadership is rational and not suicidal, it would seemingly refrain from launching a nuclear attack against Israel.

But what if the Iranian leadership is not rational, at least as the term is commonly understood in the West? There are suggestions, for example, that Iranian president Mahmoud Ahmadinejad believes that the destruction of Israel would be a transcendental good in itself, offsetting even the destruction of Iran and the loss of his own life. Ahmadinejad, it is said, maintains religious beliefs supporting the notion that the destruction of the Jewish state will pave the way for the return of the "hidden Imam" and thus usher in an era of paradise under Islamic rule. If Ahmadinejad truly believes this, and his beliefs are supported by others in the Iranian government in control of the nuclear force, then deterrence would have no meaning. Deterrence is effective only when the adversary to be deterred believes that the costs of acting outweigh the benefits. If no cost can be imposed on the Iranian leadership that is greater than the benefit of removing the hated Jewish state, then deterrence will not work. Iran will do what it is capable of doing, and that means a nuclear Iran will once and for all destroy Israel, consequences be damned.

It is, of course, far from certain that the Iranian leaders hold such fanatical beliefs or, even if some do, would act on them. Nevertheless, Iran's development of nuclear weapons places Israel in a horrible quandary. All of the choices available to forestall Iran's getting nuclear weapons either won't work or, in the case of a military strike, are fraught with risks. Allowing Iran to acquire nuclear weapons, however, places the ability to destroy Israel in the hands of those who have sworn they will do so.

Israel is surrounded by countries and groups that make no secret of their desire to destroy the Jewish state. The growth of the Arab population under Israeli control and the fear of conventional attack pose existential threats to

Israel, but in ways that can be managed for the next several decades. The acquisition of nuclear weapons by Iran, on the other hand, poses a pressing and immediate threat to Israel's survival to which there is no good response. Alone among the countries of the world, Israel's existence is threatened by forces that have the will and soon will have the ability to achieve their dream of a world without a Jewish state.

Notes

1. For an excellent overview of the 1948 war, see Nadav Safran, *From War to War: The Arab-Israeli Confrontation 1948–1967* (Indianapolis, IN: Pegasus, 1969), pp. 28–36.

2. On the problems of preemption, see Dan Reiter, "Exploding the Powder Keg Myth: Preemptive Wars Almost Never Happen," *International Security*, vol. 20 (Fall 1995), pp. 5–34; and Richard Betts, "Striking First: A History of Thankfully Lost Opportunities," *Ethics and International Affairs*, vol. 17, no. 1 (March 2003), pp. 17–24.

3. For an argument that Israel has not faced a threat to its existence since the 1948 war (due to Israeli conventional superiority and Arab disunity), see Zeev Maoz, "The Mixed Blessing of Israel's Nuclear Policy," *International Security*, vol. 28, no. 2 (Fall 2003), pp. 44–77.

4. http://www.iranfocus.com/modules/news/article.php?storyid=4164, accessed April 2007.

5. Fathi Nazila, "Wipe Israel 'Off the Map' Iranian Says," *New York Times* (October 27, 2005), p. A1.

6. For the text of the Hamas Charter, see http://www.mideastweb.org/hamas.htm, accessed April 2007.

7. Osama bin Laden, "To the Americans, October 6, 2002," in Bruce Lawrence, ed., *Messages to the World: The Statements of Osama Bin Laden* (New York: Verso, 2005), p. 162.

8. Osama bin Laden, "Terror for Terror, October 7, 2001," ibid., pp. 126, 127.

9. Noam Chomsky, *Peace in the Middle East? Reflections on Justice and Nationhood* (New York: Pantheon, 1975).

10. Tony Judt, "Israel: The Alternative," *New York Review of Books*, vol. 50, no. 16 (October 23, 2003), pp. 8–10.

11. Charles Tilly, "Reflections on the History of European State-Making," in Charles Tilly, ed., *The Formations of National States in Western Europe* (Princeton, NJ: Princeton University Press, 1975), p. 24.

12. *The Human Security Report 2005: War and Peace in the 21st Century* (New York: Oxford University Press, 2005).

13. Monty Marshall and Ted Robert Gurr, *Peace and Conflict 2005* (College Park: University of Maryland, Center for International Development and Conflict Management, 2005), p. 12.

14. This point has been made by, among others, Robert H. Jackson and Carl G. Rosberg, "Sovereignty and Underdevelopment: Juridical Statehood in the African Crisis," *Journal of Modern African Studies*, vol. 24, no. 1 (1986), esp. p. 3, and is a major theme of Robert H. Jackson, *Quasi-States: Sovereignty, International Relations and the Third World* (New York: Cambridge University Press, 1990).

15. Tilly, "Reflections on the History," p. 42.

16. In addition to Tilly, others who argue the importance of threats to national existence as engendering strong states include Jeffrey Herbst, "War and the State in Africa," *International Security*, vol. 14, no. 4 (Spring

1990), pp. 117–139; Joel Migdal, *Strong Societies and Weak States* (Princeton, NJ: Princeton University Press, 1988); and Jackson, *Quasi-States*.

17. Jackson, *Quasi-States*.

18. Jeffrey Herbst, "War and the State."

19. Central Intelligence Agency, *The World Factbook*, accessed at www.cia.gov/cia/publications/factbook/geos/is/html, p. 5.

20. Bennett Zimmerman, Roberta Seid, and Michael L. Wise, *The Million Person Gap: The Arab Population in the West Bank and Gaza*, Mideast Security and Policy Studies No. 65 (Ramat-Gan, Israel: Begin-Sadat Center for Strategic Studies, Bar-Ilan University, February 2006), p. 5.

21. An additional three hundred thousand went elsewhere, many to the United States and Canada.

22. Zimmerman et al., *The Million Person Gap*, pp. 9, 11.

23. Quoted in Jon E. Dougherty, "Will Israel Become an Arab State?" (January 12, 2004), www.newsmax.com/archives/articles/2004/1/11/124803.shtml.

24. Ibid.

25. Larry Derfner, "Sounding the Alarm about Israel's Demographic Crisis," *Forward* (January 9, 2004).

26. Zimmerman et al., *The Million Person Gap*, pp. 1–3.

27. Derfner, "Sounding the Alarm."

28. I am grateful to Professor Raymond Westbrook of the Johns Hopkins University's Department of Near Eastern Studies for this intriguing idea.

29. For numbers of forces and equipment, see *The Military Balance 2005–2006* (London: Institute of Strategic Studies, 2006), chap. 4.

30. Ibid., p. 192.

31. On the stabilizing role of nuclear weapons, including deterring conventional warfare, see Kenneth N. Waltz, "More May Be Better," in Scott D. Sagan and Kenneth N.

Waltz, eds., *The Spread of Nuclear Weapons* (New York: Norton, 2003), esp. pp. 32–33.

32. An excellent study of the background and future threat posed by biological weapons can be found in Jeanne Guillemin, *Biological Weapons: From the Invention of State-Sponsored Programs to Contemporary Bioterrorism* (New York: Columbia University Press, 2005).

33. On dirty bombs, see Peter Zimmerman and Cheryl Loeb, "Dirty Bombs: The Radiological Weapons Threat Revisited," Occasional Paper No. 54, Center for Strategy and Technology, Air University, Maxwell Air Force Base, Alabama.

34. On chemical weapons, see Jonathan B. Tucker, *Chemical Warfare from World War I to al-Qaeda* (New York: Pantheon, 2006).

35. Thomas Homer-Dixon, "The Rise of Complex Terrorism," *Foreign Policy*, no. 128 (January-February 2002), pp. 52–62.

36. For a solid, up-to-date assessment of Iran's nuclear capabilities, see the Web site of the Nuclear Threat Initiative, www.nti.org. See also *Iran: Nuclear Intentions and Capabilities, National Intelligence Estimate* (Washington, DC: National Intelligence Council, November 2007).

37. For the contrary (and minority) view that an Israeli attack against Iran's nuclear facilities might be effective, see Whitney Raas and Austin Long, "Osirak Redux? Assessing Israeli Capabilities to Destroy Iranian Nuclear Facilities," *International Security*, vol. 31, no. 4 (Spring 2007), pp. 7–33.

38. The recognition that an antiballistic missile system would not work was enshrined in the 1972 ABM Treaty, which limited each side to token defensive sites that could easily be overwhelmed. President George W. Bush abrogated this treaty in 2002.

39. On how countries can trace the source of a nuclear explosion through its isotopic identifiers, see "Preparing for the Worst," *Nature* (October 2006).

14

Israel's 2006 War with Hizbollah: The Failure of Deterrence

Elli Lieberman

STUDENTS OF INTERNATIONAL RELATIONS who are interested in the problem of deterrence must have been more than a little puzzled by statements made by Hizbollah's leader, Hassan Nasrallah, as well as by Israel's prime minister, Ehud Olmert, after the end of the Second Lebanon War in the summer of 2006. In an interview with Lebanese television NTV on August 28, 2006, Nasrallah said, "If I thought that the capture of two soldiers on July 11th would bring about this war I would certainly not have done that."[1] On September 4, Olmert indirectly replied, "It is clear now to every terrorist organization that they are dealing with a state which goes to war for two captured soldiers."[2] The puzzling aspect of these statements is that Nasrallah should not have been surprised by the Israeli reaction, and that Olmert's statement was made in conjunction with a disproportionate military response that was six years too late. These statements suggest a major Israeli failure in its application of deterrence, a rather surprising event given Israel's familiarity with and previously successful application of that strategy.

Israel is still undergoing a major soul-searching about many aspects of its conduct during the Second Lebanon War. This war is becoming one of the most analyzed wars in Israel's history, even more than the 1973 Yom Kippur War, which was one of the most traumatic wars in its history. A special commission, the Winograd Commission,[3] was established to study the preparedness and the conduct of the political and military leadership with regard to all

317

aspects of the war that began on July 12, 2006. The reason for the establishment of the commission was the great dissatisfaction in Israel with the outcome of the war. Surprisingly, however, one of the main issues missing from
the initial commission report is an analysis of Israel's decision to adopt a policy of containment and its decision not to use deterrence in the period from
its pullout from Lebanon on May 24, 2000, to the outbreak of hostilities on
July 12, 2006. The adoption of a policy of containment must be studied as
well, since it was a major policy failure that led to the July 12, 2006, challenge.

Interestingly, deterrence in this case failed not because, as is the case in most
deterrence failures, the necessary requirements for deterrence did not exist, but
because the strategy of deterrence was not properly applied. Amir Peretz, then
Israel's defense minister, was asked after the war who, in his opinion, was responsible for that situation. According to Peretz, "There was a conception
which was ongoing for many years. This conception is the responsibility of the
leaders who adhered to the conception and not those who activated it. I am in
favor of any type of inquiry, every commission should investigate [the policy]
at least over the last six years . . . at least six years, from the withdrawal from
Lebanon, if they had acted decisively when the three soldiers were captured in
2000 it is possible that we would not have reached this event."[4]

Analysts of Israel's security policies who begin their analysis on July 12, 2006,
and note Israel's disproportionate response have argued that "the trigger-happy
tendency of the Israeli political establishment"[5] and Israel's reliance on force are
the main impediments to peace and deterrence stability in the region. According to Zeev Maoz, Israel has been involved in displays and use of force during
most of its history, and this policy was "fundamentally misconceived."[6] According to Maoz, the use of force has not curbed Arab violence against Israel.

Others have argued that Israel's withdrawal from Lebanon signaled a weakness that encouraged Hizbollah to embrace violence.[7] According to Or Honig,
in the period between 1993 and 2006, and as a result of the Oslo process,
Israel abandoned its deterrence doctrine and adopted a new strategic concept
of *havlagah*, or restraint.

I will argue that in this case, Israel's reluctance to use force on the Lebanese
front, as prescribed by its long-standing deterrence doctrine, led to the failure
of deterrence and the need for a much larger war to reestablish it. Had Israel
followed its deterrence doctrine in this period, it is likely that the Second
Lebanon War would have been prevented altogether or fought on a much
smaller scale under more favorable conditions, at the time and place of Israel's
choosing. Thus, while many aspects of Israel's conduct of the war are and
should be thoroughly investigated, an evaluation and an analysis of Israel's
deterrence posture in the six years prior to the war must also be studied by the
Israeli political and military leadership because, as discussed below, a war of

such magnitude could have been prevented. Furthermore, had the Israeli political and military leadership had a deterrence framework in mind, such a framework would have provided a better guide to the decision-making process on July 12 on how to respond to the challenge by Hizbollah.

Any state must have the capability, interest, and resolve to create deterrence stability and deter challenges to its interests. But that may not be enough, and states must also follow through and apply a strategy of deterrence. When challenged, states must retaliate, and when retaliation fails, they must escalate. Ultimately, if and when escalation and attrition fail as well, states must go over the brink. As will be seen later in more detail, such a strategy was successful in 1956 on the Egyptian front when deterrence stability was established only after escalation and war. During that period, Israel's deterrence doctrine was developed, and it was later applied against other actors.

Not only did Israel have a solid understanding of and a successful experience with deterrence, but after the withdrawal from Lebanon the elements necessary for a successful application of deterrence against Hizbollah were known as well. Israel perceived correctly that Hizbollah was an independent actor acting primarily in its own interest. Israel also perceived correctly that Hizbollah was sensitive to its position in Lebanon and worried about a massive Israeli retaliation that would endanger this position. Syria, too, had no interest in a massive Israeli retaliation in Lebanon. And the Israeli intelligence community clearly understood that to create deterrence, Israel would have had to retaliate forcefully if Hizbollah did not play by the new rules of the game, which should have been established after Israel withdrew from Lebanon. Nevertheless, Israel did not tailor a deterrence strategy that addressed these sensitivities. Instead, Israel issued threats that were not always followed by action, it retaliated against Syria and Hizbollah but did so in a proportional, nonescalatory manner, or it just went through passive "days of battle" and/or "days of absorption." Israel resigned itself to border challenges in which Israeli positions were fired on and Israel either retaliated in kind or just absorbed the attacks without any retaliation.

The new rules of the game, or red lines, that were established after the Israeli withdrawal from Lebanon, and the rules that were enforced, were not the kind of rules that result in successful deterrence. Rather, the new rules of the game indicated that Israel was willing to tolerate low-intensity conflict, not always confined to the Shabba Farms region, as well as the kidnapping of Israeli soldiers. The new measure of deterrence success that was accepted was relative stability and calm. As for the kidnapping of soldiers, Israel showed that in return for her captive soldiers, it was willing to release many Lebanese and Palestinians from its prisons. Thus the July 12, 2006 failure should not have been a surprise, given Israel's conduct from May 2000 to July 2006.

The structure of this chapter is as follows: The first section briefly reviews the main elements of deterrence theory as it developed in the West during the cold war; it also describes how the incentives in the conventional and nuclear worlds are different. The next section describes Israel's perspective and practice of deterrence and summarizes the success and failure of deterrence in the Israeli case. What follows is a short review of Israel's policy in Lebanon since the 1982 invasion and the conditions that led to the decision to withdraw from Lebanon. Hizbollah's interests and strategy in response to Israel's decision to withdraw are examined. The chapter ends with an examination of Hizbollah's challenges and the Israeli response from 2000 to 2006. Finally, I examine whether Israel's deterrent reputation has eroded.

Deterrence Theory: Theoretical Considerations

The deterrence literature is extensive, and a review of the different schools in the deterrence literature is beyond the scope of this chapter.[8] The term *deterrence* refers to a rather simple and universally observed interaction in which one actor threatens another actor not to do something or to face strong punishment if the behavior continues. The threatened actor weighs the costs and benefits of its action, and if the costs outweigh the benefits, it refrains from that action. States use deterrence threats to influence the behavior of other states. They enunciate a set of interests they want to protect and commit themselves to defending these interests. The success of deterrence turns on the credibility of the threats. The key question is: What make threats credible?

The most important element is, of course, capability. The challenged state must have the capability to deny the challenger its objectives. The costs of an attack or a challenge are so great that the challenger decides to back down. If the defender cannot deny a certain action by the challenger, it has to be able to inflict such punishment that the challenger again decides that a challenge is not worth the costs.

Capability is, however, not enough. The balance of interests is also an important element in the decision-making process. A defender may have the capability to deny or punish a challenger, but the adversary may value the interests at stake enough to create a situation where the defender decides it is not in its interests to fight. Thus the defender must also have a strong interest in the conflict. Having the resolve to defend a particular issue is a function of the defender's capability and valuation of interest.

The defense of the homeland is the most obvious example of a situation in which a state will have the resolve to fight and defend itself even when the balance of capability does not clearly favor that state. Interests other than the defense of the homeland are more difficult to analyze. It is harder to establish and demonstrate the resolve to defend interests further removed from the immediate defense of the homeland, and here the balance of interests and the reputation a state develops in defending those interests become very important.

Defining the interests a state considers important is very critical. The more specific its goals are, the more clearly the target state will understand which challenges it will defend. Of course, it is important for the defender to communicate this information clearly to the adversary.[9] The state issuing the threat must also convince its adversary of its resolve.

A major element in making deterrent threats credible is demonstrating resolve. How does a state demonstrate resolve? Most of the literature dealing with the different strategies of demonstrating resolve were developed during the cold war when the main concern was showing resolve without risking escalation and war. Western strategists Bernard Brodie, Albert Wohlstetter, Herman Kahn, Henry Kissinger, and Thomas Schelling struggled with the question of how states demonstrate resolve in the nuclear world without losing control over escalation and ending up in unwanted and unacceptable war. Glenn Snyder suggested retaliating within the context of attrition and upping the ante as methods of demonstrating resolve.[10] The main theme in Western strategic thinking was demonstrating resolve in limited wars of attrition and graduated military exchanges within the confines of major restraint.[11]

Since both parties are concerned about controlling escalation and preventing nuclear war, these scholars were not able to suggest how a state establishes its reputation for resolve if the adversary responds in kind or even plans an all-out conventional war, knowing too well that neither side will escalate past a certain threshold, to avoid nuclear war.[12] The main concern, and the main obstacle to creating a reputation for resolve, was the fact that during such exchanges, miscommunications, misperceptions, poor control of battlefield situations, the fog of war, and just unintended accidents could lead to inadvertent escalation and the risk of nuclear war.[13]

Despite a concern about escalation control US deterrence theorists did advocate escalation dominance as an important element in devising a successful influence strategy. Possessing a dominant conventional as well as nuclear-war-fighting capability ensured that the opponent would eventually realize the futility and danger of escalation and would back down. Given the risk and prospect of inadvertent escalation and war, attrition and escalation dominance as tools to establish one's resolve reputation were never tested, and the focus for gaining a bargaining advantage in conflict shifted to the concept of the credibility of commitment.

Thus, in the nuclear realm, it became immediately clear that war was no longer an acceptable outcome. It became apparent rather quickly that in the nuclear world the state that would be most likely to win would not be the state that demonstrated resolve but the state that made a convincing case that it was precommitted to a course of action that would lead to an unacceptable outcome. The other state then was left with the choice of going to war or backing down, and rationality dictated backing down.

In the nuclear age, escalation can lead to nuclear war, and since war is so inconceivable, threats are made credible by the creation of commitments from which one can't back off. One concept developed by Schelling was that an actor escalates to the point at which its adversary cannot escalate further, and it then must choose war. Since war is not a rational choice, the actor is forced to back down, and the state that escalated wins. Another concept developed by Schelling was the interdependence of commitment strategy, where an actor that can make a convincing case that it cannot abandon its commitments wins. These concepts, while very important to the nuclear world, have little relevance to the conventional world.

In the conventional world the dynamic is different. War may be costly and may not be the preferred solution, but it is conceivable. Demonstrating resolve requires that an actor develop a reputation for toughness. By acting tough and risking or even fighting wars, an actor develops a reputation that separates it from a weak actor, who only tries to mimic the behavior of tough actors. Irresolute actors have impulse control problems, the tendency to prefer immediate gains at the expense of larger payoffs in the future, and they back down.[14] In conventional war, escalation and war are part of the elements that create resolve.[15]

In the conventional world the chilling effect of a possible nuclear war is absent. Leaders are not concerned about escalation control. The incentives push actors in opposite directions. If tit for tat fails, states are tempted to escalate to bring a challenge to a halt. And if escalation fails, going over the brink into an all-out war is not inconceivable. In the conventional world not only are states not restrained by fear of an all-out war but there are strong incentives to escalate and dominate the escalation ladder because resolute actors want to separate themselves from irresolute ones. Signals must be costly because any of the less costly signals in any interactions can be performed by less resolute actors as well. Needing to demonstrate resolve, states have to separate themselves from the less resolute actors who mimic their behavior. Thus there are strong incentives for states to escalate rapidly and go over the brink.

Deterrence in Israel's Strategic Doctrine

How did Israel use and apply deterrence, and how close was its deterrence doctrine to the concepts developed by Western strategists?

The foundation of deterrence theory in Israel was formed in the early 1950s, immediately after the creation of the state, by its political and military leadership: Moshe Dayan, David Ben-Gurion, Shimon Peres, and Yigal Allon. In the early 1950s Israel used disproportionate reprisals against civilian and military targets in the Arab states, and primarily against infiltration from Egypt, with the stated purpose of increasing the costs of that course of action and making it a less attractive policy choice.

In a famous 1955 article, Moshe Dayan, then chief of staff, articulated the underlying premises of that policy. The problem Israel encountered was that at the time it was unable to stop infiltration from Egypt, and Israel had no denial capability: "We cannot guard every water pipeline from explosion and every tree from uprooting."[16] What Israel was able to do was to forcefully retaliate and punish the Arab states for their infiltration: "The retaliation raids are designed to set a [high] price for our blood [a price] that no Arab village, army, or government would feel was worth paying."[17] Since Dayan concluded that Israel did not have the capability at the time to defend itself from every possible infiltration and thus could not deny the challenges from Egypt, retaliation was used as a strategy of punishment that forced Arab army commanders to evaluate whether the cost of not protecting the border was worth the humiliation they suffered at the hands of the Israelis.

The other elements of deterrence can be detected in Dayan's article.[18] One element is the development of a reputation for capability: "Clashes in the border war would determine how the Israeli soldier was perceived by the Arab public and military."[19] The other element was the cumulative effect of a reputation for capability.[20] As a result of Israel's demonstrating capability in many retaliatory acts, the Arab governments would be forced to first ask themselves whether their military could compete with the Israeli military and, in the long run, whether the destruction of the state of Israel was a realistic goal. Here is a demonstration of the cumulative effects of reputation on long-term deterrence stability, a topic to be discussed further. Thus retaliation aimed to create the right incentives for the Arab leaders to protect the border and abstain from further infiltrations, as well as to entertain doubts about the feasibility of destroying the Jewish state.

The deterrent-effect retaliation was not limited to proportional tit-for-tat exchanges. Tit for tat has, according to Maoz, a "built-in escalatory logic."[21] When tit for tat fails, there are incentives to escalate and move up the escalation ladder. The incentive to move up the escalation ladder exists for two reasons. First, an actor may actually want to provoke war and so wants to provoke a strong response from its adversary in order to have a justification to go to war.[22] Second, actors have an incentive to demonstrate resolve and to differentiate themselves from irresolute actors. In addition, they also need to make sure that the signal is clearly perceived and understood.

Israeli retaliation took the form of disproportionate retaliation.[23] The retaliatory attacks were large in magnitude and attempted to demonstrate capability and intent.[24] When the strategy of escalation dominance failed to stop infiltration across the Egyptian border, Israeli decision makers decided that only going over the brink would demonstrate Israel's resolve. As in the theoretical discussion, escalatory logic is inherent in this process because the defender needs to differentiate itself from less resolute actors that mimic the less costly behavior of tit for tat and even some escalation, but that are not willing to go to war.[25]

Reliance on the use of force through the use of retaliation, escalation, and war became the foundation of Israel's deterrence posture.[26] Throughout its history Israel applied retaliation and escalation against most Arab countries, as well as against nonstate actors that challenged it. Thus, during the early 1950s, Israel's deterrence policy was very much in line with the theoretical logic developed by Western deterrence strategists, and because it did not suffer the constraints imposed by the nuclear threshold, low-intensity warfare and wars of attrition ended in escalation and war.

Success or Failure in the Israeli Case

How successful was Israel's policy of deterrence? This is an important question because it is necessary to rule out the possibility that the reason Israel did not use a strategy of deterrence against Hizbollah was simply that Israel had learned in its fifty years of experience with deterrence that deterrence was not effective.

Indeed, some scholars look at the many wars experienced by Israel (1948, 1956, 1967, 1969–1970, 1973, and 1982), as well as the many long-term or unending low-intensity conflicts, as evidence that deterrence as a strategy does not work.[27] Elsewhere,[28] I have shown that the reason most analysts who study the Arab-Israeli conflict observe only deterrence failure is that they do not use a longitudinal perspective that captures the effects of deterrence over time. A longitudinal perspective enables scholars to detect periods of deterrence stability and how deterrence failures earlier in an enduring rivalry actually produced learning and long-term deterrence stability.

In the deterrence literature there has long been a debate regarding the discrepancy between the robustness of rational deterrence theory, on the one hand, and the rather weak empirical evidence for its propositions, on the other. The problem is that rational deterrence theorists, as well as their critics, have employed a flawed research design. Deterrence, which is a dynamic and causal phenomenon, was evaluated by studies that used "snapshots" of single deterrence episodes, focusing on crises and war to the exclusion of deterrence success. Rational deterrence theorists, while using better samples of deterrence success and failure, have relied on behavioral indicators of threats and thus have not completely solved the selection bias problem. Cases in which challengers contemplated an attack and refrained from a challenge because of a credible deterrent threat were excluded.[29]

When one looks at deterrence longitudinally, as in the Egypt-Israel case from 1948 to 1979 within the context of an enduring rivalry, one finds a better and more satisfactory explanation of deterrence outcomes. Despite the many deterrence failures, Israel's deterrence strategy produced long periods of deterrence success. The escalation period leading to the 1956 war led to a stable deterrence period between 1956 and 1967, and Israel was not challenged in that period even though the pressures on Nasser to take military action against Israel were very strong.[30] The 1956 defeat was a sobering learning experience for Nasser.[31] Similarly, the longitudinal perspective puts the deterrence failures in 1969 and 1973 in a different perspective. After the 1967 defeat Egypt learned that it no longer had the capability to challenge Israel in an all-out war and resorted to a war of attrition and a limited-aims strategy.

Thus the study of deterrence longitudinally leads to the counterintuitive finding that short-term deterrence failures may be a necessary condition for long-term deterrence success. States in an enduring rivalry and in a conventional world have to fight wars early in their interaction in order to prevent future wars. This statement would also apply to a new cycle of challenges. States need to fight or respond forcefully to clarify the balance of capability, interest, and resolve to overcome the costly-to-fake principle. As mentioned above, resolute actors need to separate themselves from irresolute ones. Their signals must be costly because less costly signals can also be performed by less resolute actors who mimic the behavior of resolute actors and try to create a reputation for resolve cheaply. Thus there are strong incentives for states that need to demonstrate resolve to escalate rapidly and go over the brink.

The longitudinal perspective is referred to in the Israeli discussion of deterrence as "cumulative deterrence."[32] In a review of Israel's deterrence practice over fifty years, Uri Bar-Joseph introduced a conceptual scheme that enables scholars to better understand the conditions under which different types of deterrence are more likely to succeed or fail.[33] Bar-Joseph argues that "strategic deterrence" (a threat to dissuade an opponent from initiating a general war) and "cumulative deterrence" (an attempt to influence the Arab states, through the combined behavior of all deterrence events, to conclude that the goal of destroying the state of Israel is not feasible) have been successful in Israel's history.[34]

That is not true, however, of other types of deterrence. Current deterrence (attempts to reduce or stop low-intensity conflict) and specific deterrence (attempts to deter the Arab countries from crossing red lines that threaten Israel's interests) do not have as good a track record. When the Arab states had reputational considerations that outweighed the military costs associated with retaliation, and when the targets were nonstate actors with little to lose and high interest motivations, most cases ended in Israel's failure. If one looks at current-deterrence interactions the success of these policies has been mixed.[35] According to Bar-Joseph, out of the eleven cases he identified, seven were failures. Retaliation failed against Jordan between March and October 1956, but the Israel-Jordan border became peaceful after the 1956 campaign. Retaliation failed against Syria between 1957–1967 and 1967–1970. It also failed against PLO (Palestine Liberation Organization) attacks between 1965 and 1967 from Lebanon, Jordan, and Syria; between 1967 and 1970 from Jordan; and between 1968 and 1981 from Lebanon.

It is important to note that while Israel was unable to end hostilities through its retaliatory campaigns, in two out of the four cases involving states the challenge stopped after Israel escalated and went to war, in 1956 and 1967.

Current deterrence was successful against Jordan between October 1953 and March 1956; against Jordan in 1970, when Jordan was compelled to take on the PLO; against Syria between 1956 and 1957, and again in 1970–1973; against the PLO in Lebanon in 1981–1982; and partially against Hizbollah.

Unlike in cases of strategic deterrence, where a challenge may occur as a result of uncertainty about both capability and will, in cases of current deterrence uncertainty about capability exists only very early in the interaction. Once challenges continue, they occur either because they serve some political function, despite the military costs associated with them, or because there is uncertainty about the defender's will to escalate the conflict—or simply because the challenger values its goals a lot more and is willing to absorb the costs of retaliation and escalation.[36]

For deterrence to succeed against state actors, the punishment must be disproportionate. For highly motivated nonstate actors, such interaction will evolve into long wars of attrition that can last until the challenger wins some tangible political gains and becomes less willing to risk those gains in future interaction. Egypt before the 1956 war is an example of the former, and the PLO and Hizbollah are examples of the latter. According to Bar-Joseph the evidence suggests that even nonstate actors in control of their territory are deterrable.

Two general patterns have important implications for the use of deterrence. First, the issue of capability, the most important issue in any deterrence encounter, was solved rather early in the Arab-Israeli conflict. Israel is perceived as more powerful, even though some uncertainties remained and emerged in later deterrence encounters. Most Israeli analysts tend to focus almost exclusively on the issue of capability, and in doing so they overlook the importance of the issue of interests and its effect on resolve. The Israeli tendency to focus on capability may have been justified in the early stages of the rivalry, but after the 1967 War, the balance-of-interests equation changed. It took Israeli analysts a long time to come to grips with the effect of the changed balance of interests on Arab states' decisions to challenge deterrence even when the issue of capability was resolved.

After 1967, the Arab states were dissatisfied with the status quo. If early in the rivalry they were willing to challenge deterrence for reputation considerations because they were not as certain about the balance of capability, once their direct interests (their territories) were at stake, they challenged deterrence in partial ways to recover their territories. Thus current deterrence failed in the early stage of the conflict, but once reputations for capability and will had been created, deterrence became stable. Current deterrence against nonstate actors, which are weak and have no control of territory, was not successful.

Israel's experience with deterrence suggests that while retaliation may not in many cases produce deterrence stability, when the balance of interests favors Israel deterrence does become stable once Israel goes over the brink. The most interesting finding of relevance to the situation in Lebanon is that a nonstate actor that is in control of its territory, military, and troops is a deterrable actor. Hizbollah had rather limited goals and risked losing many of its resources. A well-tailored deterrence strategy would have been successful.

The Deterrence Equation against Hizbollah

It is beyond the scope of this chapter to discuss Israel's entanglement in Lebanon.[37] However, to understand the current situation in the Israeli-Hizbollah deterrence relationship, a little background is in order. Israel invaded Lebanon in 1982 to destroy the PLO's state-within-a-state. The invasion led to a mixed outcome. While Israel was able to destroy the PLO and remove its threat from Israel's northern border, it created in the process a far more serious and formidable adversary: Hizbollah.

In 1985 Prime Minister Shimon Peres withdrew Israeli troops from all but a strip of southern Lebanon; however, the Israeli military also continued its presence there through its allies, the South Lebanon Army and the Christian Maronites. The Shiite community, which had initially supported Israel in its effort to uproot the PLO from south Lebanon, turned against Israel and, in the intercommunal conflicts for power and influence in Lebanon, saw that their strength and influence within Lebanon were growing in response to their conflict with Israel.

Until 1992, when Hizbollah leader Abbas Mussawi was assassinated by Israel, Hizbollah's attacks on Israeli forces in Lebanon were relatively mild.[38] Hassan Nasrallah, the new Hizbollah leader, was more militant and escalated Hizbollah's attacks on Israeli forces.[39]

Israel tried to contain the power of Hizbollah in south Lebanon in two separate operations: Operation Accountability in 1993 under Yitzhak Rabin and Operation Grapes of Wrath in 1996 under Peres. However, these operations failed to undermine Hizbollah's power and ability to challenge Israel. These campaigns led to an Israeli-Hizbollah agreement not to attack each other's civilian populations, but Hizbollah's attacks on Israeli forces within Lebanon continued.

Syria's interest was to keep the situation on the Lebanese border unresolved so it could have a lever to force Israel to come to the negotiating table and resolve the Golan Heights issue.[40] When Benjamin Netanyahu was elected the Israeli prime minister and all negotiations broke off, the Syrian position on Lebanon was that as long as the issue of the Golan Heights was unresolved, it would not support a resolution of the conflict in Lebanon, and it would use this conflict to put pressure on Israel to change its policy on the Golan Heights.[41]

Daily Israeli casualties in Lebanon created strong pressures within Israel to withdraw. In February 1997 two Israeli helicopters that were ferrying troops to south Lebanon collided, and seventy-three Israeli soldiers died. In September 1997, in a raid on Ansariya, eleven soldiers from an elite commando unit died. These events marked a turning point in the debate within Israel about whether it should continue to stay in south Lebanon until a political and a security agreement was reached with Lebanon and/or Syria, or whether it should unilaterally withdraw from Lebanon.

The Debate on Unilateral Withdrawal

Two conflicting proposals were put forward to deal with the Lebanese situation. The opponents of withdrawal argued that a unilateral withdrawal would not solve the problem, since Syria's intentions were to continue to challenge Israel and the fighting would continue. They also argued that the Lebanese government was too weak and that Hizbollah had called for a jihadist war that included not only south Lebanon but "occupied north Palestine" as well, and Israel's northern settlements would be under attack.[42]

In addition, opponents of unilateral withdrawal argued that unilateral withdrawal would create the impression in the Arab world in general and in Palestinian and Hizbollah circles in particular that Israel was weak, and its reputation for resolve would suffer.[43]

Most senior military officers opposed unilateral withdrawal.[44] Israel Defense Forces (IDF) intelligence warned that Syria would "do everything it could to heat up Lebanon and inflame the entire sector."[45] And head of IDF military intelligence Major General Amos Malka and head of intelligence research division Major General Amos Gilad argued that both Syria and Iran had an interest in perpetuating the conflict and would press Hizbollah to continue with its attacks.[46]

Proponents of unilateral withdrawal argued that Hizbollah felt it could legitimately attack Israel as long as Israel was perceived as an occupier.[47] Once Israel withdrew from south Lebanon, there would no longer be a justification for Hizbollah attacks, and Israel would be able to assume the moral high ground. In turn, Israel would be able to punish Hizbollah's transgressions more forcefully and with international support.[48] After a withdrawal, the Lebanese population might also turn against Hizbollah if it perceived that Hizbollah was responsible for Israeli retaliations. Syria, in turn, would lose a tool of leverage over Israel.[49]

During the 1999 election campaign Ehud Barak announced that, if elected, he would pull Israeli troops from Lebanon within a year, whether there was an agreement with Syria or not.[50] Barak argued that once Israel was out of Lebanon, there would be no reason for challenges by Hizbollah, and that any such challenges, should they occur, would not be legitimate and could be met with a very strong response that would undermine the incentives for any further challenges. Once in office Barak ordered the Israeli army to withdraw from Lebanon, and on May 24, 2000, Israel completed the withdrawal. Whether withdrawal would lead to deterrence stability, and whether Hizbollah was deterrable, depended on Hizbollah's goals and interests.

Hizbollah's Interests

Hizbollah's interests are first and foremost to survive as an organization and to create and cement the conditions necessary for such survival as a viable actor in Lebanon and the Middle East.[51] Surviving militarily and politically means balancing many forces, which have sometimes pulled the organization in different directions. Short of establishing a Shiite Islamic republic in Lebanon, Hizbollah would like to control the Lebanese government as much as possible. Second, Hizbollah would like to be accepted by the larger Lebanese society. Hizbollah has used challenges against Israel to justify the organization's need to survive as a powerful and independent organization. Hizbollah needs an enemy to survive politically as an independent entity. Thus it has challenged Israel and championed the Palestinian cause.[52] It has also served Syrian[53] and Iranian[54] interests to continue to give Hizbollah military and economic support. Sustaining the conflict, however, which is crucial to the organization's survival, entails the risk of massive Israeli retaliation, which could undermine Hizbollah's position in Lebanon.[55]

Relinquishing its armaments to a centralized Lebanese government threatens Hizbollah's ability to act independently in its own interests. Once it can no longer serve Syrian or Iranian interests even when these interests conflict with Lebanese interests, Hizbollah risks losing its financial and military support and becoming a weaker actor in Lebanese politics. Hizbollah has to challenge Israel to keep maintaining the support of its patrons so it can survive as an organization.

Hizbollah has to walk a fine line between challenging Israel, a prerequisite for its survival as an independent organization within Lebanon, and alienating its supporters in the Lebanese government. Before the Israeli withdrawal from Lebanon, the Lebanese supported Hizbollah's position. After the withdrawal, a challenge to Israel risked massive Israeli retaliation, and Lebanese leaders argued that Hizbollah's actions could become counterproductive and harm Lebanese interests.[56]

According to Martin Kramer, Hizbollah uses force to gain power in Lebanon but does make cost-benefit calculations.[57] While some believe that Hizbollah was emboldened by the Israeli withdrawal from Lebanon and was led to miscalculate its true capability in achieving its pronounced goals, others see the organization as being very pragmatic. It uses limited force for political goals and in the right political circumstances. It knows its limits. Hizbollah's goals are to sustain the political situation that is most likely to serve its purpose of using force to maintain its organization intact. Thus Hizbollah goals are to keep the Palestinian conflict unresolved, to support Syria but interfere with Syrian attempts to settle its conflict with Israel, to entangle the United States in Iraq, to serve Iranian interests in Iran's conflict with the United States, and to keep Lebanon weak.

Within Lebanon Hizbollah is active in supporting its Shia constituency and in promoting Lebanese reconstruction. Hizbollah has invested in the education of the Lebanese population, is providing for its medical needs, and cares about Lebanese reconstruction and the importance of tourism to Lebanon.

Hizbollah has strong interests in Lebanon's economy and tourist industry, since economic success enables Hizbollah to provide social services to its constituency and to gain legitimacy. The flip side is that any action undertaken by Hizbollah that might undermine the Lebanese economy would hurt Hizbollah's legitimacy. Hizbollah's activity on the Lebanese-Israeli border had the potential of endangering Lebanese reconstruction efforts.[58]

Given Hizbollah's interests and intentions, it is clear that Israel's decision to withdraw from Lebanon had a major effect on Hizbollah, as well as on Syria and Iran. Obviously Hizbollah's and Syria's interests more directly, and Iran's interests indirectly, were not served by Israel's withdrawal. The Israeli withdrawal made it harder for Hizbollah to challenge Israel without risking a full military retaliation, which was not in the interest of any of the parties involved.

Hizbollah needed an opening for a legitimate resistance and found it in Israel's decision not to withdraw from the Shabba Farms area. Shelling at Har Dov three days before the Israeli withdrawal was completed was an interesting signal of things to come. Hizbollah was arguing that the area at the foot of the Golan Heights called the Shabba Farms is Lebanese territory, and that therefore it was legitimate for them to continue to fight Israel until all that land was returned. Israel maintained that the land belonged to Syria, had been captured from the Syrians during the Six Day War, and would be returned to Syria after a negotiated peace settlement was reached between Israel and Syria. The UN sided with Israel on this matter.

In addition to the Shabba Farms issue Hizbollah began to use the prisoners held by Israel as an issue that justified continued attacks on Israeli forces. Nasrallah said his forces would continue to fight until Sheikh Abdel Karim Obeid and Mustafa Dirani were released from prison in Israel. He also said that the villages in northern Israel that he claimed to be Lebanese (Hunin, Malikiya, Saliha, and Tarbikha) had to be returned to Lebanon. Nasrallah argued that if the Israelis stayed in the Shabba Farms and kept any Lebanese prisoners, Hizbollah would consider the Israeli withdrawal incomplete and would have to continue the fighting to liberate their country.

While an argument can be made that the Shabba Farms area should have been considered for a return to Lebanon (or Syria), it immediately becomes clear that by mentioning the villages inside Israel, Hizbollah created a situation in which Israel had little incentive to consider the Shabba Farms issue. The demand of the villages inside Israel proper clearly made it impossible for Israel to act in a way that would completely delegitimize Hizbollah's claims. Israel's withdrawal, while not addressing every single Hizbollah claim, was clearly a major move that changed the balance-of-interests equation. Israel now held the moral high ground, and Hizbollah understood the implications of this position and tried to figure out ways to resist it.

While officially not recognizing the UN Blue Line articulated in UN Resolution 425, Hizbollah did accept the demarcation with the exception of the Shabba Farms area, which it considered occupied territory. Nasrallah announced in April 2002 that Hizbollah would respect the demarcation. Lebanon demanded the Shabba Farms on April 16, 2000, and Nabih Berri, chairman of the Lebanese parliament at the time, claimed that the resistance would continue until that area was returned to Lebanon. Israel's position was that the area is Syrian and will be negotiated between Israel and Syria during peace talks based on UN Resolution 242. Lebanon claimed that Syria had given the area to Lebanon in 1951.

Israeli Deterrent Threats

Once Israel withdrew, did Israel issue threats clearly and did Hizbollah perceive them correctly? Israel issued clear threats in case its withdrawal was misinterpreted as weakness. In interviews for the approaching Israeli independence day, Chief of Staff Shaul Mofaz said, "And after we deploy, if Hizbollah attempts to harm IDF soldiers or threatens to endanger the Northern settlements, I will propose that we retaliate with all our might."[59] He excluded returning to Lebanon to occupy a security zone but emphasized, "The moment we get out of the security zone and leave Lebanon there is no pretext for anybody to continue the guerilla actions against us. I don't think we can accept or be silent over a situation which endangers the residents of the North and strikes at IDF soldiers."[60]

Israel's threat was a specific deterrent threat. It attempted to persuade the Hizbollah to avoid taking specific actions aimed at changing the status quo, and it threatened that such action would trigger a military reaction and might even imply war. In addition to the specific threat, Israel's deterrence posture has always been that low-level warfare is a red line that could lead to an all-out war. Did Hizbollah and other relevant actors perceive the Israeli threat clearly? The Israeli threat was clearly perceived and understood by Lebanon and Hizbollah. The Lebanese, Syrian, and Hizbollah leaders actually were concerned that Israel would use any incident, minor as it might be, as a reason to retaliate forcefully: "The Israelis are saying they will turn the region into a living hell if even a single one of their soldiers or civilians was hurt."[61]

Hizbollah was clearly aware of Israel's ability to hurt the Lebanese economy and its tourist industry. According to Hussein Asgha, Hizbollah's leader, Hassan Nasrallah, is "a very cautious rational, calculating, measured, and pragmatic leader who not only knows the weaknesses of his enemy but also the limits of his and his party's power."[62] Secretary Nasrallah stated, "We have no illusions. We are very familiar with the limitations of our power. . . . we are not . . . capable of stopping the Israelis from crashing across the borders."[63]

What Should Israel's
Deterrence Policy Have Been in Lebanon?

What should Israel's strategy have been after its unilateral withdrawal, given Hizbollah's goals and strategy? Hizbollah wanted to keep itself part of the

Lebanese state system and did not want to take actions that would undermine it. Israeli intelligence evaluations before the withdrawal noted that "neither Syria, Iran, nor Hizbollah is interested in civilian destruction in Lebanon, therefore they will try to operate without supplying Israel with too many 'pretexts' for escalating and damaging the Lebanese infrastructure."[64] In 2002, Research Division Brigadier General Yossi Kuperwasser argued that Hizbollah would have to act "in the realm of deep legitimacy," meaning it could not create a crisis that would turn the Lebanese population against it.[65]

In an Israeli intelligence document, Israel's head of the Intelligence Research Division, Major General Amos Malka, realized that the creation of a deterrence regime would require confrontation and escalation to demonstrate that, for deterrence to succeed, there must be a determination to implement it. According to Malka, "I expect that an attempt to create such deterrence would entail confrontation, escalation, and loss of life in order to demonstrate that behind the idea of deterrence stands the determination to realize [it]."[66] The question was what level of violence Israel would tolerate. Would one soldier's being killed every few weeks be perceived as a tolerable level of activity, or would massive retaliation be required to bring the killing to a stop? Under such a scenario Malka doubted that Israel would have the resolve to create a strong deterrent. Malka was concerned that Hizbollah would use "salami tactics" to challenge deterrence without creating a strong enough pretext for a massive Israeli retaliation.

Thus it was clear that since a new situation was being created, Israel had to establish new red lines of acceptable behavior. And should there be challenges, tests, and escalations beyond a certain level of tolerable cost, Israel would have to apply deterrence.

But who should be the target of deterrence? Should it be Hizbollah or Syria? Israel had two options, depending on the assumptions about who would be more deterrable: Syria or Hizbollah. One school of thought within Israel argued that Israel had lost its deterrent capability against Hizbollah, that is, its tactical deterrence against irregular forces. Thus Israel would have to reestablish deterrence in Lebanon by issuing explicit threats against Syria, and Barak and Mofaz did just that by threatening to attack Syria if challenged in Lebanon.[67] Israel, they felt, had to reestablish its deterrent power against the Syrians, a strategic deterrent against a state that had something to lose.[68]

The problem with this approach was that, first, it assumed that Hizbollah was acting on Syria's instructions and did not have its own independent set of goals. And second, it assumed that Syria had control over Hizbollah's actions and had the will to stop it if necessary.

Syria did have some leverage over Hizbollah. According to some Hizbollah sources, the Syrian general Ghazi Kan'an, the head of Syrian intelligence in

Lebanon, who had great influence in Lebanon, was instrumental in convincing Hizbollah to respect the Blue Line. The head of Israel intelligence General Malka stated that Syrian threats had had a cumulative effect after a few warnings.[69] But at the same time there was equally strong evidence, as seen above, that Hizbollah was its own independent actor. Thus pressure on Syria had its limitations and was not as effective as pressure on Hizbollah.

As has been seen, Hizbollah was worried about its position and legitimacy in Lebanon, and this concern was perceived correctly by Prime Minister Barak. After the Israeli withdrawal Hizbollah's attention to Lebanese public opinion had risen. According to Uzi Dayan, "Hizbollah will not operate in a way that angers the Lebanese people."[70] If Hizbollah action provoked a serious Israeli response, Hizbollah risked losing support among the Lebanese people. Hizbollah was interested in brinkmanship but not in massive Israeli retaliation. Hizbollah was aware of its military limitations and had no illusions about what it could achieve against Israel. And in the end it had to be careful not to alienate the Lebanese population.

In an interesting case even before Israel pulled out of Lebanon, on June 24, 1999, Israel bombed an electric facility and bridges in Beirut in retaliation for Hizbollah activity in south Lebanon. Immediately after the Israeli retaliation, Hizbollah tempered its activity.[71] Ehud Barak noticed the importance of legitimacy in Hizbollah behavior: "You could see their obsession with legitimacy in each and every operation. . . . I understood that the legitimacy factor is more important than it seems.[72]

Was Hizbollah Deterrable?

Hizbollah was on a path to modernization and integration into Lebanese society. This process would have been hurt by continued attacks on Israel after Israel's withdrawal if Israeli retaliation hurt the Lebanese society.[73] The Israeli leadership understood what the requirements of deterrence were and noted Hizbollah's sensitivities. They could have established and tailored a deterrence strategy that targeted Hizbollah and could have evaluated whether Hizbollah cared enough for Lebanon's reconstruction. As will be seen soon, the summers of 2001 and 2002 were quiet. Muhammad Ra'd, a Hizbollah member of parliament, declared clearly that Hizbollah had no intention of ruining the tourist season in Lebanon:[74] "The resistance will act befitting the present conditions and will not be responsible for destroying the summer vacation season."[75]

This outcome, of course, assumed a relatively costly Israeli retaliation along the lines of the June 1999 retaliation, and not the type of retaliations that Israel actually conducted. A careful reading of the political situation and the ability to adapt to changing situations were good indicators that Hizbollah would have been deterrable as long as Israel applied the right pressures on Hizbollah's sensitivities. What should have been expected from a deterrence strategy? The theory suggested expectation of a strong response to the first challenge to clarify the new rules of the game, and an even stronger response if the challenges continued. Boaz Ganor's recommendations to use airpower against Lebanese and Syrian military facilities in Lebanon and not against civilians was a sound suggestion, but not sufficient.[76] Israel should have exploited Hizbollah's sensitivities and attacked the targets that threatened to undermine its legitimacy within the Lebanese state. As discussed in the next section, however, this logical deterrent strategy was not translated into a coherent retaliatory program after the pullout.

Challenge and Response

Before a discussion of the specific deterrence challenges, I would like to mention the general pattern of challenge and response that emerged after the Israeli withdrawal.[77] It is important to note that three challenges stand out as important test cases. The first is the October 7, 2000, ambush and kidnapping of three Israeli soldiers. This was the first challenge after Israel withdrew from Lebanon and occurred three months after that event. It was Barak's first test and his response set the tone for the remainder of his time in office. The second major test came after Sharon assumed office in February 2001. While Sharon tried to deviate from Barak's pattern of response, he, too, returned to a policy of restraint. And things did not change when the third test came in 2002, when Hizbollah escalated its attacks.

Barak's First Test: The October 7 Kidnapping

While the first Hizbollah challenge after the withdrawal occurred on October 7, 2000, it should be noted that Hizbollah had signaled its intention to use the Shabba Farms as a focal point to advance its interests three days before the withdrawal of Israeli troops from Lebanon, when it shelled the area on May 21, 2000. Israel did not respond.

On October 7, 2000, Hizbollah kidnapped three Israeli soldiers from the Mount Dov sector. Hizbollah ambushed and kidnapped the Israeli soldiers after a roadside bomb hit their vehicle. Mount Dov was shelled to distract attention from the ambush. Two weeks later it was announced that the three Israeli soldiers, Adi Avitan, Omer Suaed, and Binyamin Avraham, were dead.

Foreign Minister Shimon Peres claimed that Lebanon no longer had an excuse to act this way, and that if Lebanon behaved wildly, then Israel would also have to behave wildly.[78] While Peres was threatening Lebanon, the Israeli military had not yet formulated a response, and the Lebanese media reported that mediators were trying to establish contact between Israel and Hizbollah to arrange a prisoner exchange. Deputy Defense Minister Ephraim Sneh stated that Syria was responsible for the kidnapping, but there was a growing consensus in the defense establishment that as a result of the Palestinian uprising, Israel's deterrent power had eroded.

The Israeli situation at the time was complicated. On the Palestinian front Israel had witnessed the worst violence since 1982. Its soldiers were being lynched in the West Bank, and rioting had erupted in the occupied territories. Israel's decision to withdraw from Joseph's Tomb and allow it to be ransacked by the Palestinians was also perceived as weakness. To react forcefully to Hizbollah's challenge would have required that Israel open a second front, and that would have distracted it from the Palestinian challenge.

In the end, Israel's response to Hizbollah's attack was to rush troops to the north and to mass tank columns on the border. Warnings were issued to Beirut and Damascus that the rules of the game had changed since the withdrawal, but no painful or disproportionate punitive military action was taken.

Critics on the political right in Israel argued that the Israeli reaction had sent the wrong message to the Arab states, the message that Israel could be defeated by irregular military forces. From a deterrence perspective it was clear that the first challenge after the withdrawal should have been met with a strong signal. Israel was in a position to assume the moral high ground, since it had been attacked after it withdrew from Lebanon and Hizbollah no longer had a legitimate reason to attack. Barak should have sent a strong message that the nature and rules of the game had changed and that such attacks would not be tolerated.

Furthermore, because of the Palestinian challenge in the West Bank, which some argued had resulted from the perception of Israel's withdrawal from Lebanon as weakness, Israel should have retaliated against Hizbollah, sending a clear message that it was able and willing to fight on two fronts if necessary. Instead, the first test sent the signal that Israel, when challenged on two fronts, would use restraint rather than force. Israel's deterrent reputation was clearly sinking.

On November 16, 2000, Hizbollah attacked again, using a roadside bomb near an IDF convoy at Mount Dov, and declared that the attacks would continue. On November 26, 2000, a roadside bomb near Mount Dov killed an IDF soldier.[79]

In two other incidents, one on January 3, 2001, and the other on February 16, 2001, Hizbollah fired at Mount Dov, killing one Israeli soldier and wounding three in the latter incident. Israel did not retaliate. This case illustrates a major deviation from the finding by Kuperman that Israeli military fatalities were the best predictor of Israel's retaliation policy.[80]

Reports began to surface at the time that Hizbollah had acquired long-range missiles that could reach Haifa and the Galilee, and Hizbollah warned that it had further surprises for the Israelis. Nasrallah requested a list of all security prisoners in Israel and wanted them exchanged for the Israelis kidnapped by Hizbollah.[81]

While the Israeli response was mute, the Lebanese and the Syrians, aware of Israel's deterrent reputation, expected a strong Israeli response. Rafik Hariri, the Lebanese prime minister, was very critical of Hizbollah's actions. He argued that the Syrians also did not think that Hizbollah should give Israel a pretext to attack. Hizbollah responded by arguing that the operation had been carried out on the ninth anniversary of Abbas Musawi's assassination, and that this was a message intended for Sharon, who assumed office in February 2001.

Sharon's First Test: The April 2001 Attack

On April 14, 2001, a Hizbollah attack at Mount Dov killed an Israeli soldier. This was the first provocation handed to new Israeli prime minister Ariel Sharon. Sharon lost no time, and his immediate response was to send a message that the rules of the game under his administration would be different. Israeli warplanes attacked a Syrian radar station in Lebanon's Bekaa Valley in Dahr al-Baydar, destroying the installation and killing four Syrian soldiers.[82] This was a tit-for-tat retaliation but the target was the Syrians, who the Israelis assumed controlled Hizbollah decisions. The message also set the stage for an escalation against Syria but did not challenge Hizbollah's direct interests.

Israel retaliated strongly in Gaza, as well as sending a signal that it intended to use more force and saying that Area A, the territory controlled by the PLO, was no longer immune to Israeli retaliation.[83] The message was that Israel was willing to fight on two fronts if necessary.

The Israeli government under Sharon clearly deviated from the Barak government's mode of response. Sharon sent a clear signal that he was willing to engage the Syrians if necessary and fight on two fronts. Two issues were not clear at the time. One was the extent to which Syria was willing to control Hizbollah's actions. Second, it was not yet clear whether Sharon's government was willing and able to sustain a campaign of retaliation and escalation if the challenges continued.

In Lebanon there was mounting criticism of Hizbollah by the Lebanese, who feared an Israeli attack on their infrastructure. At the same time, Lebanon warned Israel not to attack, in order not to turn the Lebanese population against Israel and give Hizbollah more ammunition.

The Israeli retaliation had little effect on Hizbollah's activity pattern. On May 14, 2001, two antitank missiles were fired at IDF positions at Mount Dov. In response to the May 14 incident, Israeli defense minister Binyamin Ben-Eliezer warned Lebanon and Syria that Israel would attack Syrian positions in Lebanon. Hizbollah's leader, Nasrallah, stated that his organization was ready for a fight. Lebanese president Emil Lahud warned that the northern border between Israel and Lebanon would flare up if Israel intended to change the rules of the game.[84] On June 29, 2001, an Israeli soldier was wounded by an antitank missile and mortar fire from the same location. Nasrallah issued a threat that Hizbollah would strike anywhere along the border and would not confine itself to the Mount Dov area.[85]

Israel's response to these challenges was mixed. On the one hand, Israel destroyed another Syrian radar installation in Lebanon on July 1, 2001, this time much closer to the Lebanese-Syrian border. It was a signal of retaliation against Hizbollah, but it was mainly intended as a signal to Bashar Asad that Israel would hold Syria responsible. At the same time, Israel reduced its presence on the border to avoid exposing its troops, and it increased its reliance on a sophisticated electronic fence.[86]

In addition, and contrary to the earlier message that Sharon had intended to send about Israel's willingness to fight on two fronts, the Israeli defense minister declared that Israel would do everything in its power to avoid opening a second front in the north. According to Daniel Sobelman, Hizbollah was fully aware that Israel had no intention to attack in the north. Hizbollah believed that the reason was its having a deterrence of its own: missiles capable of reaching Haifa. In newspaper interviews and articles, Hizbollah leaders Muhammad Hussein Fadlallha, Na'im Qasim, Sheikh Nabil Qawuq, and others, argued that Israel was not going to open a second front.[87]

The Israeli strikes nevertheless led to the longest period of calm since the kidnapping of the Israeli soldiers: three months of quiet after the two Israeli attacks on Syrian radar installations. Israeli analysts expected Hizbollah attacks to resume in September or October as the tourist season in Lebanon ended. This was one of the pressure points Israel had against Hizbollah, but it chose not to use it in its deterrence strategy.

On October 3, 2001, Hizbollah attacked the Mount Dov sector with anti-tank missiles and mortar shells. Hizbollah announced it was helping the Palestinian uprising, the al-Aqsa Intifada. Hizbollah also tried to torpedo the American-led coalition that was being formed to fight in Afghanistan. In his speech commemorating the one-year anniversary of the intifada, Nasrallah said he wanted to join the Palestinian struggle. This was the first time Nasrallah had attributed Hizbollah's attacks to the Palestinian issue and not to a Lebanese-related issue.[88]

On October 22, 2001, Hizbollah fired at Mount Dov, and Israel responded in kind. A period of calm ended when, on January 23, 2002, Hizbollah fired again at the Mount Dov area. Israel's concern at the time was that Iran was behind the attacks by Hizbollah. Israel embarked on a diplomatic campaign to mobilize world public opinion to pressure Syria and Lebanon to control Hizbollah. Israel was also considering retaliation against Syria, but no action was taken.

As of January 24, 2002, Israel's pattern of response to Hizbollah's attacks was to enter into a mode of "absorption" and to try to mobilize international support to get the Syrians and Lebanese governments to rein in Hizbollah. Sharon reverted to Barak's restraint policies.

Sharon's Second Test: The March–April 2002 Escalation

On March 12, 2002, Hizbollah-backed Palestinians infiltrated Israel and killed an Israeli soldier and five civilians. This act occurred just before the Passover suicide bombing in the city of Netanya and Israel's retaliation against the Palestinians in Operation Defensive Shield. Hizbollah would not confirm or deny its involvement in the incident.

From March 30, 2002, through April 14, 2002, Hizbollah fired at Mount Dov, at an IDF post near Rajar, at IDF posts at Avivim in the western sector, and at the northern Golan Heights in the Hermon sector. The Hizbollah challenges in this period were a major escalation from prior activities. These attacks marked the first time since the withdrawal that Hizbollah had fired at areas other than Mount Dov. For the first time in two years, Israeli citizens slept in shelters along the border with Lebanon. Firing at Israeli settlements in the western sector and not just Mount Dov was a major escalation by Hizbollah. It was also the first time that Hizbollah had used 122-mm Katyusha rockets.

Israeli forces at the time were involved in Operation Defensive Shield in the West Bank. They returned fire but restrained themselves from any escalation or punitive measures.

On April 4, 2002, in an Israeli cabinet meeting, Sharon discussed potential Syrian and Lebanese targets for reprisal but on a tour of the Northern Command decided to abstain from an escalation along the border. Shaul Mofaz, Israel's chief of staff, declared that the "restraint we demonstrate can be strength but only up to a point."[89] Ben-Eliezer said that Syrian president Bashar Asad was "playing with fire."[90] Israel embarked yet again on a diplomatic effort to put pressure on Syria to rein in Hizbollah.

Israel did mobilize some forces. Interestingly, aware of Israel's prior reputation for not tolerating such challenges, Kamal Kharazi, Iran's foreign minister, called on Hizbollah to act with restraint. And UN Secretary General Kofi Annan declared that Syria had promised to control Hizbollah.

Israel fired on Hizbollah positions near Hazabia to signal what would follow if Hizbollah continued to attack. Israeli analysts surmised that Palestinian factions belonging to Ahmad Jibril, the leader of the Popular Front for the Liberation of Palestine–General Command, were firing at Israeli positions in solidarity with the Palestinian struggle in the West Bank, and in coordination with Hizbollah.

The Israeli National Security Council called on the Israeli leaders to retaliate by attacking targets in south Lebanon and Syrian targets on the Syrian-Lebanese border. Israel warned that if it were forced to retaliate, the retaliation would be stronger than the attacks on the radar installations. Military sources said, "It is not possible to threaten all the time. Threats must be implemented."[91]

Defense Minister Ben-Eliezer argued that Syria must realize soon that Hizbollah was actually controlling the Syrians and not the other way around. And Syria was going to be the first target of retaliation. The Lebanese government acted to stop Palestinian attacks from its border and arrested PLO members from Jibril's faction but failed to act against Hizbollah.

Israel concluded that Hizbollah had interpreted Israel's restraint as weakness. But Israel was also concerned that Haifa and Acco might be targeted this time. Despite warnings to Syria, most Israeli leaders chose a policy of restraint and continuation of diplomacy, and despite Israeli mobilization, Hizbollah continued its attacks and hit Beit Hillel. Artillery was fired also at the northern Golan Heights and Mount Dov.

Israeli intelligence also advocated restraint, believing that international pressure would bring a cessation of fighting to "tolerable" levels confined to Mount Dov. Israeli intelligence, however, assumed that Asad was behind the conflagration because the Saudi peace plan being discussed at the time made no mention of the return of the Golan Heights. By keeping up a low-level war on the Israeli border with Lebanon, Asad believed that Israel would be pressured to deal with the Golan issue as well. Asad and Nasrallah met and decided to escalate the situation on the border. The Syrians wanted to demonstrate their important role in the Middle East against the background of the Saudi initiative at the Arab summit in Beirut at the end of March.

So March and April saw increased Hizbollah activity. Nasrallah's actions, which lasted for about fifteen days, added pressure on the Israeli operations in the West Bank, but Israel kept its restraint. Despite its rhetoric, Hizbollah did not deploy its Katyusha arsenal during the Israeli-Palestinian fighting, and Nasrallah said that he had to guard the arsenal in case Israel tried to force the Palestinians into Lebanon.

This was the third major time when Hizbollah posed a serious and escalatory challenge to Israel, a challenge that went unanswered. Because Hizbollah escalated the challenge to areas beyond Mount Dov, and because it attacked Israel while Israel was preoccupied with its Operation Defensive Shield, Israel had to demonstrate that these types of actions would not go unanswered. It had to respond to the escalation and it had to demonstrate its ability to fight a two-front war. Instead, Israel continued with a policy of restraint that could only be interpreted as weakness. It is important to note the implications of Ben-Eliezer's observation that Hizbollah controlled Syria's activity. The proper target for the reestablishment of deterrence should have been Hizbollah. And the way to influence Hizbollah's behavior would have been to threaten to attack where it would hurt Hizbollah most: the Lebanese economy. Hizbollah cared about the tourist industry in Lebanon and Lebanon's reconstruction. As can be seen clearly, May 7, 2002, marked the last incident of firing by Hizbollah's forces on an Israeli patrol before a summer lull that lasted until August 29, 2002.[92]

While Israel continued with its restraint and containment policy, from the end of the summer of 2002 to the July 12, 2006, challenge, there was a consistent pattern of continuing challenges by Hizbollah.[93] Throughout the period Israel responded to Hizbollah's aggression with localized retaliation. Israel did not use any of its proven deterrence strategies, such as disproportionate retaliation, escalation, and war.

Conclusions

Since the Israeli withdrawal from Lebanon in May 24, 2000, nineteen Israeli soldiers have been killed, and seventy-seven have been wounded. There were 43 military attacks, 105 cases of antiaircraft fire, 42 cases of antitank missile fire, 5 incidents of small arms fire, 10 cases of explosives, 5 cases of Katyusha rocket fire, and 14 attempts at infiltration, some for the purpose of kidnapping.

Between 2000 and 2006, four Israeli soldiers and civilians were killed a year on average by Hizbollah attacks, a casualty rate that should not have been acceptable after Israel withdrew from Lebanon.

According to the Winograd Commission's partial report, Israel's withdrawal from Lebanon was accompanied by clear threats that any infringement by Hizbollah on Israel's sovereignty would be met with a strong response.[94] The military redeployment on Israel's northern border, however, was not properly structured to send a strong deterrent message. The opposite actually happened. To reduce the potential for friction with Hizbollah forces, Israel reduced the number of outposts it manned, and it kept the number of soldiers on the border to a minimum. The guiding operational principle for the Israeli forces was restraint even in situations where Hizbollah initiated the attacks.[95] The term used by Israeli strategists was *hachala,* which means "containment," and was understood to mean an attempt to limit the gains of an adversary and to restrain its actions without causing a major escalation or confrontation.[96]

The levers of influence over Hizbollah were assumed to be retaliatory acts against Syrian targets in Lebanon and the Lebanese infrastructure. The operating assumption was that aiming at state targets would pressure the state to act against Hizbollah and thus deter it from attacks on Israel.

This containment policy guided Israeli responses throughout 2000–2006. Why did Israel choose such a policy instead of a policy of deterrence? Undersecretary for Defense Ephraim Sneh argued that the policy of containment was adopted for two main reasons. First, the Barak government did not want to signal that the unilateral withdrawal had been a failure and had brought about an escalation in warfare instead of a period of quiet. This was a political decision that must be understood against the background of the hotly debated decision to withdraw from Lebanon. An escalation on the Lebanese front so quickly after the withdrawal would have been an admission of failure and would not have enabled the civilian population in the north to recover from the many years of harassment.

Second, Israel was reluctant to open a second front against Hizbollah at the time of the Second Intifada. The Palestinian uprising was exacting a high cost on the Israeli population and was considered the primary front. Israel preferred to focus on the Palestinian front as long as Hizbollah's challenges caused only "slow bleeding."[97]

One might add that the Sharon government was reluctant to follow through with a strategy of escalation and war, given Sharon's experience in the Lebanese quagmire and the meager results of Operation Accountability in 1993 under Rabin and Operation Grapes of Wrath in 1996 under Peres.

The general consensus in the Israeli military was that an escalation by the Israeli army would spiral into massive retaliations that would involve the civilian populations on both sides and that could be stopped only by the reinsertion of ground troops into Lebanon.

The operational implication of the containment policy was that the Israeli army, over a period of six years, limited its presence on the northern border and restrained itself from any serious response to Hizbollah's challenges. While Hizbollah's challenges increased in intensity and range, Israel moved army outposts to a back line, built back access roads, and reduced to a minimum the active patrols on the border. The policy was taken to such extremes that the chief of staff denied return-fire orders in response to Hizbollah fire.[98] According to Northern Commander Udi Adam, the practical implication of the policy was that Israel had abandoned Israeli sovereignty on the northern borders.

While the policy of containment characterized the Israeli response in the years 2000–2006 regardless of the government in power, and while it was based on some serious considerations, this policy clearly should have been examined in light of Israel's long-standing experience with the strategy of deterrence and against the background of the changed circumstances on the Lebanese border.

Israel did withdraw to the international border and Hizbollah no longer had a legitimate reason to challenge Israel and harass its population. Israel needed to establish new rules of the game, and when immediately challenged in October 2000, it should have responded forcefully. While the Palestinian uprising confronted Israel with a serious challenge, Israel should have fought on the second front to prevent the erosion of its reputation for resolve. It is important to remember that Hizbollah did care abut Lebanese reconstruction and its image as a responsible actor in that reconstruction. Thus it is clear that Hizbollah would have had little interest in an escalation that would undermine the reconstruction efforts. Hizbollah was testing the limits of acceptable behavior, and Israel should have made the red lines clear. Had escalation taken place, it would have occurred before Hizbollah became capable of significantly hitting Israeli civilians.

It is also important to note that had Israeli political and military leaders had a deterrence framework in mind, the decisions made on July 12, 2006, would have been better. The problem on July 12 was one of deterrence failure. The goal should have been the return of the captured Israeli soldiers and the reestablishment of deterrence. The use of ultimatums accompanied by graduated escalation in case of noncompliance would have been effective and would have given Israeli leaders the time necessary to prepare the ground forces in case the ultimatums did not work. In his classic book *Arms and Influence,* Thomas C. Schelling argued, "The power to hurt can be counted among the most impressive attributes of military force."[99] But this power is most effective only when it is used as bargaining power whose goal is to make the adversary behave differently to avoid it. "The power to hurt is most successful when held in reserve. It is the threat of damage, or of more damage to come, that can make someone yield or comply."[100] The power to hurt is communicated not by the use of brute force to destroy infrastructure, as was Israel's strategy, but by "some performance of it."[101] Once brute force has been used and the adversary has suffered great loss, it has no incentive to bargain. The expectation of more violence no longer influences its behavior.

Since the Second Lebanon War in 2006 the Israeli-Lebanese border has been quiet. Deterrence is working. This is actually not surprising to deterrence theorists, but it has been surprising to those who argue that Israel relies too heavily on deterrence and the use of force and to those who argue that Israel's deterrence is ending.

Zeev Maoz, for example, argues, "The culture of trigger happiness characterized all of Israel's governments, regardless of period and of the person or party in power. The effectiveness of this tool has been limited at best. Israel's national security was improved not by the use of force but by the willingness to give diplomacy a chance as a substitute for the use of military strategies."[102]

In this case, Israel withdrew to the international border, and in so doing it delegitimized any further military challenge by Hizbollah. Furthermore, Israel—contrary to its deterrence doctrine, which calls for the use of disproportionate retaliation—adopted a policy of restraint. This policy was taken to such an extreme that even when Israeli soldiers were killed, Israel did not immediately retaliate, a major deviation from its long-standing mode of operation. Yet the policy of restraint led to more rather than fewer challenges, thus proving Maoz wrong.

Critics of deterrence argue that advocates of deterrence believe only in the use of force as a method of conflict resolution. The reality, however, is that the use of force is at times a necessary evil and that policies of restraint can equally lead to more rather than less war. The question analysts must resolve is when the use of force is necessary and when the proper time for diplomacy has arrived.

Military analysts who rely only on capability indicators err in the other direction. They place too much emphasis on the military, believing that deterrence success can be obtained only through superior capability. Once a state is unable to achieve a certain military outcome, such analysts believe, deterrence erodes.[103]

The argument that Israel's experience in Lebanon and the subsequent withdrawal brought about a collapse in Israel's security concept is wrong. Analysts who rely only on capability indicators concluded that Israel's deterrence reputation eroded because Israel was not able to defeat Hizbollah in Lebanon and withdrew without getting any political or security agreement in return. The best evidence that Israel's deterrence after the withdrawal was still robust is the reaction of Lebanese, Syrian, and Iranian leaders to Hizbollah's challenges. When Hizbollah was escalating the conflict during the spring of 2002, Rafik Hariri, Lebanon's prime minister, as well as the Syrians and the Iranians, urged Hizbollah not to provide Israel with a pretext for massive retaliation. We saw that Iran sent a strong message in April 2002 and in May 2003, when both Kamal Kharazi, then Iran's foreign minister, and Mohammad Khatami, then Iran's president, called on

Hizbollah for restraint while on visits to Lebanon, warning against giving Israel a pretext to attack and hoping to prevent a strong Israeli response against Lebanon or Syria. The expectation in the Arab world was that Israel would retaliate forcefully, as it had in the past. The lesson had been well learned by the Arab leaders.

Israel's reputation suffered not as a result of its decision to withdraw but as a result of its policy of restraint. Throughout the period Nasrallah was taught that Israel was willing to accept low-level challenges and would not retaliate with disproportionate force. Thus this chapter has demonstrated that Israel's reputation for resolve vis-à-vis Hizbollah actually collapsed when the three Israeli soldiers were kidnapped early in October 2000 and Israel did not retaliate, even though it had just withdrawn from Lebanon and assumed the moral high ground in its conflict with Hizbollah. The October 2000 challenge was a major test. It should have been viewed as such, and it should have been used to create new rules of the game. The Israeli nonresponse, indeed, created a new situation in which the old rules of the game collapsed. With the balance of interests in its favor, Israel should have applied its old and tested deterrence policies. While some observers pointed out that the balance-of-interests equation had changed, and that Israel, if attacked, was perceived after the withdrawal as the more legitimate actor, this observation was not translated into a well-tailored deterrence strategy. Instead of setting the new ground rules after each challenge and instead of retaliating against the party that acted independently and had the most to lose from a serious retaliation, Israel chose to send signals to a state that may not have had the ability, interest, or will to stop Hizbollah from further attacks.

The overreliance on the analysis of the balance of capability to the exclusion of an analysis of the balance of interests led to another mistake in the analysis of the deterrence situation in the Arab-Israeli case. While the Israel-Hizbollah conflict was structurally different from the Israeli-Palestinian conflict, many analysts concluded that lessons learned in the first conflict must have implications for the second. Thus there was a growing sense in Israel that its resolve reputation had suffered as a result of Israel's withdrawal from Lebanon and its response to Palestinian challenges. The two situations influenced each other and reinforced the image of a weaker Israel.

Israel, some argued, has gotten tired of the conflict with the Palestinians. Israel has been willing to accept Palestinian demands, a behavior that was being read in the Arab world as physical and psychological exhaustion. Ami Ayalon, former head of Israel's General Security Service, suggested that the Israeli response to Palestinian violence during the "Tunnel affair" in September 1996, as well as Israeli withdrawal from Lebanon, demonstrated to the

Arabs that Hizbollah and Palestinian tactics of violence worked.[104] Not only did the withdrawal from Lebanon encourage the Palestinian intifada but Israel's response to the Palestinian uprising also further eroded Israel's reputation for resolve. In response to Palestinian riots, Israel signed the Hebron Accord, in which it agreed to withdraw from most of Hebron, and in reaction to Hizbollah attacks, Israel agreed to withdraw from Lebanon.

The situations, however, are different, and as a result, the success of deterrence in the two cases was likely to be different. The Israeli-Palestinian struggle was and continues to be a national struggle about borders, survival, and independence. Israel has failed to deter the Palestinians because at the present time Palestinians are a nonstate actor with little to lose. Israel's deterrence policies have always failed against the Palestinians. The only success that cumulative deterrence has had is Palestinian acceptance of a two-state solution. Once the Palestinians are in a position to see some future political gains, they are also likely to be deterred.

Hizbollah, on the other hand, has had limited goals. The first was to expel the IDF from Lebanon. After the withdrawal, it was to maintain the conflict at a low level to sustain itself politically as an independent organization in Lebanon. Hizbollah's actions showed a pattern of caution, operating when forced to by strategic consideration or windows of opportunity needed for organizational survival, but always cautious in preventing a massive Israeli response. Thus deterrence could have worked had Israel followed through on its threats with properly tailored retaliations.

The targeting of Syria for retaliatory attacks was an attempt at strategic deterrence against a state because of a fear that tactical deterrence against a nonstate actor would be ineffective. However, Hizbollah did control territory and had strong interests that would have been undermined by a strong Israeli response. Syria's influence over Hizbollah was questionable. Hizbollah portrayed itself as the guardian of Lebanese reconstruction against Israeli interference. A threat to interfere with the rebuilding would have deterred and weakened Hizbollah.

Israel's deterrent reputation, while weakened vis-à-vis the Hizbollah between 2000 and 2006, has been reestablished by the Second Lebanon War. During the war Israel demonstrated that it could undermine Hizbollah's position within Lebanon and that it was willing and able to fight on two fronts. If properly analyzed and applied, Israel's deterrence could continue to sustain itself and create the stability necessary for the success of diplomacy. What is needed, however, is a better understanding of the conditions for deterrence success and a political leadership willing to apply the proper lessons.

Notes

1. *Ha'aretz* (August 28, 2006).

2. *Yediot Ahronot* (September 4, 2006).

3. Eliahu Winograd, "The Commission to Investigate the Events of the Lebanon War 2006," Partial Report (April 2007) (in Hebrew).

4. Ibid.

5. Zeev Maoz, "Israel's Nonstrategy of Peace," *Tikkun* (September–October 2006), pp. 49–53, p. 52.

6. Zeev Maoz, *Defending the Holyland: A Critical Analysis of Israel's Security and Foreign Policy* (Ann Arbor: University of Michigan Press, 2006), p. 233.

7. Or Honig, "The End of Israeli Military Restraint: Out with the New, in with the Old," *Middle East Quarterly* vol. 14, no. 1 (Winter 2007).

8. For a discussion of the debates within the literature and a listing of the works on deterrence, see citations in Elli Lieberman, "The Rational Deterrence Theory Debate: Is the Dependent Variable Elusive?" *Security Studies*, vol. 3, no. 3 (Spring 1994), pp. 384–427, and Elli Lieberman, "What Makes Deterrence Work? Lessons from the Egyptian-Israeli Rivalry," *Security Studies*, vol. 4, no. 4 (Summer 1995), pp. 851–910.

9. Richard Ned Lebow, *Between War and Peace: The Nature of International Crisis* (Baltimore: Johns Hopkins University Press, 1981), pp. 57–97.

10. Glenn Snyder, *Deterrence and Defense: Toward a Theory of National Security* (Princeton, NJ: Princeton University Press, 1961), pp. 210–212.

11. Bernard Brodie, *Strategy in the Missile Age* (Princeton, NJ: Princeton University Press, 1959), p. 314, and Robert Osgood, *Limited War Revisited* (Boulder, CO: Westview Press, 1979), p. 11.

12. The use of a "demonstration shot" suggested by Morton Halperin is also problematic in a world of nuclear rivals. Halperin suggests that a demonstrative shot could signal to an opponent that if its actions are not stopped things could get out of control and escalate to nuclear war. Thus it can be used to deescalate the conflict by demonstrating the resolve to escalate to a point where neither actor is comfortable with the potential consequences. However, the same concerns about escalation, massive retaliation, loss of control, miscommunications, and misperceptions apply to this scenario as well, and it is difficult to see national leaders taking the risks of crossing this threshold; see Morton Halperin, *Limited War in the Nuclear Age* (New York: Wiley, 1963), p. 58.

13. Barry Posen, *Inadvertent Escalation* (Ithaca, NY: Cornell University Press, 1991); Thomas Schelling, *The Strategy of Conflict* (Cambridge, MA: Harvard University Press, 1960); and Halperin, *Limited War*.

14. Robert H. Frank, *Passion within Reason: The Strategic Role of the Emotions* (New York: Norton, 1988).

15. "By war, reputation was maintained." Martin Gilbert, *The Roots of Appeasement* (New York: New American Library, 1966), p. 1, quoted in Paul Gordon Lauren, "Theories of Bargaining with Threats of Force: Deterrence and Coercive Diplomacy," in Paul Gordon Lauren, ed., *Diplomacy: New Approaches in History, Theory, and Policy* (New York: Free Press, 1979), p. 185. See also Jim Fearon, "Bayesian Learning and Costly Signaling in International Crises," (PhD thesis, Berkeley, University of California, 1992), chap. 5.

16. Moshe Dayan, "Why Israel Strikes Back," in Donald Robinson, ed., *Under Fire: Israel's Twenty Year Struggle for Survival* (New York: Norton, 1968), p. 122.

17. Benny Morris, *Israel's Border Wars, 1949–1956* (Oxford: Oxford University Press, 1993), p. 176.

18. Moshe Dayan, "Military Action during Peacetime," *Ba'Mahaneh* (September 14 and 21, 1955) (in Hebrew).

19. Ibid.

20. Doron Almog, "Cumulative Deterrence and the War on Terrorism," *Parameters*, vol. 34, no. 4 (Winter 2004–2005), pp. 4–19.

21. Maoz, *Defending the Holyland*, p. 281.

22. Lebow calls that "the justification of hostilities crises"; see Lebow, *Between War and Peace*, pp. 23–41.

23. In the 1960s Prime Minister Levy Eshkol adopted an "open book policy": Not every challenge was immediately answered, and Israel chose the place and time of the response. This strategy also leads eventually to disproportionate retaliation because of the need to reverse the appearance of weakness and the need to settle scores.

24. On Israel's deterrence strategy at the time, see Israel Tal, *National Security: The Israeli Experience* (Westport, CT: Praeger, 2000); Johnathan Shimshoni, *Israel and Conventional Deterrence* (Ithaca, NY: Cornell University Press, 1988); and Avner Yaniv, *Deterrence without the Bomb: The Politics of Israeli Strategy* (Lexington, MA: Lexington Books, 1987).

25. This is not to argue that Israel has always used retaliation and escalation only to demonstrate resolve. Israel clearly used escalation as a pretext for war in 1981–1982 in Lebanon, during the al-Aqsa Intifada, and against Syria in 1965–1967. During the period leading to the 1956 war, reputational as well as war pretext considerations may have existed concomitantly.

26. On the development of the concept of red lines during the 1960s, see Yigal Allon, *A Curtain of Sand* (Tel Aviv: Ha'Kibbutz Ha'Meuchad, 1968) (in Hebrew). On Israel's deterrence approach to the nuclear issue, see Maoz, *Defending the Holyland,* and Avner Cohen, *Israel and the Bomb* (New York: Columbia University Press, 1998).

27. Richard Ned Lebow and Janice Gross Stein, "Deterrence: The Elusive Dependent Variable," *World Politics,* vol. 42, no. 3 (April 1990), pp. 336–360. Janice Gross Stein, "The Arab-Israeli War of 1967: Inadvertent War through Miscalculated Escalation," in Alexander L. George, ed., *Avoiding War: Problems of Crisis Management* (Boulder, CO: Westview Press, 1998), pp. 126–160.

28. See Lieberman, "The Rational Deterrence Theory Debate," and Lieberman, "What Makes Deterrence Work?"

29. On the rational deterrence theory debate, see Christopher H. Achen and Duncan Snidal, "Rational Deterrence Theory and Comparative Case Studies," *World Politics,* vol. 42, no. 2 (January 1989), pp. 143–169; Paul Huth and Bruce Russett, "Testing Deterrence Theory Rigor Makes a Difference," *World Politics,* vol. 42, no. 4 (April 1990), pp. 466–501; Richard Ned Lebow, "Deterrence: A Political and Psychological Critique," in Paul C. Stern, Robert Axelrod, Robert Jervis, and Roy Radner, eds., *Perspectives on Deterrence* (New York: Oxford University Press, 1989); Richard Ned Lebow and Janice Gross Stein, "Deterrence: The Elusive Dependent Variable," *World Politics,* vol. 42, no. 3 (April 1990), pp. 336–369; Janice Gross Stein, "The Arab-Israeli War of 1967: Inadvertent War through Miscalculated Escalation," in Alexander L. George, ed., *Avoiding War Problems of Crisis Management* (Boulder, CO: Westview Press, 1991), pp. 126–160; Paul K. Huth and Bruce Russett, "What Makes Deterrence Work? Cases from 1900 to 1980," *World Politics,* vol. 36, no. 4 (July 1984), pp. 496–526; Elli Lieberman, "The Rational Deterrence Theory Debate: Is the Dependent Variable Elusive?" *Security Studies,* vol. 3, no. 3 (Spring 1994), pp. 384–427; Elli Lieberman, "What Makes Deterrence Work? Lessons from the Egyptian-Israeli Rivalry," *Security Studies,* vol. 4, no. 4 (Summer 1995), pp. 851–910; Elli Lieberman, "Deterrence Theory: Success or Failure in Arab-Israeli Wars?" McNair Paper No. 45 (Washington, DC: Institute for National Strategic Studies, National Defense University, October 1995); Janice Gross Stein, "Deterrence and Learning in an Enduring Rivalry: Egypt and Israel, 1948–1973," *Security Studies,* vol. 6, no. 1 (Autumn 1996), pp. 104–152.

30. Malcolm H. Kerr, *The Arab Cold War: Gamal Abd al-Nasser and His Rivals 1958–1970* (London: Oxford University Press, 1971).

31. See Lieberman, "The Rational Deterrence Theory Debate."

32. Almog, "Cumulative Deterrence," pp. 4–19.

33. Uri Bar-Joseph, "Variations on a Theme: The Conceptualization of Deterrence in Israeli Strategic Thinking," *Security Studies,* vol. 7, no. 3 (Spring 1998), pp. 145–181.

34. Ibid., pp. 158–160.

35. See Maoz, *Defending the Holyland,* p. 282.

36. Bar-Joseph, "Variations on a Theme," pp. 145–181.

37. Maoz, *Defending the Holyland,* p. 282.

38. Between July 1985 and November 1986, most attacks by Hizbollah were directed at the South Lebanese Army forces in Lebanon and not the IDF. See Ilan Pappe, "The Strategic Logic of Suicide Terrorism," *American Political Science Review,* vol. 3, no. 97 (2003), pp. 343–361.

39. Nasrallah directed his attacks not only in Lebanon but also in Israel, across the international border, and on Jewish targets internationally in Buenos Aires in 1992 and 1994. The first Buenos Aires attack was thought to be Hizbollah's retaliation for the Mussawi assassination, and the second was retaliation for the July 18, 1994, Israeli attack on Lebanon that killed fifty Hizbollah recruits.

40. Under the leadership of Prime Minister Yitzhak Rabin negotiations were close to a resolution of the Golan Heights issue, and the Syrian position was that had Rabin not been assassinated, a peace treaty would have been reached; see the interview with Ambassador Walid al-Moualem, "Fresh Light in the Syrian Israeli Peace Negotiations," *Journal of Palestinian Studies,* vol. 26, no. 2 (Winter 1997), pp. 81–94.

41. Netanyahu's offer to Syria to pull Israeli soldiers out of Lebanon in exchange for security arrangements with Syria was not successful, since Syria had no incentive to accept a deal in which there was no mention of the final status of the Golan Heights. Syria manipulated Hizbollah's attacks on Israel depending on the status of Syria's negotiations with Israel. See Itamar Rabinovich, *The Brink of Peace* (Tel Aviv: Yediot Ahronot, 1998) (in Hebrew).

42. This negative assessment of Hizbollah's intentions was made by AMAN (Israeli Military Intelligence) based on Hizbollah's rhetoric rather than its actions; see Maoz, *Defending the Holyland,* p. 220.

43. And indeed, many in this camp argued that the intifada in September 2000 was a direct response to Israel's perceived weakness. As early as 1985, when Prime Minister Shimon Peres called for a withdrawal from Lebanon, Yitzhak Shamir, then the Israeli foreign minister, argued that such an act would be surrender. See Daniel Sobelman, "New Rules of the Game: Israel and Hizbollah after the Withdrawal from Lebanon," Jaffee Center for Strategic Studies, Memorandum No 69 (Tel Aviv: Tal Aviv University, January 2004), pp. 9–17. Opponents of the withdrawal predicted that it would lead to a cycle of Hizbollah attacks and Israeli retaliation that could engulf Syria as well. Opponents of the withdrawal included Benjamin Netanyahu; Moshe Ya'alon, army intelligence chief at the time; Yitzhak Mordechai, Israeli defense minister; Uri Lubrani, Israel's Lebanon coordinator; and Labor Party member (and later deputy defense minister) Ephraim Sneh.

44. The IDF general staff was opposed to a unilateral withdrawal. These included Chief of Staff Shaul Mofaz; General Amos Malka, head of AMAN; Amos Gilead, head of the research division; and General Gabi Ashkenazi, commander of the northern front—all were opposed to a unilateral withdrawal. Being a military man, though, enabled Barak to withstand internal military pressure and to use public support to enable the withdrawal.

45. Sobelman, *New Rules of the Game,* p. 30.

46. Ibid.

47. Advocates of unilateral withdrawal included people from both main political parties (Yossi Beilin from Labor and Michael Eitan from Likud), as well as Avigdor Kahalani, a 1973 war hero, and Gideon Ezra, former deputy head of the Shin Bet. A few Israeli politicians contemplated the idea of unilateral

withdrawal as early as the mid-1990s. See Yossi Beilin, *Guide for Withdrawal from Lebanon* (Tel Aviv: Hakibbutz HaMeuchad, 1998) (in Hebrew).

48. Proponents of unilateral withdrawal argued that the withdrawal had to be accompanied by a clear threat of severe retaliation if Hizbollah continued its challenges. Since a new situation would be created, new rules of the game would have to be established. Deterrence, which was not effective as long as Israel was perceived as an occupier of Lebanese land, might become successful if properly applied once Israel was protecting its own territory.

49. Colonel Eran Lerman, Gilad's deputy in the Research Division, argued that "if Israel's actions earn regional and international legitimacy, there is a strong possibility of deterrence against Hizbollah." See July 21, 2003, interview with Daniel Sobelman, in Sobelman, "New Rules," p. 31.

50. Barak initially opposed unilateral withdrawal. In August 1997 he called for a gradual withdrawal to test Hizbollah's intentions. Finally, during the 1999 elections, Barak's position changed to include a complete withdrawal within one year once he was elected to office.

51. The discussion of Hizbollah's interests is based on Sobelman, "New Rules"; Amal Saad-Ghorayeb, *Hizbu'llah: Politics and Religion* (London: Pluto Press, 2002); Hussein Agha, "A Note on Hizbollah," in "Hizbollah and the Lebanon-Israel Border," *Bitterlemons International*, vol. 2, no. 36 (September 23, 2004); Anat Kurtz, "Hizbollah at the Crossroads," *Strategic Assessment*, vol. 3, no. 1 (2002), pp. 14–17; Augustus Richard Norton, "Hizbollah: From Radicalism to Pragmatism?" *Middle East Policy* (January 1998); and Ely Karmon, "Hizbollah as Strategic Threat to Israel," ict.org.il/articles.

52. Hizbollah built its credentials by forcing Israel to withdraw from Lebanon without any major concessions. It claims to have done what no other Arab government had been able to do. By making such a claim, Hizbollah assumed Pan-Arab credentials, and in turn, it becomes difficult for opponents to challenge Hizbollah politically. By confronting Israel and its backer, the United States, with the intent of helping the Palestinians, Hizbollah was able to establish its Pan-Arab credentials, strengthen its Islamic credentials, and gain in the internal power struggle in Lebanon. Ironically, while Hizbollah supported the Palestinians, Hizbollah actually had no interest in a settlement of the conflict. Such a settlement would have the same effect as the Israeli withdrawal from Lebanon: It would weaken the legitimacy of Hizbollah's military actions. It can challenge Israel as long as Israel fights the Palestinians, but not once the Palestinians reach an agreement with Israel. Thus, it is important to note that Hizbollah's interest in the Palestinian cause is limited to its usefulness for its own organizational survival. Hizbollah has kept a tight lid on Palestinian activity from south Lebanon and has cooperated with the Lebanese government to prevent Palestinian infiltration from Lebanon. The Lebanese government has a strong interest in preventing a return to Palestinian control of south Lebanon. Therefore, in October 2000, Hizbollah adopted a position of rejecting any settlement between Israel and the Palestinians. One of its main interests became supporting the Palestinian rejectionist front. Hizbollah expanded its infiltration of Palestinian groups in the West Bank and Gaza and used spies within Israel for intelligence gathering and acts of terror, with the purpose of realizing its goal of continuing conflict.

53. Syria's main interest is the return of the Golan Heights. Syria has very little military leverage over Israel, and the border at the Golan Heights has been very quiet. Syria's only available military pressure on Israel to return the Golan Heights is Hizbollah attacks from Lebanon. Thus Syria provides Hizbollah with equipment, technology, and logistics. While low-level warfare on the Israeli-Lebanese border serves Syria's interest, Syria does not have an interest in Israeli escalation against itself or Lebanon. Syria needs a strong Lebanese economy that employs many Syrians. And Syria wants to rebuild its relationship with Lebanon and put it on a better

footing. Alienating Lebanon through actions that lead to a massive Israeli response could backfire against Syria. For its part, Hizbollah has declared that its goal is not only the liberation of Shabba Farms but Palestine and the Golan Heights as well. Despite its military dependence, Hizbollah maintains its independence from the parties it supports, and Syria is no exception. Since Hizbollah is useful to Syria only as long as it provides Syria with a means of challenging Israel, any agreement between Syria and Israel would undermine Hizbollah's position. When in 1996 there was talk of a possible Israeli-Syrian accommodation, Hizbollah escalated the conflict with Israel to torpedo the negotiations. See Amal Saad-Ghorayeb, *Hiz'bullah: Politics and Religion*, pp. 187–188.

54. Iran's interests in the Middle East, besides regime survival, are to counter US policies aimed at weakening Iran, and to undermine a peace process in the region, which, if successful, would weaken Iran's influence. Therefore Iran supports Hizbollah and Hamas, which reject negotiations and peace with Israel. Iran supports Hizbollah militarily. Iran's and Hizbollah's goals converge in their interests to put pressure on Israel—Hizbollah as a tool to justify its existence as a separate organization, and Iran as a leverage point in its struggle against the United States. However, Iran is not interested in escalation and tries to control Israel's actions so Israel will not have a pretext to attack Hizbollah or Syria. In 2002, for example, when Hizbollah escalated its activity on the border with Israel, Foreign Minister Kamal Kharazi arrived in Beirut and called for restraint. As in other relationships, Hizbollah maintains its independence in its relations with the Iranians. The April 2002 military activity at Mount Dov was criticized by Iran's foreign minister, who said in Beirut that Hizbollah should not give Israel a reason to attack it or Syria. Nasrallah continued the military activity even after the Iranian warning; see Sobelman, "New Rules of the Game," p. 24. Elsewhere, when Israel's defense minister Iztzhak Mordechai floated for the

first time the idea that Israel might pull out of Lebanon, Iran declared that this act would be considered an important achievement of Hizbollah's goals. Nasrallah responded by saying that this was the Iranian position and "is not binding upon Hizbollah"; quoted in Sobelman, "New Rules of the Game," p. 27.

55. Agha, "A Note on Hizbollah."

56. On the constraints and moderating effects imposed on Hizbollah by the Lebanese public, see Kurtz, "Hizbollah at the Crossroads," and Norton, "Hizbollah: From Radicalism to Pragmatism?"

57. Karmon, "Hizbollah as Strategic Threat to Israel," p. 19.

58. Ofer Shelah and Yav Limor, *Captives of Lebanon* (Tel Aviv: Miskal-Yediot Ahronot Books and Chemed Books, 2007), pp. 142–143 (in Hebrew).

59. Shaul Mofaz interview with Areh O'Sullivan, *Jerusalem Post* (May 19, 2000), p. 32.

60. Ibid.

61. Azim Bishara interview, *Al-Kuds Al-Arabi*, quoted in *Jerusalem Post* (June 9, 2000), p. 2.

62. Agha, "A Note on Hizbollah," p. 2.

63. Sobelman, "New Rules of the Game," p. 46.

64. Ibid., p. 32.

65. Ibid., p. 13.

66. Ibid., p. 33.

67. *Yediot Ahronot* (May 26, 2000).

68. *Ha'aretz* (January 11, 2001).

69. Sobelman, "New Rules of the Game," p. 54.

70. Ibid., p. 44.

71. Ibid.

72. Ibid.

73. Anat Kurtz, "Hizbollah at the Crossroads," *Strategic Assessment*, vol. 3, no. 1 (2000), pp. 14–17, and Augustus Richard Norton, "Hizbollah: From Radicalism to Pragmatism?" *Middle East Policy* (January 1998).

74. Sobelman, "New Rules of the Game," p. 93.

75. Ibid.

76. Boaz Ganor, "Lebanon—Defining a New Redline" (January 4, 1999), ict.org.

77. I used a few databases for information on Hizbollah challenges. Sobelman's data extend only to October 27, 2003. The data set of the Israeli ministry of foreign affairs stops on August 10, 2003. The Center of Knowledge on Intelligence and Terror has data up to January 17, 2005, and the Jewish Virtual Library has information through the last challenge just before the war, on May 27, 2006. For the Israeli responses, I relied on *Ha'aretz* and *Yediot Ahronot* (in Hebrew), 2000–2006.

78. *Ha'aretz* (October 13, 2000), p. 3.

79. Mercaz Hameida Lemodiin Veleterror, Hamercaz Lemoreshet Hamodiin (Intelligence and Terrorism Center, Information Office, May 28, 2006).

80. Ranan D. Kuperman, "Rules of Military Retaliation and Their Practice by the State of Israel," *International Interactions,* vol. 27 (2001), pp. 29–326.

81. *Jerusalem Post* (February 16, 2001), p. 7.

82. *Jerusalem Post* (April 27, 2001), p. 3.

83. The signal was weakened, however, by the Israeli withdrawal from Gaza in response to US State Department criticism of Israel and despite Israel's stated intention to stay in Gaza as long as necessary.

84. *Yedioth Ahronot* (May 25, 2001), p. 5.

85. *Jerusalem Post* (June 1, 2001), p. 9.

86. Ibid.

87. Sobelman, "New Rules of the Game," pp. 60–61.

88. *Yediot Ahronot* (October 4, 2001), p. 7.

89. *Yediot Ahronot* (April 5, 2002), p. 8.

90. Ibid.

91. Ibid., p. 3.

92. The August 29 attack occurred at a time when there were US congressional discussions of the Syria Accountability Act and increased US rhetoric about Iraq. According to Israeli analyst Ely Karmon, the intended message was to deter Israel from acting against the Palestinians at the time that the United States was invading Iraq.

93. On December 8, 2002, two Israeli soldiers were wounded by Hizbollah fire near Zarit in the Western Sector. Hizbollah considered this an act of revenge for the roadside killing of Ramzi Nahra, who had connections with Hizbollah. Hizbollah blamed Israel for the car bomb. In 2003, on January 21, August 8 and 10, and October 6 and 27, Hizbollah engaged in military attacks and Israel responded with proportional retaliation. The year 2003 was relatively calm on Israel's northern border. In 2004, every two months on average, there was intensive Hizbollah military activity. In November 2004, a UAV crossed into Israel over the Galilee. And in 2004, Hizbollah initiated sixty-eight attacks, in which twenty-four Israeli soldiers and civilians were killed. On January 29, 2004, Israel sent a different type of weak signal to Hizbollah, its willingness to negotiate the release of the bodies of the 3 kidnapped Israeli soldiers and a reserve colonel kidnapped in Dubai in May 2000 in exchange for the release of 400 Palestinian and 30 Lebanese prisoners. The Palestinian prisoners were released to the Palestinian Authority. Another 29 prisoners from Arab nations were flown to Germany, and then most went to Lebanon. In addition, the bodies of approximately 60 Lebanese were handed over to the International Committee of the Red Cross at the Israeli-Lebanese border. Sharon was not the first Israeli leader to exchange prisoners. In 1985, Israel freed 1,150 prisoners in exchange for 3 Israeli soldiers kidnapped in Lebanon by the Popular Front for the Liberation of Palestine (PFLP) General Command. Israel is deeply divided over the wisdom of prisoner exchanges. While Israel has long tried to establish that it will go to great lengths to rescue its captured soldiers, a norm that plays an important role in its soldiers' motivation to fight, some have argued that exchanging hundreds or thousands of terrorists for one Israeli soldier encourages the kidnapping of other Israelis and frees terrorists who return to terrorist acts. On January 9, 2005, an Israeli officer was killed at the Shabba Farms. On January 14 and 17 additional devices exploded without casualties. According to Sheikh Nabil Qawuq, Hizbollah's commander in the south, Hizbollah tried to remind the Israelis that they were still in occupied lands

and that Hizbollah wanted the Shabba Farms and Kfar Shuba Hills liberated. On April 12, 2005, another unmanned surveillance craft flew over northern Israel. It was timed with Sharon's and Bush's news conference and the pressure on Syria to withdraw from Lebanon. At that time, Syria ended its presence in Lebanon, and Hizbollah attempted to show that it wouldn't change its strategy toward Israel. Hizbollah signaled that the Syrian withdrawal would not influence its decision to disarm and become an arm of the Lebanese government. Hizbollah's goal was to maintain its independence from Syria, and its military actions signaled that strategy. Hizbollah feared that once it became part of the Lebanese government, it would not be able to resist Israel and act independently. On June 29, 2005, 1 Israeli soldier was killed and 4 wounded when Hizbollah fired more than twenty mortars. On November 21, an attempt to kidnap an Israeli soldier failed, and subsequent Hizbollah attacks injured 9 soldiers and 2 civilians. The last attack in 2005 occurred on December 27 but was unleashed by a Palestinian organization. May 27, 2006, was the last attack by Hizbollah before the July 12, 2006, infiltration. An IDF soldier was wounded when Katyushas were fired at an army base at Mount Meron in the Galilee.

94. Winograd, "The Commission to Investigate," p. 39.

95. Ibid.

96. Ibid., p. 41. See also Shelah and Limor, *Captives of Lebanon*, p. 128.

97. General Gabi Ashkenazi in testimony before the Winograd Commission, November 7, 2006; see Winograd, "The Commission to Investigate," p. 45.

98. Ibid., p. 47.

99. Thomas C. Schelling, *Arms and Influence* (New Haven, CT: Yale University Press, 1988), p. 2.

100. Ibid., p. 3.

101. Ibid.

102. Maoz, *Defending the Holyland*, pp. 552–553.

103. Chief of Staff Dan Halutz argued, for example, that Israel's deterrent capability suffered as a result of Israel's inability to defeat Hizbollah decisively. See Halutz, "The War Impacted Negatively on Israel's Deterrence Capability," *Ha'aretz* (January 3, 2007).

104. 104 Eyal Zisser, "Is Anyone Afraid of Israel?" *Middle East Quarterly*, vol. 8, no. 2 (Spring 2001).

Appendix:
Election Results

Israeli Election Results, 1996–2006

	2006	2003	1999	1996
Kadima	29	—	—	—
One Israel (Labor Party)	19	19	26	34
Likud (added Yisrael B'aliya after 2003 election)	12	38 (40)	19	32
Shas (religious party)	12	11	17	10
Meretz	5	6	10	9
Shinui	0	15	6	Part of Meretz
Yisrael B'aliya (joined Likud after 2003 election)	—	2	6	7
Center Party	—	0	6	—
National Religious Party (MAFDAL) (joined Nat'l Union in 2006)	0	6	5	9
United Torah Judaism (religious party)	6	5	5	4
United Arab List (Ra'am Ta'al) (Arab party)	4	2	5	4
National Union (joined by MAFDAL 2006)	9	7	4	—
Yisrael Beiteinu (joined National Union 2003)	11	—	4	—
Hadash (Arab party) (DFPE)	3	3	3	5
Balad (Arab party)	3	3	2	—
Am Ehad	—	3	2	—
Pensioners	7	—	—	—
Third Way	—	—	—	4
Moledet	—	—	—	2
Total	**120**	**120**	**120**	**120**

Final Election Results: Knesset 2006 (Seats)

Kadima	29
Labor	19
Shas	12
Likud	12
Yisrael Beiteinu	11
NRP/National Union	9
Pensioners	7
United Torah Judaism	6
Meretz	5
United Arab List	4
Balad	3
Hadash	3
Total	*120*

(61 needed to govern)

Initial Coalition

Kadima	29
Labor	19
Shas	12
Pensioners	7
Total	*67*

Coalition (October 2007)

Kadima	29
Labor	19
Shas	12
Pensioners	7
Yisrael Beiteinu	11
Total	*78*

Coalition (February 2008)

Kadima	29
Labor	19
Shas	12
Pensioners	7
Total	*67*

Bibliography

Books

Aharoni, Yair, *The Israeli Economy: Dream and Realities* (New York: Routledge, 1993).

Albright, Madeleine, *Madam Secretary: A Memoir* (New York: Miramax Books, 2003).

Allon, Yigal, *A Curtain of Sand* (Tel Aviv: Ha'Kibbutz Ha'Meuchad, 1968) (in Hebrew).

Arian, Asher, *Politika Umishtar Beyisrael* [Politics and Government in Israel] (Tel Aviv: Zmora Bitan, 1985).

_____, *The Second Republic: Politics in Israel* (Washington, DC: CQ Press, 2004).

Avineri, Shlomo, *The Making of Modern Zionism: Intellectual Origins of the Jewish State* (New York: Basic Books, 1981).

Avnery, Arie, *The Defeat: The Disintegration of Likud's Rule* (Tel Aviv: Midot, 1993).

Barzilai, Gad, *Communities and Law* (Ann Arbor: University of Michigan Press, 2003).

Bass, Warren, *Support Any Friend: Kennedy's Middle East and the Making of the U.S.-Israel Alliance* (New York: Oxford University Press, 2003).

Bassat, Avi Ben, *The Israeli Economy 1985–1998: From Government Intervention to Market Economics* (Jerusalem: Israel Democracy Institute, 2002).

Begin, Menahem, *The Revolt*, rev. ed. (New York: Nash, 1977).

Beilin, Yossi, *Guide for Withdrawal from Lebanon* (Tel Aviv: Hakibbutz HaMeuchad, 1998) (in Hebrew).

_____, *The Path to Geneva: The Quest for a Permanent Agreement 1996–2004* (New York: RDV Books, 2004).

Ben-Ami, Shlomo, *Scars of War, Wounds of Peace: The Israeli-Arab Tragedy* (New York: Oxford University Press, 2006).

Benjio, Ofra, *The Turkish-Israeli Relationship* (New York: Palgrave, 2004).

Benziman, Uzi, *Rosh Memshala Be'Matzor* [A Prime Minister under Siege] (Tel Aviv: Adam, 1981).

Bickel, Alexander M., *The Least Dangerous Branch* (Indianapolis, IN: Bobbs-Merrill, 1962).

Brecher, Michael, *The Foreign Policy System of Israel* (London: Oxford University Press, 1972).

Chomsky, Noam, *Peace in the Middle East? Reflections on Justice and Nationhood* (New York: Pantheon, 1975).

Cleveland, William L., *A History of the Modern Middle East* (Boulder, CO: Westview Press, 2004).

Clifford, Clark, *Counsel to the President: A Memoir* (New York: Random House, 1991).

Clinton, Bill, *My Life* (New York: Knopf, 2004).

Cohen, Asher, and Baruch Susser, *Mahashlama Lehaslama—Hashesa Hadati-Chiloni Befe-tach Hame'a ha–21* [From Reconciliation to Escalation—The Religious-Secular Rift at the Dawn of the 21st Century] (Tel Aviv: Schocken, 2003).

_____, *Shas—Periferya Belev Hamerkaz* [Shas—Periphery in the Heart of the Main-stream] (Tel Aviv: Am Oved, 2006).

Cohen, Avner, *Israel and the Bomb* (New York: Columbia University Press, 1998).

Don-Yehiya, Eliezer, *Hapolitika shel Hahasdara—Yishuv Sichuschim Benos'ey Dat Beyisrael* [The Politics of Regulation—Conflict Settlement on Religious Questions in Israel] (Jerusalem: Floersheimer Institute for Policy Studies, 1997).

_____, *Shituf Vekonflikt beyn Machanot Politiyim—Hamachane Hadati Utnu'at Ha'avoda Umashber Hachinuch Beyisrael* [Cooperation and Conflict among Political Camps—The Religious Camp and the Labor Movement and the Crisis of Education in Israel] (PhD thesis, Jerusalem, Hebrew University, 1977).

Dowty, Alan, *The Jewish State: A Century Later* (Berkeley: University of California Press, 2001).

Drezon-Tepler, Marcia, *Interest Groups and Political Change in Israel* (New York: State University of New York Press, 1990).

Feldman, Anat, *Gormin Bitsmichat Miflaga—Shas* [Factors in the Growth of a Party—Shas] (PhD thesis, Ramat Gan, Israel, Bar-Ilan University, 2002).

Feldman, Eliezer, *Russian Israel: Between Two Polls* (Moscow: Market DC, 2003).

Frank, Robert H., *Passion within Reason: The Strategic Role of the Emotions* (New York: Norton, 1988).

Freedman, Robert O., *Israel's First Fifty Years* (Gainesville: University Press of Florida, 2000).

_____, *Moscow and the Middle East: Soviet Policy since the Invasion of Afghanistan* (Cambridge: Cambridge University Press, 1991).

_____, *Russia, Iran, and the Nuclear Question: The Putin Record* (Carlisle, PA: Strategic Studies Institute of the U.S. Army War College, 2006).

_____, ed., *Israel under Rabin* (Boulder, CO: Westview Press, 1995).

Frish, Ronni, *The Causal Effect of Education on Earnings in Israel* (Jerusalem: Bank of Israel Research Department, February 2007).

Fromkin, David, *A Peace to End All Peace* (New York: Avon Books, 1990).

Frum, David, *The Right Man: The Surprise Presidency of George W. Bush* (New York: Random House, 2003).

Ganin, Zvi, *An Uneasy Relationship: American Jewish Leadership and Israel 1948–1967* (Syracuse, NY: Syracuse University Press, 2005).

Gavison, R., M. Kremnitzer, and Y. Dotan, *Judicial Activism: Pro and Con* (Jerusalem: Magnes, 2000) (in Hebrew).

Gilbert, Martin, *Israel: A History* (New York: William Morrow, 1998).

Goldberg, Giora, *Hamiflagot Beyisrael—Mimiflagot Hamon Lemiflagot Electoralliyot* [The Parties in Israel—From Mass Parties to Electoral Parties] (Tel Aviv: Ramot, 1992).

Gonen, Jay, *A Psychohistory of Zionism* (New York: Plume, 1976).

Gronau, Reuben, *Globalization: The Israeli Economy in the Shadow of Global Economy* (Jerusalem: Israel Democracy Institute, 2002).

Guillemin, Jeanne, *Biological Weapons: From the Intervention of State-Sponsored Programs to Contemporary Bioterrorism* (New York: Columbia University Press, 2005).

Hahn, Peter L., *Caught in the Middle East: U.S. Policy toward the Arab-Israeli Conflict 1945–1961* (Chapel Hill: University of North Carolina Press, 2004).

Hakan, Yavuz, *Islamic Political Identity in Turkey* (New York: Oxford University Press, 2003).

Herzberg, Arthur, ed., *The Zionist Idea: A Historical Analysis and Reader* (New York: Jewish Publication Society, 1997).

Herzog, Chaim, *The Arab-Israeli Wars: War and Peace in the Middle East* (New York: Random House, 1982).

Hirshler, Gertrude, and Lester S. Eckman, *From Freedom Fighter to Statesman: Menachem Begin* (New York: Shengold, 1979).

Horowitz, Dan, and Moshe Lissak, *Myishuv Lemedina* [From Yishuv to State] (Tel Aviv: Am Oved, 1977).

Inbar, Efraim, *Rabin and Israel's National Security* (Washington and Baltimore: Wilson Center Press and Johns Hopkins University Press, 1998).

Jabotinsky, Vladimir (Ze'ev), *Samson* (Tel Aviv: Shikmona, 1976) (in Hebrew).

_____, *The Story of the Jewish Legion* (New York: B. Ackerman, 1945).

Jackson, Robert H., *Quasi-States: Sovereignty, International Relations and the Third World* (New York: Cambridge University Press, 1990).

Kerr, Malcolm H., *The Arab Cold War: Gamal Abd al-Nasser and His Rivals 1958–1970* (London: Oxford University Press, 1971).

Khalidi, Rashid, *Resurrecting Empire: Western Footprints and America's Perilous Path in the Middle East* (Boston: Beacon Press, 2004).

Khanin, Vladimir (Ze'ev), *The "Russians" and Power in the State of Israel: The Establishment of the USSR/CIS Immigrant Community and Its Impact on the Political Structure of the Country* (Moscow: Institute for Israel and Middle Eastern Studies, 2004) (in Russian).

Kirisci, Kemal, *Turkey's Foreign Policy in Turbulent Times,* Chaillot Papers No. 92 (Paris: Institute for Security Studies, September 2006).

Klein, Yitzhak, and Daniel Polisar, *Choosing Freedom: Economic Policy for Israel, 1997–2000* (Jerusalem: Shalem Center, 1997).

Kumaraswami, P. R., *Israel and India: Evolving Strategic Partnership*, Mideast Security and Policy Studies No. 40 (Ramat Gan, Israel: Begin-Sadat Center for Strategic Studies, September 1998).

Lahav, Pnina, *Judgement in Jerusalem* (Berkeley: University of California Press, 1995).

Laqueur, Walter, *A History of Zionism* (New York: Holt, Rinehart & Winston, 1972).

Laqueur, Walter, and Barry Rubin, *Israel-Arab Reader* (New York: Penguin Books, 2001).

Lebow, Richard Ned, *Between War and Peace: The Nature of International Crisis* (Baltimore: Johns Hopkins University Press, 1981).

Lesch, David W., *The New Lion of Damascus: Bashar al-Asad and Modern Syria* (New Haven, CT: Yale University Press, 2005).

_____, *The Arab-Israeli Conflict: A History* (New York: Oxford University Press, 2007).

_____, ed., *The Middle East and the United States,* 4th ed. (Boulder, CO: Westview Press, 2007).

Levey, Zach, *Israel and the Western Powers* (Chapel Hill: University of North Carolina Press, 1997).

Levitzky, Nomi, *Your Honor (A Biography of Aharon Barak)* (Tel Aviv: Keter, 2001).

Mahler, Gregory, *Politics and Government in Israel* (New York: Rowan & Littlefield, 2004).

Makovsky, David, *Engagement through Disengagement: Gaza and the Potential for Renewed Israeli-Palestinian Peace-Making* (Washington, DC: Washington Institute for Near East Policy, 2005).

Maoz, Zeev, *Defending the Holyland: A Critical Analysis of Israel's Security and Foreign Policy* (Ann Arbor: University of Michigan Press, 2006).

Marshall, Monty, and Ted Robert Gurr, *Peace and Conflict 2005* (College Park: University of Maryland, Center for International Development and Conflict Management, 2005).

Meital, Yoram, *Peace in Tatters: Israel, Palestine and the Middle East* (Boulder, CO: Lynne Reinner, 2006).

Mishal, Shaul, and Avraham Sela, *The Palestinian Hamas: Vision, Violence and Coexistence* (New York: Columbia University Press, 2006).

Mizrahi, Shlomo, and Assad Meidani, *Public Policy between Society and Law: The Supreme Court, Public Participation and Policy-making* (Tel Aviv: Carmel, 2006) (in Hebrew).

Morris, Benny, *Israel's Border Wars, 1949–1956* (Oxford: Oxford University Press, 1993).

_____, *Righteous Victims: A History of the Zionist-Arab Conflict, 1881–1998* (New York: Vintage Books, 2001).

Netanyahu, Benjamin, *A Place among the Nations: Israel and the World* (New York: Bantam, 1993).

Nitzan, Jonathan, and Shimshon Bichler, *The Global Political Economy of Israel* (London: Pluto Press, 2002).

Oren, Michael, *Six Days of War: June 1967 and the Making of the Modern Middle East* (New York: Oxford University Press, 2002).

Oz, Amos, *In the Land of Israel* (New York: Harcourt Brace, 1993).

Ozacky-Lazar, Sara, *Habhirot la-Knesset ha–13 Bekerev Haaravim be-Israel, Yuni 1992* [The 13th General Elections among the Arabs in Israel, June 1992] (Givat-Haviva, Israel: Ha-Machon Le-Limudim Araviim, 1992).

Peleg, Ilan, *Begin's Foreign Policy, 1977–1983: Israel's Move to the Right* (Westport, CT: Greenwood Press, 1987).

_____, *Human Rights in the West Bank and Gaza* (Syracuse, NY: Syracuse University Press, 1995).

Podeh, Elie, *From Fahd to Abdullah: The Origins of the Saudi Peace Initiatives and Their Impact on the Arab System and Israel* (Jerusalem: Harry S. Truman Research Institute for the Advancement of Peace, 2003).

Posen, Barry, *Inadvertent Escalation* (Ithaca, NY: Cornell University Press, 1991).

Quandt, William, *Peace Process: American Diplomacy and the Arab-Israeli Conflict since 1967*, 3rd ed. (Los Angeles: University of California Press, 2005).

Rabinovich, Itamar, *The Brink of Peace: The Israeli-Syrian Negotiations* (Princeton, NJ: Princeton University Press, 1998).

_____, *Waging Peace, Israel and the Arabs 1948–2003* (Princeton, NJ: Princeton University Press, 2004).

Ram, Uri, *The Changing Agenda of Israeli Sociology: Theory, Ideology and Identity* (Albany: State University of New York Press, 1995).

_____, *The Globalization of Israel* (Tel Aviv: Resling, 2005) (in Hebrew).

Ram, Uri, and Dani Filk, eds., *The Power of Property: Israeli Society in a Global Age* (Jerusalem: Van Leer Institute, 2004).

Ross, Dennis, *The Missing Peace: The Inside Story of the Fight for Middle East Peace* (New York: Farrar, Straus, Giroux, 2005).

Ross, Dennis, Margaret Warner, and Jim Hoagland, "From Oslo to Camp David to Taba: Setting the Record Straight," *Peacewatch,* No. 349 (August 14, 2001).

Rubinstein, Amnon, *The Constitutional Law of the State of Israel,* 6th ed. (Tel Aviv: Schocken, 2005)(in Hebrew).

Saad-Ghorayeb, Amal, *Hizbu'llah: Politics and Religion* (London: Pluto Press, 1992).

Sachar, Howard, *A History of Israel from the Rise of Zionism to Our Time,* 3rd rev. ed. (New York: Knopf, 2007).

Safran, Nadav, *From War to War: The Arab-Israeli Confrontation 1948–1967* (Indianapolis, IN: Pegasus, 1969).

Sandler, Shmuel, *The State of Israel, the Land of Israel, the Statist and Ethnonational Dimensions of Foreign Policy* (Westport, CT: Greenwood Press, 1994).

Schiff, Ze'ev, and Ehud Ya'ari, *Milhemet Sholal* [A War of Deception] (Tel Aviv: Schocken, 1984), published in English as *Israel's Lebanon War* (New York: Simon & Schuster, 1984).

Segev, Tom, *One Palestine Complete: Jews and Arabs under the British Mandate* (New York: Henry Holt, 2001).

Seigel, Dina, *The Great Immigration: Russian Jews in Israel* (New York and Oxford: Berghan Books, 1998).

Sharansky, Natan, *The Case for Democracy: The Power of Freedom to Overcome Tyranny and Terror* (New York: PublicAffairs, 2004).

Sher, Gilead, *The Israeli-Palestinian Peace Negotiations, 1999–2001* (London: Routledge, 2006).

Shiloach, Zvi, *Eretz Gdola Le'am Gadol: Sipuro Shel Maamin* [A Great Land for a Great Nation: The Story of a Believer] (Tel Aviv: Orpaz, 1970).

Snyder, Glenn, *Deterrence and Defense: Toward a Theory of National Security* (Princeton, NJ: Princeton University Press, 1961).

Spiegel, Steven, *The Other Arab-Israeli Conflict: Making America's Middle East Policy, From Truman to Reagan* (Chicago: University of Chicago Press, 1985).

Sprinzak, E., *The Ascendance of Israel's Radical Right* (London: Oxford University Press, 1991).

Sweet, Alec Stone, *Governing with Judges: Constitutional Politics in Europe* (Oxford: Oxford University Press, 2000).

Tal, Israel, *National Security: The Israeli Experience* (Westport, CT: Praeger, 2000).

Tenet, George, *At the Heart of the Storm: My Years at the CIA* (New York: HarperCollins, 2007).

Tessler, Mark, *A History of the Israeli-Palestinian Conflict* (Bloomington: Indiana University Press, 1994).

Tessler, Riki, *Beshem Hashem: Shas Vehamahapecha Hadatit* [In the Name of God: Shas and the Religious Revolution] (Tel Aviv: Keter, 2003).

Tuchman, Barbara, *Bible and Sword: England and Palestine from the Bronze Age to Balfour* (New York: Ballantine Books, 1984).

Tucker, Jonathan B., *Chemical Warfare from World War I to al-Qaeda* (New York: Pantheon, 2006).

Woodward, Bob, *Bush at War* (New York: Simon & Schuster, 2002).

Yona, Yossi, and Yehuda Shenhav, *Rav Tarbutiyut Mahi? Al Hapolitika shel Hashonut Beyisra'el* [What Is Multiculturalism? On the Politics of Difference in Israel] (Tel Aviv: Bavel, 2005).

Zeira, Joseph, *Reducing Unemployment and Closing Income Gaps on the Road to Economic Growth* (Jerusalem: Israel Democratic Institute, 2004).

Zimmerman, Bennett, Roberta Seid, and Michael L. Wise, *The Million Person Gap: The Arab Population in the West Bank and Gaza,* Mideast Security and Policy Studies No. 65 (Ramat Gan, Israel: Begin-Sadat Center for Strategic Studies, Bar-Ilan University, February 2006).

Articles and Chapters in Books

A'id, Khalid, "Al-Taswit al-Falastiniyyi Ahl–48 fi al-Intikhabat al-Israiliyya: Nata'ij wal-Dalalat" [The 1948 Palestinian Vote in the Israel Elections: Results and Meaning], *Majallat Al-Dirasat al-Falastiniyya* (Summer 1996).

Almog, Doron, "Cumulative Deterrence and the War on Terrorism," *Parameters* (Winter 2004–2005).

Arian, Asher, and Michael Shamir, "The Primarily Political Functions of the Left-Right Continuum," *Comparative Politics,* vol. 15, no. 2 (1983).

Aronoff, Myron J., "Labor during Fifty Years of Israeli Politics," in Robert O. Freedman, ed., *Israel's First Fifty Years* (Gainesville: University of Florida Press, 2000).

Bar-Joseph, Uri, "Variations on a Theme: The Conceptualization of Deterrence in Israeli Strategic Thinking," *Security Studies,* vol. 7, no. 3 (Spring 1998).

Barzilai, Gad, and Ilan Peleg, "Israel and Future Borders: Assessment of a Dynamic Process," *Journal of Peace Research,* vol. 31, no. 1 (1994).

Benjio, Ofra, and Gencer Ozcan, "Old Grievances, New Fears: Arab Perceptions of Turkey and Its Alignment with Israel," *Middle Eastern Studies,* vol. 37, no. 2 (April 2001).

Betts, Richard, "Striking First: A History of Thankfully Lost Opportunities," *Ethics and International Affairs,* vol. 17, No. 1 (March 2003).

Cohen, Asher, "Hazionut Hadatit Vehamafdal BaBichirot 2003: She'ifa Lemifleget Machane Lenochach Etgarey Hapilug Hadati, Ha'adati Vehapoliti" [Religious Zionism and the Mafdal in the 2003 Elections: Aspiration for a Camp Party in the Face of the Challenges of the Religious, Ethnic, and Political Rift], *Habchirot Beyisrael—2003* (Jerusalem: Israel Democracy Institute, 2004).

———, "Shas Vehashesa Hadati-Chiloni" [Shas and the Religious-Secular Rift], *Shas— Etgar Hayisre'eliyut* [Shas—The Challenge of Israeliness] (Tel Aviv: Yedioth Aharonot and Sifre Chemed, 2001).

Cohen-Gildner, Sarit, and M. Daniele Paserman, "The Dynamic Impact of Immigration on Natives' Labor Market Outcomes: Evidence from Israel" (London: Center for Economic Policy Research, 2005).

Dayan, Moshe, "Why Israel Strikes Back," in Donald Robinson, ed., *Under Fire: Israel's Twenty Year Struggle for Survival* (New York: Norton, 1968).

Don-Yehiya, Eliezer, "Dat, Zehut Le'umit Upolitika: Hamashber Bish'elat 'Mihu Yehudi'— 1958" [Religion, National Identity and Politics: The Crisis over the Question of 'Who Is a Jew—1958'), in Mordechair Bar-On and Zvi Zameret, eds., *Shney Evrey Hagesher— Dat Umedina Bereshit Darka shel Yisrael* [Both Sides of the Fence—Religion and State at the Beginning of the State of Israel] (Jerusalem: Yad Ben-Zvi, 2002).

———, "Religion and Coalition: The National Religious Party and Coalition Formation in Israel," in Asher Arian, ed., *The Elections in Israel—1973* (Jerusalem: Academic Press, 1975).

Elazar, Daniel, and Shmuel Sandler, "The Battle over Jewishness and Zionism in the Post-modern Era," in Daniel Elazar and Shmuel Sandler, eds., *Israel at the Polls, 1996* (London: Frank Cass, 1998).

_____, "The Two-Bloc System—A New Development in Israeli Politics," in Daniel J. Elazar and Shmuel Sandler, eds., *Israel's Odd Couple: The 1984 Knesset Elections and the National Unity Government* (Detroit, MI: Wayne State Press, 1986).

File, Dani, and Udi Lebel, "The Post-Oslo Israeli Populist Radical Right in Comparative Perspective: Leadership, Voter Characteristics and Political Discourse," *Mediterranean Politics*, vol. 10, no. 1 (March 2005).

Freedman, Robert O., "The Bush Administration and the Arab-Israeli Conflict: The First Term and Beyond," in David W. Lesch, ed., *The Middle East and the United States: A Historical and Political Reassessment*, 4th ed. (Boulder, CO: Westview Press, 2007).

_____, "Sharon: The Evolution of a Security Hawk," *Midstream* (May–June 2004).

Hacohen, Dvora, "Habrit Hahistorit—Beyn Ideologia Lipolitika" [The Historical Alliance—Between Ideology and Politics], *Beyn Masoret Lachidush* [Between Tradition and Renovation] (Ramat Gan, Israel: Bar-Ilan Press, 2005).

Heller, Mark, "Begin's False Autonomy," *Foreign Policy*, vol. 37, no. 1 (Winter 1979–1980).

Herbst, Jeffrey, "War and the State in Africa," *International Security*, vol. 14, no. 4 (Spring 1990).

Hinnebusch, Raymond, "Does Syria Want Peace? Syrian Policy in the Syrian-Israeli Negotiations," *Journal of Palestine Studies*, vol. 26, no. 1 (Fall 1996).

Inbar, Efraim, "Arab-Israeli Coexistence: Causes, Achievements and Limitations," *Israel Affairs*, vol. 6, nos. 3 and 4 (Summer 2000).

_____, "The Indian-Israeli Entente," *Orbis*, vol. 48, no. 1 (Winter 2004).

_____, "The Need to Block a Nuclear Iran," *Middle East Review of International Affairs*, vol. 10, no. 1 (Spring 2006).

Isakova, Anna, "Izrail'skaya cul'tura XXI veka: kuda I kak?" [Israeli Culture of the 21st Century: Which Way Ahead?), *Vesti-Okna* (February 17, 2000).

Judt, Tony, "Israel: The Alternative," *New York Review of Books*, vol. 50, no. 16 (October 23, 2003).

Khanin, Vladimir (Ze'ev), "The Israeli 'Russian' Community and Immigrant Party Politics in the 2003 Elections," *Israel Affairs* (London), vol. 10, nos. 1 and 2 (Summer 2004).

_____, "Israeli 'Russian' Parties, and the New Immigrant Vote," in Daniel Elazar and Ben Mollow, eds., *Israel at the Polls, 1999* (London: Frank Cass, 2001).

_____, "The Jewish Right of Return: Reflections on the Mass Immigration to Israel from the Former Soviet Union," in Ian Lustick and Ann Lesch, eds., *Exile and Return: Predicaments of Palestinian Arabs and Jews* (Philadelphia: University of Pennsylvania Press, 2005).

_____, "The New Russian Jewish Diaspora and 'Russian' Party Politics in Israel," *Nationalism and Ethnic Politics*, vol. 8, no. 4 (December 2002).

_____, "The New Russian-Speaking Elite in Israel," in E. Ben Rafael, Y. Steinberg, et al., eds., *New Elites in Israel* (Jerusalem: Bialik Institute 2007) (in Hebrew).

_____, "Revival of 'Russian' Politics in Israel: The Case of 2006 Elections," *Israel Affairs* (London), vol. 13, no. 2 (April 2007).

Kimmerling, Baruch, "State Building, State Autonomy, and the Identity of Society—The Case of Israel," *Journal of Historical Sociology*, vol. 6, no. 4 (1993).

Kretzmer, D., "Judicial Review of Knesset Decisions," *Tel-Aviv University Studies in Law,* vol. 8 (1988).

Kumaraswami, P. R., "India-Israel: Emerging Partnership," *Journal of Strategic Studies,* vol. 25, no. 4 (December 2002).

Kuperman, Ranan D., "Rules of Military Retaliation and Their Practice by the State of Israel," *International Interactions,* vol. 27 (2001).

Kurtz, Anat, "Hizbollah at the Crossroads," *Strategic Assessment,* vol. 3, no. 2 (2000).

Lasensky, Scott, "Paying for Peace: The Oslo Process and the Limits of American Foreign Aid," *Middle East Journal,* vol. 58, no. 2 (Spring 2004).

Lieberman, Eli, "The Rational Deterrence Theory Debate: Is the Dependent Variable Elusive?" *Security Studies,* vol. 3, no. 3 (Spring 1994).

_____, "What Makes Deterrence Work? Lessons from the Egyptian-Israeli Rivalry," *Security Studies,* vol. 4, no. 4 (Summer 1995).

Lijphart, Arend, "Consociational Democracy," *World Politics,* vol. 21, no. 2 (1969).

Lustick, Ian S., "Kill the Autonomy Talks," *Foreign Policy,* vol. 41, no. 1 (Winter 1980–1981).

_____, "To Build and to Be Built By: Israel and the Hidden Logic of the Iron Wall," *Israel Studies,* vol. 1, no. 1 (Summer 1996).

Malley, Robert, "A New Middle East," *New York Review of Books,* vol. 53, no. 14 (September 21, 2006).

Maoz, Zeev, "Israel's Nonstrategy of Peace," *Tikkun* (September-October 2006).

_____, "The Mixed Blessing of Israel's Nuclear Policy," *International Security,* vol. 28, no. 2 (Fall 2003).

Mirsky, Georgiy, "The Soviet Perception of the U.S. Threat," in David W. Lesch, ed., *The Middle East and the United States: A Historical and Political Reassessment* (Boulder, CO: Westview Press, 2007).

Niznik, Marina, "The Dilemma of Russian-Born Adolescents in Israel," in Ben Rafael, E. Gorny, and Y. Ro'i, eds., *Contemporary Jewries: Convergence and Divergence* (Leiden/Boston: Brill, 2003).

Oliker, Olga, "Conflict in Central Asia and South Caucasus," in Olga Oliker and Thomas S. Szayna, eds., *Faultlines of Conflict in Central Asia and the South Caucasus: Implications for the U.S. Army* (Santa Monica, CA: RAND, 2003).

Olson, Robert, "Turkey-Iran Relations, 2000–2001: The Caspian, Azerbaijzan and the Kurds," *Middle East Policy,* vol. 9, no. 2 (June 2002).

Ozacky-Lazar, Sara, and As'ad Ghanem, "HaTzba'aa Ha'Aravit BaBehirot LaKnesset Ha–14, 29 May 1996" [The Arab Vote for the 14th Knesset] (May 29, 1996).

Pak, Namik Kemal, "Changing Concepts of National Security in the Post–Cold War Era and the Turkish Defence Industry," *Perceptions,* vol. 7, no. 2 (June–August 2002).

Peled, Yoav, "Hatslachata He'elektoralit Hamitmashechet shel Shas: Nituach al pi Model Chalukat Ha-avoda Hatarbutit" [Shas's Electoral Success: An Analysis According to the Model of the Cultural Division of Labor], *Habchirot Beyisrael—1999* (The Elections in Israel—1999) (Jerusalem: Israel Democracy Institute, 2000).

_____, "Strangers in Utopia: Ethno-Republican Citizenship and Israel's Arab Citizens," *American Political Science Review,* vol. 88, no. 2 (June 1992).

Peleg, Ilan, "The Likud under Rabin II: Between Ideological Purity and Pragmatic Readjustment," in Robert O. Freedman, ed., *Israel under Rabin* (Boulder, CO: Westview Press, 1995).

Peters, Joel, "Europe and the Arab-Israeli Peace Process: The Declaration of the European Council of Berlin and Beyond," in Sven Behrendt and Christian-Peter Hanelt, eds., *Bound to Cooperate: Europe and the Middle East* (Gutersloh, Germany: Bertelsmann Foundation, 2001).

Raas, Whitney, and Austin Long, "Osirak Redux? Assessing Israeli Capabilities to Destroy Iranian Nuclear Facilities," *International Security,* vol. 31, no. 4 (Spring 2007).

Reich, Bernard, "The United States and Israel: A Special Relationship," in David W. Lesch, ed., *The Middle East and the United States* (Boulder, CO: Westview Press, 2007).

Remennick, Larissa, "Transnational Community in the Making: Russian-Jewish Immigrants of the 1990s in Israel," *Journal of Ethnic and Migration Studies,* vol. 28, no. 3 (July 2002).

Sandler, Shmuel, "Rabin and the Religious Parties: The Limits of Power Sharing," in Robert O. Freedman, ed., *Israel under Rabin* (Boulder, CO: Westview Press, 1995).

_____, "The Religious Parties," in Howard R. Penniman and Daniel J. Elazar, eds., *Israel at the Polls, 1981*((Bloomington: Indiana University Press, 1986).

Sandler, Shmuel, and Jonathan Rynhold, "Introduction," in S. Sandler, B. Mollow, and J. Rynhold, eds., *Israel at the Polls,* 2003 (London: Routledge, 2004).

Sayigh, Yezid, "Arafat and the Anatomy of a Revolt," *Survival,* vol. 43, no. 3 (Autumn 2001).

Seale, Patrick, and Linda Butler, "Assad's Regional Strategy and the Challenge from Netanyahu," *Journal of Palestine Studies,* vol. 26, no. 1 (Fall 1996).

Seliktar, Ofira, "The Changing Political Economy of Israel: From Agricultural Pioneers to the 'Silicon Valley' of the Middle East," in Robert O. Freedman, ed., *Israel's First Fifty Years* (Gainesville: University of Florida Press, 2000).

Shamir, Ronen, "Landmark Cases and the Reproduction of Legitimacy: The Case of Israel's High Court of Justice," *Law and Society Review,* vol. 24 (1990).

Shichor, Yitzhak, "China's Upsurge: Implications for the Middle East," in Efraim Inbar, ed., *Israel's Strategic Agenda* (New York: Routledge, 2007).

Shimoni, Yaakov, "India—The Years of Estrangement," in Moshe Yager, Yoseph Govrin, and Aryieh Oded, eds., *Ministry of Foreign Affairs: The First Fifty Years* (Jerusalem: Keter, 2002) (in Hebrew).

Slater, Jerome, "Netanyahu, a Palestinian State, and Israeli Security Reassessed," *Political Science Quarterly,* vol. 112, no. 4 (1997–1998).

Sobelman, Daniel, "New Rules of the Game: Israel and Hizbollah after the Withdrawal from Lebanon," Jaffee Center for Strategic Studies Memorandum No. 69 (Tel Aviv: Tel Aviv University, January 2004).

Sprinzak, Ehud, "Netanyahu's Safety Belt," *Foreign Affairs,* vol. 77, no. 4 (July-August 1998).

Sultani, Nimr, and Arij Sabagh Khuri, "Muqawamat al-Haimana: Muhakamat Azmi al-Bishara" [The Factors behind Hegemony: The Trial of Azmi Bishara], *Majallat al-Dirasat al-Filastiniyya,* no. 54 (Spring 2003).

Tilly, Charles, "Reflections on the History of European State-Making," in Charles Tilly, ed., *The Formation of National States in Western Europe* (Princeton, NJ: Princeton University Press, 1975).

Walt, Stephen M., "Why Alliances Endure or Collapse," *Survival,* vol. 39, no. 1 (Spring 1997).

Waltz, Kenneth N., "More May Be Better," in Scott D. Sagan and Kenneth N. Waltz, eds., *The Spread of Nuclear Weapons* (New York: Norton, 2003).

Warschawski, Michel, "The 2006 Israeli Elections: A Drive to Normalcy and Separation," *Journal of Palestine Studies,* vol. 35, no. 4 (2007).

Index